Lecture Notes in Computer Science 5859

Commenced Publication in 1973
Founding and Former Series Editors:
Gerhard Goos, Juris Hartmanis, and Jan van Leeuwen

Manfred Tscheligi   Boris de Ruyter
Panos Markopoulus   Reiner Wichert
Thomas Mirlacher   Alexander Meschtscherjakov
Wolfgang Reitberger (Eds.)

Ambient Intelligence

European Conference, AmI 2009
Salzburg, Austria, November 18-21, 2009
Proceedings

 Springer

Volume Editors

Manfred Tscheligi, Thomas Mirlacher, Alexander Meschtscherjakov,
Wolfgang Reitberger
University of Salzburg
ICT&S Center
Sigmund-Haffner-Gasse 18
5020, Salzburg, Austria
E-mail: {manfred.tscheligi, thomas.mirlacher, wolfgang.reitberger,
alexander.meschtscherjakov}@sbg.ac.at

Boris de Ruyter
Philips Research Europe
User Experiences Department, High Tech Campus 34, WB - 5.27
5656 AE Eindhoven, The Netherlands
E-mail: Boris.de.Ruyter@philips.com

Panos Markopoulos
Technische Universiteit Eindhoven
Industrial Design
HG 2.54, P.O. Box 513, Den Dolech 2
5600 MB Eindhoven, The Netherlands
E-mail: p.markopoulos@tue.nl

Reiner Wichert
Fraunhofer-Institut für Graphische Datenverarbeitung IGD
Fraunhoferstrasse 5
64283 Darmstadt, Germany
E-mail: reiner.wichert@igd.fraunhofer.de

Library of Congress Control Number: 2009937579

CR Subject Classification (1998): H.5, I.2.11, C.2.4, H.5.1, I.3.7, K.8

LNCS Sublibrary: SL 3 – Information Systems and Application, incl. Internet/Web
and HCI

ISSN	0302-9743
ISBN-10	3-642-05407-2 Springer Berlin Heidelberg New York
ISBN-13	978-3-642-05407-5 Springer Berlin Heidelberg New York

springer.com

© Springer-Verlag Berlin Heidelberg 2009
Printed in Germany

Typesetting: Camera-ready by author, data conversion by Scientific Publishing Services, Chennai, India
Printed on acid-free paper   SPIN: 12789429   06/3180   5 4 3 2 1 0

Preface

Celebrating its 10th anniversary, the vision of Ambient Intelligence has been widely adopted as a human-centric approach to application and technology development. While the Ambient Intelligence vision was initially conceptualized as a reply to technological developments that enabled the embedding of intelligence in electronic environments with a focus on information, communication and entertainment applications, the vision has not been agnostic to the rising needs in society. Today, the Ambient Intelligence vision represents also a holistic approach to technology-supported health and wellbeing systems.

Going back to 2003, the annual Ambient Intelligence conference has established a well-recognized academic and industrial community. The first Ambient Intelligence conference presented a program built around four themes: *ubiquitous computing, context awareness, intelligence* and *natural interaction.* Reflecting the evolution of the Ambient Intelligence vision, this year's conference included additional themes such as *assisted living, methods and tools,* and *applications and studies.*

These AmI 09 proceedings include the latest research into technologies and applications that enable and validate the deployment of the Ambient Intelligence vision. With 21 full papers and 10 short papers, these proceedings provide a good insight into the state-of-the art of Ambient Intelligence research and development.

Organizing an event such as the AmI 09 conference would not have been possible without the support of a highly qualified Program and Review Committee as well as an efficient Organizing Committee. We greatly appreciate the effort of all authors submitting their contribution to AmI 09 and express our gratitude to all people who supported us in this event.

November 2009

Manfred Tscheligi
Boris de Ruyter
Panos Markopoulos
Reiner Wichert
Thomas Mirlacher
Alexander Meschtscherjakov
Wolfgang Reitberger

Organization

The 3rd European Conference on Ambient Intelligence, AmI 09, was organized by the HCI&Usability Unit, ICT&S Center, University of Salzburg, Austria.

Organizing Committee

Conference Chairs	Manfred Tscheligi (University of Salzburg, Austria)
	Boris de Ruyter (Philips Research, The Netherlands)
Papers	Manfred Tscheligi (University of Salzburg, Austria)
	Boris de Ruyter (Philips Research, The Netherlands)
Short Papers	Panos Markopoulos (TU Eindhoven, The Netherlands)
	Reiner Wichert (Fraunhofer, Germany)
Posters & Demos	John Soldatos (AIT, Greece)
	Alexander Meschtscherjakov (University of Salzburg, Austria)
Visions	Emile Aarts (Philips Research, The Netherlands)
	Albrecht Schmidt (University of Duisburg-Essen, Germany)
Workshops	Cristina Buiza (Ingema, Spain)
	Wolfgang Reitberger (University of Salzburg, Austria)
Industrial Case Studies	Maddy Janse (Philips Research, The Netherlands)
	Marianna Obrist (University of Salzburg, Austria)
Landscapes	Norbert Streitz (Smart Future Initiative, Germany)
Local Organization	Alexander Meschtscherjakov (University of Salzburg, Austria)
	Wolfgang Reitberger (University of Salzburg, Austria)
	Thomas Mirlacher (University of Salzburg, Austria)
	David Wilfinger (University of Salzburg, Austria)
	Marianna Obrist (University of Salzburg, Austria)
	Axel Baumgartner (University of Salzburg, Austria)
	Hermann Huber (University of Salzburg, Austria)
	Carina Bachinger (University of Salzburg, Austria)
	Elke Beck (University of Salzburg, Austria)

Program and Reviewing Committee

Oliver Amft	TU Eindhoven, The Netherlands
Martin Becker	Fraunhofer IESE, Germany
Gregor Broll	DOCOMO Euro-Labs, Germany
Karin Coninx	Hasselt University, Belgium
Pavan Dadlani	Philips Research, The Netherlands
Boris de Ruyter	Philips Research, The Netherlands
Monica Divitini	IDI-NTNU, Norway
Elisabeth Eichhorn	Potsdam University of Applied Sciences, Germany
Markus Eisenhauer	Fraunhofer FIT, Germany
Bernadette Emsenhuber	Johannes Kepler University Linz, Austria
Ben Fehnert	Vodafone Group Services, UK
Owen Noel Newton Fernando	National University of Singapore, Singapore
Peter Fröhlich	FTW - Telecommunications Research Center, Austria
Arjan Geven	CURE - Center for Usability Research Engineering, Austria
Thomas Grill	Austria
Sergio Guillen	ITACA Institute, Spain
Clemens Holzmann	Johannes Kepler University Linz, Austria
Vassilis Javed Khan	Eindhoven University of Technology, The Netherlands
Thomas Kleinberger	Fraunhofer IESE, Germany
Hannu Korhonen	Nokia Research, Finland
Joke Kort	TNO ICT, The Netherlands
Matthias Kranz	Technische Universität München, Germany
Antonio Krüger	DFKI, Germany
Joyca Lacroix	Philips Research, The Netherlands
Andras Lörincz	Eotvos Lorand University, Hungary
Artur Lugmayr	Tampere University of Technology (TUT), Finland
Kris Luyten	Hasselt University, Belgium
Panos Markopoulos	Eindhoven University of Technology, The Netherlands
Alexander Meschtscherjakov	University of Salzburg, Austria
Thomas Mirlacher	University of Salzburg, Austria
Florian Michahelles	ETH Zurich, Switzerland
Laurence Nigay	University of Grenoble, LIG, France
Christoph Obermair	Bernecker & Rainer, Austria
Fabio Paternó	CNR-ISTI, Italy
Marianne Graves Petersen	University of Aarhus, Denmark
Marten Pijl	Philips Research, The Netherlands

Table of Contents

Ambient Assisted Living

Applications and Studies

Methods and Tools

Reasoning and Adaptation

Ambient Intelligence 2.0: Towards Synergetic Prosperity

Emile Aarts[1] and Frits Grotenhuis[2]

[1] Philips Research, High Tech Campus 34, 5656AE, Eindhoven, The Netherlands
[2] Nyenrode Business University, P.O. Box 130, 3620AC, Breukelen, The Netherlands
`emile.aarts@philips.com`, `f.grotenhuis@nyenrode.nl`

Abstract. Ten years of research in Ambient Intelligence have revealed that the original ideas and assertions about the way the concept should develop no longer hold and should be substantially revised. Early scenario's in Ambient Intelligence envisioned a world in which individuals could maximally exploit personalized, context aware, wireless devices thus enabling them to become maximally productive, while living at an unprecedented pace. Environments would become smart and proactive, enriching and enhancing the experience of participants thus supporting maximum leisure possibly even at the risk of alienation. New insights have revealed that these brave new world scenarios are no longer desirable and that people are more in for a balanced approach in which technology should serve people instead of driving them to the max. We call this novel approach *Synergetic Prosperity*, referring to meaningful digital solutions that balance mind and body, and society and earth thus contributing to a prosperous and sustainable development of mankind.

Keywords: People-Centric Design, Ambient Intelligence, Synergetic Prosperity.

1 Developing Ambient Intelligence

Ambient Intelligence (AmI) is about creating environments that are sensitive and responsive to the presence of people [1]. The user of all new AmI technologies is placed in the centre of the environment moving technology into the background. The concept aims at taking the original Ubiquitous Computing ideas of Mark Weiser [2] one step further in the sense that users are centrally positioned and devices are fully integrated into their physical environments, In 2001, the Information Society Technology Advisory Group (ISTAG) of the European Commission [3] proposed the concept of Ambient Intelligence to be used as the central theme for the 6th Framework Program in IST. Several years later, ISTAG described Ambient Intelligence as 'a stable, yet evolving vision' [4]. Over the years, Ambient Intelligence developed itself primarily as a technology enabler for participation of users in society.

On the one hand, the AmI vision promises many exciting opportunities. On the other hand, several new issues related to the vision have surfaced that need to be dealt with, related to social, business, and technological aspects. Many different papers

M. Tscheligi et al. (Eds.): AmI 2009, LNCS 5859, pp. 1–13, 2009.

and books address such aspects and visions on Ambient Intelligence. The New Everyday by Aarts and Marzano [5], for instance, provides a broad overview of directions and major questions in Ambient Intelligence. Today, for some of these questions there are appropriate answers, but most of them have not been adequately addressed, however.

In their book 'True Visions', Aarts and Encarnacao [6] recognize the early stage of Ambient Intelligence from where we are in a transition stage, from 'articulating and evangelizing' the vision towards its implementation, where different challenges have risen. Many relevant aspects of Ambient Intelligence are discussed and elaborated thus presenting a good overview of the state of the art of the technology developments that have been accomplished. At the same time the authors argue that we are still a great leap away from Ambient Intelligence being fully accepted and integrated in our daily lives. Aarts and Encarnacao describe two parallel research tracks that should be followed in order to realize the vision:

1. The further development of specific technologies, and
2. The development and implementation of AmI scenarios in which user needs, preferences, and cultural demands are leading.

Major challenges in Ambient Intelligence until today are the use of the physical world as the interface, the development of smart environments, the development of environmental programming, the problem of making environments situational aware, giving environments the ability to handle context, and eventually to master the experience itself. In the next decade, the challenge is not so much to embed Ambient Intelligence into people's lives, but more importantly will it to be able to find answers to provide people with ambient solutions that address their real-life problems.

More recently in 2009, ISTAG issued a Report on Revising Europe's ICT Strategy [7] where they analyze individual, business, and societal trends, as well as ICT trends and their impact. Based on these insights ISTAG developed a vision for future ICT related to sustainability, productivity, and society. For Ambient Intelligence this implies that social intelligence and design are being recognized as crucial aspects next to cognitive intelligence and computing.

In conclusion, the development of Ambient Intelligence shows real progress, but at the same time it calls for a repositioning of the vision in terms of its application. Despite all efforts and intentions, the major challenge in Ambient Intelligence remains the understanding and anticipating of what people really want and to build solutions that really impact their lives.

2   Towards People-Centric Design

Aarts and Diederiks [8] report in 'Ambient Lifestyle: from Concept to Experience' on five years of research in ExperienceLab, the experience and application research center of Philips. More than forty projects from the Philips Research Laboratories are described. They report on of few killer applications of which the AmbI Light

The People Age [9]

"Just as the industrial era was characterized by consumption, so the next era will be characterized by context. The industrial era is giving away to a new economy, based more on knowledge and context than on material assets and consumption. While some call this the Knowledge Age, perhaps it would be simpler and more sense-making to call it the People Age. The democratization of information, production, and power means inevitably that people are becoming the principal drivers and actors of their own futures, aided and abetted by the flexibility and adaptability of the new technologies. It is people who generate knowledge, and not only knowledge, but also creativity, imagination and sense of purpose, all qualities that we need as we go forward. As people, rather than the economy or technology, drive the future, so the emphasis in terms of why we do things, what we do and how we do them is shifting".

television is by far the most successful one. Several concepts were transferred into incubator projects leading to startup companies including amBX, Serious Toys, and Lumalive. Nevertheless, most concepts developed in ExperienceLab did not lead to any business activity, for the simple reason that it could not be made clear what the true added value for people would be and which business model should be applied to put the concept in the market.

Generally speaking, the promise of Ambient Intelligence of a truly user centered technology has not been fulfilled over the past decade. The major reason is that most of the newly proposed prototypes are still based on what is known as technology-push, despite new approaches such as user-centric design. They are still not focused at solving real problems and they are still too deeply rooted in the classical western materialistic needs. Ambient Intelligence can significantly contribute to the development of a sustainable society through its dematerialized approach to technology resulting from the full embedding of devices in its environment.

Green has identified this new opportunity by stating [9]: "The dematerialization of happiness is matched by the ability of the new ambient technologies to dematerialize benefits". Context has become more important than consumption. People should be the drivers, where ambient technology is enabling. Ultimately, only users know and determine what makes sense, what really provides value to them.

In order to better understand what people want or need, different forms of research have been practiced. To this end, the so-called *Experience Research* approach was developed which identifies three levels of user-centric research: Experience@Context, Experience@Laboratory, and Experience@Field [10]. This approach is useful in separating concerns, i.e., needs from solutions and controlled from uncontrolled user studies.

Research into AmI products and services introduces the need for test infrastructures that can be used to involve people who will be using those products and services in the early stages of the development. Only by such an approach AmI products and services will be adopted eventually by users. Experience and Research is a means to organize this people-centric R&D process.

The major new aspect, compared to previous testing of existing products and services, is that users are involved from the very beginning of research and development through the whole lifecycle. Within Experience Research different types can be discerned: user-related research, development of prototypes, usability tests, and feasibility tests and validation [11]. Experience Research offers new opportunities for multidisciplinary centers of excellence for research, development, and design.

Living Labs are another recent means to better understand what factors make innovation successful in relation to different environmental, social and cultural settings. They can be defined as: "Collaborations of public-private-civic partnerships in which stakeholders co-create new products, services, businesses and technologies in real life environments and virtual networks in multi-contextual spheres" [12]. They can be seen as a new and promising instrument for communities conducting Experience Research.

3 The 'Dark Side' of Ambient Intelligence

Next to the many positive advances and perspectives of Ambient Intelligence, criticism has surfaced leading to a counteracting movement. People have started to investigate the consequences of the AmI vision and its implementation. Many relevant issues have been raised that need to be resolved in an AmI world such as, for instance, property rights on personal data or virtual identities [13].

In 2005 the European Commission launched the SWAMI (Safeguards in a World of Ambient Intelligence) project [14], in order to identify and analyze issues in relation to the 'dark side' of Ambient Intelligence in a structured way. As a result, Wright et al [15] present in their book 'Safeguards in a World of Ambient Intelligence' a direct warning about the threats in current and future developments in Ambient Intelligence. After years of positive news about the technological potential, issues were addressed regarding the vulnerabilities of Ambient Intelligence related to important social issues such as privacy, identity, trust, security, and inclusion.

Gary Marx describes two major risks in his foreword of the book: bad or incompetent people and/or organizations with good technology, and good people and/or organizations with bad or inappropriate technology. The SWAMI group developed four 'dark' scenarios to illustrate their concerns. These scenarios have had both a technology check (regarding probability of referenced technologies) as well as a reality check (regarding similarities to existing press reports).

Wright et al conclude that an ambient intelligent world can only be successful if all stakeholders recognize the threats and vulnerabilities, and cooperate in ensuring the necessary technological, socio-economic, and legal and regulatory safeguards. The SWAMI project has played an important role in integrating these early warning signals in new research projects, as well as in policy making. It is our true conviction that these warnings should be taken very seriously in the future development of Ambient Intelligence.

Dark Scenarios [15]

"Dark Scenario 1, *the AmI family*, presents AmI vulnerabilities in the life of a typi-cal family moving through different environments. It introduces dark situations in the smart home, at work and during a lunch break in a park.

Dark Scenario 2, *a crash in AmI space*, also references a family but focuses more specifically on senior citizens on a bus tour. An exploited vulnerability in the traffic system causes an accident, raising many different problems related to both travel and health AmI systems.

Dark Scenario 3, *what is a data aggregator to do*, involves a data-aggregating company that becomes victim of theft of personal data which it has compiled from AmI networks and which fuel its core business. Given its dominant position in the market, the company wants to cover this up but ends up in court two years later. The scenario draws attention to the digital divide between developed countries with AmI networks and developing countries that do not have such networks.

Dark Scenario 4, *an early morning TV programme reports on AmI*, portrays an AmI risk society from the studios of a morning news programme. It presents an action group against personalized profiling, the digital divide at a global scale and related to environmental concerns, the possible vulnerabilities of AmI-based traffic management systems and crowd control in an AmI environment".

---

4 More on Scenarios in Ambient Intelligence

Ducatel et al., [16] developed in 2001 visions on Ambient Intelligence for the year 2010 influencing work and daily life of people. The Information Society Technolo-gies Advisory Group commissioned four different possible scenarios. The results of these scenarios were used at that time to structure the discussions about ICT research under the sixth framework.

Next to future technology requirements, Ducatel et al., also took business, eco-nomic, and socio-political implications into account. Regarding business and eco-nomic issues, they considered new business models that will be needed to adjust to changing customer demands, and they analyzed the competitive landscape that will evolve accordingly. Concerning socio-political impact, they addressed issues related to privacy, control and social cohesion. In their scenario analysis they used contrast-ing dimensions such as economic and personal efficiency versus sociability (goals), and communal versus individual (actors). These differentials resulted in four types of scenarios for Ambient Intelligence in the year 2010.

The first scenario is about 'Maria', a successful business woman, who travels to a Far Eastern country for a business meeting. With the help of ambient technologies, 'a personal and ambient communicator', she is able to manage her trip in a very efficient and personal way, both under way as well as on location while being in (virtual) touch with her family. Upon its introduction almost ten years ago, this scenario was quite compelling because it referred to a solution that could be readily achieved. Actually, by now it became reality to a large extent with the Blackberry and I-phone giving people access to context-aware services, enabling them to schedule or change a flight or hotel, videoconference with clients or family members, and so on.

The second scenario, about 'Dimitrios' and his 'Digital Me', deals with connectivity of people and different identities. This scenario is also close to realization through the recent development of virtual and augmented technologies, allowing people to life a separate digital life, but at the same time to integrate real and virtual worlds.

The other two scenarios are further out in time. The third scenario 'Carmen' is about intelligent traffic systems and the fourth scenario 'Annette and Solomon" predicts shared presence, enhancing social learning by digital connection and a collective community memory. For these two latter scenarios large infrastructural changes would be required, next to the complexity of social, economic, and political aspects that need to be dealt with. This pushes the implementation of these scenarios further out in time.

Five technology requirements were extracted from the four scenarios: very unobtrusive hardware, a seamless mobile and or fixed communication infrastructure, dynamic and massively distributed device network, natural user interfaces, and dependability and security. However, the real question is, is this what we want: ambient technology that enables us to have even busier lives?

One can argue that the ISTAG scenarios have played a significant role in the development of Ambient Intelligence over the past years towards 2010, giving direction to the community's thinking, especially in the technology domain. One may, however, question whether the scenarios still reflect the way people want to life by 2010. In our opinion this is indeed not the case; there are strong indications that people have shifted their desires profoundly. This is partly due to the current financial crisis and partly due to the growing awareness that a sustainable development of our society calls for an approach different from the technology push of the past decades. The key issue is that AmI solutions simply should make sense. Technology should support and enable meaningful balanced lives. After a decade of developing and experimenting with the AmI vision, we need a new paradigm.

5 Visions of a New Paradigm

Ambient Intelligence should be implemented in people's lives in such a way that technology enables what people really want. Therefore the innovative playground needs to be repositioned. To this end we use three basic elements, i.e. People, Planet, and Profit that have been frequently used to describe innovation. *Synergetic Prosperity* is about the balance between these elements. Only in the presence of a balanced situation, Ambient Intelligence can truly contribute, using its inherent properties such as its dematerialized embedding and its ability to tailor towards people's needs. The basic elements of Synergetic Prosperity are presented in Figure 1.

Using People, Planet, and Profit as the basic elements we introduce the following views.

'People' reflects Body and Mind and the needs resulting from them in terms of health and wellbeing. The Latin saying 'mens sanem in corpe sanem' (a healthy mind in a healthy body) already recognized the relation between both.

'Body' is directly related to *Personal Healthcare* and is concerned with diagnostics, monitoring, and treatment of diseases in a way that is tailored to the individual patient. Personal healthcare addresses sustainable healthcare solutions in which the patient outcome and the quality of life play a central role. Health care has become

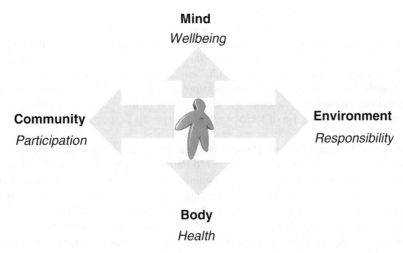

Fig. 1. Putting people in the center of Synergetic Prosperity

more and more personal over the past years. The concept of ambient assistant living plays an important role in this perspective.

'*Mind*' is related to *Balanced Lifestyle* and focuses on an integral way that brings peace of mind in a demanding society. Balanced lifestyle addresses the need to cope with the personal, mental, and physical demands of a modern lifestyle. In this perspective, Antonovsky [17] discerns between *pathogenesis* and *salutogenesis*. Pathogenesis looks at health from a disease point implying a binary state of a person being either sick or well. Salutogenesis applies a more continuous scale to a person's health condition, representing a mixture of elements related to our general state, such as happiness, motivation, and coping with change.

'*Planet*' reflects Environment and Community, where Environment can be viewed as the Body, and Community as the (collective) Mind. Community and Environment refer to our participation and responsibility towards our Planet.

'*Community*' refers to common welfare and taking care of each other. Every person should be able to participate and to make use of his or her capabilities, and so to contribute to our society. Due to globalization and the Internet, society has become more and more open over the past decades. Furthermore, our economy has developed over time from agricultural, via industrial to knowledge based. In the current knowledge-based society, the so-called creative class plays a major role. From this perspective, creative industries focus on creating and exploiting creative services in an open societal setting where every person can participate into. Creative Industries are not only consisting of a white elite part of our population, as some criticisms may like us to believe. In contrast, also in many developing countries creative industries play a major role in economic growth and (digital) infrastructure. Think about the rapidly growing mobile phone network in Africa, or the rise of creative industries in Indonesia contributing 6,3% on average to the GDP between 2002-2006 [18].

'*Environment*' relates to sustainable development of the planet which demands a global change in the use of resources in such a way that their use is consistent with future as well as present needs. Sustainable development is about meeting the needs of the present generation without comprising the needs of future generations. Evidently, the issue of the development of a more sustainable planet was brought to the attention of society in the large by Al Gore in his compelling movie "An Inconvenient Truth" a few years ago. In the mean time there is a rapidly growing group of people called the *Cultural Creatives* who are challenging materialistic lifestyles and asking for a sustainable alternative building upon novel concepts such as *Cradle-to-Cradle*. Andrew Price introduces the concept of *Slow Tech* in his recent book offering us an alternative vision on the use of technology in the twenty-first century [19].

Profit should be replaced with Prosperity. True prosperity may result from the right mixture of the various components related to People and Planet as described above. It is important to note that in our view the components related to the components People (Mind and Body) and to Planet (Community and Environment), respectively, are intertwined and interrelated in the sense that they reflect two different views of the corresponding elements, but they cannot be separated and consequently should be balanced. The aspect of balancing can be well understood from the groundbreaking work of Max-Neef et al., [20] who introduced the concept of *Synergic Satisfiers*. Their vision is rooted in the belief that *needs* can be separated from *satisfiers*. According to their argumentation, needs are independent of contextual elements such as culture, geography, and social embedding and they are more or less independent of time. Satisfiers, however, are strongly dependent of context and one should aim at the development of solutions that satisfy multiple needs at the same time. As an example they mention breast feeding which satisfies both the need of subsistence as well as the needs of protection, and affection. With their theory, Max-Neef et al., illustrate that human needs can be well integrated with the process of human development.

Based on the framework presented above we arrive at the following informal definition of Synergetic Prosperity:

"Synergetic Prosperity refers to the development and application of eco-affluent innovations that allow all people to flourish"

The key element of the new vision on AmI2.0 is that the development of Ambient Intelligence should be geared towards the development of concepts that can act as Synergic Satisfiers ultimately contributing to Synergetic Prosperity.

6 Implementing the New Vision

Below we present a number of examples of ambient intelligent concepts that can be viewed as proof points of the existence of synergic satisfiers, thus illustrating contributions of AmI2.0 to Synergetic Prosperity.

Example 1: My Reading Light

In the beginning of 2009, Philips launched a new ambient intelligent, solar powered, Led based reading light, called 'My Reading Light'. This device enables people to read and write in the dark when the night falls, without using a power grid or disposable batteries. Only in Africa, around half a billion people live without electricity. This means that after sunset, people are barely able to read or study. Candles and kerosene lamps have been the only tools till recently. As a result, children could not study in the evening hours, realising that at the equator night falls around 6PM already. With My Reading Light, people are provided an innovative solution. The costs of the device itself are low, and during daytime, the reading light recharges by using daylight.

My Reading Light [21]

"Offering new LED based, solar lighting solutions offers a triple-win: the lives of people in Africa will be generally improved, LEDs result in a very low carbon footprint and companies offering the right solutions stand to gain".

My reading light is a fine example of a lighting solution which is ready and usable anywhere, and anytime at zero costs. It contributes to the simultaneous satisfaction of the various elements of Synergetic Prosperity in the following way.

Body: the device enables people to study under physically better circumstances. Candlelight or kerosene lamps are not good for the eyes. Without this product people would only be able to read in bad light in countries and areas that still lack electricity.

Mind: young people are able to study or do their homework in the evening hours, where older people can read for enjoyment or personal development as well. This provides people with knowledge that will result into self enrichment and enrichment of society.

Community: education is the major driver of today's knowledge economy. When new generations can continue education, and go to university, society as a whole will benefit.

Environment: My Reading Light does not need any resources except for the production of it. The device will be charged by daylight, which generates reading light for several hours in the evening, thus enabling people to read or write.

Example 2: TagTiles

Intelligent Toys helps children to learn social and other kinds of skills while the fun element remains intact. The company Serious Toys produces and sells educational products that match the need for playing and personal development by applying tangible objects in an ambient intelligent setting. TagTiles is an electronic board game where both fine motor skills, cognitive, and social skill are being challenged. The development of (individual) children is the central focus. Children can experiment with different (team) roles in the games at different levels which they select themselves. First results indicate that shy children can become more assertive and accepted by peers [22].

TagTiles [23]

"TagTiles can be described best as a game computer in the form of a tablet, without keyboard, without mouse, without screen. Children play with the board by placing play pieces on them. It is very easy to use, because the pieces you use to control the computer form an integral part of the game that is played. This makes task easy to understand and a lot of fun to carry out".

TagTiles contributes to Synergetic Prosperity in the following way.

Body: while playing TagTiles, children develop motoric skills because the game requires to pick-up, touch, and mover objects in a controlled way.

Mind: during the play, children develop cognitive skills improving their learning behavior and developing their intelligence.

Community: TagTiles stimulates children to learn, play, and work together already at an early stage which will be fruitful when they become older and actively partici-pate in society.

Environment: different children can play at the same time with the same device. The device embeds a multitude of games at different levels, so can save in materials compared to 'old-fashioned' toys.

Example 3: MyHeart

The 'MyHeart' project is one of the largest health care research projects within the European Union of the past years. It is aimed at developing concepts for ambient as-sisted living in relation to heart failure. Within a consortium of 33 partners from indus-tries, knowledge institutes, and governments spread over 10 European countries, research was conducted into a variety of solution related to a number of different as-pects of cardio-vascular diseases. With the help of AmI technology, such as wearable electronics and integrated services, vital body functions can be monitored and proc-essed. Cardio-vascular diseases (CVDs) are the major cause of death in our western world. In Europe more than 20% of the people suffer from chronic cardio-vascular diseases. Around 45% of all deaths can be related to fatal heart failure. As a result, Europe spends billions of Euro's a year on CVD treatment. Society is aging at grate pace which urgently demands for a healthier and more preventive lifestyle. A different lifestyle in combination with early diagnosis could save us millions of live-years.

MyHeart [24]

"The MyHeart mission is to empower citizen to fight cardio-vascular diseases by preventive lifestyle and early diagnosis.

The starting point is to gain knowledge on a citizen's actual health status. To gain this info continuous monitoring of vital signs is mandatory. The approach is therefore to integrate system solutions into functional clothes with integrated tex-tile sensors. The combination of functional clothes and integrated electronics and process them on-body, we define as intelligent biomedical clothes. The processing consists of making diagnoses, detecting trends and react on it. Together with feed-back devices, able to interact with the user as well as with professional services, the MyHeart system is formed.

This system is suitable for supporting citizens to fight major CVD risk fac-tors and help to avoid heart attack, other acute events by personalized guidelines and giving feedback. It provides the necessary motivation the new life styles. My-Heart will demonstrate technical solutions. The outcome will open up a new mass market for the European industry and it will help prevent the development of CVD, meanwhile reduce the overall EU healthcare costs".

MyHeart contributes to Synergetic Prosperity in the following way.

Body: MyHeart helps people preventing heart diseases, and enables a healthy life style. People are provided with information about how to work on a vital life, enjoy a healthier life, and live longer.

Mind: people will feel more at ease as they know what is good for their body, when they better understand what their lifestyle does with their health and how to improve their health. People are motivated to adopt to a healthy life style.

Community: people will stay healthy longer and they will be able to live independently longer, thus leading to reduced costs of the healthcare system. Furthermore, strengthen the healthy labor force, on the one hand because people can work longer and on the other hand because less people will be disabled to work.

Environment: MyHeart may result in a substantial reduction of medication thus reducing the footprint of the pharmaceutical industry worldwide. Furthermore, wearable electronics and integrated services contribute to dematerialization.

Example 4: One Laptop per Child

The association 'One laptop per child' was founded by MIT professor Negroponte. He discovered in 2002 how connected laptops can transform lives of children and their families in remote areas. The mission from One Laptop per Child (OLPC) is: "to empower the children of developing countries to learn by providing one connected laptop to every school-age child. In order to accomplish our goal, we need people who believe in what we're doing and want to help make education for the world's children a priority, not a privilege" [26].

One Laptop per Child [26]

"A small machine with a big mission. The XO is a potent learning tool designed and built especially for children in developing countries, living in some of the most remote environments. It's about the size of a small textbook. It has built-in wireless and a unique screen that is readable under direct sunlight for children who go to school outdoors. It's extremely durable, brilliantly functional, energy-efficient, and fun".

Body: children in remote areas are safer, because they do not need to travel large distances anymore to get education.

Mind: the XO supports learning, thus enabling children to educate them selves by collecting knowledge that stimulates their minds and provides meaning to their lives.

Community: by enabling children, but also elder people, with a laptop, people become connected, and can actively participate in today's global society. Next to enabling participation, educated people can also contribute to society by sharing and exploiting their knowledge and skills.

Environment: the XO operates at extremely low energy levels and is environmentally friendly.

This is just an arbitrarily chosen collection of examples that explain the AmI2.0 paradigm related to Synergetic Prosperity. There are currently many more interesting developments that provide ground breaking AmI technologies which eventually may contribute to new Synergetic Prosperity solutions. One of the most intriguing ones is the MIT's Medialab recently introduced SixthSense [26], "a wearable gestural interface that augments the physical world around us with digital information and lets us use natural hand gestures to interact with that information". The SixthSense seamlessly integrates information with reality, and enables real time interaction with the environment. The challenge is to further develop such prototypes into balanced products that make sense to users and contribute to synergetic prosperity.

7 The Message

Ten years of development of Ambient Intelligence has raised some serious concerns with respect to its development. Besides technology and user requirements, also economic and socio-political issues have to be taken into account. On the one hand AmI technology makes it possible to provide people with flexible, embedded, and adaptable products and services. On the other hand it should also be about sense-making concepts that result in a balance of body and mind, and society and earth.

We believe that Ambient Intelligence requires a new innovation direction that supports the sustainable development of our society. We call this paradigm AmI2.0: Towards Synergetic Prosperity. Synergetic Prosperity will be the key for the future development of Ambient Intelligence. Only when products and services make sense to the users, with the right balance between body, mind, society and earth, Synergetic Prosperity can be realized.

References

1. Aarts, E., Harwig, H., Schuurmans, M.: Ambient Intelligence. In: Denning, J. (ed.) The Invisible Future, pp. 235–250. McGraw Hill, New York (2001)
2. Weiser, M.: The computer for the Twenty-First Century. Scientific American 165(3), 94–104 (1991)
3. http://cordis.europa.eu/fp7/ict/istag/home_en.html
4. ISTAG, Ambient Intelligence: From vision to reality, Report, European Commission, Luxemburg (2003), ftp://ftp.cordis.europa.eu/pub/ist/docs/istag-ist2003_consolidated_report.pdf
5. Aarts, E.H.L., Marzano, S. (eds.): The New Everyday: Visions on Ambient Intelligence. 010 Publishers, Rotterdam (2003)
6. Aarts, E.H.L., Encarnacao (eds.): True Visions: The Emergence of Ambient Intelligence. Springer, Berlin (2006)
7. ISTAG, Revising Europe's ICT Strategy, Report, European Commission, Luxemburg (2009), ftp://ftp.cordis.europa.eu/pub/ist/docs/istag-revising-europes-ict-strategy-final-version_en.pdf
8. Aarts, E.H.L., Diederiks, E. (eds.): Ambient Lifestyle: from Concept to Experience. BIS Publishers, Amsterdam (2006)

9. Green, J.: Thinking the Unthinkable: In the Long Run (Corporate Foresight und Langfrist-denken in Unternehmen und Gesellschaft), Burmeister, K., Neef, A. (Hrsg.) (2005)
10. Aarts, E.H.L., de Ruyter, B.: New research perspectives on Ambient Intelligence. Journal of Ambient Intelligence and Smart Environments 1(1), 5–14 (2009)
11. ISTAG, Experience and Application Research: Involving Users in the Development of Ambient Intelligence, Report, European Commission, Luxemburg (2004), ftp://ftp.cordis.europa.eu/pub/ist/docs/2004_ear_web_en.pdf
12. Feurstein, K., Hesmer, A., Hribernik, K.A., Thoben, K.-D., Schumacher, J.: Living Labs: a new development strategy. In: Schumacher, J., Niitamo, V.P. (eds.) European Living Labs. Springer, Heidelberg (2008)
13. Prins, J.E.J.: When Personal Data, Behaviour and Virtual Identities Become a Commodity: Would a Property Rights Approach Matter? The ICFAI Journal of Cyber Law 6(4), 48–77 (2007)
14. http://is.jrc.ec.europa.eu/pages/TFS/SWAMI.html
15. Wright, D., Gutwirth, S., Friedewald, M., Vildjiounaite, E., Punie, Y. (eds.): Safeguards in a World of Ambient Intelligence. Springer, Berlin (2008)
16. Ducatel, K., Bogdanowicz, M., Scapolo, F., Leijten, J., Burgelman, J.C.: Scenarios for Ambient Intelligence in 2010, ISTAG report for the European Commission, Luxemburg (2001)
17. Antonovsky, A.: Health, Stress and Coping. Jossey-Bass, San Francisco (1979)
18. Suharmoko, A.: Govt plans blueprint for creative industries, The Jakarta Post (2008)
19. Price, A.: Slow Tech: Manifesto for an Overwound World. Atlantic Books, London (2009)
20. Max-Neef, M.A., Elizalde, A., Hopenhayn, M.: Development and Human Needs. In: Max-Neef, M.A. (ed.) Human Scale Development. The Apex Press, New York (1991)
21. http://www.newscenter.philips.com/about/news/press/20090216_sesa.page
22. Hendrix, K., Van Herk, R., Verhaegh, J., Markopoulos, P.: Increasing Children's Competence Through Games, an Exploratory Study, IDC, Como, Italy (2009)
23. http://www.serioustoys.com/en/home.aspx
24. http://www.hitech-projects.com/euprojects/myheart/
25. http://www.laptop.org
26. Maes, P., Mistry, P.: Unveiling the "Sixth Sense", game-changing wearable tech. In: TED 2009, Long Beach, CA, USA (2009)

Behavior Analysis Based on Coordinates of Body Tags

Mitja Luštrek[1], Boštjan Kaluža[1], Erik Dovgan[1],
Bogdan Pogorelc[2,1], and Matjaž Gams[1,2]

[1] Jožef Stefan Institute, Dept. of Intelligent Systems,
Jamova 39, 1000 Ljubljana, Slovenia
[2] Špica International d. o. o., Pot k sejmišču 33,
1231 Ljubljana, Slovenia
{mitja.lustrek,bostjan.kaluza,erik.dovgan}@ijs.si,
{bogdan.pogorelc,matjaz.gams}@ijs.si

Abstract. This paper describes fall detection, activity recognition and the detection of anomalous gait in the Confidence project. The project aims to prolong the independence of the elderly by detecting falls and other types of behavior indicating a health problem. The behavior will be analyzed based on the coordinates of tags worn on the body. The coordinates will be detected with radio sensors. We describe two Confidence modules. The first one classifies the user's activity into one of six classes, including falling. The second one detects walking anomalies, such as limping, dizziness and hemiplegia. The walking analysis can automatically adapt to each person by using only the examples of normal walking of that person. Both modules employ machine learning: the paper focuses on the features they use and the effect of tag placement and sensor noise on the classification accuracy. Four tags were enough for activity recognition accuracy of over 93 % at moderate sensor noise, while six were needed to detect walking anomalies with the accuracy of over 90 %.

Keywords: Activity recognition, fall detection, gait, machine learning.

1 Introduction

The population of developed countries is aging at an alarming rate, threatening to overwhelm the society's capacity for taking care of its elderly members. New technical solutions are being sought worldwide to ensure that the elderly can live longer independently with minimal support of the working-age population. This is also the primary goal of the Confidence project [3] discussed in this paper.

The Confidence project aims to develop a ubiquitous care system for monitoring users in order to detect health problems. Such problems can be immediate (fall), short-term (limping due to injury, dizziness) or long-term (hemiplegia, Parkinson's disease, age-related deterioration of movement).

The user of the Confidence system will wear a number of radio tags placed on the body. The coordinates of the tags will be acquired by sensors situated in the apartment and a portable device carried outside. This will make it possible to reconstruct the user's posture and movement and analyze his/her behavior. Radio technology is a departure from the more common video surveillance. It was chosen for being thought

M. Tscheligi et al. (Eds.): AmI 2009, LNCS 5859, pp. 14–23, 2009.

a lesser threat to privacy by the users – in interviews carried out in the Confidence project the elderly accepted wearing tags even during activities such as bathing.

This paper describes two modules of the Confidence system. The first module recognizes the user's activity as one of the following: walking/standing, sitting, lying, the process of sitting down, the process of lying down and falling. Activity recognition is needed for further analyses specific to each activity. In addition, recognizing falls is important in itself.

The second Confidence module analyzes walking. It computes a general-purpose walking signature intended to detect changes in the user's gait. This signature is used to recognize abnormal walking based on the knowledge of normal walking alone. This is an advantage since obtaining examples of abnormal walking of a particular person can be difficult. Other Confidence modules are not discussed in the paper.

We also present a classifier for recognizing a few of the most common and critical health problems of the elderly that manifest in walking: Parkinson's disease, hemiplegia, pain in the leg and pain in the back.

The objective of our research was twofold. First, to find out if the coordinates of radio tags worn on the body are suitable for health-related behavior analysis. And second, to investigate the classification accuracy achievable using various numbers and placements of tags on the user's body and various amounts of noise in tag coordinates. Both the findings regarding noise and tag placement can affect hardware selection and further development and applications of care systems for the elderly.

2 Data Acquisition

We used 370 recordings of 5 persons performing the activities of interest:

- 45 recordings of falling.
- 30 recordings of lying down.
- 30 recordings of sitting down.
- 85 recordings of walking normally (30 of them with a burden).
- 80 recordings of walking limping (25 due to pain in the leg, 25 due to pain in the back and 30 of unspecified type).
- 50 recordings of walking dizzily.
- 25 recordings of walking with hemiplegia (the result of stroke).
- 25 recordings of walking with Parkinson's disease.

Due to the unavailability of persons with the diseases, those recordings were made under the supervision of a physician by healthy volunteers imitating patients. The physician demonstrated the behaviors and provided guidance during recording.

The recordings consisted of the coordinates of 12 tags worn on shoulders, elbows, wrists, hips, knees and ankles, sampled with 10 Hz. Tag coordinates were acquired with Smart infrared motion capture system. The Smart system adds negligible noise to the coordinates (under 1 mm), which allowed us to control the total amount of noise by adding varying degree of Gaussian noise to the raw coordinates. It also supports an unlimited number of tags, so we could explore various tag placements. The closest approximation to the hardware planned for the Confidence project is Ubisense real-time location system, which was used to determine the amount of noise to be added to the coordinates. The standard deviation of the noise measured in the Ubisense system was 4.36 cm horizontally and 5.44 vertically, to which we refer as Ubisense noise.

3 Activity Recognition

The first step in our analysis of user behavior is to classify the user's activity into walking/standing, sitting, lying, the process of sitting down, the process of lying down or falling. This is accomplished by training a classifier that can recognize the activity from a one-second interval of the user's behavior (other durations were tried, but one second proved most suitable). The feature vector for machine learning is a concatenation of the features belonging to the ten snapshots of the user's posture in that interval. Six feature sets described in the following subsection were considered. We tested multiple machine learning algorithms [8], with Support Vector Machine (SVM) offering the highest classification accuracy.

3.1 Features

Reference Features. The reference coordinate system is immobile with respect to the environment. The reference features consist of the z coordinates and the velocities of all the tags in each of the ten snapshots of the user's posture within the one-second interval to be classified. The x and y coordinates were omitted because the location where an activity takes place is not important. Additional features are the absolute distances and the distances in the z direction between all pairs of tags.

Body Features. The body coordinate system described in our previous work [8] is affixed to the user's body. It enables the observation of the x and y coordinates of the user's body parts, since these coordinates no longer depend on the location in the environment. We considered four variants of the body coordinate system differing in two characteristics. First, the coordinate system may be either fully affixed to the body or it may use reference z coordinates. Second, it may be computed for each snapshot in the one-second interval separately or it may be computed for the first snapshot in the interval and the coordinates in the remaining snapshots expressed in the coordinate system of the first snapshot. The main features are the x, y and z coordinates, the velocities, and the angles of movement of all the tags.

Angle Features. These are the angles between adjacent body parts: the shoulder, elbow, hip and knee angles and the angle between the lower and upper torso.

3.2 Machine Learning Experiments

The data for machine learning were prepared as follows. The recordings described in Section 2 were first labeled with the six activities of interest. Then a sliding window passed over each recording, splitting it into overlapping one-second intervals (one interval starting every one-tenth of a second). Afterwards, the features described were extracted from these intervals. This resulted in 5,760 feature vectors consisting of 240–2,700 features each (depending on the combination of features used). An activity was assigned to each feature vector. Finally, these vectors were used as training data for the SVM learning algorithm. The algorithm was implemented in Weka [12] and used default settings. The results were obtained with ten-fold cross validation.

Machine learning experiments proceeded in two steps. In the first step we compared the classification accuracy of the six single feature sets: reference features, the four types of body features and angle features. In the second step we discarded the less promising feature sets and compared the remaining sets in all reasonable combinations at three levels of noise. The results of the second step are shown in Table 1; the classification accuracy of the best feature set combination is in bold.

Table 1. Classification accuracy of feature set combinations

Features \ Noise	None	Ubisense	Ubisense × 2
Reference + body with body z	96.7	94.9	93.4
Reference + body with reference z	96.9	95.4	93.5
Reference + angle	**97.7**	**96.5**	**94.7**
Body with body z + angle	95.6	91.3	87.8
Body with reference z + angle	95.5	92.5	89.6
All (body z)	96.9	95.0	93.7
All (reference z)	96.9	95.5	93.8

Table 1 indicates that the reference + angle features are the best feature set combination. It is what we used in all the following experiments. The angle features alone performed rather poorly, but they seem to complement the reference features well. The more difficult to compute body features are apparently not worth the effort.

3.3 Tag Placement and Noise Level

Even though interviews carried out in the Confidence indicated that the users would accept many tags if the benefit was clear, wearing the full complement of 12 tags may be annoying. Therefore we investigated ways to reduce the number of tags and studied the interplay between tag placement and noise level.

The experimental results were obtained by leave-one-person-out method, which means that the recordings of all the persons but one were used for training and the recordings of the remaining person for testing. The intention was not to overfit the classifiers to the specific persons in the training recordings, so the results show the expected classification accuracy on a previously unseen person. This is the setting for the Confidence system, which should work on a new user without a training session.

The classification accuracies for activity recognition were compared for all $2^{12} - 1$ = 4095 combinations of 1 to 12 tags and all noise levels from none to Ubisense × 2 in increments of Ubisense × 0.2. The best tag placement for each number of tags is shown in Fig. 1. The accuracy of the best tag placement for each number of tags and each noise level is shown in Fig. 2. The highest classification accuracy of over 93 % is achieved with four to eight tags at low noise levels. One would expect higher numbers of tags to always perform better than lower numbers, but this turned out not to be the case. The reason is probably that more tags yield more features, which make

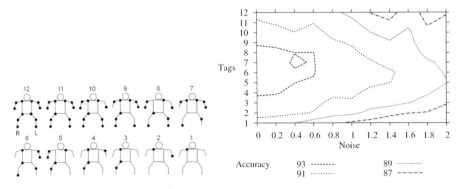

Fig. 1. Best tag placement for each number of tags for activity recognition

Fig. 2. Classification accuracy with respect to the number of tags and noise level for activity recognition

overfitting to the persons in the training recordings more likely. Since we test with the leave-one-person-out method, such overfitting is punished with a lower accuracy.

Fall Detection. We used a simple rule that recognized a fall when at least three classifications of falling were followed by at least one classification of lying. The accuracy of fall detection was mostly independent of noise. It rarely exceeded 95 %, but it was above 94 % for more than six tags and above 93 % for more than three tags.

4 Analyses of Walking

In the following two subsections we present a classifier for the detection of specific health problems and a Confidence module for the detection of abnormal walking.

4.1 Detection of Specific Health Problems

The specific health problems for detection were suggested by a medical expert based on the incidence in the elderly aged 65+, medical significance and the feasibility of recognition from movement. Four health problems were chosen: Parkinson's disease, hemiplegia, pain in the leg and pain in the back. A physician usually diagnoses such health problems while observing a patient's gait. For the computer to do the same, the relevant gait characteristics must be transformed into computable features [4].

Features. The features for identification of the four health problems were designed with the help of a medical expert. They assume the person is affected on the right side of the body; if he/she were affected on the left side, the sides would be reversed:

- Absolute difference of average distances right elbow – right hip and right wrist – left hip.
- Average angle of the right elbow.
- Quotient between maximal angle of the left and maximal angle of the right knee.
- Difference between maximal and minimal angle of the right knee.

- Difference between maximal and minimal height of the left shoulder.
- Difference between maximal and minimal height of the right shoulder.
- Quotient between {difference between maximal and minimal height of the left and maximal and minimal height of the right ankle}
- Absolute difference of {difference of maximal and minimal speed of the left and difference of maximal and minimal speed of the right ankle}
- Absolute difference of average distances of right shoulder – right elbow and left shoulder – right wrist.
- Average speed of the right wrist.
- Frequency of angle of the right elbow passing average angle of the right elbow.
- Average angle between the vector {right shoulder – right hip} and the vector {right shoulder – right wrist}
- Absolute difference of average heights of the right and the left shoulder.

Machine Learning, Tag Placement and Noise Levels. The machine learning task was to classify walking into five classes: four types of walking with the chosen health problems and the fifth without health problems as a reference. The classifier was trained on the recordings described in Section 2, which were labeled with the type of walking. For each recording the feature vector consisted of the 13 features averaged over the recording. These vectors were used as training data for several machine learning algorithms, of which the SVM learning algorithm achieved the best performance. The algorithm was implemented in Weka [12] and used default settings. Testing was performed with the leave-one-person-out method.

The classification accuracy with respect to the tag placement and noise level was computed. First, various numbers and positions of tags were tested. We started with all 12 tags and then removed them in the order that achieved the best performance. The best tag placement for each number of tags is shown in Fig. 3. Noise level was varied from none to Ubisense × 2 in increments of Ubisense × 0.2. Fig. 4 shows the classification accuracy for each tag placement and noise level. At Ubisense noise, the classification accuracy of 95 % is just out of reach, and to exceed 90 %, at least six

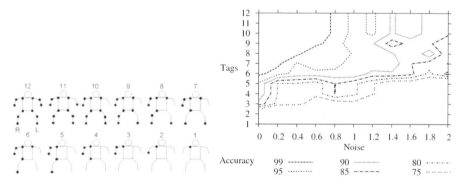

Fig. 3. Best tag placement for each number of tags for detection of specific health problems

Fig. 4. Classification accuracy with respect to the number of tags and noise level for detection of specific health problems

tags are needed. In the upper left corner of the graph there is an area with an extremely high accuracy. It requires more tags and lower noise than expected in the Confidence system, but it may be interesting in a clinical setting.

4.2 Walking Signature

Gait is an important indicator of general health condition, particularly in the elderly, and a large body of medical literature is devoted to its study [4, 5, 9]. Walking signature consists of a number of features characterizing the way a person walks. It can be used to detect changes in a person's gait that may be related to a health problem. Unlike the features from the previous subsection, they are not geared towards any specific health problems. Most features refer to a pair of steps, so to compute them we had to develop an algorithm for step detection.

Step Detection. We detect steps by observing the x and y coordinates of the user's ankles (the signal-to-noise ratio in the z coordinates is too low). For each snapshot of the user's posture, the distance in the xy plane an ankle has travelled from the previous snapshot is computed first. The snapshots are then sorted by this distance. The snapshots in the group with the lowest 30 % of distances are considered standing still. Each period of standing still is refined by moving its boundaries to the first and last snapshot with an above-average distance for the group.

Features. The features were adapted from medical literature [5, 9]. Each feature refers to two steps, one with each leg. Wherever applicable, the features are computed for each leg separately and the difference in the values for both legs is also included:

- Support (foot on the ground), swing (foot off the ground) and step (support + swing) times.
- Double support time (both feet on the ground).
- Step length and width.
- Maximal distance of the foot from the ground.
- Ankle, knee and hip angles upon touching the ground.
- Knee angle when the ankle of the leg on the ground is directly below the hip, and knee angle of the opposite leg at that time.
- Minimal and maximal knee and hip angles, the angle of the torso with respect to the ground, and the range for each.
- Hip and shoulder sway (the difference between the extreme left and right deviation from the line of walking).

Machine Learning, Tag Placement and Noise Levels. Since the walking signature was not intended for the recognition of specific health problems, but rather to detect any type of abnormal walking, we used the Local Outlier Factor (LOF) algorithm [2]. This algorithm can recognize abnormal walking based on examples of normal walking alone. It computes a degree of 'outlierness' or abnormality of each example. If the degree exceeds a certain bound for a given example, the example is considered abnormal. The algorithm can thus recognize abnormal walking of a Confidence user by only observing him/her walk normally. Thus it can adapt to each user without needing examples of that user walking abnormally, which can be difficult to obtain.

The training of the LOF algorithm was carried out on the recordings described in Section 2, which were labeled with the type of walking. The step detection algorithm first extracted pairs of steps, after which the walking signature was computed for each pair. This resulted in around 534 feature vectors (depending on how many steps were detected), consisting of up to 58 features (depending on tag placement). The experimental results were obtained with the leave-one-person-out method.

We again studied the classification accuracy with respect to tag placement and noise level. Four tag placements were considered. Ankles tags were always used, since they are needed for step recognition. They were first used alone, then knee tags were added (four tags in all), then hip tags (six) and finally shoulder tags (eight). Noise level was varied from none to Ubisense × 2 in increments of Ubisense × 0.2. The classification accuracy with respect to the number of tags and noise level is shown in Fig. 5. At Ubisense noise, the accuracy with eight tags is above 95 %, with six tags above 90 %, with four tags around 80 % and with two tags still above 75 %.

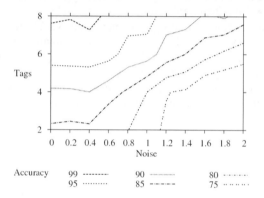

Fig. 5. Classification accuracy with respect to the number of tags and noise level for recognizing normal and abnormal walking with the walking signature

5   Related Work

Related work on fall detection and activity recognition can be broken down by the choice of hardware (sensors and possibly tags): accelerometers (measure linear acceleration), gyroscopes (measure angular velocity), cameras (not discussed here) and cameras + visible tags (measure tag coordinates). It should be noted that the hardware used in the experiments described in this paper actually belongs to the last category. However, since we added noise to the results, we did not unfairly take advantage of its main strength, which is accuracy.

Fall detection with accelerometers is quite common, particularly using simple threshold algorithms [6]. With a more advanced approach using the One-Class SVM learning algorithm, the accuracy of 96.7 % was reported [13]. A fall detector using a gyroscope attached to the torso achieved the accuracy of 100 % [1]. In both cases falls and the activities from which falls were being distinguished were performed by the same persons in training and in testing, which may account for the high accuracies. Our person-independent testing resulted in accuracies around 94 %.

Accelerometers can also be used for activity recognition. Five tri-axial accelerometers distinguished 30 physical activities of various intensities with the accuracy of 94.9 % with person-dependent training and 56.3 % with person-independent training [11]. We used person-independent training, which resulted in accuracy above 90 %, although the number of activities in our experiments was admittedly lower.

The related work described so far had objectives similar to ours, but the data it used were significantly different due to the sensors employed. As a consequence, the methodology was different as well, particularly when using video as the source of the data. The approaches belonging to the cameras + visible tags category, however, use cameras to locate tags and thus – like us – work with tag coordinates. The work most similar to ours [10] used 43 body tags sampled with 30 Hz to distinguish between seven activities related to military operations, reporting the accuracy of 76.9 %. This was achieved with the SVM learning algorithm whose features were the tag coordinates belonging to two postures separated by 1/3 second. Our accuracies exceeded 90 % despite more noise and fewer tags, so apparently our features are better suited to activity recognition from tag coordinates.

Motion capture systems consisting of cameras and visible tags are also used for medical research. They commonly provide data for human experts to evaluate, but they can also be used automatically [7]. In distinguishing between health problems such as hemiplegia and diplegia, the accuracy of 92.5 % was reported. Our accuracies were comparable despite more noise and fewer tags (and probably also lower sampling frequency – this is not reported in the related paper).

6 Conclusion

We have investigated the feasibility of using the coordinates of radio tags worn on the body for fall detection, activity recognition and the detection of health problems. The performance of fall detection with person-independent accuracy of around 94 % seems to be comparable to the competitive approaches. The accuracy of activity recognition (over 90 %) often exceeds the alternatives, although admittedly the recognized activities were quite basic. More complex activities will be investigated in the future. Finally, the detection of health problems, which is rarely addressed outside of clinical setting in this form, is quite promising (accuracy 85–95 %). Radio tags and sensors combined with the methods presented in this paper can tackle all these tasks in a single package. They are a viable alternative to inertial and other sensors that can serve the same purpose. At the moment the greatest barrier to the acceptance of such an approach is the price and maturity of the available hardware. However, we are hopeful that this problem will be solved before long.

We have studied the impact of tag placement and noise level on the accuracy of fall detection, activity recognition and the detection of health problems. In general more noise resulted in lower accuracy, as expected. The number of tags sometimes also behaved as expected, i.e., fewer tags resulted in lower accuracy. In activity recognition, however, a moderate number of tags performed best, probably because too many tags caused overfitting to the persons in the training recordings. These results can be used as guidance in further development of the Confidence system and potentially in other projects in the area of ambient assisted living.

Last but not least, the paper describes and compares various features for machine learning. The relatively straightforward features in the reference coordinate system and angles combined with the SVM learning algorithm proved best for activity recognition. For the detection of specific health problems, specific features turned out to be needed. For recognizing abnormal walking, the walking signature consisting of general gait features was sufficient.

Acknowledgments. The research leading to these results has received funding from the European Community's Framework Programme FP7/2007–2013 under grant agreement n° 214986. Operation was partially financed by the European Union, European Social Fund. We thank Martin Tomšič, Bojan Nemec and Leon Žlajpah for their help with data acquisition, project partners for the aid in the development of the walking signature, Anton Gradišek for lending us his medical expertise, Rok Piltaver and Zoran Bosnić for discussion, and Barbara Tvrdi for programming assistance.

References

1. Bourke, A.K., Lyons, G.M.: A threshold-based fall-detection algorithm using a bi-axial gyroscope sensor. Medical Engineering & Physics 30(1), 84–90 (2006)
2. Breunig, M.M., Kriegel, H.-P., Ng, R.T., Sander, J.: LOF: Identifying density-based local outliers. In: 2000 ACM SIGMOD International Conference on Management of Data, pp. 93–104 (2000)
3. Confidence: Ubiquitous Care System to Support Independent Living, http://www.confidence-eu.org
4. Craik, R., Oatis, C.: Gait Analysis: Theory and Application. Mosby-Year Book (1995)
5. Heiden, T.L., Sanderson, D.J., Inglis, J.T., Siegmund, G.P.: Adaptations to normal human gait on potentially slippery surfaces: The effects of awareness and prior slip experience. Gait & Posture 24, 237–246 (2006)
6. Kangas, M., Konttila, A., Lindgren, P., Winblad, P., Jamsa, T.: Comparison of low-complexity fall detection algorithms for body attached accelerometers. Gait & Posture 28(2), 285–291 (2008)
7. Lakany, H.: Extracting a diagnostic gait signature. Pattern recognition 41, 1627–1637 (2008)
8. Luštrek, M., Kaluža, B.: Fall detection and activity recognition with machine learning. Informatica 33(2), 205–212 (2009)
9. Paróczai, R., Bejek, Z., Illyés, Á., Kocsis, L., Kiss, R.M.: Gait parameters of healthy, elderly people. Facta Universitatis 4(1), 49–58 (2006)
10. Sukthankar, G., Sycara, K.: A cost minimization approach to human behavior recognition. In: The Fourth International Joint Conference on Autonomous Agents and Multi-Agent Systems (AAMAS), pp. 1067–1074 (2005)
11. Tapia, E.M., Intille, S.S., Haskell, W., Larson, K., Wright, J., King, A., Friedman, R.: Real-time recognition of physical activities and their intensities using wireless accelerometers and a heart rate monitor. In: The 6th International Semantic Web Conference, pp. 37–40 (2007)
12. Witten, I.H., Frank, E.: Data Mining: Practical Machine Learning Tools and Techniques, 2nd edn. Morgan Kaufmann, San Francisco (2005)
13. Zhang, T., Wang, J., Liu, P., Hou, J.: Fall detection by wearable sensor and One-Class SVM algorithm. In: Nossum, R.T. (ed.) ACAI 1987. LNCS, vol. 345, pp. 858–863. Springer, Heidelberg (1988)

MobiDiC: Context Adaptive Digital Signage with Coupons

Jörg Müller and Antonio Krüger

University of Münster, DFKI Saarbrücken
Joerg.Mueller@uni-muenster.de, Antonio.Krueger@dfki.de

Abstract. In this paper we present a field study of a digital signage system that measures audience response with coupons in order to enable context adaptivity. In the concept for context adaptivity, the signs sense their environment; decide which content to show, and then sense the audience reaction to the content shown. From this audience measurement, the strategies which content to show in which situation are refined. As one instantiation of audience measurement, we propose a novel simple couponing system, where customers can photograph the coupons at the signs. Thus, it can be measured whether customers really went to the shop. To investigate the feasibility of this approach, we implemented a prototype of 20 signs in the city center of Münster, Germany. During one year of deployment, we investigated usage of the system through interviews with shop owners and customers. Our experiences show that customer attention towards the signs is a major hurdle to overcome.

1 Introduction

As display prices continue to fall and new display technologies emerge, public space is increasingly penetrated by digital signs. Many stores use them for branding to improve the shopping experience, but increasingly digital signage is used to present advertisements from multiple advertisers. Digital signs already exist in airports, train and subway stations as well as some public places, but we believe they will eventually replace paper signs everywhere. Because on digital signs the content can be exchanged every moment, the content can then be tailored to the context and the interests of the audience. Thus, scheduling becomes much more complex than for paper signs, and new technologies are needed to automatically decide which ad to show where and when. To enable such technology, it is useful to measure the audience reaction to content shown. We hope that the approach presented here is a first step towards providing more interesting content on digital signs while preserving customer privacy.

In this paper we present a field study of an audience measurement system, which uses coupons to determine what content is popular in different situations. This information can be used to automatically select the most interesting content for each situation.

M. Tscheligi et al. (Eds.): AmI 2009, LNCS 5859, pp. 24–33, 2009.

2   Related Work

Research prototypes of digital signage or Situated Public Displays have both been deployed in labs or in the public. Many such systems are presented in [7], and good survey is provided in [4].

A few research prototypes have been deployed for large public audiences and are used to evaluate the public reaction to the prototypes. E-campus [10] is an effort to deploy displays throughout a whole university campus. Currently, mostly artistic content is shown. News & Reminder Displays [6] are also a deployment at a university to study how users can be supported in deciding whether or not to act upon shown information. Mobile phones present an opportunity to pick up information presented on a public display. Shoot & Copy [1] is a technique to take photos of a digital sign, process these with image recognition and copy the photographed content in electronic form to the mobile phone. A method to collect coupons on a mobile phone has been presented in [3]. Several commercial systems that copy coupons to the user's mobile phone already exist. Bluespot[1] provides kiosks where users can copy a coupon to their mobile phone via Bluetooth. MarketEye[2] is a device that can be attached to paper signs. Via Infrared or Bluetooth it causes the mobile phone to send a SMS that requests a coupon.

Less work has been done regarding the scheduling of content on digital signage. Storz [9] proposes a technical solution to manage the scheduling in the eCampus deployment. BluScreen [8] was the first system to use auctions to sell advertising space on digital signage, similar to Google AdSense[3].

An approach to schedule content depending on the context by using audience measurement has been presented in the ReflectiveSigns system [5]. While the ReflectiveSigns system uses face detection to measure audience attention towards the displays, in this study we present a field study to measure audience preferences with coupons.

3   Context Adaptive Scheduling

For scheduling the content, we propose a system similar to Google AdSense, where advertisers would pay for a certain user reaction (e.g. a coupon being redeemed) and the system would automatically schedule content (depending on the context) such that utility (for the display owner) is being maximized. For each of the possible audience reactions j (e.g. somebody looking at the content, interacting with it or converting a coupon), the advertiser would specify his utility u_j that somebody shows this reaction. The current measurable context of the sign can be described by a number of features $F_1 \dots F_n$. The sign senses its context with the available sensors and computes the current context feature values $f_1 \dots f_n$. The function $A_j(f_1 \dots f_n)$ is then used to predict how many people actually show behavior j if the content is shown.

---

[1] http://www.bluespot.de
[2] http://www.accinity.de
[3] http://adsense.google.com

The expected utility of showing a content item ('ad') in a given context with different possible audience reactions j can then be simply described as

$$EU(ad \mid f_1 \ldots f_n) = \sum_{j=1}^{m} A_j(f_1 \ldots f_n)u_j .$$

The sign would then simply present the content with the highest utility. The central difficulty is then to determine the function $A_j(f_1 \ldots f_n)$. We propose that this function can automatically be learned by observing actual audience behaviour, e.g. whether the audience converted a coupon. We use a simple Bayesian classifier to predict the number of converted coupons in a certain context from the number of converted coupons in previous similar situations.

4 Requirements Analysis

We decided to deploy the prototype in the only digital signage network that was available and was spanning a considerable area. At public telephones throughout the city, 13" advertising signs were deployed. We used 20 of these signs to deploy the MobiDiC system (see Figure 1). In the deployment, we used coupons as the only feedback channel. The idea is simple: The customer can pick up a coupon at the sign that contains a code. This code encodes the time and location where he has seen the ad. The customer then presents the coupon at the shop and is given a rebate or promotion. The shop feeds the code back into the system. A complete history is kept on which ad is shown on which sign at what time together with the values of the context features and how many coupons were converted. This database can then easily be used to apply the proposed learning procedure to learn the function $A_j(f_1 \ldots f_n)$.

Fig. 1. Deployed MobiDiC sign (Screenshot translation: "Coupon: 1. Photograph display, 2. Show Photo in store. Coupon is for free gummi bears.)

Advertisers

We conducted a questionnaire with potential advertisers to see their requirements on such a system. We distributed the questionnaire to all shops in the important shopping streets of the city. In total 97 questionnaires were distributed. The shops were asked that the shop owner should fill in the questionnaire. Where possible, it was filled in immediately together with the shop owner. If that was not possible, the questionnaire was left in the shop to be filled in later. One and two weeks later we went to the shops again to collect the questionnaires. In total we could collect 39 questionnaires. The results are presented in Table 1. Not all shops answered all questions. In these cases, we state the number of yes and no answers separately.

Table 1. Results of the Advertiser Questionnaire

Already use Coupons	**Yes**: 23, No: 16
Main Benefits for Coupons	New Customers, Increased Sales, Measurability of Success
Interested in Digital Signage Advertising	**Yes**: 26, No: 13
Interested in Using Coupons	**Yes**: 25, No: 14
Share Feedback Data with other Advertisers	**Yes**: 23, No: 7
Select location for ad	Automatically: 5, Manually: 12, **Manually with Recommendations**: 16
Select time for ad	Automatically: 3, Manually: 11, **Manually with Recommendations**: 19
Show ad together with other advertisers	Yes: 10, No: 9, **Select certain businesses with whom not**: 14
Submit Coupon to System	**Web Form**: 13, Email: 10, Mail: 5, Scanner at Counter: 4
Limit Number of Coupons	Yes: 11, **No**: 17
Would like to use System	**Interested**: 27, Not interested: 11
Most important System features	**Measurability of Advertising Success**: 20, Optimization of Location: 17, Show Ads on Digital Signs: 16, Optimization of Time: 13, Coupons: 13

The measurability of advertising success was perceived as the most important system feature. Interestingly however, most shops disliked the automatic ad placement that we proposed and instead preferred manual placement with recommendations from the system. It is very promising that advertisers are willing to share effectiveness data of their ads so that the corpus of all ads can be optimized. Clearly, for a commercial system a constraint system would be necessary that allows advertisers to specify certain ads with which they do not like to appear on the same screen. Also, for a commercial system automatic scanning of the coupon from the mobile phone screen would be necessary. While distributing the questionnaires, we noticed that almost none of the small shops were equipped with a barcode scanner. While half of the shops had a PC with Internet connection, this was almost always placed in the back office behind the sales room. Therefore we decided for the prototype to use paper sheets where employees would manually write down the code, which shops could upload via a Web form, or could also be collected by us. It is convenient that most shops see no need to limit the number of coupons that are issued, so we do not need to care about this, which would be difficult if the user only takes a photo of the coupon. Because the measurability of advertising success was mentioned as the most important feature by the advertisers we implemented an extensive interface to view the statistics. Interestingly, after deployment of the system we found that actual advertiser behavior differed widely from these stated preferences (see Section "Experiences").

Customers

From informal prototype tests and the advertisers study, we considered an alphabetic code that is transferred from the advertising sign to the customers' mobile phone via Bluetooth, SMS or camera the best solution. We suspected that SMS would not be very popular, because each coupon possibly has a low monetary value, and forcing the customer to send a SMS for which he has to pay would further decrease this value. We decided to conduct an experiment to compare the usability of the Bluetooth mechanism versus the photo mechanism and conduct structured interviews to ask for the preferences of photo versus Bluetooth versus SMS.

In an experiment, two mechanisms to issue the coupons were compared. A mockup of the advertising sign was created using PowerPoint on a convertible tablet PC. The tablet PC was attached to a real phone pillar in the city center. On the mockup, a coupon for a belt of the value of 10€ was presented together with operating instructions. The system was not explained to the participants, instead they were asked to just read the operating instructions and get the coupon. In the photo condition, participants would have to take a photo of the sign using their own mobile phone. In the Bluetooth condition, they would have to activate Bluetooth and set it to 'visible'. A hidden wizard-of-oz would then send them the coupon via Bluetooth using a mobile phone. The participant would have to accept the incoming connection. The time needed from the first key press on the user's mobile phone until the coupon was saved on the mobile phone was measured. In both conditions, participants would then go to the shop, which was approx. 60m away, and participate in the interview. They would then get a bag with the belt. A between-subjects design was used. N=24 participants were recruited from passers-by, 12 for each condition. 22 participants were interviewed. Passers-by were asked randomly, but most of the older people rejected, resulting in participants from age 15-30 years, $\mu=20.9$ years. 10 participants were male and 12 female; there were 11 pupils, 6 students and 5 other professions. When asked to participate in the camera condition, 5 passers-by rejected because they had no camera on their mobile phone. In the Bluetooth condition, 8 rejected because Bluetooth was not supported, 4 had security concerns and in 3 cases the Bluetooth did not work.

Except for 3 participants where Bluetooth failed, all participants could understand the operating instructions on the sign and use the system. In the photo condition, participants needed 5-25 seconds to get the coupon ($\mu=15.3s$, $\sigma=6.5s$). In the Bluetooth condition, participants needed 5-30 seconds to get the coupon ($\mu=10.75s$, $\sigma=7.72s$). During the experiment, most of the time 1-2 other visible Bluetooth devices were in range, which would have received the coupon unintentionally if the coupons would have been sent automatically. Several participants in the photo condition were surprised that merely taking the photo was sufficient ('Ok. What do I do now?'). Also, some participants spontaneously started copying the coupon to each other via Bluetooth. One woman refused to participate in the Bluetooth condition because she was afraid we would get her phone number.

In the interview, 21 participants stated they would use the system, and only 1 declined. On a Likert scale from 1 to 5, where 1 would mean 'do not like' and 5 would mean 'do like', the photo condition was rated with 4, Bluetooth was rated with 3.95, and an imaginary mechanism where the coupon would be transferred via SMS was rated with 2.04. Interestingly, most participants liked the mechanism best that they used in the experiment. From those who participated, 18 stated to have no security concerns regarding Bluetooth, and 4 stated to have concerns. 12 participants stated they had already seen the signs at public phones, and 10 stated they had not seen them. Many said not to pay attention to public phones because they own a mobile phone.

From the experiences of the experiment we decided to implement the photo mechanism. One reason to reject the Bluetooth mechanism is that we want customers to pull the coupon instead of pushing it to them to gain bigger user acceptance. Simply pushing the coupon to all visible Bluetooth devices could result in many users getting coupons accidentally and possibly being annoyed. Although pull-based Bluetooth mechanisms are possible, they would probably be more effort to use. The main reason to reject the SMS mechanism is the low rating in the interview and the possible costs. We favor the photo mechanism because many mobile phones have a camera and most users have already tried this camera. Instead of being buried in a submenu like Bluetooth, the camera can usually be activated with a dedicated button on the mobile phone. We hope that we gain better user acceptance with the camera mechanism, because unlike SMS or Bluetooth it is obvious that this is a unidirectional data transfer from the sign to the mobile phone and no private data like the phone number is revealed. In addition, the process of taking a photo is a common process of making something in the environment your own. Because the user has taken the photo himself, it should feel more personal and fit better to a personal device like the mobile phone.

As we noticed in the experiment, the photo mechanism is simpler than most users expect. Therefore we point out in the instructions that the user can go directly to the shop after taking the photo. One dilemma that remains with the displays on public phones is that the owners of mobile phones do not use public phones and the users of public phone can not use the system if they do not own a mobile phone or camera. This problem however is specific to the kind of signs used and will be overcome if users go to the public phones specifically to look for coupons.

5 Experiences

The described system was deployed in the city center of Münster, Germany from September 20, 2007 to September 2008. It was running on 20 public signs at 10 different locations in the city center.

Over the course of one year, 17 shops participated in the MobiDiC system. Of these shops, only 2 created their own coupons and uploaded them via the Web application. For the other shops, the coupons were designed by us. Unfortunately, the feedback loop never worked quite as intended: over one year, only 37 coupons were registered as converted. In order to make context adaptive scheduling work, much more data were needed, and for this reason, the actual scheduling used never went beyond random. It is however still interesting to look at the coupons that were converted. There was a strong preference for coupon type: One coupon (free gummi bears) was converted 17 times, and four others (free coffee, 10€ rebate on clothes, solarium and tea rebate) were converted 10, 7, 2 and 1 times, the other 12 coupons were never converted. There also was a strong preference by location: The most effective signs generated 10,6,4,4,4,3,2,2,1,1 and 1 coupons, while 9 signs generated no coupons at all. The majority of coupons (26) were photographed between 2 and 8 pm. However, we could not find any strong correlations between the kind of coupon and time, location, weather, day of week or anything similar. Additionally, we could find a strong novelty effect. In September, October and November 2007 9, 19 and 6 coupons were registered, respectively, and only 4 coupons were registered since then.

Customers

Semi-structured interviews were conducted asking 26 customers for their opinion. We shortly explained the system to random passers-by and showed them the signs. 13 participants were male, 13 female. The age of participants was 16-32 years, $\mu=25.7$. The interviews were conducted at two different days in front of signs at the main market and train station. Interview duration was 3-15 minutes.

22 participants stated that they like the system, 4 participants disliked it. 20 participants owned a mobile phone with camera, 6 did not. When asked whether they would use the system regularly, 19 said they would and 7 said they would not. 17 participants said they would tell their friends about it, and 9 said they would probably not. All 4 participants who disliked the system were male, 26-32 years old, and only one of them owned a mobile phone with camera. Only one participant stated he had seen the system before, and he had thought that it was merely a clock consisting of letters, what he considered funny (the coupon code changes every second). One participant considered the system useless, but found it creative at least. The young participants were particularly enthusiastic about the system, and two immediately gathered their friends to show them the system. Many said they would from now on look at the signs whenever they pass them. Some even said they would go to the sign specifically to look for new coupons, and one said jokingly that she would from now on spend the entire day in front of it. Some said they would use them while they wait for the bus. Some young participants considered the coupons incredible and asked why the shops would submit them so easily. Almost all participants stated spontaneously that it was a bad idea to place the signs at public phones because people who own mobile phones ignore them. They also mentioned that the idea that they could benefit from doing something at the sign would never have occurred to them. Some participants mentioned that they had no idea that 'there are not only ads at the display but instead something useful'. Some stated that the screen content should invite more to take a photo. Almost all participants said the screens were not eye-catching enough, and suggested to surround them with paper signs. Many suggested advertising with flyers

and in newspapers. Many participants immediately tried the system and all of them managed to take the photo effortlessly within a few seconds.

As we saw in the requirements analysis, it is again striking that the younger the participants, the more they liked the system. We found it very promising that so many participants liked the system. It seems important, however, that customers know about the coupons beforehand, because the screens are too small and not eye-catching enough to make somebody look at the screen. From the users we interviewed, nobody expected anything interesting at the signs, and nobody stated to look at the signs all by himself. While we observed about 15 people making phone calls at the public phones, none of them looked at the screen just in front of their eyes. In order to make the system used more, more visible signs (e.g. bigger, better angle to walking direction, better contrast) clearly are necessary. We posted paper signs around the displays, but this had no apparent effect. Additionally, a paradigm shift needs to be necessary, to make the users expect something useful at the signs. Otherwise, most users seemed to expect nothing interesting at the signs (i.e. boring advertisements, telephone book) and ignored them. In order to advertise the system, we distributed 5000 flyers in the city center. This however seemed to have had no effect in mitigating the lower visibility of the signs.

Advertisers

Although many advertisers were interested, it was pretty difficult to make them actually register on the system, create ads and submit them. Except for two shops, the actual ads were finally created and submitted by us.

Semi-structured interviews were conducted repeatedly asking all participating shops regarding their experiences, opinions, and proposals for improvement. Despite the low response to the system, all shops were very satisfied (partially because it was free for them). All of them mentioned that the system should be advertised better, for example with flyers, labels at the shops doors or in newspapers. In the beginning, all shops believed that it would only take some time until word-of-mouth would make the system popular. However, after one year of deployment, this hope had waned. Two shops explicitly mentioned that they plan to change their target audience towards younger people using the system. Two shops mentioned that it could be a problem if only young people use the coupons who do not become customers. One shop would like to see added services, like maps, weather forecast or emergency pharmacy locations on the signs. One shop said he would prefer a printer at the sign printing out paper based coupons. He also would like to collect the phone numbers of coupon users. Also, it was proposed to use a touch screen to stop the sign while showing a particular coupon. Asked whether it was more important to them that customers see the ad or go to the shop, one shop stated it was more important that customers see the ad, one shop considered it more important that customers come to the shop, and the rest considered both equally important. The participating shops stated that they do not like to put a lot of work into the ad, and it is ok for them if it is scheduled automatically. They stated that it is ok for them to write down the codes at the counter. It became clear however that only a small fraction of converted coupons were actually written down. One vendor for example stated that 30-40 coupons were converted at his shop, but he did not write down a single one. When we interviewed customers, some of them had also already converted coupons, but for most of them the codes were not written down.

Interestingly, advertisers' opinions before and after the deployment of the system show some striking differences. Before deployment, what advertisers were most interested in was control. They wanted to control where and when their ads were shown, wanted to upload a detailed graphic as coupon, as well as check and upload coupon codes via a web form. In addition, they were interested in detailed statistics where their ad was shown and from which signs coupons were converted. After deployment of the system, this preference changed completely. Advertisers did not care about control anymore, but only about convenience and effort. Only two advertisers used the web application at all, to upload their coupon templates. For all other advertisers, they told us on the telephone how the coupon should look like and we created it for them. They did not care about deciding where and when it was shown, and not a single coupon code was submitted via the web form. Advertisers wrote down the code on a paper form (if they did), and we collected these forms. Analogous to the automatic ad placement on the web, we experienced that after a short time, automatic scheduling was well accepted.

6 Conclusion

In this paper, we presented an approach to automatically tailor content on digital signage to the context. This approach involves a feedback loop to sense the sign's context, decide which content to show and measure the audience reaction to the content shown. A context adaptive scheduling strategy was presented that determines the optimal content for each context. To parameterize this scheduling strategy, a learning mechanism was developed that can learn how well content works in certain contexts. In order to create a corpus for this learning mechanism, we proposed to measure content effectiveness by using coupons, which customers can pick up at the signs. The requirements analysis showed that the coupons should be photographed at the signs and should contain an alphabetic code, which encodes where and when the photo was taken. A deployment using 20 signs in a city showed the feasibility of this approach. Experiences from the deployment show that generating enough feedback data to make this approach work keeps problematic. Major hurdles are the relatively low visibility of the signs, the fact that customers ignore the signs because they expect nothing interesting, the apparently to low attractiveness of the coupons and the fact that advertisers don't record the coupon codes.

References

1. Boring, S., Altendorfer, M., Broll, G., Hilliges, O., Butz, A.: Shoot&Copy: Phonecam-Based Information Transfer from Public Displays onto Mobile Phones. In: Proc. Mobility 2007 (2007)
2. Brignull, H., Rogers, Y.: Enticing People to Interact with Large Public Displays in Public Spaces. In: Proc. INTERACT 2003, pp. 17–24. IOS Press, Amsterdam (2003)
3. Ferscha, A., Swoboda, W., Wimberger, C.: En passant Pick-up of Digital Give-Aways. In: Adjunct Proceedings of ISWC 2009, OCG (2009)

4. Huang, E.M., Mynatt, E.D., Russell, D.M., Sue, A.E.: Secrets to success and fatal flaws: The design of large-display groupware. IEEE Computer Graphics and Applications 26(1), 37–45 (2006)
5. Müller, J., Exeler, J., Buzeck, M., Krüger, A.: ReflectiveSigns: Digital Signs that Adapt to Audience Attention. In: Proc. Pervasive 2009. LNCS, vol. 5538, pp. 17–24. Springer, Heidelberg (2009)
6. Müller, J., Krüger, A.: Situated Public News and Reminder Displays. In: Schiele, B., Dey, A.K., Gellersen, H., de Ruyter, B., Tscheligi, M., Wichert, R., Aarts, E., Buchmann, A. (eds.) AmI 2007. LNCS, vol. 4794, pp. 248–265. Springer, Heidelberg (2007)
7. O'Hara, K., et al. (eds.): Public and Situated Displays. Kluwer International, Dordrecht (2003)
8. Payne, T.R., David, E., Jennings, N.R., Sharifi, M.: Auction mechanisms for efficient advertisement selection on public displays. In: Proc. ECAI, pp. 285–289. IOS Press, Amsterdam (2006)
9. Storz, O., Friday, A., Davies, N.: Supporting Content Scheduling on Situated Public Displays. Computers & Graphics 30(5), 681–691 (2006)
10. Storz, O., Friday, A., Davies, N., Finney, J., Sas, C., Sheridan, J.: Public ubiquitous computing systems: Lessons from the e-campus display deployment. Personal and Ubiquitous Computing 5(3), 40–47 (2006)

Slice&Dice: Recognizing Food Preparation Activities Using Embedded Accelerometers

Cuong Pham and Patrick Olivier

Culture Lab, School of Computing Science, Newcastle University

Abstract. Within the context of an endeavor to provide situated support for people with cognitive impairments in the kitchen, we developed and evaluated classifiers for recognizing 11 actions involved in food preparation. Data was collected from 20 lay subjects using four specially designed kitchen utensils incorporating embedded 3-axis accelerometers. Subjects were asked to prepare a mixed salad in our laboratory-based instrumented kitchen environment. Video of each subject's food preparation activities were independently annotated by three different coders. Several classifiers were trained and tested using these features. With an overall accuracy of 82.9% our investigation demonstrated that a broad set of food preparation actions can be reliably recognized using sensors embedded in kitchen utensils.

1 Introduction: Ambient Intelligence in the Kitchen

Ambient intelligence has seen significant progress since Weiser's original vision of ubiquitous computing [1], a world in which computers and sensors disappear as they are woven into the fabric of our surroundings. The technical basis and infrastructure to realize miniaturized computing and sensory devices, connected by wireless networks, is already apparent. However, it is not enough simply to demonstrate that miniaturization and networking are possible. If this technology is to find its way into our homes it must be made to fit into existing home environments and then be able to support the things people wish to do there.

Kitchens offer a unique challenge for the development of the situated services envisaged by Weiser, not only because there is a readily identifiable user group in people with dementia, whose lives would be transformed by effective situated support, but because kitchens are not typical sites for the deployment of digital technologies. Whilst the kitchen contains much existing technology in the form of appliances for cooking, washing and food preparation the level of integration of such devices is minimal and the very notion of the "appliance" emphasizes the stand alone character and well defined function of each device. Unlike many aspects of modern life, the kitchen is still a space where physical interaction with real objects (food and kitchen utensils) is valued and information access is furnished through traditional media such as cookbooks.

In particular, the development of cognitive prosthetics lies at the heart of our interest in activity recognition in the kitchen. Specifically, the clinical problem of prompting people in the early stages of dementia through multi-step tasks [2, 3].

M. Tscheligi et al. (Eds.): AmI 2009, LNCS 5859, pp. 34–43, 2009.

Carefully conducted interviews with people with dementia and their carers, and in depth observational studies have revealed both the nature of the support that people with dementia require in the kitchen, and just how important being able to prepare food and drink was to their sense of their own autonomy. The development of a system to support a person with dementia undertaking even quite simple food and drink preparation requires intelligent technologies that are still well beyond the state-of-the-art, in particular, the detection of a user's actions and intentions, and the provision of situated prompts when things go awry.

The literature contains many proposals as to how one might use ambient intelligence to support people with dementia complete daily tasks. Only a few of these have been implemented as research prototypes, and none so far are commercial products. There are significant problems to be solved before such technologies can become a commercial reality. An effective prompting system has to infer context: what activity the user is engaged in, what have they done so far, and what is the current state of the environment. For example, the COACH hand washing system [4] has to sense that someone is at the sink oriented in such a way that there is a high probability that they want to wash their hands. It has to track the steps in carrying out this activity and prompt only when necessary. It has to sense whether the tap is on or off and where the soap is. The COACH system is sensitive to errors in this process of sensing and inference. Our goal is to provide the sensing foundations for a system that can support people undertaking food preparation activities and we therefore concentrate on the detection and classification of activities in which cooking utensils (in this case knives and spoons) are involved.

2   Previous Work: Activity Recognition

A key element of intelligent situated support technology is context recognition, how a system can understand when and where a service should be provided and furnishing this service in a manner that is sensitive to the current location, activity and characteristics of the user. The notion of *context* is typically very broad and includes any information that characterizes a situation, but in particular, the activity that the user is engaged in. Representing and automatically recognizing activity remains a fundamental challenge and plays a vital role in a broad range of applications such as automated prompting, preventive health care systems, proactive service provision, and visual surveillance. Such applications are often proposed as being particularly valuable for assisting elderly and cognitively impaired people.

Previous work has often approached the problem of activity recognition through sensors worn on different parts of the users body to detect activities such as running, and walking. Although much of this prior work has yielded significant results, it is well understood that users are generally not comfortable wearing such sensors. Moreover, the actions performed in the kitchen context relating to food preparation (such as chopping, peeling, slicing and coring ingredients) are highly dependent on the motions of the kitchen instruments themselves (i.e. kitchen uten-sils such as knives and spoons) which are rather distinct from the movements of the user's body. Wearable sensor research, and computer vision based approaches [8, 15] have generally explored sets of body-level activities such as lying, standing, sitting, walking, running and cycling. The majority of these studies [7, 9, 13] col-lected data under controlled laboratory conditions, with the minority [5, 6] using only semi-realistic conditions.

A small number of previous projects [8, 10, 11] have utilized embedded sens-ing in objects to recognize human activities. For example, by attaching RFID tags to everyday items such as sugar bowls, cups and kettles [12] and requiring users to wear a sensor in the form of a wrist worn RFID reader. Such systems aim to identify everyday kitchen task performance such as boiling water, making tea, making cereal or other activities of daily living such as making a phone call, having a drink or taking medicine. Such worn RFID sensor systems are notori-ously noisy, but can provide an accurate picture of activity levels in a kitchen (characterized in terms of the number of object manipulations). However, fine grained activity support with RFID is not feasible; it might be possible to detect that a knife is in use, but not to distinguish between a user's chopping or peeling actions.

3   Detecting Food Preparation Activities

Our examination of a wide range of sensor-based activity recognition systems (see Table 1) shows that existing systems are not always evaluated independently of the subjects for which the underlying models have been trained. Even the best subject independent evaluations achieve accuracies for the detection of high level activities of around 80-85%. Furthermore, participatory design activities with users usually reveal two key requirements for activity recognition systems: that

Table 1. Summary of examples of previous work on human activity recognition

	Ind.	Dep.	Example activities	No.	Sensors
[5]	81%	94%	Walking, lying, cycling	21	Worn
[6]	84%	n/a	Walking, lying, cycling	20	Worn
[7]	73%	99%	Standing, walking, brushing	2	Worn
[8]	81%	n/a	Boiling water, making tea	n/a	Embedded
[9]	n/a	79-92%	Driving, sitting, ironing	n/a	Worn
[10]	25-89%	n/a	Watching TV, preparing dinner	2	Worn
[11]	n/a	88%	Toileting, washing	14	Worn
[12]	n/a	63-99%	Vacuuming, ironing, mopping	12	Worn
[13]	n/a	98%	Sitting, standing, lying	18	Worn
[14]	80%	98%	Drinking, phoning, writing	4	Embedded

the sensing infrastructure should not intrude on the conduct of the activity itself (i.e. sensors hidden from users) and that the cost and ease of deployment (and maintenance) of such systems should be minimal. Even the most unobtrusive worn sensor system would appear to be in conflict with these needs and are not a practical solution for cognitively impaired users for who many situated support systems are targeted.

The level of abstraction of activity that existing systems are capable of detecting (e.g. walking, sitting, drinking) is also out of kilter with the granularity of action with which a system aimed at supporting cognitively impaired users requires. Wherton and Monk's studies of people with dementia [3] demonstrated that so-called failures in task completion occurred when low-level actions were unexpectedly suspended or prolonged, and fine-grained prompts to complete a low-level action were performed by carers (e.g. putting a tea bag in a tea pot, or buttering a piece of toast). Even situated support systems that are not targeted at cognitively impaired users, require prompts (and therefore action detection) at the sub-task level, for example, prompting the next step in a recipe based on the detection of the completion of the previous step. Such boundaries between subtasks might be the break between chopping one ingredient and scraping it off the chopping board to make space for the next ingredient. We can therefore see that situated support systems for food preparation require low-level recognition of food preparation activities that is beyond the theoretical capability of a worn sensor system.

3.1 Slice&Dice: Instrumented Utensils

With a view to detecting low-level food preparation activities we have developed Slice&Dice, a set of custom made cooking utensils created using FDM rapid prototyping, in which we embedded accelerometers. Slice&Dice comprises three knives and a serving spoon (see Figure 1) into which we have embedded

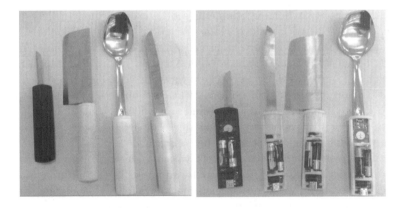

Fig. 1. Modified Wii Remotes embedded in specially designed handles

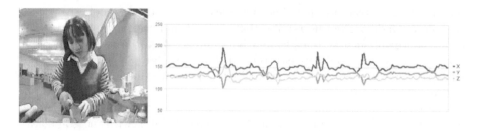

Fig. 2. X, Y and Z acceleration data for dicing with the big knife

the electronics of modified Wii Remotes [16]. An ADXL330 accelerometer, which is able to sense acceleration along three axis, is integrated in a Wii Remote. An ADXL330 is a thin, low power, 3-axis accelerometer with signal conditioned voltage outputs. The dynamic acceleration can be measured from motion, shock or vibration. An ADXL330 accelerometer can measure acceleration with a minimum full-scale range -3g to 3g. While we envisage that future versions of Slice&Dice might use the ADXL330 as a component of a smaller wireless sensor, the Wii Remote provides an excellent platform for developing and evaluating classifiers in utensils that can still retain a usable form factor.

Wii Remotes yield 3-axis values X, Y and Z. As the frequency for the embedded Wii Remotes was set to 40 Hz, this provided approximately 40 triples (samples) of acceleration data every second. The handles of the Slice&Dice utensils were designed so that they comfortably contained the Wii Remote board after its casing and the infrared camera were removed. Informal post-experiment discussions with users revealed that they were generally not aware of the embedded electronics inside the utensils while they were performing their food preparation actions.

3.2   Data Collection and Annotation

There are five IP cameras installed in the Ambient Kitchen [17], our laboratory-based instrumented kitchen environment (see Figure 3). Three of these cameras directly focus on the work surface where the food is prepared. The food ingredients used for the salad and sandwich preparation task that we set users included: potatoes, tomatoes, lettuce, carrots, onions, garlic, kiwi fruit, grapefruit, pepper, bread and butter. Twenty subjects without professional experience of food preparation were recruited from our institution. Subjects were asked to freely perform any actions relating to salad and sandwich preparation, with the ingredients provided, without any further direction from the experimenter, and subjects were not placed under any time constraint.

The time taken to complete the task varied widely, resulting in lengths of recorded sessions that varied from 7 to 16 minutes. To synchronize the videos with acceleration data, we recorded one time stamp for each sample written into the log files. In contrast to previous studies [5, 6], the subjects of our experiment were unencumbered by worn sensors, and were free to act as if they were in their home kitchens (to the extent that this is possible in a university research lab).

Subjects signed privacy waivers and the resulting accelerometer data and the annotated video (see next section) is freely available to other researchers. A set of 11 activity labels were decided upon based on an informal survey of language used in several hours of English language cooking videos found on YouTube, these were: *chopping, peeling, slicing, dicing, coring, spreading, eating, stirring scooping, scraping* and *shaving*. The recorded videos showed that all subjects performed a significant number of chopping, scooping, and peeling actions. Only small subsets of subjects performed eating (i.e. using the knife or spoon to eat ingredients), scraping (i.e. rather than peeling) or dicing (i.e. fine grained rapid chopping) actions.

The collected videos were independently annotated by 3 coders using the Anvil multimodal annotation tool [18]. Each annotator was provided with an informal description of the 11 activities for which we had labels, and were asked to independently annotate the video of each subject. After annotation, we created two data sets for training and testing the classifiers. Dataset A was the intersection of the 3 coded data sets where only labeled data for which all 3 annotators agreed was extracted. This corresponds to data where there is complete agreement between the annotators as to the action being performed. It should be noted that the boundaries between the 11 activity labels is often unclear. While dataset A is a subset of the data for which all the annotators agree, we also repeated our experiments on a second dataset (B) which is the complete data set coded by one annotator. Dataset B is therefore a larger single dataset corresponding to a single annotator's interpretation of the labels and the video data.

Although previous research on activity recognition used window sizes ranging from 4.2 seconds [5] to 6.7 seconds [6], our problem domain is quite different as our sensors are attached to the utensils themselves and we are well aware of the relatively short time window within which some actions might be best characterized. However, we still needed to determine the window size with which the best result could be achieved. Therefore, the collected data were grouped into windows sized: 0.8 seconds (i.e. 32 samples), 1.6 seconds (i.e. 64 samples), 3.2 seconds (i.e. 128 samples), 6.4 seconds (i.e. 256 samples) and 12.8 seconds (i.e. 512 samples). A 50% overlap between two consecutive windows was used. For each triple X, Y, Z, we also computed the pitch and roll of the Wii Remotes and made these available to our classifiers.

For each window, we computed *mean, standard deviation, energy* and *entropy* [19] as follows:

- *energy*: computed for values on the X-axis by: $energy(X) = \frac{\sum\limits_{i=1}^{N} x_i^2}{N}$
- *mean*: computed by summing all values in an axis of a sliding window and divided by the window size.
- *standard deviation*: $\Delta_x = \sqrt{energy(X) - mean(X)^2}$
- *entropy*: for values on the X-axis, where N is the window size, $0 \ log_2(0)$ is assumed to be 0; and $p(x_i) = Pr(X = x_i)$ the probability mass function of x_i: $entropy(X) = - \sum\limits_{i=1}^{N} p(x_i)log_2 p(x_i)$

For each utensil, 12 features were computed for the X, Y, Z axes; 4 features were computed for pitch, and 4 features for roll. Therefore a total of 20 features are computed for one utensil within one window. As we used 4 utensils, a vector composed of all 80 features was used for training the classifiers.

4   Results

Feature vectors computed from 32, 64, 128, 256 and 512-sample windows were trained for the Bayesian Network, Decision Tree (C4.5) and Naïve Bayes classifiers found in Weka [20, 21]. The classification algorithms were evaluated on the two different data sets A and B. Since subject dependent evaluations have only very limited application in the contexts that we envisage we only evaluated our algorithms under the subject independent protocol. Under this protocol, we trained 19 subjects, tested the one remaining subject, and repeated the process.

Where n_i is the number of test instances of an activity a_i, $Acc(a_i)$ is the accuracy of an activity a_i, and M is the total number of test instances for all activities, the overall accuracy was computed as follows:

$$Overall\ Accuracy = \frac{\sum_i (n_i \times Acc(a_i))}{M} \tag{1}$$

The overall accuracy of classifiers evaluated on dataset A (data for which all three annotators agree) is given in Table 2 and this shows that the Decision Tree with window sizes of 128 (3.2 seconds) and 256 (6.4 seconds) exhibit the highest accuracies (i.e. over 80%). Table 3 shows a summary of the results for dataset B which has significantly more data (i.e. corresponding one annotator's mark-up of all the data), here a 128-sample windows demonstrated marginally better accuracy.

Table 2. Summary of results for three classifiers on dataset A

Algorithm	Window size				
	32	64	128	256	512
Decision Tree (C4.5)	77.7	78.7	80.3	82.9	80.2
Bayesian Net	70.8	72.5	79.7	78.9	69.1
Naïve Bayes	47.5	45.6	50.5	52.4	51.3

Table 3. Summary of results for three classifiers on dataset B

Algorithm	Window size				
	32	64	128	256	512
Decision Tree (C4.5)	77.0	76.8	80.2	77.5	80.1
Bayesian Net	67.5	70.2	73.6	71.3	74.5
Nave Bayes	61.3	61.8	62.2	73.5	72.7

5   Reflections

The aggregated results tell us little of the accuracy of the classifiers across the different actions and tables 4 and 5 reveal the performance of the Decision Tree classifier for different window sizes across the different activities. As one might expect, the classifier performs worst for actions which are intuitively less well defined and in themselves hard to label. Classifier performance for relatively unambiguous activities such as chopping, peeling, coring, stirring and scooping is above 80%, while classification of less distinct activities is significantly less accurate. This may in part be due to the low number of training instances for activities such as slicing, dicing and scraping. We also see significant improvements in accuracy for these activities in dataset B, where the number of

Table 4. Detailed results for the Decision Tree classifier on dataset A

	Window size									
	32		*64*		*128*		*256*		*512*	
Action	instances	%	instances	%	instances	%	instances	%	instances	%
chopping	2040	87.3	986	87.5	476	86.1	220	87.7	102	86.5
peeling	712	96.9	342	95.9	170	97.1	80	97.5	36	94.4
slicing	160	19.4	64	26.6	36	30.3	10	80.0	4	0.0
dicing	184	19.6	86	18.6	38	15.8	12	4.2	4	0.0
coring	354	73.4	170	77.7	80	76.3	36	80.6	10	60.0
spreading	224	46.0	126	44.4	56	57.1	26	53.9	10	40.0
eating	94	10.6	44	31.8	18	27.2	8	50.0	0	n/a
stirring	392	78.6	192	85.9	86	90.7	36	91.7	14	100.0
scooping	906	89.5	460	86.3	222	89.2	98	86.7	42	92.9
scraping	98	50.0	48	56.3	22	18.2	8	75	2	0.0
shaving	388	60.3	176	59.7	120	72.3	60	69.9	28	60.3

Table 5. Detailed results for Decision Tree classifier on dataset B

	Window size									
	32		*64*		*128*		*256*		*512*	
Action	instances	%	instances	%	instances	%	instances	%	instances	%
chopping	6184	88.0	3116	86.7	1510	88.1	726	86.6	328	90.9
peeling	472	72.5	230	75.7	86	67.4	50	70.0	16	75.0
slicing	788	31.6	378	27.5	150	35.3	82	24.4	36	19.4
dicing	162	3.7	78	14.1	38	15.3	16	12.5	4	12.5
coring	1246	94.5	612	94.8	300	92.7	130	86.9	64	82.8
spreading	2177	88.0	1034	90.5	498	90.4	260	86.9	116	82.8
eating	326	21.5	164	10.4	82	31.7	28	35.7	18	4.2
stirring	1122	74.7	558	70.8	190	77.4	134	70.9	64	81.3
scooping	796	37.3	390	39.5	186	51.1	76	47.2	32	81.3
scraping	716	62.2	364	64.3	172	65.2	82	65.8	32	56.3
shaving	848	75.9	416	79.6	200	90.5	88	86.4	42	92.9

Fig. 3. The Ambient Kitchen is pervasive computing prototyping environment

training samples is higher (this is particularly true for scraping). Notably, as one might expect, the activities themselves have different temporal scales (e.g. dicing vs. eating), and thus the window size for which a classifier is most accurate varies across the activities.

Slice&Dice is a first step in the development of a low-level activity recognition framework for fine-grained food preparation activities. As such it forms one component of the heterogenous sensor framework that we are developing in the Ambient Kitchen [17]. The Ambient Kitchen (Figure 3) also utilizes extensively deployed RFID readers (and tags associated with all moveable non-metallic objects), five IP cameras integrated into the walls of the kitchen, a mote-based wireless network of accelerometers attached to other kitchen objects, and a pressure sensitive floor. Projectors and speakers embedded in the environment facilitate the generation of spatially embedded cues. The current configuration uses blended projection from four small projectors placed under up-lighters in the main workbench. The projection is reflected by a mirror under the over-head cabinets onto the kitchen wall. Integrating spatially situated auditory cueing allows us to explore the various configurations by which auditory and visual cues can be realized. In this way we can explore the practical problems of creating technologies that are robust and acceptable in the home.

References

[1] Weiser, M.: The computer for the 21st century. Scientific American 265(3), 93–104 (1991)
[2] Wherton, J., Monk, A.: Designing cognitive supports for dementia. SIGACCESS Access. Comput. (86), 28–31 (2006)
[3] Wherton, J., Monk, A.: Technological opportunities for supporting people with dementia who are living at home. International Journal of Human-Computer Studies 66(8), 571–586 (2008)
[4] Mihailidis, A., Boger, J., Canido, M., Hoey, J.: The use of an intelligent prompting system for people with dementia. interactions 14(4), 34–37 (2007)
[5] Tapia, E.M., Intille, S.S., Haskell, W., Larson, K., Wright, J., King, A., Friedman, R.: Real-time recognition of physical activities and their intensities using wireless accelerometers and a heart rate monitor. In: Proceedings of 11th IEEE International Symposium on Wearable Computers, October 2007, pp. 37–40 (2007)

[6] Bao, L., Intille, S.S.: Activity recognition from user-annotated acceleration data. In: Ferscha, A., Mattern, F. (eds.) PERVASIVE 2004. LNCS, vol. 3001, pp. 1–17. Springer, Heidelberg (2004)

[7] Ravi, N., Dandekar, N., Mysore, P., Littman, M.L.: Activity recognition from accelerometer data. In: Proceedings of the Seventeenth Conference on Innovative Applications of Artificial Intelligence (IAAI), pp. 1541–1546. AAAI Press, Menlo Park (2005)

[8] Wu, J., Osuntogun, A., Choudhury, T., Philipose, M., Rehg, J.M.: A scalable approach to activity recognition based on object use. In: Proceedings of the International Conference on Computer Vision (ICCV), Rio de (2007)

[9] Huynh, T., Blanke, U., Schiele, B.: Scalable recognition of daily activities with wearable sensors. In: Hightower, J., Schiele, B., Strang, T. (eds.) LoCA 2007. LNCS, vol. 4718, pp. 50–67. Springer, Heidelberg (2007)

[10] Tapia, E.M., Intille, S.S., Larson, K.: Activity recognition in the home using simple and ubiquitous sensors. In: Ferscha, A., Mattern, F. (eds.) PERVASIVE 2004. LNCS, vol. 3001, pp. 158–175. Springer, Heidelberg (2004)

[11] Philipose, M., Fishkin, K.P., Perkowitz, M., Patterson, D.J., Fox, D., Kautz, H., Hahnel, D.: Inferring activities from interactions with objects. IEEE Pervasive Computing 3(4), 50–57 (2004)

[12] Stikic, M., Huynh, T., Van Laerhoven, K., Schiele, B.: Adl recognition based on the combination of rfid and accelerometer sensing. In: Second International Conference on Pervasive Computing Technologies for Healthcare. PervasiveHealth 2008, 30 2008-February 1 2008, pp. 258–263 (2008)

[13] Kim, I., Im, S., Hong, E., Ahn, S.C., Kim, H.-G.: ADL classification using triaxial accelerometers and RFID. In: Proceedings of the International Workshop on Ubiquitous Convergence Technology (November 2007)

[14] Wang, S., Yang, J., Chen, N., Chen, X., Zhang, Q.: Human activity recognition with user-free accelerometers in the sensor networks. In: International Conference on Neural Networks and Brain (ICNN&B 2005), October 2005, vol. 2, pp. 1212–1217 (2005)

[15] Robertson, N., Reid, I.: A general method for human activity recognition in video. Computer Vision and Image Understanding 104(2-3), 232–248 (2006); Special Issue on Modeling People: Vision-based understanding of a person's shape, appearance, movement and behaviour

[16] Wii Remote: http://en.wikipedia.org/wiki/Wii_Remote

[17] Olivier, P., Xu, G., Monk, A., Hoey, J.: Ambient kitchen: designing situated services using a high fidelity prototyping environment. In: PETRA 2009: Proceedings of the 2nd International Conference on PErvsive Technologies Related to Assistive Environments, pp. 1–7. ACM, New York (2009)

[18] Kipp, M.: Anvil – a generic annotation tool for multimodal dialogue. In: Proceedings of In EUROSPEECH 2001, pp. 1367–1370 (2001)

[19] Shannon, C.E.: A mathematical theory of communication. SIGMOBILE Mob. Comput. Commun. Rev. 5(1), 3–55 (2001)

[20] Weka: http://www.cs.waikato.ac.nz/ml/weka/

[21] Witten, I.H., Frank, E.: Data Mining: Practical machine learning tools and techniques. Morgan Kaufmann, San Francisco (2005)

The Ambient Tag Cloud: A New Concept for Topic-Driven Mobile Urban Exploration

Matthias Baldauf, Peter Fröhlich, and Peter Reichl

Telecommunications Research Center Vienna (ftw.)
Donau-City-Strasse 1, 1220 Vienna, Austria
{baldauf,froehlich,reichl}@ftw.at

Abstract. Today's mobile phones are increasingly used as mediators between the real world and georeferenced digital information. However, common 2D maps as the most often applied visualization method are bearing inherent limitations when presenting a vast amount of data on a small screen. Therefore, in this paper, we propose 'ambient tag clouds' as an abstract alternative visualization approach for spatial information. Ambient tag clouds are designed as an extension of their Web counterparts exploiting the context-awareness of mobile devices. In our prototype implementation this novel concept has been combined with a gesture-based interaction method and thus enables mobile users to scan their current surroundings and make summarizing snapshots of adjacent areas.

Keywords: Mobile Spatial Interaction, Visualization, Tag cloud, Location-based services.

1 Introduction

Beyond their original purpose of communication on the move, mobile devices are nowadays increasingly used also for interaction with our physical environment. They provide information about our surroundings, they guide us to remote places, and let us communicate with real-world objects. This trend is strongly supported by the massive growth of georeferenced data. Large community websites attract hundreds of thousand user-submitted and geotagged photos, and countless websites make use of map mashups. However, exploring these masses of data on the spot with a present-day mobile phone application often will result in a disappointing experience, mainly because static 2D maps with georeferenced points of interest (POIs) bear inherent limitations: the more information is presented, the more difficult it is for a user to overview, browse and search suitable information [1].

Therefore, we propose 'ambient tag clouds' as a visualization technique that we believe to be better suited for addressing this challenge, especially for mobile urban exploration. Usually, tag clouds are used for visualizing the most-assigned tags on a website in the form of a weighted list of tag names, while the textual attributes such as size, weight and color, as well as the word placement may indicate a specific tag's properties. In the most common implementation, a tag's frequency is represented via its font size: the larger a tag name is visualized, the more often it has been assigned.

M. Tscheligi et al. (Eds.): AmI 2009, LNCS 5859, pp. 44–48, 2009.

Our key idea is to transfer this broadly known visualization concept to mobile devices and to make such clouds dynamically adapt to the current spatial surroundings. To prove this concept, we have built a prototype that displays a weighted list of tags that are associated to the portion of the environment where the user is pointing to with her mobile device. When the user turns around or moves along, this ambient tag cloud dynamically morphs according to the changing information landscape delivering a foretaste of what the user can expect in that area. If a tag of interest is selected, a conventional map of this area helps to explore the corresponding POIs.

The remainder of the paper is structured as follows: First, we report on related work and define the concept of ambient tag clouds. We then describe our current prototype implementation, and finally highlight some upcoming research issues.

2   Related Work

Tagged user-generated data and tag clouds recently have become subject of scientific research. Examples include studies to measure a tag cloud's effectiveness for various tasks such as presented by Rivadeneira et al. [6]. A novel visualization approach which combines common 2D maps with tag overlays resulting in so-called tag maps has been proposed by Jaffe et al. [4]. Slingsby et al. [8] defined an exploratory cycle for filtering content via a spatial map as well as via an aspatial cloud representation. Nevertheless, scientific work investigating the use of tagged data and its representations in a mobile spatial context is scarce. A representation technique similar to tag maps is proposed by Jones et al. [5] where the authors placed recently conducted Web search queries of nearby mobile users on a map providing insights into a location's character. Yahoo's ZoneTag is a well-known project supporting mobile users with location-aware tagging suggestions for submitted photo [9].

Natural ways to interact with spatially referenced content are investigated in the research field of Mobile Spatial Interaction (MSI) [3]. In early work Egenhofer [2] proposed the concepts of so-called Smart Compasses pointing the user into the direction of a particular geographic object and Smart Horizons presenting additional information beyond the user's current field of view. More recent work such as presented by Simon et al. [7] includes real-world applications investigating the use of pointing gestures to fetch digital content attached to a real-world object.

3   Ambient Tag Clouds

As already mentioned above, conventional tag clouds are used to arrange the most-assigned tags on a website. Our proposed 'ambient tag clouds' are based on an underlying set of georeferenced tagged items. Therefore, they serve as an abstract visualization for a given area's digital content. Just as their counterpart on the Web [6], ambient tag clouds may provide advantages for several generic types of exploration, as compared to conventional map- or list-based POI presentations.

- **'Gisting'.** Getting the gist of what is available is certainly one of our main needs when starting to explore a new place. Ambient tag clouds appear to be an ideal tool for such purposes, as they aim at recapitulating the information on one single screen while providing a unique picture of its currently prevailing key aspects.

- **Browsing.** Exploration of the urban surroundings is often inspired by an overall interest in learning more about the surrounding objects and related opportunities. In such a rather unspecific browsing attitude, the 'topic-orientation' offered by ambient tag clouds may be more appropriate than the usual 'target-orientation' with a map.
- **Searching.** Also in more targeted search, such as when a user is looking for a popular restaurant in the area, the efficient selection among a multitude offers can be a considerable challenge. The weighted and overview tag descriptions could be advantageous compared to generic category listings. In addition, pre-selection of tags promises to be a relatively intuitive and direct filtering method to reduce the number of POI on a map.

Moreover, the application of such tag clouds on a mobile device enables the additional integration of contextual information to further tailor the appearance of the cloud. Thus, location-aware devices are able to restrict a cloud's underlying items to the currently nearby ones. Built-in compasses even allow the restriction of items to a certain direction of view.

Due to the dynamic nature of the involved data, the resulting ambient tag clouds are not static as their conventional website counterparts but constantly change their appearance according to the underlying items and new contextual information.

Based on these features, we define and summarize the concept of ambient tag clouds as follows.

- Ambient tag clouds are based on georeferenced items, therefore providing an abstract location description for a given area.
- Ambient tag clouds are context-sensitive with emphasis on location- and orientation-awareness. Thus, they are usually applied on mobile devices.
- Ambient tag clouds present their dynamic nature in a suitable way in order to visually notify the user about context changes.

4 Prototype Implementation

We have implemented this new visualization approach as a prototype which combines the concept of ambient tag clouds with a gesture-based interaction method as follows. While the user holds the mobile device parallel to the ground as depicted in Figure 1, the application is running in 'scanning mode': The displayed ambient tag cloud is consistently updated according to the device's current location and orientation. Thus, the user may 'scan' her environment by pointing and turning at the same time while pursuing the changes on the display. Note that, in order to support the experience of 'scanning' and conspicuously visualize these adaptations, an appropriate ambient cloud does not simply pop up but the former cloud gradually turns into the new one: old tag labels may disappear, new ones may be revealed, remaining ones may change their appearance (cf. Figure 3).

As soon as the user is content with the ambient cloud's structure and interested in more detailed information about the visualized area, she usually moves her mobile closer to her face. Therefore, tilting the device in a more upright position as depicted in Figure 2 disables the scanning mode, i.e. the application ignores further changes of the device's location and orientation in order to allow additional interaction with the currently visible ambient cloud.

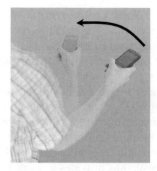

Fig. 1. Scanning the environment by pointing and turning

Fig. 2. Disabling scanning mode by tilting the mobile

Fig. 3. Morphing from source to target cloud

At this stage, the cloud's tag labels may be selected via the touch screen. The touch of a tag switches from the cloud view to a common 2D map. Turning the former abstract and aspatial cloud visualization into this spatial map representation now reveals the tag's underlying POIs with their corresponding positions for detailed search and browsing tasks.

Pressing the appropriate hardware button brings the user back to the current ambient tag cloud; tilting the device forwards re-enables the scanning mode.

5   Conclusion and Outlook

The concept of 'ambient tag clouds' presented in this paper enables topic-oriented exploration of a user's urban surroundings. It combines dynamic tag cloud visualization with mobile spatial interaction techniques to provide quick and individual snapshots of areas and directions of interest in the user's immediate surroundings.

Our prototype is deliberately designed for experimentation. The natural next step is now to systematically investigate the benefits and usage practices related to such an abstract, topic-based exploration and to evaluate its complementarity to conventional target-based map visualizations. In addition, we aim at better understanding how to realize the most innovative aspect of the ambient tag cloud, i.e. the dynamic morphing of abstract visualizations due to a user's spatial movements. For example, recommendations are needed regarding an optimal style of tag rearrangement that is dynamic enough to support fine-grained context-adaptation but stable enough to support efficient tag selection.

The current ambient tag cloud prototype is devised for accessing volunteered geographic information organized by user-assigned tags. However, in principle, ambient tag clouds complementing standard maps with more abstract information representations might serve as a worthwhile exploration tool for other information types as well, such as extracted commercial travel and restaurant guide recommendations. Grounding ambient tag clouds on a broader information basis thus provides a viable promising direction for further research.

Acknowledgments. This work has been carried out within the projects WikiVienna and U0, which are financed in parts by Vienna's WWTF funding program, by the Austrian Government and by the City of Vienna within the competence center program COMET. The authors would like to thank all members of these project teams for many fruitful discussions.

References

1. Chittaro, L.: Visualizing Information on Mobile Devices. IEEE Computer 39(3), 40–45 (2006)
2. Egenhofer, M.J.: Spatial Information Appliances: A Next Generation of Geographic Information Systems. In: 1st Brazilian Workshop on GeoInformatics, Campinas, Brazil (1999)
3. Fröhlich, P., Simon, R., Baillie, L.: Mobile spatial interaction. Personal and Ubiquitous Computing 13(4), 251–253 (2009)
4. Jaffe, A., Naaman, M., Tassa, T., Davis, M.: Generating summaries and visualization for large collections of geo-referenced photographs. In: Proceedings of the 8th ACM international workshop on Multimedia information retrieval (2006)
5. Jones, M., Buchanan, G., Harper, R., Xech, P.: Questions not answers: a novel mobile search technique. In: Proceedings of the SIGCHI Conference on Human Factors in Computing Systems, CHI 2007, pp. 155–158. ACM, New York (2007)
6. Rivadeneira, A.W., Gruen, D.M., Muller, M.J., Millen, D.R.: Getting our head in the clouds: toward evaluation studies of tagclouds. In: Proceedings of the SIGCHI conference on Human factors in computing systems (2007)
7. Simon, R., Fröhlich, P., Obernberger, G., Wittowetz, E.: The Point to Discover GeoWand. In: Krumm, J., Abowd, G.D., Seneviratne, A., Strang, T. (eds.) UbiComp 2007. LNCS, vol. 4717. Springer, Heidelberg (2007)
8. Slingsby, A., Dykes, J., Wood, J., Clarke, K.: Interactive Tag Maps and Tag Clouds for the Multiscale Exploration of Large Spatio-Temporal Datasets. In: Proceedings of the 11th International Conference Information Visualization (2007)
9. Yahoo! Research Berkeley: ZoneTag (June 16, 2009),
   http://zonetag.research.yahoo.com

Constructing Topological Maps of Displays with 3-D Positioning Information

Donald J. Patterson

University Of California, Irvine, USA
djp3@ics.uci.edu

Abstract. To better coordinate information displays with moving people and the environment, software must know the locations and *three dimensional alignments* of the display hardware. In this paper we describe a technique for creating such an enhanced topological map of networked public displays using a mobile phone. The result supports a richer user experience, without the cost of maintaining a high resolution reconstruction of a smart environment.

1 Introduction and Related Work

Digital displays are relied upon to provide location and situation specific information to a wide variety of viewers (*e.g.*, [1]). Despite their cost, power and maintenance requirements, they are often preferred to non-digital signage in high-traffic venues [2]. The presence of multiple networked digital displays creates a class of navigation applications which can coordinate the display of dynamic content in a way that is not possible with static or isolated digital signage. This class of applications does not require complete knowledge of the physical environment to be effective.

An example of such an application is a hospital that guides patients to the appropriate office. Imagine that Martha must visit a cardiac specialist for the first time. She indicates her high-level goal to a kiosk, "Appointment with Dr. Theophilus" She is requested to follow a yellow arrow which appears on a series of cooperating displays [3] that guide her to the correct office. Other patients are given different colors to follow. Martha can follow her arrows without needing to be familiar with the layout of the hospital, or knowing that Dr. Theophilus has a complicated schedule that has him seeing patients in several locations during the course of the day. Incorporating tracking technology [4] would support showing the yellow arrows only on displays that Martha can actually see.

To realize this scenario, displays must know their location and position relative to each other. Location alone is not sufficient because two displays in the same location would show an arrow pointing in opposite directions (for the same destination) depending on which side of the hallway they were mounted. An expensive infrastructure in which displays contain a digital compass, a 3-axis accelerometer, and in which the environment contains a fine-grained indoor localization technology [5] would be sufficient to address this problem. In this paper we demonstrate that this additional heavyweight capability is not required.

M. Tscheligi et al. (Eds.): AmI 2009, LNCS 5859, pp. 49–54, 2009.

Müller and A. Krüger [4] have done similar work in learning device topologies. Their goal was to identify the distance between devices to enable displays to show sequential content to a moving person. They detected and centrally analyzed passing Bluetooth signals from cooperating subjects to calculate distance estimates between displays. Our work builds on theirs by focusing on developing techniques for orienting the devices to enable richer *spatial* interactions to complement their temporal interactions. Our use of camera sensors provides useful additional spatial data for reducing errors in estimates that are caused by the limited spatial granularity at which Bluetooth devices can be detected.

2 System Overview

Our system requires a single cooperating administrator, using a cell-phone camera, to walk the entire floor plan of the building while the system displays unique 2-D barcodes on each display for calibration and identification. The camera is mounted in a small "image splitter" bracket containing two mirrors, angled at 45 degrees, that are aligned to the lens of the camera. The mirrors reflect images from both sides of the hallway allowing synchronized information from two streams of video to be leveraged during analysis (see Fig. 1). Utilizing techniques (from augmented reality research) that orient barcodes in space, the timing between frames, and the synchronized observations of opposite sides of a hallway, we are

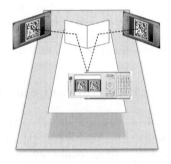

Fig. 1. A user's view of two mounted displays as seen through the camera and image splitter

able to create accurate building topologies including display location and orientation. We evaluated our approach on simulated and real-world floor plans.

Determining a barcode's orientation from an image is a well understood problem in augmented reality [6] when the following two reasonable assumptions are made: First, the image splitter is being held parallel to the floor. Second, the display is mounted flush on the wall, parallel to the floor, so that the orientation of the barcode matches the orientation of the wall, allowing us to relax the assumption of orthogonal walls.

To test our system we deployed several Nokia N800's as displays. We used a Nokia N95 cell phone for video capture (640x480, 30fps) and sent the data wirelessly to a server for real-time analysis. We converted the dual video streams into time-stamped observations indicating the absence or identity of a barcode in both channels as well as the 3D orientation of the barcode. A remote server subsequently constructed candidate topologies of the floor plan that were consistent with the observations and ranked them according to a scoring model.

Alternatively, we could have used RFID tags or Bluetooth beacons to identify and calibrate the displays. However, they do not provide self-orientation nor directionality information between the reader and the tag/beacon. They also incur additional complexity and cost. In contrast, 2-D barcodes work well for calibration; they provide orientation information, camera line-of-sight provides directionality, they can be *temporarily* shown on displays during calibration, they are feasible for large deployments and id's can be dynamically assigned.

3   Topology Reconstruction Algorithm

To reconstruct a representation of the building with displays positioned on the topology, we present a generate-and-score style algorithm that is run in real-time as an administrator walks through the building. This algorithm maintains a list of physically feasible topologies that is updated with each new display observation. The list is ranked according to Occam's razor such that the simplest floor plan, consistent with the observations, is preferred. We assume that floor plans can be represented as planar graphs and that the administrator completes a full walk-through of the area and observes every display.

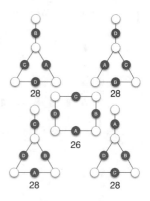

Fig. 2. Candidate topologies made from observing (A,B,C,D,A)

We represent topologies as a *display connectivity graph* (DCG), an undirected graph in which displays, intersections and dead-ends are represented as nodes (black, white and white respectively), and edges represent physical adjacency (roughly hallways). Display nodes contain the 3-D orientation as meta-information (See Figure 2).

Scoring Model. During a walk-through, when a new display is observed we inductively generate all possible candidate graphs from the graphs previously under consideration. After removing non-planar and isomorphic graphs, we score the graphs according to floor plan complexity and likely user walking behavior (see equation 1).

$$S = \alpha_1 \sum_N degree(N)^2 + \alpha_2 * |loops| + \alpha_3 * bktracks \qquad (1)$$

Our scoring function is a weighted sum of two structural penalties and one behavior penalty. The first term is a sum of the squares of the degree of the structure nodes, N. This term favors simpler intersections as explanations for data. The second term penalizes graphs which contain more loops. The final term is the number of backtracks that the user must have made during the walk-through. (This corresponds to leaving a structure node by the same edge by which it was entered when the degree of the structure node > 1). In our experiments we used weighting factors of $\alpha_1 = 1$, $\alpha_2 = 10$, and $\alpha_3 = 1$. Better topologies receive lower scores. Figure 2 shows the top 5 possible graphs after observing four displays in sequence (A, B, C, D, A).

4   Analysis

The first analysis we present assumes the algorithm only has knowlege of the *presence* of a display as would be the case if the displays were augmented with RFID or Bluetooth. Later we include the additional orientation information that is afforded by our visual system.

Simulated Floor Plan Results. We generated 25 physically possible DCGs and a simulated walk-through as test cases.

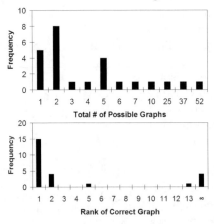

Fig. 3. Top: Histogram showing how many possible floor plans were generated for each of the 25 simulations. Bottom: Histogram of the rank of the true floor plan among all those generated and scored.

We measured the number of candidate graphs the algorithm created during simulated walk-throughs (see Figure 3-top).

Figure 3-bottom shows that 80% of the time the true floor plan was ranked first or second. In four cases the observations were not sufficient to close a loop in the true floor plan, so the algorithm did not have enough information to generate the correct answer. For example, in Figure 2, none of the floor plans would be generated if the walk-through observed only {A, B, C, D}. This sequence does not capture the link from D to A, and so, none of the generated floor plans would show that connection either. A "complete" walk-through is therefore necessary for optimal results, although sub-optimal results will support our motivating scenario but not produce the shortest path through the building for a user.

Removing the user model component from the scoring caused two of the correct graphs to be ranked lower.

Video Augmented Results. Our second analysis included orientation and dual-channel video as well. When a display is seen a second time, we compare the orientation to its previously observed state. If it is on the same side of the hallway, we know we have experienced a loop. If its orientation is reversed, we have turned around, and the previous display should be linked to the appropriate side. This is only possible because of our image splitter tool and choice of visual tags for landmarks. As an example, if we assumed that all displays in Figure 2 were on the outside of the hallways and seen on the left side of the camera splitter, the four graphs with score 28 are impossible.

Using the same simulated data, our analysis is now strongly constrained and only produces one viable, correct floor plan for each case.

Real Floor Plans. Finally we obtained the floor plans of 5 research institutions. We simulated the placement of displays around 4 of them and conducted a real analysis on the fifth. We asked two participants familiar with the buildings to provide us with paths through the space that would observe all the displays. We simulated 4 outcomes and empirically evaluated the fifth. The resulting number of potential graphs is reported in Table 1. In all five cases, the dual-video algorithm correctly identified the real-world topology.

5 Discussion and Future Work

Using split-screen video capture of 2D barcodes to locate displays provides a rapid, effective and low-cost way to calibrate a smart environment. The resulting display connectivity graph, augmented with 3D display orientation, supports rich user interface applications such as providing directional user navigation in a coordinated fashion.

Although we clearly demonstrated the value of orientation as provided by the split-screen camera, there are improvements that

Table 1. Real-world buildings analyzed for complexity. The correct floor plan was identified in each case.

Building Name	# of Potential Graphs
Sieg (UW)	4
Microsoft(Seattle)	6
Allen (UW)	12
Bren Hall (UCI)	32
Intel (Seattle)	100+

should be made. First we assume 100% recognition of our displays. If a display is never seen, but known to be in the building, the model cannot provide any information about where the display might be located. Additionally, if a display is seen once, but later missed the floor plans will be sufficient but sub-optimal. A hybrid approach that mixed visual and RFID/Bluetooth beaconing might alleviate some of these challenges.[1]

References

1. Huang, E.M., Koster, A., Borchers, J.: Overcoming assumptions and uncovering practices: When does the public really look at public displays? In: Indulska, J., Patterson, D.J., Rodden, T., Ott, M. (eds.) PERVASIVE 2008. LNCS, vol. 5013, pp. 228–243. Springer, Heidelberg (2008)
2. Cheverst, K., Dix, A.J., Fitton, D., Friday, A., Rouncefield, M.: Exploring the utility of remote messaging and situated office door displays. In: Chittaro, L. (ed.) Mobile HCI 2003. LNCS, vol. 2795, pp. 336–341. Springer, Heidelberg (2003)
3. Kray, C., Cheverst, K., Fitton, D., Sas, C., Patterson, J., Rouncefield, M., Stahl, C.: Sharing control of dispersed situated displays between nomadic and residential users. In: Nieminen, M., Röykkee, M. (eds.) Mobile HCI, pp. 61–68. ACM, New York (2006)
4. Müller, H.J., Krüger, A.: Learning topologies of situated public displays by observing implicit user interactions. In: Stephanidis, C. (ed.) UAHCI 2007 (Part II). LNCS, vol. 4555, pp. 158–167. Springer, Heidelberg (2007)

---

[1] This work was supported by NSF award: HCC:0713562.

5. Stuntebeck, E.P., Patel, S.N., Robertson, T., Reynolds, M.S., Abowd, G.D.: Wide-band powerline positioning for indoor localization. In: UbiComp 2008: Proceedings of the 10th international conference on Ubiquitous computing, pp. 94–103. ACM, New York (2008)
6. Zhou, F., Duh, H.B.L., Billinghurst, M.: Trends in augmented reality tracking, interaction and display: A review of ten years of ismar. In: 7th IEEE/ACM International Symposium on Mixed and Augmented Reality. ISMAR 2008, September 2008, pp. 193–202 (2008)

Activity Recognition for Personal Time Management

Zoltán Prekopcsák, Sugárka Soha, Tamás Henk, and Csaba Gáspár-Papanek

Budapest University of Technology and Economics, Hungary
prekopcsak@tmit.bme.hu, sugarka.soha@gmail.com,
henk@tmit.bme.hu, gaspar@tmit.bme.hu
http://prekopcsak.hu

Abstract. We describe an accelerometer based activity recognition system for mobile phones with a special focus on personal time management. We compare several data mining algorithms for the automatic recognition task in the case of single user and multiuser scenario, and improve accuracy with heuristics and advanced data mining methods. The results show that daily activities can be recognized with high accuracy and the integration with the RescueTime software can give good insights for personal time management.

1 Introduction

Activity recognition is a popular research area since the 1980s, when camera based methods have been developed, but due to the fast advancement in small sensor technology, it is gaining even more attention in the past few years. Since the first sensor based results [11], activity recognition has been used for the surveillance of medical patients [7], providing context-aware information [2,9] and many more in military and public domains [3]. The algorithmic results are very promising and activity information could be used in many ways, but so far there is no widespread application of this recognition technology.

Furthermore, our life is getting faster and information workers try to be as efficient as possible which made a hype for time management theories, like GTD (Getting Things Done [1]) and gave birth to many software applications which track the time that we spend in front of our computers (e.g. RescueTime). They can give detailed statistics about the time spent with specific applications and documents, and they can even provide suggestions on managing our time better.

As computer usage is continuously shifting towards mobile, we have no information about the context in which we are using our devices, and of course there is a significant amount of time that we spend without using them. Mobile activity recognition solutions can provide additional information about our context and activities even when we are not using electronic devices.

2 System Description

Our goal was to design an activity recognition system that can be used in real life for personal time management. We have used a regular mobile phone and a

M. Tscheligi et al. (Eds.): AmI 2009, LNCS 5859, pp. 55–59, 2009.

small external accelerometer sensor (SparkFun WiTilt v3.0) which was accessed via Bluetooth connection and placed in a belt case, so we could easily track its orientation which makes the recognition easier. It is not a serious limitation as many people uses belt cases, but it is possible to extend our recognition tests in the future for other mobile wearing habits.

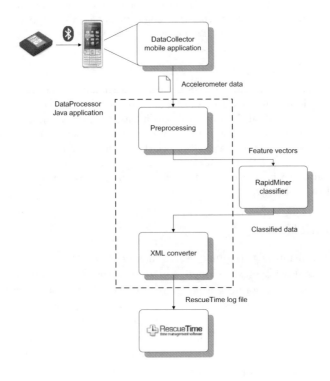

Fig. 1. Building blocks of the system

For the data collection period, we have created a mobile application that helps to collect annotated data about our lives that can serve as training data for the recognizer algorithms. We have decided to pre-define 10 daily (or weekly) activities: walking, running, working (while sitting), watching television, cooking, vacuuming, taking stairs, using the elevator, traveling on a bus, lying. These activities have been selected because they are done frequently and they might be of interest from a personal time management perspective. On the mobile screen, the user can select from the list of these activities, which starts the data collection to the memory card or the phone's internal memory. The user can always change the activity in the list or stop the data collection. The application is written in mobile Java, so it can run in the background and seamlessly track longer activities too.

The accelerometer data files are synchronized to a computer where the recognition software operates. After some data preprocessing, we use the RapidMiner open source data mining framework [8] for the recognizer algorithm, which produces time stamps and activity labels as its output. This is then converted to a special file format for the RescueTime time management software, which adds these activities to its statistics. The whole system can be seen on Figure 1.

3 Activity Recognition

3.1 Data Preprocessing

To be able to use the continuous 3-dimensional accelerometer and the one dimensional gyroscope data for recognition, we had to preprocess it first. We have decided to take two seconds long chunks from the data which resulted 40 data points for each dimension, as the sensor was working on 20Hz. The optimal window length was investigated in earlier papers and they concluded that different activities have different optimal window lengths, but the global optimum is around 2 seconds [5].

From these 4x40 data points, we have calculated many statistical features for the recognition. Previous works suggested minimum, maximum, average and variance values for each dimension [6,9,5], energy measures from the Fourier transformation [2,9,5], and Pearson correlation between the different dimensions [2,9,5]. We believe that these features should well describe the underlying activities, and the classification performance proved our assumptions.

3.2 Classification

With these features, we have tested three different classifier algorithms from the RapidMiner framework: decision tree (DT), support vector machine (SVM), k-nearest neighbor (k-NN). These standard machine learning and data mining algorithms are part of the framework, so we only needed to optimize their parameters. The cross-validation results show that SVM has the highest accuracy, but all methods have the recognition rate around 90%. It is an excellent result considering that there are 10 different activities to be recognized, so random guessing would produce 10% accuracy. We have to note, that for an application that runs only on mobile, decision tree can be the best choice, as it is easy to program on mobile devices and needs low resources.

We have also tried some heuristics to enhance our results. The most successful from these was the usage of a 10 seconds long moving window, which included five 2-second pieces and calculated the most frequently predicted class of these 5 classifications. As it is impossible to have a 2 seconds long cooking activity in minutes of walking, this moving window could correct these errors. This simple heuristic improved the accuracy and sometimes corrected more than half of the errors. Results can be seen on Table 1.

Table 1. Recognition accuracy

Classifier	Accuracy	Accuracy with heuristics
Decision Tree	87.42%	91.97%
Support Vector Machine	93.28%	96.57%
k-Nearest Neighbor	91.27%	95.77%

3.3   Advanced Data Mining Methods

The above mentioned methods are standard data mining algorithms usually used for activity recognition. However, in the past decade, there has been a lot of development in classification algorithms. One of the most important trends is boosting, which is a combination method for a set of weak decision rules to form a highly accurate classifier. A comprehensive overview of boosting methods is written by Schapire [10] and the LogitBoost algorithm is described by Friedman et al. [4]. We have used the latter algorithm with iteratively training small decision trees and combining them for the final model.

Cross-validation was used to optimize the iteration number of LogitBoost to avoid overfitting. The optimal iteration number was 60, which resulted an accuracy of 95.53% on its own and 97.59% when using the heuristics described above. The iteration number means that the final model includes 60 small decision trees. It seems complex, but these 60 trees can be programmed to a mobile phone with code generation.

In case of 97.59% accuracy, the error rate is only 2.41%, so we have analyzed these errors to get some ideas about further improvements. It turned out that most of these errors come from using the elevator being misclassified as cooking which makes sense, as these are very similar activities. We do not consider using the elevator as a very important activity, so by removing it from the study, the accuracy exceeds 99%.

3.4   Multiuser Scenario

These results apply for the case of a single user, when training and test data was collected from the same person. To test the generalization performance of the system, we have made a measurement with training on one user and testing on another. As expected, accuracy drops significantly to around 58–63% for all four algorithms, but we achieved 68.39% with combining them with simple majority voting. This result can be improved if we collect more data from different users.

4   Conclusion

We have shown an activity recognition system that can be used with everyday mobile phones. We have compared standard data mining algorithms and boosting methods, and presented some heuristics to improve the results. The recognition accuracy is over 99% for a single user and 68% for a new user, but there is a huge potential of improving the latter result by additional data collected from more users. Similar results can be achieved with a mobile implementation using low resources.

This system is mainly intended for personal time management, so there is no need for perfect recognition, mistakes are not critical, because its goal is only to track important trends and provide overall statistics. We have found that it can give interesting insights to our personal lives and help us manage better the everyday tasks that we face.

Personal time management is a popular application area, so we believe that it will help spreading activity recognition components for mobile phones in the next few years. If activity recognition becomes a basic service in the mobile, all applications will know much more about our context and they can adapt to us.

References

1. Allen, D.: Getting Things Done: The Art of Stress-Free Productivity. Viking, New York (2001)
2. Bao, L., Intille, S.S.: Activity Recognition from User-Annotated Acceleration Data. In: Ferscha, A., Mattern, F. (eds.) PERVASIVE 2004. LNCS, vol. 3001, pp. 1–17. Springer, Heidelberg (2004)
3. Choudhury, T., Borriello, G., et al.: The Mobile Sensing Platform: An Embedded System for Activity Recognition. In: IEEE Pervasive Magazine - Special Issue on Activity-Based Computing (2008)
4. Friedman, J., Hastie, T., Tibshirani, R.: Additive Logistic Regression: a Statistical View of Boosting. Annals of Statistics 28 (1998)
5. Huynh, T., Schiele, B.: Analyzing Features for Activity Recognition. In: Proceedings of Smart Objects & Ambient Intelligence Conference (2005)
6. Kern, N., Schiele, B., Schmidt, A.: Multi-Sensor Activity Context Detection for Wearable Computing. In: Aarts, E., Collier, R.W., van Loenen, E., de Ruyter, B. (eds.) EUSAI 2003. LNCS, vol. 2875, pp. 220–232. Springer, Heidelberg (2003)
7. Mathie, M.J., Celler, B.G., Lovell, N.H., Coster, A.C.: Classification of basic daily movements using a triaxial accelerometer. Medical & Biological Engineering & Computing 42, 679–687 (2004)
8. Mierswa, I., Wurst, M., Klinkenberg, R., Scholz, M., Euler, T.: YALE: Rapid Prototyping for Complex Data Mining Tasks. In: Proceedings of the 12th ACM SIGKDD International Conference on Knowledge Discovery and Data Mining, KDD 2006 (2006)
9. Ravi, N., Dandekar, N., Mysore, P., Littman, M.L.: Activity recognition from accelerometer data. In: Proceedings of IAAI 2005 (2005)
10. Schapire, R.: The Boosting Approach to Machine Learning: An Overview. In: MSRI Workshop on Nonlinear Estimation and Classification (2003)
11. Uiterwaal, M., Glerum, E.B.C., Busser, H.J., Van Lummel, R.C.: Ambulatory monitoring of physical activity in working situations, a validation study. Journal of Medical Engineering & Technology 22 (1998)

Getting Places:
Collaborative Predictions from Status

Mohamad Monibi and Donald J. Patterson

University Of California, Irvine, USA
{mmonibi,djp3}@ics.uci.edu

Abstract. In this paper we describe the use of collaborative filtering to make predictions about *place* using data from custom instant messaging status. Previous research has shown accurate predictions can be made from an individual's personal data. The work in this paper demonstrates that community data can be used to make predictions in locations that are completely new to a user.

1 Introduction and Related Work

The practice of online status setting has evolved into a form of informal interaction and information exchange. It is an indicator of interruptibility in instant messaging (IM) clients [1] and expresses current mood in social networking applications [2]. The popularity of status messages has given rise to services dedicated to status setting and sharing (e.g., twitter.com, ping.fm). We are primarily interested in its use to indicate the current place of a user (i.e., "micro-presence").

To provide an accurate and useful indication of place, users must frequently update their status, for example every time they enter a new location [3] or engage in a new activity, which is cumbersome. Automating this task can greatly assist the user in maintaining up-to-date status. Accuracies of 80-90% can be achieved in automatically predicting a user's place and activity from their *own* history of status setting behavior [4]. However, these techniques do not address how to make predictions when a user arrives at a place for the first time.

In this paper, we describe the use of collaborative filtering techniques for recommending socially appropriate and relevant place descriptions for mobile IM status using the history of an entire community of users. These place labels often incorporate colloquial understandings of place, putting them outside the ability of commercial point-of-interest databases for choosing appropriate labels.

Recent work has combined sensing with semantic labeling to provide lightweight interpretation of sensor data. WatchMe is a tool based on interpreting sensors as graphical icons to communicate remote context between members of close relationships [5]. Reno allowed users to associate labels to cell tower connections and then to activate rules based on entering those zones [6]. Finally, Connecto allows users to associate labels with combinations of cell-phone towers [7] and IMBuddy with combinations of WiFi access points [8].

Zonetag [9] is a context-aware media annotation system that uses sensor data to provide tag suggestions to annotate photos taken with a cell phone. Zonetag

M. Tscheligi et al. (Eds.): AmI 2009, LNCS 5859, pp. 60–65, 2009.

suggestions come from the tag history of the user, the user's social circle, and the public. Scoring of tags generated by others depends on the social distance between users. Our research builds on ideas of using community labels from ZoneTag but uses wifi access points instead of cell towers and collaborative filtering for label prediction.

2 Methodology

Dataset. To develop effective techniques for predicting status we first obtained data collected for the Nomatic*IM project [10]. The data was collected over approximately 3 months by 72 users. It contains 19,664 status entries each of which consists of a set of sensor readings paired with 390 unique place labels. Although several sensors were available, we utilized only wifi access point mac addresses. Our data contained sightings of 2352 unique wifi access points. Users had *connected* to 501 of those access points.

Collaborative Filtering. We applied collaborative filtering as a method for making place label predictions from this data. Collaborative filtering is a method for recommending items of interest to a user based on the interests of other similar users [11]. It had much early success in movie recommender systems [12] and remains an active area of research. Our approach treats place labels as the item which is "recommended."

Collaborative filtering assumes that given the data, a *ranking* function exists for ordering recommendations for one user based on one other user. Then, a user *similarity* function describes how to order recommendations from multiple users for a global recommendation.

As a baseline we created a recommendation based on Equation 1, which simply calculates the most **probable** label for a wifi access point across all users. $\psi(l, w, u)$ is a function which counts the number of times a label, l, is used at a given wifi access point, w, by a user, u.

$$P_B(l|w) = \frac{1}{|U|} \sum_{u \in U} \left[\frac{\psi(l, w, u)}{\sum_{l' \in L} \psi(l', w, u)} \right] \quad (1)$$

Ranking Functions. When making a recommendation for a user, u^*, the first ranking function, Equation 2, ranks the most probable labels used at his current **single wifi** access point, w_{u^*} based on one other user, u.

$$P_{R_1}(l|w_{u^*}, u) = \frac{\psi(l, w_{u^*}, u)}{\sum_{l' \in L} \psi(l', w_{u^*}, u)} \quad (2)$$

The second ranking function, Equation 3, ranks the most probable labels using the same wifi access point, w_{u^*} and then incorporates the chance that the same label was generated by **all visible wifi** access points, $\widehat{w_{u^*}}$, which u^* can also currently see. The trade-off between w_{u^*} and $\widehat{w_{u^*}}$ is managed by $0 < \alpha < 1$.

$$P_{R_2}(l|w_{u^*}, \widehat{w_{u^*}}, u) = \alpha \; P_{R_1}(l|w_{u^*}, u) + \frac{(1-\alpha)}{|\widehat{w_{u^*}}|} \sum_{w \in \widehat{w_{u^*}}} P_{R_1}(l|w, u) \qquad (3)$$

Similarity Functions. To combine the results of the ranking functions, we formulated two distinct user similarity metrics. Since we were looking to predict place labels, the first metric, Equation 4, asserts that similar users are often **co-located**. The function, $\phi(u, w)$, returns the number of times user u, entered *any* label at a wifi access point, w, from the set of all wifi access points, $\widehat{w}$.

$$S_1(u_1, u_2) = \frac{1}{|\widehat{w}|} \sum_{w \in \widehat{w}} \left[1 - \frac{|\phi(u_1, w) - \phi(u_2, w)|}{max(\phi(u_1, w), \phi(u_2, w))} \right] \qquad (4)$$

In this method the similarity between users is the average of the percentage of times that two users entered any status at the same location.

The second metric, Equation 5 combines how often two users were in the same physical location and *also* labeled the location the same way. This metric captures **place agreement**. We calculate this as the product of the probability of u_1 and u_2 using the same label, l, at the same location and sum that over all labels at all wifi access points. $\widehat{l_w}$ is the set of labels used at an access point, w.

$$S_2(u_1, u_2) = \frac{1}{|\widehat{w}|} \sum_{w \in \widehat{w}} \frac{1}{|\widehat{l_w}|} \sum_{l \in \widehat{l_w}} \left[\frac{\psi(l, w, u_1)}{\sum_{l' \in \widehat{l_w}} \psi(l', w, u_1)} \frac{\psi(l, w, u_2)}{\sum_{l' \in \widehat{l_w}} \psi(l', w, u_2)} \right] \qquad (5)$$

While it is possible (and may indeed be useful) to incorporate external user profile or demographic data into similarity metrics, for the purposes of this research and evaluation, we assumed the only data available to us for determining similarity is the data actively generated by the users, namely the status messages and the sensor data that accompanies them.

3   Results and Discussion

In our dataset, there were 746 user-location combinations (location here is based on connected access points). Only 344 of these instances consisted of a location that was visited by more than one user; these are the only cases where community based suggestions were possible. A recommendation for a user, u^*, at a wifi access point, w, was calculated by combining similarity and ranking scores as follows:

$$R(u^*, w) = \arg \max_{l \in L} \left(\sum_{u \in U} P(l|w, u) S(u^*, u) \right) \qquad (6)$$

Figure 1 shows the percentage of times the label that the test user chose was in the top n recommended labels by combinations of ranking functions and similarity functions.

Our best case prediction accuracy is 23%, much better than the 0.2% which would be expected by random. Our technique shows a clear improvement over our baseline and it appears that our similarity metrics are a more important consideration than our ranking techniques.

To more deeply understand our results we categorized and counted the prediction errors as follows:

Syntactical. These errors result from different phrasings of the same label. For example, "peets" and "peet's coffee". Errors resulting from use of abbreviations or acronyms also fall into this category, e.g. "technology garden" and "tech garden."

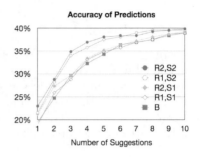

Fig. 1. Prediction accuracy graphed against the number of suggestions included

Technical. These errors result from technical limitations of the system such as the limited accuracy of our positioning mechanism, which resulted in multiple locations being recognized as one. For example, "tech garden" and "galen lab" are across from each other in the hallway of our department, beneath the resolution of our location recognition.

Conceptual. Four error categories are due to variations in conceptualization of place a–mong different users and situations:

Activity Bleed. The concept of place is often intermingled with activity, resulting in labels that actually describe activity rather than place. E.g. "dbh 1300" and "class", "austria" and "ubicomp."

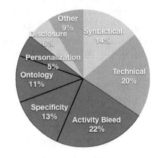

Fig. 2. Types of errors

Specificity. Many locations have labels describing both a larger place and a specific subsection of that place, for example a room within a building. E.g. "engineering tower" and "et 201", "austria" and "Innsbruck."

Ontology. A place may have different names depending on the ontology used by users. For instance, one user, e.g. a college student, may elect to label a place "seminar room" while another user, e.g. from building's facilities staff, may label the same place is "5011."

Personalization. Some places are attributed to a unique person or group of persons, resulting in a personalized approach to labeling. E.g. "office" and "André's office."

Disclosure. In some instances, users may elect to leave the place label blank when updating status which we do not allow as a suggestion.

Other. Errors that we could not interpret/categorize due to lack of information.

Figure 2 shows the percentage of each type of error when evaluating the top ranking suggestions ($n = 1$) generated using the R2, S2 prediction method.

Based on our results, we hypothesize that actually suggesting collaboratively filtered suggestions for place labels will lead to a convergence of place labels among groups of similar users driving accuracy numbers even higher. We expect this to eliminate virtually all syntactical and many conceptual errors.

4   Conclusion

Existing point-of-interest databases don't provide much flexibility in addressing individual users' place-naming style, and existing techniques based on personal histories don't provide labels in new places. The collaborative filtering methods described in this paper allow for both of these capabilities. By combining personal and community data sources, it should be possible to make good predictions when a user first visits a place.

References

1. Fogarty, J., Lai, J., Christensen, J.: Presence versus availability: the design and evaluation of a context-aware communication client. Int. J. Hum.-Comput. Stud. 61(3), 299–317 (2004)
2. Smale, S., Greenberg, S.: Broadcasting information via display names in instant messaging. In: GROUP 2005: Proceedings of the 2005 international ACM SIG-GROUP conference on Supporting group work, pp. 89–98. ACM, New York (2005)
3. Lehikoinen, J.T., Kaikkonen, A.: PePe field study: constructing meanings for locations in the context of mobile presence. In: MobileHCI 2006: Proceedings of the 8th conference on Human-computer interaction with mobile devices and services, pp. 53–60. ACM, New York (2006)
4. Patterson, D.J., Ding, X., Kaufman, S.J., Liu, K., Zaldivar, A.: An ecosystem for learning and using sensor-driven IM messages. In: IEEE Pervasive Computing: Mobile and Ubiquitous Systems (to appear)
5. Marmasse, N., Schmandt, C., Spectre, D.: Watchme: Communication and awareness between members of a closely-knit group. In: Davies, N., Mynatt, E.D., Siio, I. (eds.) UbiComp 2004. LNCS, vol. 3205, pp. 214–231. Springer, Heidelberg (2004)
6. Smith, I.E., Consolvo, S., LaMarca, A., Hightower, J., Scott, J., Sohn, T., Hughes, J., Iachello, G., Abowd, G.D.: Social disclosure of place: From location technology to communication practices. In: Gellersen, H.-W., Want, R., Schmidt, A. (eds.) PERVASIVE 2005. LNCS, vol. 3468, pp. 134–151. Springer, Heidelberg (2005)
7. Barkhuus, L., Brown, B., Bell, M., Sherwood, S., Hall, M., Chalmers, M.: From awareness to repartee: sharing location within social groups. In: CHI 2008: Proceeding of the twenty-sixth annual SIGCHI conference on Human factors in computing systems, pp. 497–506. ACM Press, New York (2008)
8. Hsieh, G., Tang, K.P., Low, W.Y., Hong, J.I.: Field deployment of IMBuddy: A study of privacy control and feedback mechanisms for contextual im. In: McCarthy, J., Scott, J., Woo, W. (eds.) UbiComp 2008, pp. 91–108. ACM, New York (2008)
9. Naaman, M., Nair, R.: Zonetag's collaborative tag suggestions: What is this person doing in my phone? IEEE MultiMedia 15(3), 34–40 (2008)

10. Patterson, D.J., Ding, X., Noack, N.: Nomatic: Location by, for, and of crowds. In: Hazas, M., Krumm, J., Strang, T. (eds.) LoCA 2006. LNCS, vol. 3987, pp. 186–203. Springer, Heidelberg (2006)
11. Goldberg, D., Nichols, D., Oki, B.M., Terry, D.: Using collaborative filtering to weave an information tapestry. Commun. ACM 35(12), 61–70 (1992)
12. Miller, B.N., Albert, I., Lam, S.K., Konstan, J.A., Riedl, J.: Movielens unplugged: experiences with an occasionally connected recommender system. In: IUI 2003: Proceedings of the 8th international conference on Intelligent user interfaces, pp. 263–266. ACM, New York (2003)

Place Enrichment by Mining the Web

Ana O. Alves[1,2], Francisco C. Pereira[2], Assaf Biderman[3], and Carlo Ratti[3]

[1] ISEC, Coimbra Institute of Engineering, Portugal
aalves@isec.pt
[2] CISUC, University of Coimbra, Portugal
{ana,camara}@dei.uc.pt
[3] SENSEable City Lab, MIT, USA
{abider,ratti}@mit.edu

Abstract. In this paper, we address the assignment of semantics to places. The approach followed consists on leveraging from web online resources that are directly or indirectly related to places as well as from the integration with lexical and semantic frameworks such as Wordnet or Semantic Web ontologies. We argue for the wide applicability and validity of this approach to the area of Ubiquitous Computing, particularly for Context Awareness. We present our system, KUSCO, which searches for semantics associations to a given Point Of Interest (POI). Particular focus is provided to the experimentation and validation aspects.

1 Introduction

The vision of Ubiquitous Computing is rapidly becoming a reality as our environment grows increasingly replete with different sensors, widespread pervasive information, and distributed computer interfaces. New challenges still emerge, however, in creating coherent representations of information about places using this multitude of data. These challenges are being addressed in the various areas that involve *Data Fusion*. Significant progress has been made in Data Fusion at specific levels of representation. Many off-the-shelf products integrate GPS, Wi-Fi, GSM, accelerometer, and light sensor data and furthermore employ elaborate software that is capable of integrated contextual processing. Many have noted, however, that a piece in this puzzle is missing without which it is difficult to enable context-aware scenarios: semantic information. While semantic information has been available for centuries, the Internet has dramatically increased its abundance and availability. In each of the four dimensions of context-awareness (*where, what, who, when*), semantics are present at various degrees. In this paper, we focus on the "where" dimension: the semantics of place.

The problem with the semantics of place has already been noted by many in the field of Ubiquitous Computing [1,2,3] as a valid research challenge. We stand in agreement with their perspective and aim in our work to further explore this topic with particular emphasis on methodology and short-term real-world applications. Our focus is on the most elementary and unambiguous information about a place: its latitude/longitude. Our question is: what does a specific position *mean* from a common sense perspective? The answer we propose involves

M. Tscheligi et al. (Eds.): AmI 2009, LNCS 5859, pp. 66–77, 2009.

the representation of concepts through a *tag cloud*, where a concept here is a noun in a given context and this context is given by its near concepts in the tag cloud. Our task is thus to define the most accurate method to find that set of concepts from a given source, i.e. the Internet. Our method is based on the hypothesis that the tag cloud of any given point in space will be a function of the semantics of its surrounding points of interest (POI). A POI is a tuple with a latitude/longitude pair, a name and, optionally, a category such as restaurant, hotel, pub, museum, etc. It represents a place with meaning to people. The work presented here focuses on the semantic enrichment of POI data.

We believe that such information is highly relevant to the majority of context-aware systems. For example, navigation systems: searching for a place that has specific characteristics; route planning using locations with specific functionalities; inferring users activities, etc. We refer to this process as "Semantic Enrichment of Place". It involves using available common sense ontologies and Web information to build a collection of generic and instant facts about places.

The main contributions described in this paper are: (1) A modular methodology for the assignment of semantics to a place; (2) An implemented system, KUSCO, that will become available online; (3) An independent validation method that compares KUSCO's performance with the Yahoo! terms Information Extraction service, currently being used in many projects.

This paper starts with an overview of the approaches that involve the semantics of place within several areas: Ubiquitous Computing, location-based Web search, and Information Extraction. Our system, KUSCO, is presented in the following section, which includes a detailed description of its processes in addition to several examples. Before finishing with a conclusion, we present our project results and validation experiments and raise a number of important questions.

2   Literature Review

2.1   Semantics of Place

As argued in [1], absolute position such as the pair latitude/longitude is a poor representation of place. From the human perspective places are often associated with meaning, and different people relate to places in different ways. The meaning of place derives from social conventions, their private or public nature, possibilities for communication, and many more. As argued by [2] on the distinction between the concept of place from space, a place is generally a space with something added - social meaning, conventions, cultural understandings about role, function and nature. Thus, a place exists once it has meaning for someone and the perception of this meaning is the main objective of our research. In [4], the authors propose a semi-automatic process of tag assignment which integrates knowledge from Semantic Web ontologies and the collection of Web2.0 tags. This approach should be the theoretically correct one: it shares the formal soundness of Ontologies with the informal perspective of social networks. However it is essentially impracticable: the main choice points have to be made manually, and for each new POI/category. The dynamics of this kind of information, particularly when depending on Web 2.0 social networks, would demand drastic resources to keep the information up to date, and the compliance to semantic standards by individual users also seems a lost battle, of which the lack of success of the Semantic Web as a global vision is the most salient expression.

On a different direction, Rattenbury et al [5] identify place and event from tags that are assigned to photos on Flickr. They exploit the regularities on tags in which regards to time and space at several scales, so when "bursts" (sudden high intensities of a given tag in space or time) are found, they become an indicator of event of meaningful place. Then, the reverse process is possible, that of search for the tag clouds that correlate with that specific time and space. They do not, however, make use of any enrichment from external sources, which could add more objective information and their approach is limited to the specific scenarios of Web 2.0 platforms that carry significant geographical reference information.

Other attempts were also made towards analysing Flickr tags [6,7] by applying ad-hoc approaches to determine "important" tags within a given region of time [6] or space [7] based on inter-tag frequencies. However, no determination of the properties or semantics of specific tags was provided [5].

In the Web-a-Where project, Amitay et al [8] associate web pages to geographical locations to which they are related, also identifying the main "geographical focus". The "tag enrichment" process thus consists of finding words (normally Named Entities) that show potential for geo-referencing, and then applying a disambiguation taxonomy (e.g. "MA" with "Massachusetts" or "Haifa" with "Haifa/Israel/Asia"). The results are very convincing, however the authors do not explore the idea other than using explicit geographical references. An extension could be to detect and associate patterns such as those referred above in [5] without the need for explicit location referencing.

While our work focuses on the semantic aspect of location representation, we also take advantage of information available on the Web about public places. With the rapid growth of the World Wide Web, a continuously increasing number of commercial and non-commercial entities acquire presence on-line, whether through the deployment of proper web sites or by referral of related institutions. This presents an opportunity for identifying the information which describes how different people and communities relate to places, and by that enrich the representation of Point Of Interest. Notwithstanding the effort of many, the Semantic Web is hardly becoming a reality, and, therefore, information is rarely structured or tagged with semantic meaning. Currently, it is widely accepted that the majority of on-line information contains unrestricted user-written text. Hence, we become dependent primarily on Information Extraction (IE) techniques for collecting and composing information on the Web, as described below.

2.2 Location-Based Web Search

Location-based web search (or *Local Search*) is one of the popular tasks expected from the search engines. A location-based query consists of a topic and a reference location. Unlike general web search, in location-based search, a search engine is expected to find and rank documents which are not only related to the query topic but also geographically related to the location which the query is associated with. There are several issues for developing effective geographic search engines and, as yet, no global location-based search engine has been reported to achieve them[9]. Location ambiguity, lack of geographic information on web pages, language-based and country-dependent addressing styles, and multiple locations related to a single web resource are notable difficulties.

Search engine companies have started to develop and offer location-based services. However, they are still geographically limited, mostly to the United States, such as Yahoo!Local, Google Maps and MSN Live Local, and have not become as successful and popular as general search engines. Despite this, lot of work has been done in improving the capabilities of location-based search engines [10], but it is beyond of the scope of this paper to develop them. Instead of this, we make use of generally available search engines and formulate queries using the geographical reference to retrieve information about places (section 3.1). The role of our work in this context is more on the side of contributing to the indexing capabilities of such engines in terms of local search (finding an inspiration in [11]) than on becoming any alternative form of search.

2.3   Information Extraction

The role of the Information Extraction (IE) task is to obtain meaningful knowledge out of large quantities of unstructured data. In which regards to textual information, IE is a task much linked to Text Mining, being both subtopics of the wider area of Information Retrieval (IR). IE applies classic Natural Language Processing (NLP) techniques and resources over unstructured pages written in natural language. Differently, Text Mining usually applies machine learning and pattern mining to exploit the syntactical patterns or layout structures of the template-based documents. However, it is impossible to guarantee that public places are only represented in structured pages from directory sites (e.g. from directory sites such as http://www.tripadvisor.com or http://www.urbanspoon.com). In fact, some important places may have their proper pages.

Nowadays, freely available common sense lexicon resources (such as WordNet, OpenCyc or others) are helpful tools to deduce semantic meaning of several concepts, including places, in that they carry relational networks that allow for new associations. Normally, these concepts and their semantic relationships are built with a generic perspective, thus rarely representing any instance in themselves. For example, the concept of *library* can be generically described as *a building that houses a collection of books and other materials* (in WordNet), but if we talk about a specific library (e.g. U.S. National Library of Medicine), further exploration beyond those resources is needed to grab a more precise meaning of that place. It is at this point that Information Extraction is mandatory in the inference of the semantics of a place: the concepts that are specific to that place are the ones that best distinguish it from others.

Within IE, and excluding some of the projects referred to above, the Artequakt [12] system is the one that is closest to KUSCO. It uses natural language tools to automatically extract knowledge about artists from multiple Web Pages based on a predefined and hand-crafted ontology to generate artist biographies. The system uses a biography ontology, especially built for this purpose, which defines the data for an artist biography. Information is collected by parsing text found on the Web and is subsequently presented using templates. Diferently from our approach, it assumes that Web pages are syntactically well-constructed in order to extract knowledge triples (concept - relation - concept). Web pages are divided into paragraphs, and consequently in sentences. Each sentence, which heuristically corresponds to a grammatical construction of the form Subject-Verb-Concept, is then used to fulfill a triple.

3   KUSCO

When given a Point Of Interest, KUSCO [13] searches the Web for related pages by using reverse geocoding to formulate the query. Afterwards, Information Extraction is applied to those Web pages in order to extract meaningful concepts related to the intendend Place referred by the POI. We name this output as a Semantic Index since it contains concepts contextualized in two distinct types: *common concepts* for that place (e.g. smooking room, wheelchair access) which can be found on Common Sense Ontologies (e.g. WordNet) and *specific concepts* or related Named Entities (e.g. Carlsberg, Rissoto) generally as proper nouns. For example, the POI (52.212944, 0.119241, Arundel House Hotel) will trigger KUSCO to build a Semantic Index for that Place composed by Named Entities like Cambrige Guide, Conservatory Brasserie, Cambridgeshire; and some Word-Net concepts like airport: "an airfield equipped with control tower and hangars as well as accommodations for passengers and cargo", comfort: "a state of being relaxed and feeling no pain", cleanliness: "diligence in keeping clean". In this paper, we describe in detail the two main processes responsible for mining the *meaning of the place*: Geo Web Search and Meaning Extraction.

3.1   Geo Web Search

This module is responsible for finding Web pages using only POI data as keywords: place name and geographical address. This last element is composed by the City name (where the POI is located) and is obtained from Gazetteers[1] available on Web). The search is made by the freely available Yahoo!Search API. KUSCO applies a heuristic that uses the geographical reference as another keyword in the search. Thus, assuming a POI is a tuple (Latitude, Longitude, Name), the final query to each search will be: <City Name> <Name>. To automatically select only pages centered on a given Place, we apply also the following heuristics to filter out unuseful Web Pages:(1) The title must contain the POI name; (2) The page body must contain an explicit reference to the POI geographical area; (3) Out of date pages will not be considered.

---

[1] A geographical dictionary generally including position and geographical names like Geonet Names Server and Geographic Names Information System [14].

3.2   Meaning Extraction

Having the set of Web pages found earlier, keyword extraction and contextualization on Wordnet is made at this point. This process includes Part-of-Speech
tagging, Noun Phrase chunking and Named Entity Recognition (NER) using
available NLP tools [15,16,17]. Linguistic analisys of text typically proceeds in a
layered fashion. Texts are broken up into paragraphs, paragraphs into sentences,
and sentences into words. Words in a sentence are then tagged by *Part-of-Speech*
(POS) *taggers* which label each word as a noun, verb, adjective, etc. *Noun Phrase
chunking* is made typically by partial (sometimes called 'shallow') parsers and go
beyond part-of-speech tagging to extract clusters of words that represent people
or objects. They tend to concentrate on identifying *base* noun phrases, which
consist of a *head* noun, i.e., the main noun in the phrase, and its *left modifiers*,
i.e, determiners and adjectives occurring just to the left of it.

Named Entity Recognition tries to identify proper names in documents and
may also classify these proper names as to whether they designate people, places,
companies, organizations, and the like. Unlike noun phrase extractors, many
NER algorithms choose to disregard part of speech information and work directly
with raw tokens and their properties (e.g., capitalization clues, adjacent words
such as 'Mr.' or 'Inc.'). The ability to recognize previously unknown entities
is an essential part of NER systems. Such ability hinges upon recognition and
classification rules triggered by distinctive features associated with positive and
negative examples.

On completion of these subtasks for each web page, KUSCO ranks the concept
either with TF-IDF [18] (Term Frequency × Inverse Document Frequency) value
in order to extract the most relevant terms (only common or proper nouns) that
will represent a given place. These nouns are contextualized on WordNet and
thus can be thought not only as a word but more cognitively as a concept
(specifically a synset - family of words having the same meaning, i.e., synonyms
[19]). Given that each word present in WordNet may have different meanings
associated, its most frequent sense is selected to contextualize a given term.
For example, the term "wine" has two meanings in WordNet: "fermented juice
(of grapes especially)" or "a red as dark as red wine"; being the first meaning
the most frequent used considering statiscs from WordNet annotated corpus
(Semcor[20]).

When using data from different sources, integration of information is imper-
ative to avoid duplicates. To solve this problem we treat differently common
nouns (generally denoting concepts) from proper nouns (generally Named Entities found). Although we use WordNet to find synonyms in the first group, we
don't have a list of all possible entities in the world to match words from the
second group. So, we take advantage of the relatively mature field of *String metrics* to find the distance between strings using an open-source available library
with different algorithms implementations [21]. The importance of each concept
is computed by tf weighting considering all pages related to a POI. As result of
the system, each POI is represented by a list of more relevant WordNet concepts
and NE terms, or, in other words, by its *Semantic Index*.

3.3   Illustrative Example

To follow the whole process of Semantic Enrichment of Places of Interest here described, we propose an illustrative example with a bar restaurant. In the beginning of the process, it is only a point in the map having a name associated:*(40.708925,-74.005111, Whitneys J Byrne Bar & Restaurant)*. The reverse geocoding gives us the city where it belongs to. So the next phase is to browse the Web using the Yahoo!Search API with the following queries in the for-mat [City] + POI Name: *"New York"+Whitneys+J+ Byrne+Bar+Restaurant*.

For each query a set of relevant pages is retrieved and downloaded to the next phase. From 20 Web pages only 10 at most are selected following the criteria described above. Table 1 presents the Web pages selected for this POI, with the corresponding Yahoo! search ranking. Due to page size limitations, we only provide the domain for each page (a simple search query yields the exact page to the interested reader).

Table 1. Most relevant pages obtained by Yahoo!

ID	Title - Url		Rank
A	*Whitneys' J Byrne Bar - Restaurant* *New York, NY : Reviews and maps...*	http://local.yahoo.com	1
B	*Whitneys' J Byrne Bar - Restaurant,* *New York City, NY : Reviews of...*	http://travel.yahoo.com	3
C	*Whitneys' J Byrne Bar & Restaurant* *New York, NY on Yahoo! Local*	http://local.yahoo.com	4

As we can see from table 1, there are sites pointing out to the same informa-tion, only differing the server where the page is hosted. In these cases, we see a possible solution by using *string metrics* between urls found. Analysing more deeply, the content is the same, only differing, in some cases, for a few characters - say, a notation showing the date and time at which the page was last modified. This widespread phenomenon on the Web, named *near duplication*, can be de-tected by a technique, *shingling*, that creates contiguous subsequences of tokens in a document, that can be used to gauge the similarity of two documents [22].

The Meaning Extraction module receives as input for each POI a set of N most relevant pages and extract in the first place the Named Entities as it works about raw text. For the example above, we can find the following relevant Named Entities (enclosed by brackets with their respective context excerpt in raw text):

Categories: [Steak Houses], Restaurants, American Restaurants, Irish Restau-rants Reviews of New York Restaurants on Yelp.com New York City Guide > Food & Dining > Restaurants > [Steak Houses] > Whitneys' J Byrne Bar & Restaurant (site A) You Might Also Like [Nebraska Beef] 15 Stone St, New York, NY (site A)

To find common concepts, POS tagging is applied to recognize nouns and NP chunking to isolate Noun Phrases on text. For our POI in the example above, relevant concepts were found and contextualized in WordNet (table 2).

Table 2. Wordnet meaning for each concept associated to "Whitneys J Byrne Bar Restaurant"

Hotels	a building where travelers can pay for lodging and meals and other services
Irish	the Celtic language of Ireland
American	a native or inhabitant of the United States
Attractions	he force by which one object attracts another
Travel	the act of going from one place to another
Deals	(often followed by 'of') a large number or amount or extent
Services	(sports) a stroke that puts the ball in play; "his powerful serves won the game"
Steaks	a slice of meat cut from the fleshy part of an animal or large fish
Reservations	a district that is reserved for particular purpose
Plan	a series of steps to be carried out or goals to be accomplished

As a result, the semantic index produced comprises the union of Named Entity concepts and Wordnet concepts. The ordering follows Term Frequency (TF) ranking and, in this POI, it is composed by the follwoing concepts: *Hotels, Steak Houses, Irish, American, Attractions, Travel, Deals, Nebraska Beef, Services, Steaks.*

4 Avoiding Noise

The identification of all valuable concepts regarding a POI given a set of web pages seems to be an achieved goal within KUSCO. However, the emergence of large quantities of redundant, lateral, or simply page format data hinders the determination of accurate semantics. In other words, while recall is very high, precision is very low. We rely on statistical evidence to find very frequent words that bring little information content, as well as some heuristics to filter out insignificant words (e.g. geographical description of the place, such as the name of the city, which becomes redundant).

The list obtained at this point carries large quantities of *noise*, which corresponds to any word that does not contribute in any way to the meaning of the place. This includes technical keywords (e.g. http, php), common words in web pages (e.g. internet, contact, email, etc.) as well as geographically related nouns that become redundant when describing the place (e.g. for a POI in Brooklyn Bridge, NY, nouns like "New York" or "Brooklyn" are unnecessary). We apply a filter that gathers a set of fixed common words (a "stopword list") as well as a variable set of "redundant words". The latter set is obtained from an analysis of a large set of texts: we group all original texts retrieved, tokenize them to isolate words, apply a stemmer algotithm [23] to deduce the root of each word and define IDF (Inverse Document Frequency) value for each stem. We then select all words relatively commom occurring in at least 30% or more of our corpus to become also "special stopwords", in the sense that if the stem of some candidate word is present in this last list, it is considered a common word and not elegible to be a descriptive concept. These "special stopwords", in our case, only represent 3% of our stem list of all words processed. This can be supported by Zipf's Law [24] which states that frequency decreases very rapidly with rank.

5 Results and Experimental Evaluation

In the development process, we put an emphasis on assuring short-term applicability of this project. It is an online resource for extracting semantic information about places, intended for use by other projects and applications. Both the choice of POI types and dataset samples was motivated by our desire to make the system relevant to a wide user-community, and to ensure it reflects the unstructured nature of the internet. No priority or special emphasis was given to POIs that provide more information than the average. In other words, we present a basic scenario that demonstrates the behavior of the system in an uncontrolled environment.

The POI categories we chose to analyze were restaurants and hotels. They are described mostly in dedicated listing websites pages such as Tripadvisor.com, hotels.com, lastminute.com, and more. While these websites can provide rich content for each POI, in the majority of cases they provide only limited detail as well as plenty of noise. There is a very large number of hotels and restaurants described online and these categories do not represent a set of hand-picked points. These conditions make hotels and restaurants a good basis for our analysis. Also, the Internet is widely used by the public to explore these POIs, which increases the relevance of the metadata our system creates.

A set of experimental results was obtained for over 215 POIs which were randomly selected from 4989 POIs of hotels and restaurants in the U.K., Australia and New York city. They were collected from different POI sharing websites[2] and also from Yahoo!Local search directory. We also address a few questions about the effectiveness of the Kusco System. The following sections describe our experimental evaluation of two distinct modules of the system: Geo Web Search and Meaning Extraction.

5.1 GeoWeb Search Results

For the 215 POIs, 1091 Web pages were processed by Kusco. With a great diversity of Web pages sources, 477 different domains were retrieved, most of which were directory Web sites. Following our initial queries with Yahoo search engine, we repeated an identical process using Google search. For our POI set, we automatically selected 864 pages from the total retrieved, using the same heuristic described above. Table 3 presents statistics from different sets of pages, one group retrieved by Yahoo and the other retrieved by Google. The Yahoo results exhibit greater diversity than Google, which could be explained by the fact that more than 50% of Web pages retrieved by Yahoo were not considered relevant by Google.

5.2 Meaning Extraction Results

The Meaning Extraction module is expected to bring out relevant concepts and entities mentioned in the POI Web pages. As there is location-based semantics

---

[2] Such as POIfriend.com, Pocket GPS World, GPS Data Team, POI Donwload UK.

Table 3. Geo web search results from two Search APIs: Yahoo and Google

	Yahoo	Google
Web Pages per POI (in 10 possible)	5.07	4.02
Distinct Domains	477	300
Common Web pages (from the total of each side)	48.96	73.23
POIs with common Web pages from two sides	215 (All)	

benchmark dataset to test and validate our results, we chose to use Yahoo!Term Extraction API (Yahoo!TE) [25] to examine the diversity and richness of our module. Yahoo!TE API provides a list of significant words or phrases extracted from a larger content and is currently used to create indexes over Web pages for Information Retrieval purposes.

Using the same Web pages for both systems, we need to understand *the contribution of Meaning Extraction module compared to Yahoo!TE API*. Once Yahoo!TE doesn't receive location as a parameter neither does search over the Web, we will apply the same selected Web pages (downloaded for each POI) as input to this API output. To each text, Yahoo!TE extracts most relevant terms, which are then contextualized in WordNet as KUSCO does. Considering a threshold baseline of equal value for both Extraction Meaning systems, Semantic Indexes produced by KUSCO have an average size of 35 terms (both concepts and named entities), while those built using Yahoo!TE API have 44 terms on average. For further comparison with Yahoo!TE, we applied the Information Content (IC) measure from Wordnet concepts (a combination of specificity and term frequency of each term in relation to large corpora [26]) to both semantic index lists. In this respect, KUSCO and Yahoo! have very similar results (71% and 70% respectively), with similar standard deviation (aprox. 6.0). Looking for the same perspective for Named Entities, we sought for the average TF measure for these concepts in both approaches. Here, KUSCO slightly outperforms Yahoo (59% and 50% respectively). These measures, however, mean that both systems have the same level of efficiency (with slight advantage for KUSCO) in getting valid concepts regardless of being or not significant for the meaning of the place (e.g. concepts like "New York" or "address", present in the Yahoo!TE index, get high IC value or high frequency, but they don't add novel information about the place).

6   Conclusions

In this paper, we presented an approach to the problem of "Semantics of Place". We developed a system, Kusco, which builds a semantic index associated to a given Point Of Interest (a latitude/longitude pair and a name). For each POI, Kusco executes a sequence of Information Extraction and Natural Language Processing steps based on algorithms and tools that have been thoroughly tested. The system has also been subject to a series of tests. In comparison with related work, specifically, the generic term extraction tool from Yahoo! (Yahoo!Terms Extraction), Kusco has shown better results. Kusco is expected be launched as an open platform on-line in the near future.

The main contribution in this work includes a clear and well defined methodology for creating semantic information about place from web pages, a stable tool that will be available online, and a new set of benchmarking datasets (semantic indexes) that allow for future comparisons and gradual improvements on the current results and methods. Kusco is currently being applied in the context three different research projects as a semantic enrichment source: an intelligent route planner; a project for analysis of correlations of cell-phone activity and events in the city; a platform for data fusion with traffic and land use data.

The future steps for this system include the exploitation of structured knowledge resources (e.g. openmind, framenet, wikipedia) that can provide broader common sense semantics as well as specific information on the idiosyncrasies of each POI (e.g. Restaurants have a menu; Museums have a topic; etc.). This, we expect, should show better results than using OWL ontologies, a process we tried before with the several categories of POIs studied previously [13,27,28].

References

1. Hightower, J.: From position to place. In: Proc. of LOCA, pp. 10–12 (2003); Ubicomp
2. Harrison, S., Dourish, P.: Re-place-ing space: the roles of place and space in collaborative systems. In: Proc. of CSCW 1996, pp. 67–76. ACM Press, New York (1996)
3. Aipperspach, R., Rattenbury, T., Woodruff, A., Canny, J.F.: A quantitative method for revealing and comparing places in the home. In: Dourish, P., Friday, A. (eds.) UbiComp 2006. LNCS, vol. 4206, pp. 1–18. Springer, Heidelberg (2006)
4. Lemmens, R., Deng, D.: Web 2.0 and semantic web: Clarifying the meaning of spatial features. In: Semantic Web meets Geopatial Applications. AGILE 2008 (2008)
5. Rattenbury, T., Good, N., Naaman, M.: Towards automatic extraction of event and place semantics from flickr tags. In: SIGIR 2007, pp. 103–110. ACM, New York (2007)
6. Dubinko, M., Kumar, R., Magnani, J., Novak, J., Raghavan, P., Tomkins, A.: Visualizing tags over time. In: WWW 2006, pp. 193–202. ACM, New York
7. Jaffe, A., Naaman, M., Tassa, T., Davis, M.: Generating summaries and visualization for large collections of geo-referenced photographs. In: MIR 2006, pp. 89–98 (2006)
8. Amitay, E., Har'El, N., Sivan, R., Soffer, A.: Web-a-where: geotagging web content. In: SIGIR 2004, pp. 273–280. ACM, New York (2004)
9. Asadi, S., Zhou, X., Jamali, H., Mofrad, H.: Location-based search engines tasks and capabilities: A comparative study. Webology, vol. 4 (December 2007)
10. Ahlers, D., Boll, S.: Location-based web search. In: Scharl, A., Tochtermann, K. (eds.) The Geospatial Web. Springer, London (2007)
11. Tanasescu, V., Domingue, J.: A differential notion of place for local search. In: LOCWEB 2008, pp. 9–16. ACM, New York (2008)

12. Alani, H., Kim, S., Millard, D., Weal, M., Hall, W., Lewis, P., Shadbolt, N.: Automatic extraction of knowledge from web documents (2003)
13. Alves, A., Antunes, B., Pereira, F.C., Bento, C.: Semantic enrichment of places: Ontology learning from web. Int. J. Know.-Based Intell. Eng. Syst. 13(1), 19–30 (2009)
14. GNS: Geonet names server. national imagery and mapping agency (2009)
15. Toutanova, K., Klein, D., Manning, C.: Feature-rich part-of-speech tagging with a cyclic dependency network
16. Ramshaw, L., Marcus, M.: Text Chunking using Transformation-Based Learning. In: Proc. of WVLC 1995, Cambridge, USA (1995)
17. Finkel, J.R., Grenager, T., Manning, C.: Incorporating non-local information into information extraction systems by gibbs sampling. In: ACL 2005, pp. 363–370 (2005)
18. Salton, G., Buckley, C.: Term-weighting approaches in automatic text retrieval. Information Processing and Management 24(5), 513–523 (1988)
19. Fellbaum: WordNet: An Electronic Lexical Database, May 1998. MIT Press, Cambridge (1998)
20. Mihalcea, R.: Semcor semantically tagged corpus. Technical report (1998)
21. Cohen, W., Ravikumar, P., Fienberg, S.: A comparison of string distance metrics for name-matching tasks. In: IJCAI 2003 Works. on Information Integration, pp. 73–78 (2003)
22. Manning, C.D., Raghavan, P., Schütze, H.: Introduction to Information Retrieval. Cambridge University Press, Cambridge (2008)
23. Porter, M.: An algorithm for suffix stripping, pp. 313–316 (1997)
24. Zipf, G.K.: Human Behaviour and the Principle of Least Effort: an Introduction to Human Ecology. Addison-Wesley, Reading (1949)
25. Yahoo!: Term extraction documentation for search web (2009), http://developer.yahoo.com/search/content/v1/termextraction.html
26. Resnik, P.: Using information content to evaluate semantic similarity in a taxonomy. In: IJCAI, pp. 448–453 (1995)
27. Antunes, B., Alves, A., Pereira, F.C.: Semantics of place: Ontology enrichment. In: Geffner, H., Prada, R., Machado Alexandre, I., David, N. (eds.) IBERAMIA 2008. LNCS (LNAI), vol. 5290, pp. 342–351. Springer, Heidelberg (2008)
28. Alves, A.O.: Semantically enriched places: An approach to deal with the position to place problem. In: Doctoral Colloquium of Ubicomp - Adjunct Proceedings (2007)

Sensor-Based Human Activity Recognition in a Multi-user Scenario

Liang Wang[1], Tao Gu[2], Xianping Tao[1], and Jian Lu[1]

[1] State Key Laboratory for Novel Software Technology, Nanjing University
[2] Department of Mathematics and Computer Science, University of Southern Denmark
wangliang@ics.nju.edu.cn, gu@imada.sdu.dk, txp@nju.edu.cn, lj@nju.edu.cn

Abstract. Existing work on sensor-based activity recognition focuses mainly on single-user activities. However, in real life, activities are often performed by multiple users involving interactions between them. In this paper, we propose Coupled Hidden Markov Models (CHMMs) to recognize multi-user activities from sensor readings in a smart home environment. We develop a multimodal sensing platform and present a theoretical framework to recognize both single-user and multi-user activities. We conduct our trace collection done in a smart home, and evaluate our framework through experimental studies. Our experimental result shows that we achieve an average accuracy of 85.46% with CHMMs.

Keywords: Multi-user activity recognition, probabilistic model.

1 Introduction

The problem of recognizing human actions and activities based on video camera has been studied in computer vision since a decade ago [18, 7]. With the availability of low-cost sensors and the advancement of wireless sensor networks, researchers in ubiquitous computing are recently interested in deploying various sensors to collect observations, and recognizing activities based on these observations. This in turn supports many potential applications such as monitoring activities of daily living (ADLs) [8] for the elderly.

Recognizing human activities based on sensor readings is interesting since sensors can capture many useful low-level features of human users, their living environments and human-to-environment interactions. It is also a challenging task because sensor data are noisy and human activities are complex in nature. Existing work on sensor-based activity recognition mainly focuses on recognizing activities of a single user [10, 9, 13, 15]. However, activities involving multiple users collaboratively or concurrently are common in our daily lives, especially in a home setting. For example, family members always watch TV together in a living room, and prepare meals together in a kitchen.

From social psychology point of view, people often form groups to perform certain activity collectively not only because they share socially relevant features but also because they interact and rely on each other to achieve specific goals. Among others, two distinctive features – social interdependence and task interdependence – are salient [14]. Foremost, they are socially interdependent because they rely on one another for feelings of connectedness and positive emotional outcomes. This is especially demonstrated in a

M. Tscheligi et al. (Eds.): AmI 2009, LNCS 5859, pp. 78–87, 2009.

home environment among family members whether affiliated by consanguinity, affinity, or co-residence.

Understanding activities of multiple users is important for not only psychologists, but also for computer scientists. In the vision of ambient intelligence, to a great extent, people who share socially relevant characteristics or features like gender, age, or an interest in the environment are brought together to form a group. Then, the focus and interaction again are often on multiple human users within the group instead of single ones.

Recognizing activities of multiple users is more challenging than that of a single user. The challenge is to find a suitable model to capture the interactions between users and perform inference using these observations. In this paper, we propose a temporal probabilistic models – Coupled Hidden Markov Models (CHMMs) – to model user interactions and recognize multi-user activities. CHMMs are a multi-chained variant of the basic Hidden Markov Models (HMMs); it couples HMMs with temporal, asymmetric influences. We design a wearable sensor platform capable of capturing observations of human users and their interactions. Based on this platform, we conduct real-world trace collection, and evaluate our model through comprehensive experiments to demonstrate the effectiveness.

In summary, the paper makes the following contributions.

- We investigate the problem of sensor-based, multi-user activity recognition in a smart home setting, and propose a temporal probabilistic model to recognize activities in a multi-user scenario.
- We develop a multimodal, wearable sensor platform to capture observations of both users and their interactions, and conduct trace collection involving two users in a real smart home.
- We conduct experimental studies to evaluate our proposed model for multi-user activity recognition.

The rest of the paper is organized as follows. Section 2 discusses the related work. In Section 3, we present the design of our wearable sensor platform. Section 4 describes our proposed activity model, and Section 5 reports our empirical studies. Finally, Section 6 concludes the paper.

2   Related Work

In ubiquitous computing, researchers are recently interested in recognizing activities based on sensor readings. Recognition models are typically probabilistic based, and they can be categorized into static classification or temporal classification. Typical static classifiers include naïve Bayes used in [10], decision trees used in [10], k-nearest neighbor (k-NN) used in [6], and Support Vector Machine used in [6]. In temporal classification, state-space models are typically used to enable the inference of hidden states (i.e., activity labels) given the observations. We name a few examples here: HMMs used in [9, 16], Dynamic Bayesian Network (DBN) used in [13] and Conditional Random Fields (CRFs) used in [15].

Some work has been done in modeling interaction process in computer vision. Oliver et al. [11] proposed and compared HMMs and CHMMs for modeling interactions between people and classifying the type of interaction based on observations collected from video camera. Gong et al. [4] developed a dynamically multilinked HMMs model to interpret group activities based on video camera. Park et al. [12] presented a synergistic track- and body-level analysis framework for multi-person interaction and activity analysis in the context of video surveillance. An integrated visual interface for gestures was designed in [2] as a platform for investigating visually mediated interaction with video camera. However, their system only tackled simple gestures like waving and pointing.

Most of the existing work on multi-user activity recognition used video data only. One possible reason is that it is rather hard to determine hidden parameters of HMMs in the case of multimodal group action or activity recognition, where features from each modal are concatenated to define the observation model [19]. Wyatt et al. [17] presented a privacy-sensitive DBN-based unsupervised approach to separating speakers and their turns in a multi-person conversation. They addressed the problem of recognizing sequences of human interaction patterns in meetings with two-layer HMMs using both audio and video data. Different from these work, we deploy a multimodal sensor platform, and show that how sensor modality plays a role in multi-user activity recognition.

3   Multimodal Wearable Sensor Platform

We built our wearable sensor platform as shown in both Figure 1 and Figure 2. This platform measures user movement (i.e., both hands), user location, human-object interaction (i.e., objects touched and sound), human-to-human interaction (i.e., voice) and environmental information (i.e., temperature, humidity and light). To capture acceleration data, we used a Crossbow iMote2 IPR2400 processor and radio board with the ITS400 sensor board, as shown in Figure 1d. The ITS400 sensor board also captures environmental information such as temperature, humidity and light. To capture object use,

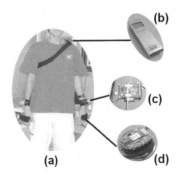

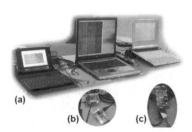

Fig. 1. (a) Wearable sensor set, (b) Audio recorder, (c) iMote2 with ITS400, (d) RFID wristband reader

Fig. 2. (a) Servers for logging sersor readings, (b) iMote2 receiver, (c) Mica2Dot receiver

we built a customized RFID wristband reader which incorporates a Crossbow Mica2Dot wireless mote, a Skyetek M1-mini RFID reader and a Li-Polymer rechargeable battery. The wristband is able to detect the presence of a tagged object within the range of 6 to 8 cm. To capture the vocal interaction between users, we use a commercial audio recorder to record audio data as shown in Figure 1b. To determine user identity, the device IDs of each iMote2 set and RFID reader are logged and bound to a specific user.

The sampling rate of the RFID readers is set to 2 Hz and the sampling rate of the 3-axis accelerometer in each iMote2 is set to 128 Hz, and the sampling rate of audio recorder is set to 16 KHz. When a user performs activities, the acceleration readings from each iMote2 set are transmitted wirelessly to a local server (shown in Figure 2a, left or middle) which runs on a laptop PC with an iMote2 IPR2400 board connected through its USB port. When a user handles a tagged object, the RFID wristband reader scans the tag ID and sends it wirelessly to another server (shown in Fig. 2a, right) that can map the ID to an object name. In addition, human voice and environmental sound are recorded by the audio recorder. All the sensor data are logged separately with timestamps, and will be merged into a single text file as the activity trace for each user.

4   Multi-chained Temporal Probabilistic Model

In this section, we first describe our problem statement, then present a multi-chained temporal probabilistic activity model.

4.1   Problem Statement

We formulate our multi-user activity recognition problem as follows. We assume that there are a number of training datasets, where each training dataset corresponds to each user. Each training dataset O consists of T observations $O = \{o_1, o_2, \dots, o_T\}$ associated with activity labels $\{A_1, A_2, \dots, A_m\}$, where there are m activities and activities can be single-user ADLs or multi-user ADLs. For a new sequence of observations corresponding to a user, our objective is to train an appropriate activity model that can assign each new observation with the correct activity label.

4.2   Feature Extraction

After obtaining sensor readings, we first need to extract appropriate sensor features. We convert all the sensor readings to a series of *observation vectors* by concatenating all of the data observed in a fixed time interval which is set to one second in our experiments. Our feature extraction process generates a 47-dimensional *observation vector* every second. Different types of sensors require different processing to compute various features.

For acceleration data, we compute the features including mean, variance, energy, frequency-domain entropy, and correlation. The DC feature is the mean acceleration value over the window. Variance is used to characterize the stability of the signal. The energy feature captures the data periodicity, and is calculated as the sum of the squared discrete FFT component magnitudes of the signal. Frequency-domain entropy helps to discriminate activities with similar energy values, and is calculated as the normalized information entropy of the discrete FFT component magnitudes of the signal. Correlation is calculated between every two axes of each accelerometer and between all pairwise combinations of axes on different accelerometers. This feature aims to find out the correlation among the different axes of the two accelerometers.

For audio data, we compute both time-domain and frequency-domain features. The time-domain features measure the temporal variation of audio signal, and consist of three features. The first one is the standard deviation of the reading over the window, normalized by the maximum reading in the window. The second one is the dynamic range defined as (max - min) / max, where min and max represent the minimum and maximum readings in the window. The third is Zero-Crossing Rate (ZCR), which measures the frequency content of the signal and is defined as the number of time-domain zero crossings in the window. In the frequency-domain, we compute two features – centroid (the midpoint of the spectral power distribution) and bandwidth (the width of the range of frequencies that the signal occupies).

For RFID reading or location information, we use object name or location name directly as features. For each RFID wristband reader, we choose the first object in a one-second window since a user is unlikely to touch two or more objects in such a short interval. If no RFID reading is observed or in the presence of a corrupted tag ID, the value will be set to NULL.

We then transform these observation vectors into feature vectors. A feature vector consists of many feature items, where a feature item refers to a feature name-value pair in which a feature can be numeric or nominal. We denote a numeric feature as $numfeature_i$. Suppose its range is $[x, y]$ and an interval $[a, b]$ (or in other forms, $(a, b]$, $[a, b)$, or (a, b)) is contained in $[x, y]$. We call $numfeature_i@[a, b]$ a numeric feature item, meaning that the value of $numfeature_i$ is limited inclusively between a and b. We denote a nominal attribute as $nomfeature_j$. Suppose its range is $\{v_1, v_2, ..., v_n\}$, we call $nomfeature_j@v_k$ a nominal feature item, meaning the value of $nomfeature_j$ is v_k.

The key step of transformation is to discretize numeric features. We follow the entropy-based discretization method [3], which partitions a range of continuous values into a number of disjoint intervals such that the entropy of the partition is minimal.

Then we can directly combine the feature name and its interval into a numeric feature item. For the nominal feature, the feature name and its value are combined as a nominal feature item. For the *LEFTOBJ* and *RIGHTOBJ* features, we merge them into one feature by computing *LEFTOBJ* ∪ *RIGHTOBJ* without losing any essential objects during the user-object interaction due to user's handedness. All the feature items will be indexed by a simple encoding scheme and used as inputs to the probabilistic model described in the next section.

4.3   Coupled Hidden Markov Models

After feature extraction, we obtain a sequence of feature vectors for each user, where a feature vector $f = \{f_1, f_2, ... , f_T\}$ is associated with activity labels $\{A_1, A_2, ... , A_m\}$. A typical temporal probabilistic framework to model each user's sequence is HMMs which consist of a hidden variable and an observable variable at each time step. In this case, the hidden variable is an activity label, and the observable variable is a feature

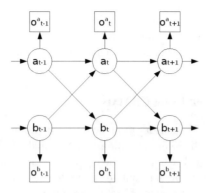

Fig. 3. Structure of CHMM

vector. For multiple sequences of observations corresponding to multiple users, we can factorize the basic HMMs into multiple channels to model interaction processes. We exploit CHMMs to model multi-user sequences involving user interactions. The CHMMs was originally introduced in [1], and it couples HMMs to capture inter-user influences across time.

To illustrate, as shown in Figure 3, there are two sequences of states A and B with observation O^a and O^b, respectively, at each time slice t. A two-chain CHMMs can be constructed by bridging hidden states of its two component HMMs at each time slice with the crosswork of conditional probabilities $P_{a_t|b_{t-1}}$ and $P_{b_t|a_{t-1}}$.

Inference for CHMMs. The posterior of a state sequence through fully coupled two-chain CHMMs is defines as follows.

$$P(S|O) = \frac{\pi_{a_1} P(o_1^a|a_1)\pi_{b_1} P(o_1^b|b_1)}{P(O)} \prod_{t=2}^{T} [P_{a_t|a_{t-1}} P_{b_t|b_{t-1}} P_{a_t|b_{t-1}} P_{b_t|a_{t-1}} P(o_t^a|a_t)P(o_t^b|b_t)] \quad (1)$$

where π_{a_1} and π_{b_1} are the initial probabilities of states, $P_{a_t|a_{t-1}}$ and $P_{b_t|b_{t-1}}$ are the inner-chain state transition probabilities, $P_{a_t|b_{t-1}}$ and $P_{a_t|b_{t-1}}$ are the inter-chain state transition probabilities modeling the interactions, $P(o_t^a|a_t)$ and $P(o_t^b|b_t)$ are the output probabilities of the states, we employ the Gaussian distribution in this case.

The CHMMs inference problem is formulated as follows. Given an observation sequence O, we need to find a state sequence S which maximizes $P(S|O)$. The inference algorithm – Viterbi – for HMMs could be applied to CHMMs as well with some modifications. The key point is, for each step, we need to compute both the inner-chain and inter-chain state transition probability, i.e., $P_{a_t|a_{t-1}} P_{b_t|b_{t-1}}$ and $P_{a_t|b_{t-1}} P_{b_t|a_{t-1}}$. The algorithm outputs the best state sequence S which involves two state sequences S_a and S_b corresponding to the recognized activity sequences for the two users.

Parameter Estimation in CHMMs. There are many existing algorithms for training HMMs such as Baum-Welch. Since a two-chain CHMM C can be constructed by joining two component HMMs A and B and taking the Cartesian product of their states, we define our training method as follows. We first train A and B following the maximum likelihood method, and then, we couple A and B with inter-chain transition probabilities which can be learnt from training datasets. This method is efficient since we do not need to re-train the CHMMs.

4.4 Activity Recognition Using CHMMs

For each user, the wearable sensors produce an observation sequence. The observation sequence will be divided into a training sequence and a testing sequence. We first compute a feature vector extracted from the observation sequence in every one second interval, which each feature vector contains many feature values as described in Section 4.2. We then obtain a sequence of feature vectors for each user. These sequences, corresponding to multiple users, will be the inputs to a CHMM.

To apply CHMMs for recognizing activities of multiple users, the model will be first trained from multiple training sequences corresponding to multiple users, and the trained models is then used to infer activities given multiple testing sequences. For example, to apply CHMMs, we build a CHMM for multiple users where each single-chain HMM is used for each user and each hidden state in the HMM represents one activity for the user. Given multiple training sequences, we train the CHMM using the parameter estimation method described in Section 4.3. When testing, the multiple testing sequences are fed into the trained CHMM, the inference algorithm then outputs multiple state sequences for each single-chain HMM as the labeled sequences for each of the users.

5   Experimental Studies

We now move to evaluate our proposed activity recognition models. We use the dataset collected in [5]. The dataset contains the observations of two subjects performing a total number of 21 activities (shown in Table 1) over a period of two weeks.

5.1 Evaluation Methodology

We use ten-fold cross-validation to generate our training and test datasets. We evaluate the performance of our methods using the time-slice accuracy which is a typical technique in time-series analysis. The time-slice accuracy represents the percentage of correctly labeled time slices. The length of time slice Δt is set to 1 second as our experiment shows different Δt doest not affect accuracy much. This time-slice duration is short enough to provide precise measurements for most of activity recognition applications. The metric of the time-slice accuracy is defined as follows.

$$Accuracy = \frac{\sum_{n=1}^{N} [predicted(n) == ground\_truth(n)]}{N} \qquad (2)$$

where $N = \frac{T}{\Delta t}$.

Table 1. ADLs Performed in Our Trace Collection

Single-user ADLs				Multi-user ADLs
0	brushing teeth	8	vacuuming	15	making pasta
1	washing face	9	using phone	16	cleaning a dining table
2	brushing hair	10	using computer	17	making coffee
3	making pasta	11	reading book/magazine	18	toileting (with conflict)
4	making coffee	12	watching TV	19	watching TV
5	toileting	13	eating meal	20	using computer
6	ironing	14	drinking		
7	making tea				

Table 2. Accuracy for CHMMs

User	CHMMs		
	Single-user ADLs	Multi-user ADLs	Overall
user 1	74.79%	96.91%	82.22%
user 2	85.11%	95.91%	88.71%
overall	79.95%	96.41%	**85.46%**

5.2 Results

In this experiment, we evaluate the accuracy of our proposed model. Table 2 shows the result. We achieve an accuracy of 85.46% for CHMMs. CHMMs perform better in multi-user ADLs than single-user ADLs. This probably can be explained as follows. For multi-user ADLs, the observations from both users are useful in the model since both users are performing the same activity. Hence, coupling two single-chain HMMs is effective to recognize multi-user activities. However, when recognizing single-user ADLs for one user, the observations from other users will become background noise, and hence they will have negative effects in model prediction. In this case, coupling two single-chain HMMs may weaken the posterior probability we compute for single-user activities.

Table 3 presents the confusion matrix for CHMMs. The activity serial numbers in both tables are identical to the numbers in Table 1. The values in each table are percentages, indicating that the percentage of the entire observation sequence for each activity is predicted correctly, and the percentages are predicted as other labels. For CHMMs, the activities such as *brushing hair* (single-user ADL), *toileting* (single-user ADL), *using computer* (single-user ADL), *toileting* (multi-user ADL) and *watching TV* (multi-user ADL) give the highest accuracies, and the activities *brushing teeth* (single-user ADL), *reading book/magazine* (single-user ADL), *watching TV* (single-user ADL) perform the worst. Most confusion takes place in the following cases:

Case 1: A single-user ADL is predicted as another single-user ADL. For example, the result shows that, for *making coffee*, while 74.7% of its entire observations are predicted correctly, 25.3% of them are predicted as *making pasta*.

Case 2: A single-user ADL is predicted as a multi-user ADL. For example, the result shows that, for *reading book/magazine* (single-user ADL), 24.4% of its observations are predicted as *watching TV* (multi-user ADL).

Case 3: A multi-user ADL is predicted as another multi-user ADL. For example, for *making pasta* (multi-user ADL), the result shows that 10.0% of its observations are predicted as *cleaning a dining table* (multi-user ADL).

Table 3. Confusion Matrix of CHMMs

	0	1	2	3	4	5	6	7	8	9	10	11	12	13	14	15	16	17	18	19	20
0	27.8	2.4	0	0	0	0	0	0	0	0	0	0	0	0.1	0	0	0	0	0	0	0
1	72.2	97.6	0	0	0	0	0	0	0	0	0	0	0	5.0	0	0	0	0	0	0	0
2	0	0	100.0	0	0	0	0	0	0	0	0	0	0	0	0	0	0	0	0	0	0
3	0	0	0	92.9	25.3	0	0	0	0	0	0	0	0	0	0	0	0	0	0	0	0
4	0	0	0	7.1	74.7	0	0	0	0	0	0	0	0	0	0	0	0	0	0	0	0
5	0	0	0	0	0	100.0	0	0	0	0	0	0	0	0	0	0	0	0	0	0	0
6	0	0	0	0	0	0	93.7	1.1	0	0	0	0	0	0	0	0	0	0	0	0	0
7	0	0	0	0	0	0	1.7	93.9	3.5	0	0	0	0	0	0	0	0	0	0	0	0
8	0	0	0	0	0	0	0	0	95.6	0	0	0	0	0	0	0	0	0	0	0	0
9	0	0	0	0	0	0	0	0	0	100.0	0	0	0	0	0	0	0	0	0	0	0
10	0	0	0	0	0	0	0	0	0	0	100.0	0	0	0	0	0	0	0	0	0	0
11	0	0	0	0	0	0	0	0	0	0	0	68.0	1.7	0	0	0	0	0	0	0	0
12	0	0	0	0	0	0	0.4	0	0	0	0	4.8	43.3	0	0	0	0	0	0	0	0
13	0	0	0	0	0	0	0.4	0	0	0	0	0.4	0	84.9	0	0	0	0	0	0	0
14	0	0	0	0	0	0	0.3	0	0	0	0	0.4	0.1	0	90.2	0	0	0	0	0	0
15	0	0	0	0	0	0	2.5	0	0	0	0	0.6	0.1	0	0	90.0	4.9	0	0	0	0
16	0	0	0	0	0	0	0.3	0	0	0	0	0.4	0	5.5	0	10.0	95.1	8.8	0	0	0
17	0	0	0	0	0	0	0.3	5.0	0	0	0	0.6	0.1	0.1	0	0	0	91.2	0	0	0
18	0	0	0	0	0	0	0.2	0	0	0	0	0.4	0.1	4.4	0	0	0	0	100.0	0	0
19	0	0	0	0	0	0	0	0	0.1	0	0	24.4	54.4	0	0.2	0	0	0	0	100.0	0
20	0	0	0	0	0	0	0	0	0.8	0	0	0	0.1	0	9.7	0	0	0	0	0	100.0

(Row labels: Predicted Activities. Column group header: Ground Truth Activities)

6   Conclusions and Future Work

In this paper, we study the fundamental problem of recognizing activities of multiple users from sensor readings in ubiquitous computing, and propose a multi-chained temporal probabilistic model. Our evaluation results demonstrate the effectiveness of our model.

For our future work, we will investigate a possible future research direction – to recognize activities in a more complex scenario where single-user ADLs and multi-user ADLs are mixed with *interleaved* (i.e., switching between the steps of two or more activities) or *concurrent* (i.e., performing two or more activities simultaneously) activities. Recognizing activities in such a complex situation can be very challenging while we consider both single-user and multi-user activities at the same time, and hence, an in-depth study is required.

Acknowledgments. This work is supported by the National 973 project of China under Grant 2009CB320702, the National Natural Science Foundation of China under Grants NSFC 60721002 and NSFC 60736015, and the Jiangsu Natural Science Foundation under Grant BK2008017.

References

1. Brand, M.: Coupled hidden markov models for modeling interacting processes. Technical Report (November 1997)
2. Du, Y., Chen, F., Xu, W., Li, Y.: Recognizing interaction activities using dynamic bayesian network. In: Proc. of ICPR 2006, Hong Kong, China (August 2006)

3. Fayyad, U., Irani, K.: Multi-interval discretization of continuous-valued attributes for classi-fication learning. In: Proc. Int'l. Joint Conf. on Artificial Intelligence, San Francisco (1993)

4. Gong, S., Xiang, T.: Recognition of group activities using dynamic probabilistic networks. In: Proc. of ICCV 2003, Nice, France, October 2003, pp. 742–749 (2003)

5. Gu, T., Wu, Z., Wang, L., Tao, X., Lu, J.: Mining Emerging Patterns for Recognizing Activi-ties of Multiple Users in Pervasive Computing. In: Proc. of the 6th International Conference on Mobile and Ubiquitous Systems: Computing, Networking and Services (MobiQuitous 2009), Toronto, Canada (July 2009)

6. Huynh, T., Blanke, U., Schiele, B.: Scalable recognition of daily activities from wearable sensors. In: Hightower, J., Schiele, B., Strang, T. (eds.) LoCA 2007. LNCS, vol. 4718, pp. 50–67. Springer, Heidelberg (2007)

7. Ivanov, Y.A., Bobick, A.F.: Recognition of visual activities and interactions by stochastic parsing. IEEE Trans. Pattern Recognition and Machine Intelligence 22(8), 852–872 (2000)

8. Katz, S., Ford, A.B., Moskowitz, R.W., Jackson, B.A., Jaffe, M.W.: Studies of illness in the aged. the index of adl: A standardized measure of biological and psychological function. Journal of the American Medical Association 185, 914–919 (1963)

9. Lester, J., Choudhury, T., Borriello, G.: A practical approach to recognizing physical activ-ities. In: Fishkin, K.P., Schiele, B., Nixon, P., Quigley, A. (eds.) PERVASIVE 2006. LNCS, vol. 3968, pp. 1–16. Springer, Heidelberg (2006)

10. Logan, B., Healey, J., Philipose, M., Munguia-Tapia, E., Intille, S.: A long-term evaluation of sensing modalities for activity recognition. In: Krumm, J., Abowd, G.D., Seneviratne, A., Strang, T. (eds.) UbiComp 2007. LNCS, vol. 4717, pp. 483–500. Springer, Heidelberg (2007)

11. Oliver, N., Rosario, B., Pentland, A.: A Bayesian computer vision system for modeling hu-man interactions. IEEE Transactions on Pattern Analysis and Machine Intelligence 22(8), 831–843 (2000)

12. Park, S., Trivedi, M.M.: Multi-person interaction and activity analysis: A synergistic track-and body- level analysis framework. Machine Vision and Applications: Special Issue on Novel Concepts and Challenges for the Generation of Video Surveillance Systems 18(3), 151–166 (2007)

13. Philipose, M., Fishkin, K.P., Perkowitz, M., Patterson, D.J., Fox, D., Kautz, H., Hähnel, D.: Inferring activities from interactions with objects. IEEE Pervasive Computing 3, 50–57 (2004)

14. Smith, E.R., Mackie, D.M.: Social Psychology. Routledge, London (1999)

15. van Kasteren, T.L.M., Noulas, A.K., Englebienne, G., Kröse, B.: Accurate activity recog-nition in a home setting. In: Proc. of International Conference on Ubiquitous Computing (Ubicomp 2008), Korea (September 2008)

16. Wang, S., Pentney, W., Popescu, A.M., Choudhury, T., Philipose, M.: Common sense based joint training of human activity recognizers. In: Proc. Int'l. Joint Conf. on Artificial Intelli-gence, Hyderabad (January 2007)

17. Wyatt, D., Choudhury, T., Bilmes, J., Kautz, H.: A privacy sensitive approach to modeling multi-person conversations. In: Proc. IJCAI, India (January 2007)

18. Yacoob, Y., Black, M.J.: Parameterized modeling and recognition of activities. In: Proc. of International Conference on Computer Vision, ICCV 1998 (1998)

19. Zhang, D., Gatica-Perez, D., Bengio, S., McCowan, I., Lathoud, G.: Modeling individual and group actions in meetings: A two-layer hmm framework. In: Proc. of CVPRW 2004, Washington, DC, USA (2004)

Amelie: A Recombinant Computing Framework for Ambient Awareness

Georgios Metaxas[1], Panos Markopoulos[1], and Emile Aarts[2]

[1] Eindhoven University of Technology, The Netherlands
[2] Philips research, The Netherlands
{g.metaxas,p.markopoulos}@tue.nl,
emile.aarts@philips.com

Abstract. This paper presents Amelie, a service oriented framework that supports the implementation of awareness systems. Amelie adopts the tenets of Recombinant computing to address an important non-functional requirement for Ambient Intelligence software, namely the heterogeneous combination of services and components. Amelie is founded upon FN-AAR an abstract model of Awareness Systems which enables the immediate expression and implementation of socially salient requirements, such as symmetry and social translucence. We discuss the framework and show how system behaviours can be specified using the Awareness Mark-up Language AML.

Keywords: Awareness, Focus Nimbus, Recombinant computing, Symmetry, Social Translucence, Ambient Intelligence, AML, FN-AAR.

1 Introduction

Awareness systems, can be broadly defined as systems intended to help people construct and maintain an awareness of each others' activities, context or status, even when these individuals are not co-located[4]. Awareness can bring important, if subtle, benefits, such as effectiveness of collaborative work, fostering social relationships. Awareness has been approached traditionally as a benefit deriving from the use of systems supporting cooperation between groups, messaging, and, more recently, social networking and micro-blogging.

Supporting awareness in the field of Ambient Intelligence has prompted researchers to consider how to integrate the capture of awareness information, its dissemination and display within heterogeneous collections of devices and services comprising Ambient Intelligence Environments. Example applications of such systems address well known scenarios such as awareness of a lone elderly relative living independently [10]. Existing implementations of awareness systems of this latter kind, which we call *ambient awareness systems* have so far been of very limited scale. In advancing towards realistic deployments and actual use, devices and services need to be used often in configurations and for purposes that are not foreseen by their designers and developers [8]. Eventually such a dynamic configuration and repurposing of the multitude of devices and applications in an Ambient Intelligence environment requires

M. Tscheligi et al. (Eds.): AmI 2009, LNCS 5859, pp. 88–100, 2009.

that they operate collectively, using information and intelligence that is hidden in the interconnection network [1]. A clear consequence of this statement is that interoperability and dynamic aggregations of devices and services are needed, a technical ambition that has been pursued consistently by the Ambient Intelligence community in the past ten years.

This paper introduces Amelie, a recombinant computing framework designed to meet this challenge. First related work is summarized and the theoretical foundations of Amelie are introduced: the Focus-Nimbus Aspects Attributes and Resources (FN-AAR) model [11], and the concept of recombinant computing [5]; then Amelie is described and the paper concludes with an illustration the advantages it offers for implementing ambient awareness systems.

2 Related Work

An early and influential model of awareness systems was the *'event propagation model'* (EPM) [14] which identifies three basic information processing functions they should support: capturing information regarding a particular individual, group, or location, disseminating it, and displaying it to the intended receivers. GroupDesk [7] is a prototype implementation of the EPM that allows users to stay informed dynamically about events, that happen currently or that have happened in the past in the surroundings of their actual position. Despite that this model did not originally target ambient intelligence it has been adopted for most implementations of ambient awareness prototypes to date, e.g., the InfoCanvas [17] and Nessie [18].

Confab [15] is a prototypical toolkit for facilitating the development of privacy-sensitive ubiquitous computing applications; building on the *Approximate Information Flows model* [16] Confab affords basic support for building ubiquitous computing applications, providing features to allow the easy implementation of a spectrum of trust and privacy levels.

3 FN-AAR

The FN-AAR model [11] is a model of awareness systems that extends the Focus/Nimbus model [2, 13] that models (the magnitude of) awareness in terms of the overlap between the focus of one entity upon another and the information that other entity is prepared to share with the first - which is termed the 'nimbus' of this latter entity. Where the focus-nimbus model describes **how much aware** two entities are about each-other in a particular *space,* FN-AAR describes **of what** are the entities **aware** in a particular situation in relation to each other, and illustrates[11, 12] how this departure is instrumental for modelling concisely awareness systems, and the social aspects pertaining to their use.

The FN-AAR model extends the focus-nimbus model, with the notions of *entities, aspects, attributes, resources and observable items.*

- *Entities* are representations of actors, communities, and agents.
- *Aspects* are any characteristics that refer to an entity's state; they are easily thought of as the complement to the statement "*I want to be aware of your... *".

- ***Attributes*** are place-holders for the information exchanged between *Entities* by binding *aspects* with values. An entity makes its state available to other entities using attributes.
- ***Resources*** are bindings of *aspects* with ways of rendering (displaying) one or more relevant attributes. In any situation an entity might employ one or more resources to express its 'interest' about certain aspects of other entities.
- ***Observable items*** are the result of displaying some attributes about an aspect using a *resource*. Roughly speaking an *observable item* contains the answer to the question *"How are these attributes displayed to you?"*.

To reflect the fact that awareness is dynamic, the FN-AAR model populates one's ***nimbus*** with *attribute-providers*; i.e. functions that return those attributes that one makes available to other entities in a specific situation. Likewise one's *nimbus*, ***focus*** is populated with *resource-providers*; i.e. functions that return one's *resources* that display information about other entities in a specific situation. Conforming to the original *focus/nimbus* model, the negotiation of the reciprocal *foci* and *nimbi* of two entities in a given situation (i.e. the corresponding 'produced' *attributes* and *resources*) is a function which returns the *observable-items* that are displayed to the two entities about each other's states, effectively characterizing their reciprocal awareness.

4 Recombinant Computing

Edwards et al. [5, 6] pointed out that ubiquitous computing research has considered enabling technologies in isolation, e.g., location sensing, multi-device user interfaces, ad hoc network protocols, and so on, overlooking fundamental software architectural issues relating to their composition. They outline an approach that they call *"recombinant computing"* which allows the dynamic extension of computational entities through the use of mobile code. As they point out existing component frameworks (e.g., JavaBeans, DCOM, UPnP) are insufficient to enable arbitrary software interconnection because the users of such frameworks (i.e., application developers) are required not only to have knowledge of the interconnected components' interfaces but also of their semantics.

The recombinant computing approach proposes a limited set of *recombinant interfaces* that provide the foundation for allowing components to interact with one another dynamically. For that to succeed it is the users who provide the semantic understanding of what components actually do. The initial prototypical architectural framework supporting recombinant computing, Speakasy [6], outlays three general functional requirements:

- ***Connection***: How components exchange information with each other
- ***Context***: How components reveal information about themselves
- ***Control***: How components allow users and other components to effect changes

5 Recombinant Implementation of the FN-AAR

FN-AAR can serve as a conceptual model, but it can also be mapped to executable semantics following and benefiting from the recombinant computing approach discussed above.

Attribute and Resource providers (i.e. the functions that return one's focus and nimbus in a situation) are abstracted with a single recombinant interface and implemented as web services. An entity's profile comprises a set of service instances (i.e. recombinant components) that interact with one another, effectively characterizing an entity's focus-on and nimbus-to other entities. Rendering functions are abstracted as web services that implement a simple interface which provides methods for displaying information.

Amelie services communicate by exchanging attributes or resources which are the fundamental carriers of information within an awareness system; attributes and resources conform to a simple xml schema that encompasses a wide range of semantics. They are used not only to characterize effectively one's nimbus-to and focus-on others but also to characterize one's awareness of others.

The behaviour of an awareness application but also of an entity within an awareness system is defined by manipulating the services of the entity's profile. Amelie provides the necessary components that allow registration and modification of services in an entity's profile; for the same purpose services are free to provide interactive mechanisms that target any medium.

5.1   How Are the Attributes and Resources Mapped on the Architecture?

The FN-AAR model introduces the notion of attributes, and resources; the first are the elements of information exchanged between entities hence defining one's nimbus in some situation, and resources are the elements of information comprising one's focus on other entities. Bellow we will describe how these notions are mapped on Amelie.

5.1.1   Mapping Attributes

In terms of the model, an attribute is a binding of an aspect to a value. Amelie follows the model's notion of attributes through a simple XML schema. Bellow we can see an example of a simple attribute denoting that someone's activity is walking for the last hour:

```
<aml:attribute>
  <aml:aspect>activity</aml:aspect>
  <aml:value>walking for 1 hour and 25 minutes</aml:value>
</aml:attribute>
```

The value of an attribute is considered by default as a simple text. This allows heterogeneous services to display for example the attribute's information in a human-readable way. However, attribute values may be defined as structured types. Bellow we can see the same attribute value as above extended with richer semantics of a custom type.

```
<aml:value type="aml-state-duration">
 <state duration="1h25m" state="walking">
 walking for 1 hour and 25 minutes
 </state>
</aml:value>
```

The above declaration is quite richer semantically for services that are able to handle the "*aml-state-duration*" type. For example, an ambient display can benefit from the detailed semantics to make a graphical representation of the duration. On the other hand, a service that does not support the introduced value-type can still use the text part of the value only; this eliminates type-errors in the information propagation for either services, and addresses *"the tyranny of types"* one of the problems that recombinant computing is aimed at tackling.

For an entity to express its nimbus (i.e. the attributes that it exposes to others), attributes are adorned with a list of entities that they are exposed to. For example the attribute declaration below instructs the system to expose to *"John"* and *"Anna"* that our location is downtown.

```
<aml:attribute>
 <aml:aspect>location</aml:aspect>
 <aml:value>downtown</aml:value>
 <aml:access>
  <aml:entity>John</aml:entity>
  <aml:entity>Anna</aml:entity>
 </aml:access>
</aml:attribute>
```

5.1.2 Mapping Resources

Resources as described in the FN-AAR model are bindings of aspects with ways of rendering information. In terms of Amelie a resource is described with a simple XML schema, which we call Awareness Mark-up Language (AML). Bellow we can see a simple resource declaring one's focus on John's activity.

```
<aml:resource>
  <aml:entity>John</aml:entity>
  <aml:aspect>activity</aml:aspect>
  <aml:renderer target="http://home-server/picture-frame"/>
</aml: resource>
```

The above declaration instructs the system that we are acquiring John's activity, and given that he is exposing to us any information (i.e. attributes) concerning this aspect we would like to use it for displaying it using the specified renderer (in this case a "picture-frame")

In order to allow richer interaction with the rendering services the *aml: renderer* tag allows also the declaration of render-specific parameters:

```
<aml:resource>
  <aml:entity>John</aml:entity>
  <aml:aspect>activity</aml:aspect>
  <aml:renderer target="http://home-server/picture-frame">
   <color for="walking">blue</color>
      ...
   <color for="driving">green</color>
  </aml:renderer>
</aml: resource>
```

In the example above the same resource is also populated with renderer specific parameters that instruct the picture-frame to colour code different activities.

5.1.3 Enabling Seamful Design

A requirement for ambient awareness system pertains to what has been termed seamful design [3]. In most cases the 'seams' by which technological components are aggregated do not interest users and should therefore be transparent; however, the complex nature of Ambient Intelligence environments and the uncertainty that is bound to be associated with sensing and networking infrastructures, mean that it is often important to allow users to inspect and understand the nature of these seams and even to exploit them in the design of such systems. Metaxas et al. [10] argued how letting users inspect the basis of the inferences made from sensed data can let them better deal with erroneous information and can be essential for their use.

To do so, attributes may contain an optional confidence index and a section that contains information about the attribute's seams, both of which are populated by the underlying services that generate the attributes. In the above example it could be that the attribute is adorned with some seams:

```
<aml:attribute confidence="0.9">
  <aml:aspect>activity</aml:aspect>
  <aml:value>walking</aml:value>
  <aml:seams content-type="text/plain">
    the activity was detected as walking because the
    accelerometer is detecting that there is frequent
    change of the accelaration vector.
  </aml:seams>
</aml:attribute>
```

As one can observe the seams define also their content-type (above plain text) so that services can further benefit from the seams' semantic information. This is particularly useful when attributes are used to describe an entity's Observable-Items; seams allow the system not only to describe what information is displayed, but also to describe how this information is displayed (e.g. the medium, the timing, the abstraction level etc…).

5.1.4 Supporting Symmetrical Constraints

The aforementioned semantics of attributes and resources are sufficient to define one's focus and nimbus at some point in time with regards to others. At first sight, the services that generate such information are adequate protections for one's privacy considerations by choosing when, what, and to whom information should be exposed-to and when, what, and how information should be acquired-from other entities. Although this approach has been traditionally followed by relevant application-frameworks, e.g., [15] it is not sufficient to address privacy control when this is considered at a social level rather than as an issue of security or access control.

Consider for example the following scenario:

"John, an office worker seeks some distraction and a break from work. He would like to let his colleague Anna to know in case she wishes to join him. He hesitates however, as he does not want to be perceived as lazy. He would like to know Anna's mood, but would not like his interest to be known or to be public, so that he will not be perceived as prying."

This scenario above describes guardedness to disclose that characterizes many social interactions (e.g., dating, confiding) and even business transactions. Reciprocity is paramount and there is high cost at revealing intentions to others, especially in case where these are unmatched. The Amelie framework supports the application of constraints that are applied prior to the exchange of information among entities, and within the boundaries of the focus-nimbus composition, in order to support this kind of requirement regarding disclosure. In the scenario above a constraint could require the system to check whether Anna and John are sharing their feelings, before actually exposing any related information to each other.

To apply such equity constraints attributes and resources may be adorned with relevant semantic information. The attribute declaration bellow, for example, is instructing the system to expose John's mood to Anna if she is also bored

```
<aml:attribute>
 <aml:aspect>mood</aml:aspect><aml:value>bored</aml:value>
 <aml:access><aml:entity>Anna</aml:entity></aml:access>
 <aml:contstrains>
  <ctx:symmetry mode="affirmative" xmlns:ctx="…">
   <match>
    aml:attribute[aml:aspect='mood']/aml:value='bored'
   </match>
  </ctx:symmetry>
 </aml:contstrains>
</aml:attribute>
```

The above declaration uses a contextual symmetry constraint that defines an affirmative symmetrical constraint regarding sharing John's mood with Anna. The xml namespace *"xmlns: ctx"* provides the necessary executable semantics for the interpretation of the constraints; in the example above the constraints are described using XPath to define the context that needs to be matched. Similarly we could define a negative symmetrical constraint regarding the exposure of John's desire for a break to Anna, in order to reassure that John's desire for a break will only be exposed to Anna if she is not busy.

Likewise with attributes, resources may be adorned with symmetrical constraints. We could for example adorn John's resources focusing on Anna to inquire her mood only if she is focusing on his location.

Such level of symmetrical constraints both on the side of the observed and on the side of the observer support the definition of nuanced participation structures addressing privacy requirements of individuals and groups, rather than just different levels of access control.

5.2   How Are Attribute Providers, Resource Providers, and Renderers Mapped on the Architecture?

As mentioned in the introduction all the functional parts of the FN-AAR model are mapped as web services on the Amelie framework. One can imagine that an Amelie service may return attributes, when acting as an attribute-provider, resources when acting as resource-provider or even both. Similarly, attribute renderers are implemented as web services on the Amelie platform. More specifically Amelie services are implemented as SOAP (*Simple Object Access Protocol*) services over HTTP.

SOAP is a widely adapted protocol specification that is supported by all modern application development kits. Moreover its close binding to XML makes it inherently suitable to support the semantics of the XML schemes of Amelie.

In order to minimize the effort to write, configure, interconnect and use Amelie services a single WSDL (Web Services Description Language) interface is required to be implemented by all services whether acting as Attribute-providers, Resource-providers, or Render-functions. Amelie services apart from providing a core functionality (e.g. to display or return attributes and/or resources), should provide mechanisms that allow end-users to configure their instances, mechanisms that allow persistence for their instances, and methods to describe the range of output (in terms of attributes & resources) they can produce and handle.

This limited set of functional requirements along with the choice to follow well established internet standards and protocols make the development and integration of new services with in Amelie a relatively straightforward and simplified process; by allowing developers and designers of such services freely to use any toolkit, programming language, or medium that they feel more comfortable with, Amelie provides enough space to focus on their concepts.

Services that extract contextual information through wireless -sensor networks, that define and manage one's social network, that extract activities and status from one's desktop, that capture images and videos from one's context, that extract location using existing Wi-Fi infrastructure, that allow information decoration through artefacts, that allow end-users to define rules and constraints for generating meta-information, sharing and acquiring information from others, are only a small fragment of services that have been implemented on the Amelie framework addressing various end-user requirements for building up awareness systems in the past 2 years.

5.3 How Are Entities Mapped on the Architecture, What Is an Amelie Profile Like?

Each Amelie entity is assigned a profile that describes its focus-on and nimbus-to other entities in terms of the services that act as attribute and resource providers. The Amelie framework provides the necessary component infrastructure which we term Profile-Processor that handles an entity's profile semantics and produces the corresponding focus and nimbus instance in any situation (i.e. the set of attributes that the entity exposes to its contacts, and the set of resources that define what kinds of information it acquires from the rest). The structure and semantics of an Amelie profile, allows services to interconnect and cross-reference each other in order to generate meta-information and demonstrate intelligent behaviours.

Let us walk through the features of an Amelie profile, using the following simple profile that represents the focus and nimbus of some entity:

```
<aml:profile xmlns:aml="…" xmlns:inv="…">
…
<inv:service id="gps-location" uri="http://device.to.gps">
 <deviceid>01-234-56-789</deviceid>
</inv:service>
<inv:service id="myweather" uri="http://weather.forecast">
 <location>
```

```
      <inv:service ref="*"
         select="aml:attribute[aml:aspect='location']"/>
    </location>
  </inv:service>
  <inv:service id="forjohn" uri="http://expose.some.info">
    <attributes>
      <inv:service ref="myweather" select="aml:attribute"/>
    </attributes>
    <contacts>John</contacts>
  </inv:service>
  ...
</aml:profile>
```

The profile above declares three service instances, each of which defines its persistent
information and its relevant service URL. The first declaration is a service instance
"gps-location", that instructs the profile processor that the service should be instantiated for some device with an identifier *"01-234-56-789"*. The *<deviceid>* is specific
to the *gps-location* service, and the profile processor doesn't need to "care" about its
semantic value: the profile serves as a store for the service specific parameters. The
deviceid xml tag will be used internally by the service residing at the URL
"http://device.to.gps" to retrieve the GPS coordinates from the specified device. Using the service declaration the profile processor prepares the connection with the
service and invokes it with the provided parameters; consequently the gps-location
service returns the coordinates of the device "01-234-56-789":

```
<aml:attribute>
  <aml:aspect>location</aml:aspect>
  <aml:value type="latitude-longtitude">
    <lat value="51.4366">51 degrees,26.2 minutes North</lat>
    <long value="5.4780">5 degrees,28.7 minutes East</long>
  </aml:value>
</aml:attribute>
```

In a similar manner the profile processor is instructed to instantiate the second service
(*myweather*) with its specific parameters. We can imagine that this service implements a weather service that returns an attribute describing the weather conditions and
forecast at some geo-location. Yet, notice the contents of the tag '*<location>*':

```
<inv:service ref="*"
   select="aml:attribute[aml:aspect='location']"/>
```

This declaration instructs the profile processor to instantiate *"myweather"* passing to
it the result of all services (*<inv:service ref="*"...*), that return attributes regarding
"location" (*aml:attribute[aml:aspect='location']*). Given that the service "gps-
location" returns a matching attribute, *"myweather"* could return an attribute such as:

```
<aml:attribute>
  <aml:aspect>weather</aml:aspect>
  <aml:value>partly cloudy, 26° C</aml:value>
</aml:attribute>
```

The last declaration in the profile instructs the processor to instantiate the service "*for-john*" passing to it the attributes that the service "myweather" returned previously, and an entity identifier "*John*". Once invoked, the service at "*http://expose.some.info*" could then adorn the above attributes and contact list to define that the weather information should be exposed to John.

5.3 How Is the Focus-Nimbus Composition Function Mapped on the Architecture?

The carrier of the communication objective, both in the original focus/nimbus model, and in the FN-AAR model is the focus-nimbus composition function; i.e. the function that negotiates the foci and nimbi of entities and defines the communicational outcome among them. The actual implementation of this function lies in the kernel of the Amelie framework, the Awareness Manager module. The Awareness Manager polls periodically the foci and nimbi of its registered entities pushing the appropriate attributes to the identified renderers.

For the awareness manager the profile storage of an entity and its underlying mechanisms of expressing the entity's focus and nimbus are not important. Of importance is the information each entity exposes to others (nimbus) and the information each entity acquires from other (focus) entities in a given situation. Each entity registers in the awareness manager, a service URI that identifies the entity's current focus and nimbus (i.e. its profile-processor). The awareness manager, periodically invokes the registered entities' profile-processor service URIs, and combines their instances in order to invoke the appropriate renderers according to the FN-AAR model.

Moreover, entities registered within the awareness-manager can optionally provide a URI that indicates a web service which identifies the entity's ontological model regarding the space of awareness information. This design choice not only allows an entity to observe others in its own view, but also allows the awareness manager to protect one's privacy in a more efficient way; for example it could be that Anna exposes to John that she is in the kitchen. At the same time it could be that John is focusing on Anna's activities. The ontology of John could facilitate the inference that any person who is in a kitchen is probably cooking. This way John would become aware that Anna's activity is cooking (leaving aside for the moment whether this inference would be sound or not). By having each entity register its relevant ontology, Amelie provides the required flexibility in order to use simple or more complex ontologies that relate available information to information that is needed or may be inferred. Implementation wise, third party software for defining and managing ontologies can be integrated transparently into Amelie.

The following pseudocode summarizes how the Awareness-Manager invokes the appropriate renderers while applying the focus of an entity x, on an entity y.

Let f_{xy} = last pulled focus of x on y (i.e. the resources that x occupies for observing y)
Let n_{yx} = nimbus of y to x (i.e. the set of attributes that y exposes to x)
Let n_{yx}' = apply ontology of x on n_{yx} (i.e. transform y's nimbus using x's point of view)
//to apply the symmetry contstrains we need also the observer's nimbus:
Let n_{xy} = nimbus of x to y (i.e. the set of attributes that y exposes to x)
Let n_{xy}' = apply ontology of y on n_{xy}
//having the reciprocal nimbi of x, and y apply the symmetry constraints

Let n_{yx}''=filter n_{yx}' after applying constraints in relation to n_{xy}'
//now match the resources of f_{xy} with the corresponding attributes in n_{yx}
For each resource r in f_{xy} do
*   Let a = set of attributes in n_{yx}'' about the aspects of the resource r*
*   //Invoke the renderer of the resource r passing to it the set of attributes a*
*   Let o = set of observable items returned from the renderer*

Consider for example that the last known instance of John's focus at some time in-
quires from Anna's activity, while at the same time Anna's nimbus corresponds to an
attribute that exposes to John that her location is in the kitchen. Given that John
would have registered some ontology corresponding to an inference engine like the
one described earlier, the Awareness-Manager would populate Anna's nimbus with
the attribute that exposes to John that her activity is cooking. Consequently, and
since there are not constraints that the manager needs to validate, and based on the
fact that the infered attribute is exposed to John and its aspect(i.e. "activity")
matches John's resource that focus on Anna, the manager would invoke the service
pointed by john's resource (e.g. *"http://some.actuator.at.home"*) passing to it the
abovementioned attribute.

6 Conclusions

We have presented Amelie, a framework for developing Awareness Systems based on
the FN-AAR model [11] and the notion of recombinant computing [5]. Amelie leaves
enough space for exploratory technologies both though its openness regarding ontology engines, and through its openness through the recombinant approach. Amelie
framework and AML provide the necessary semantics to directly implement systems
that ensure socially salient properties for awareness systems, namely symmetry, divergent ontologies, and social translucency.

Amelie embraces desktop, pervasive, and ubiquitous services both for context-
sensing and for information-decoration; the recombinant design of Amelie allows
seamless and rapid integration of third-party services (they only need to support a very
small set of functional requirements to complement and benefit from the framework).

Amelie respects and uplifts the designers' and end-users' role in the development
of applications, allowing the first to explore the design space more easily, and the
latter to control their participation and project their view on the system's intelligence.

Apart from the examples and case studies presented above the Amelie framework
has been used by extensively by other research projects in the past 2 years, e.g., to
support experience sampling as a research method [8], to develop and deploy a pervasive aware system [9].

Amelie's strength lies in its theoretical foundation that has been discussed extensively in this paper, its language independent implementation that allows the composition of heterogeneous components. Its focus upon modelling awareness systems
provides a foundation for enabling end-users to programme awareness systems, addressing one of the challenges for Ambient Intelligence discussed in [1]. Higher level

programming tools based upon Amelie are the subject of current research that aims to provide some of the power for controlling information disclosure and the social aspects of awareness directly to end-users.

Acknowledgements

This work is supported by the European Community under the "Information Society Technologies" Programme, FP6, project ASTRA IST 29266.

References

1. Aarts, E.H.L., Ruyter, B.E.R.: New research perspectives on Ambient Intelligence. J. Ambient Intelligence and Smart Environments 1, 5–14 (2009)
2. Benford, S., Fahlen, L.: A Spatial Model of Interaction in Large Virtual Environments. In: Proc. ECSCW 1993, pp. 109–124 (1993)
3. Chalmers, M., Galani, A.: Seamful Interweaving: Heterogeneity in the Theory and Design of Interactive Systems. In: Proc. DIS 2004, pp. 243–252. ACM Press, New York (2004)
4. Dourish, P., Bellotti, V.: Awareness and coordination in shared workspaces. In: Proceedings of the 1992 ACM Conference on Computer-Supported Cooperative Work. CSCW 1992, Toronto, Ontario, Canada, November 01 - 04, pp. 107–114. ACM, New York (1992)
5. Edwards, W.K., Newman, M.W., Sedivy, J.Z.: The Case for Recombinant Computing. Tech. report CSL-01-1, Palo Alto Research Center (2001)
6. Edwards, W.K., Newman, M.W., Sedivy, J.Z., Smith, T.F., Izadi, S.: Challenge: Recombinant computing and the Speakeasy Approach. In: Proc. MobiCom 2002, pp. 279–286 (2002)
7. Fuchs, L., Pankoke-Babatz, U., Prinz, W.: Supporting cooperative awareness with local event mechanisms: The GroupDesk system. In: Proc. ECSCW 1995, pp. 247–262 (1995)
8. Khan, V., Markopoulos, P., Eggen, B., IJsselsteijn, W., de Ruyter, B.: Reconexp: a way to reduce the data loss of the experiencing sampling method. In: Proc. MobileHCI 2008, pp. 471–476. ACM, New York (2008)
9. Khan, V., Metaxas, G., Markopoulos, P.: Pervasive awareness. In: Proc. MobileHCI 2008, pp. 519–521. ACM, New York (2008)
10. Metaxas, G., Metin, B., Schneider, J.M., Markopoulos, P., de Ruyter, B.: Daily activities diarist: Supporting aging in place with semantically enriched narratives. In: Baranauskas, C., Palanque, P., Abascal, J., Barbosa, S.D.J. (eds.) INTERACT 2007. LNCS, vol. 4663, pp. 390–403. Springer, Heidelberg (2007)
11. Metaxas, G., Markopoulos, P.: Aware of what? A formal model of Awareness Systems that extends the focus-nimbus model. In: Gulliksen, J., Harning, M.B., Palanque, P., van der Veer, G.C., Wesson, J. (eds.) EIS 2007. LNCS, vol. 4940, pp. 429–446. Springer, Heidelberg (2008)
12. Metaxas, G., Markopoulos, P.: Abstractions of Awareness. In: Markopoulos, P., de Ruyter, B., Mackay, W. (eds.) Awareness Systems: Advances in Theory, Methodology and Design. Springer, Heidelberg (2008)
13. Rodden, T.: Populating the Application: A Model of Awareness for Cooperative Applications. In: Proc. CSCW 1996, pp. 87–96 (1996)

14. Sohlenkamp, M., Fuchs, L., Genau, A.: Awareness and Cooperative Work: The POLITeam Approach. In: Proc. HICSS'30, pp. 549–558. IEEE Computer Society Press, Los Alamitos (1997)
15. Hong, J.I., Landay, J.A.: An architecture for privacy-sensitive ubiquitous computing. In: Proc. MobiSys 2004, pp. 177–189. ACM, New York (2004)
16. Jiang, X., Hong, J.L., Landay, J.A.: Approximate Information Flows: Socially-based Modeling of Privacy in Ubiquitous Computing. In: Borriello, G., Holmquist, L.E. (eds.) UbiComp 2002. LNCS, vol. 2498, pp. 176–193. Springer, Heidelberg (2002)
17. Miller, T., Stasko, J.: Artistically Conveying Information with the InfoCanvas. In: Proc. AVI 2002, pp. 43–50 (2002)
18. Prinz, W.: NESSIE: An Awareness Environment for Cooperative Settings. In: Proc. ECSCW 1999, pp. 391–410. Kluwer, Dordrecht (1999)

Bug-Free Sensors: The Automatic Verification of Context-Aware TinyOS Applications

Doina Bucur and Marta Kwiatkowska

Computing Laboratory, Oxford University, UK
{doina.bucur,marta.kwiatkowska}@comlab.ox.ac.uk

Abstract. We provide the first tool for verifying the logic of context-aware applications written for the mainstream sensor network operating system TinyOS; we focus on detecting programming errors related to incorrect adaptation to context.

1 Introduction

Intelligent ambients often include *sensors* in their designs; sensor hardware reads the current value of a specific *context*, such as a patient's cardiogram, skin temperature, blood pressure and oxygen saturation. The decision-making is then left to the software, which infers decisions based on contextual inputs, actuates in output, and is required to gracefully adapt to highly dynamic contexts, in *context-aware* fashion.

For the mainstream sensor operating system TinyOS [1], a programmer writes concurrent, shared-memory software in either nesC or the recent C *TosThreads* API [2], with both languages inheriting C's low-level features. Such software runs in an execution environment in which there is no user-kernel boundary and no guards against *memory violations*. Much more elusive, *concurrency bugs* arise because of the nondeterministic thread interleavings, while *context-awareness bugs* are due to the application's inability to deal with unexpected context. All bug categories can render a deployed sensor node unusable.

To prevent the occurence of context-awareness and concurrency bugs in sensor software *before* deployment time, we provide the very first verification tool for multithreaded, adaptive TinyOS 2.x applications written in TinyOS's C TosThreads API. We *statically verify* a TinyOS application running on a sensor node against a *context-aware safety specification* requiring the program to be in a "safe" state w.r.t actuation and memory configuration, given a—possibly nondeterministic—pattern of incoming context data.

The method our tool employs is *scalable*: We verify a given application modularly, by extracting it from the rest of the TinyOS kernel, and replacing the latter with interface-preserving models. While this requires reviewing the TinyOS code base to learn the semantics of all system calls, the method is good value for developers: it only needs to be provided once, is reusable by all applications and (given that TinyOS is fairly stable) requires little maintenance over time.

Our tool builds on SATABS [3], a generic software verification tool for ANSI C; SATABS takes specifications written as user-specified assertions of boolean

M. Tscheligi et al. (Eds.): AmI 2009, LNCS 5859, pp. 101–105, 2009.

conditions inserted in the code. The verification is *sound* (and *complete* for finite-state applications): The program's state space is exhaustively explored for violations of the specification, including e.g. behaviours triggered by unexpected, but possible, events such as scrambled incoming network packets. An execution trace is returned as a bug witness, allowing the programmer to correct the fault before deploying the application.

We (i) add native support for the C TosThreads API to SATABS, (ii) implement a SATABS-readable C model of the TinyOS system calls to stand in for the OS kernel, and finally (iii) verify application and kernel model against context-aware safety specifications written as SATABS assertions. We report benchmarks on running our tool on standard applications distributed with TinyOS's sources, and on a more complex healthcare application; we find routine violations of safety requirements in staple TinyOS code.

2   The Automatic Verification of TinyOS Applications

This section presents our verification method. We first overview TinyOS and the structure of a TinyOS application, which then allows us to underline possible sources of TinyOS software bugs. Finally, we assess performance with a set of benchmarks and point to the cause and nature of the bugs found.

Modelling the TinyOS Kernel

A TinyOS application programmed in the TosThreads C API [2], as depicted in Fig. 1, is tightly connected to the rest of the operating system's kernel by calling kernel services; these either manage execution scheduling (e.g. thread creation

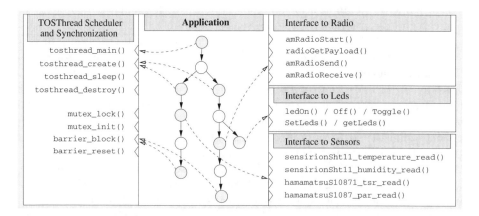

Fig. 1. A TinyOS application programmed in the TosThreads C API, calling TinyOS kernel services, as available on a Tmote Sky sensor node with integrated sensors for temperature, humidity and light intensity

and suspending) or access hardware (e.g. the radio port, sensor chips or resident leds) on their respective software interfaces.

When analysing all possible execution traces of a program to check for violations of a specification, the complexity of the analysis increases with the number of program instructions; when the program is concurrent, the complexity increase is exponential, due to having to explore all possible context switches between threads (a problem known as *state explosion*). Given this fact, we choose to verify a TinyOS application modularly: instead of analysing the application code together with the existing, sizable implementation of the kernel services from Fig. 1, we *model* these services, ensuring that their interface behaviour is preserved; e.g., if amRadioSend([..]) can fail returning EBUSY, so can its model.

Categories of Bugs in Context-Aware Software

In addition to generic memory violation issues, a concurrent context-aware program will also exhibit additional programming errors, which are the focus of our verification. We categorise these from two points of view: generic concurrency (as in Table 2) and correct awareness of context (Table 1). One particular bug can be seen from both viewpoints: an application blocked in waiting for a network packet from a network neighbour which unexpectedly moved away exhibits a bug categorized both as a *network exception* and as *deadlock*.

Table 1. Categories of bugs in context-aware, TinyOS applications

Table 2. Categories of bugs in generic concurrent software

Sensing exceptions Incomplete treatment of sensing errors.	**Data race** Multithreaded (write) access to shared resource. Not necessarily a bug.
Network exceptions Incomplete treatment of network errors.	**Atomicity violation** Failure to enforce the atomicity of a code region.
Interface use Incorrect use of interface to kernel services.	**Order violation** Failure to enforce execution order between two code regions.
False reasoning Incorrect decision-making given a context situation.	**Deadlock** A thread's failure to release a lock-like resource, halting execution.

Case Studies

We first look at *SenseAndSend*, the staple monitoring application in the TinyOS source tree. Four working threads monitor the Tmote Sky on-board sensors, and each write a fresh value in the data field of a network message; a fifth thread sends the message on the radio. The program's specification states that such messages should be sent periodically, containing valid readings, and accompanied by led signalling. The *claims* are specifications written in assertion form.

We give the results of our verification runs in Table 3. LOC stands for Lines of Code in the application's control-flow graph, including the kernel model; whenever a bug exists, it is categorised as in Tables 1,2. Claim 79 uncovers a misuse of the radio interface; thread 0 fails to ensure that the radio is turned on by not checking amRadioStart's returned error code, before a call to amRadioSend:

Table 3. Verification benchmarks. *Blink* is a simple led actuating application; we give its run for comparison. *SenseAndSend* is an application monitoring on-board sensors; *PatientNode* is an extension including distributed monitoring. Verification times are given for runs on a Mac OS X with a 2.4GHz Duo Intel Core and 2GB RAM.

Application (Threads/LOC)	Claim line	Verified?	Time	Bug: context awareness	Bug: concurrency
Blink 4/64	66	yes	2.9s	-	-
SenseAndSend 6/347	79	**no**	32.2s	interface use	order violation
	136	**no**	1m08s	sensing exception	-
	146	yes	4m25s	-	-
PatientNode 6/439	172	yes	29.9s	(interface use)	(order violation)
	254	yes	3m55s	(sensing exception)	-
	230	**no**	35m07s	network exception	deadlock
	268	yes	2m38s	(false reasoning)	-
	262	yes	61m12s	(false reasoning)	-

```
amRadioStart();                                          // thread 0, main
if(amRadioSend(AM_BROADCAST_ADDR, &send_msg, ..) // thread 5, sending
```

More importantly, claim 136 detects that a radio message could be sent with an outdated (temperature) reading. This is the case when the memory location in which the sensing call stores its reading (`sensor_data->temp`) is considered valid even if the sensing call itself failed, and no reading was written in:

```
sensor_data = radioGetPayload(&send_msg, [..]);  // thread 0, main
read_sensor(sensirionSht11_temperature_read,     // thread 2, sensing
            &(sensor_data->temp));
amRadioSend(AM_BROADCAST_ADDR, &send_msg, [..]); // thread 5, sending
```

PatientNode is a SenseAndSend extension tailored for monitoring patients in a pervasive healthcare wireless network [4]. A number of biosensors monitor each patient; a PatientNode application resident on one such sensor collects readings from all of the patient's sensors, sends them in a network message, and signals an abnormal condition by a lit-led configuration. Claims 172 and 254 are re-verifications of SenseAndSend's corrected bugs; claim 230 uncovers that a misplaced closing brace brings the program into a deadlock on a barrier, if a message expected to be received doesn't show up:

```
if(amRadioReceive(&recv_msg, [..]) == SUCCESS) { // thread 3, receiving
  barrier_block(&send_barrier);
}
barrier_block(&send_barrier);                     // thread 5, sending
barrier_reset(&send_barrier, [..]);
amRadioSend(AM_BROADCAST_ADDR, &send_msg, [..]);
```

Claims 268 and 262 verify application logic: the first, that an abnormal received reading is treated as a false alarm if it is not confirmed by a subsequent reception, and the second, that the maximum span of time between outgoing packets is bounded, regardless of the contents of incoming packets.

3   Related Work and Conclusions

While we know of no verification tools for context-aware specifications, there exist tools which bring a degree of memory and interface-use safety to existing sensor code. TinyOS's own nesC compiler has a built-in simplistic data-race detector. *Safe TinyOS* [5] is an established TinyOS extension which enforces memory safety *at runtime*. It checks e.g. dereferencing null pointers and buffer overflows, which SATABS also provides to our tool; e.g. the verification of a null-pointer claim for PatientNode takes 24.5s. The *interface contracts* [6] act like our own checks of interface use, only at runtime. Both differ from our tool in providing safety at runtime—when the sensor node is possibly deployed out of reach.

Our contribution is a tool for the verification of the logic of context-aware programs written in TinyOS 2.x's C API. It supports complex program features such as dynamic thread creation and ANSI-C pointer use; the program is statically checked before deployment, ensuring reliability to a greater extent than simply verifying against memory violations and interface use.

We keep the verification runs reasonably short by analysing our case studies scalably, against an informed model of the TinyOS kernel services; this precludes the need to explore the execution traces of the entire kernel, monolithically, and gives our method scalability. Finally, in the longer term, we aim at (i) extending this method to nesC, and (ii) verifying *networks* of sensor nodes, by checking individual nodes against specifications in assume-guarantee style.

Acknowledgments. The authors are supported by the project *UbiVal: Fundamental Approaches to Validation of Ubiquitous Computing Applications and Infrastructures*, EPSRC grant EP/D076625/2.

References

1. TinyOS: An Open-Source Operating System for the Networked Sensor Regime: http://www.tinyos.net/ (accessed August 2009)
2. Klues, K., Liang, C.J., Paek, J., Musăloiu, R., Govindan, R., Terzis, A., Levis, P.: TOSThreads: Safe and Non-Invasive Preemption in TinyOS. In: SenSys (2009)
3. Clarke, E., Kroening, D., Sharygina, N., Yorav, K.: SATABS: SAT-based Predicate Abstraction for ANSI-C. In: Halbwachs, N., Zuck, L.D. (eds.) TACAS 2005. LNCS, vol. 3440, pp. 570–574. Springer, Heidelberg (2005)
4. Varshney, U.: Pervasive healthcare and wireless health monitoring. Mobile Networks and Applications (MONET) 12(2-3), 113–127 (2007)
5. Cooprider, N., Archer, W., Eide, E., Gay, D., Regehr, J.: Efficient Memory Safety for TinyOS. In: ACM SenSys, pp. 205–218 (2007)
6. Archer, W., Levis, P., Regehr, J.: Interface Contracts for TinyOS. In: Information Processing in Sensor Networks (IPSN), pp. 158–165. ACM Press, New York (2007)

Semi-automatic Story Creation System in Ubiquitous Sensor Environment

Shohei Yoshioka[1], Yasushi Hirano[2], Shoji Kajita[3], Kenji Mase[1], and Takuya Maekawa[4]

[1] Graduate School of Information Science, Nagoya University, Japan
[2] Information Technology Center, Nagoya University, Japan
[3] Information and Communication Technology Services, Nagoya University, Japan
[4] NTT Communication Science Laboratories, Japan

Abstract. This paper proposes an agent system that semi-automatically creates stories about daily events detected by ubiquitous sensors and posts them to a weblog. The story flow is generated from query-answering interaction between sensor room inhabitants and a symbiotic agent. The agent questions the causal relationships among daily events to create the flow of the story. Preliminary experimental results show that the stories created by our system help users understand daily events.

1 Introduction

Human beings use stories to present, memorize and recall important events or useful information. For instance, people experience interesting events as stories related to family members, time spent at school or during commutes. Story-telling is a very strong and effective method for telling other people events and experiences within an episodic context. Even though such events may be gradually forgotten and lost forever, events encapsulated in an episodic story will often remain people's memory. We propose a method that enables users to semi-automatically create event stories daily by human/agent interaction. In this paper, we focus on story creation based on daily life information sensed and recorded by indoor ubiquitous sensors.

Event detection as the source of such story creation is becoming easier. Lifelog studies are now receiving much attention due to the advances of sensing technologies. This trend will enable us to log important daily events and useful information as memorable. However, most existing lifelog systems do not provide stories but only search methods for lifelog data. Lamming et al. [1] implemented a system that presents a sequence of icons that represent people met and places visited in a day. Understanding of the semantics of events in the system depends on the user's interpretation of the icon sequences. Maekawa et al. [2] proposed a system where a personified object with a sensor node posts weblog entries about events involving the objects. In their system, for example, a slipper posts a report that includes a graph that shows a wearer's daily activity level. The posted report is a simple event log, but is not provided with a story.

M. Tscheligi et al. (Eds.): AmI 2009, LNCS 5859, pp. 106–111, 2009.

We focus on creating a story that explains causal relationships among detected events to form a meaningful narrative. Other relationships such as chronology or topic commonality can be found fairly easily. However, developing a causal relationship requires common sense knowledge, for which computer agents need to ask humans for help to acquire. Thus, we propose a human/agent co-working paradigm for knowledge acquisition through the interaction based on the agent observed event data.

In the rest of the paper, related works are briefly addressed in section 2, followed by the story creation method in section 3. Section 4 explains the details of the interactive story-creation system design. A preliminary experimental result is presented in section 5 and the conclusion is given in section 6.

2   Related Works

Because people remember daily events as stories and tell these stories to others in their lives [3,4], narrative is an acceptable medium for presenting lifelog data to users. Byrne et al. [5] argue that further improvement of lifelogging is important for creating stories with digital lifelog data. In fact, Gemmell et al. [6] implemented tools for supporting story creation by photos, location information, and other sensor data. A mapping tool creates travel stories using GPS tracking points and photos. Appan et al. [7] created photo-based stories by categorizing and connecting photos into five categories including an introduction and ending. In these studies, since users are expected to create stories manually, the task imposes a burden on users, so they may forget to create stories in their daily lives.

3   Story Creation in Ubiquitous Sensor Environments

Story creation connects related events [8]. For example, assume that a person missed a bus and was late for a meeting. A story is created by connecting two important events: "missed a bus" and "late for a meeting."

By a questionnaire survey in [2], we previously obtained 66 answers that subjects wanted to record, such as the breeding records of pets and logs for taking medicine. Most subjects wanted to find *unusual events* such as forgetting to feed pets and taking too much medicine (65%). Bacause we can regard such events as errors taking note of them can improve life.

Therefore, we define an unusual event as a situation where the occurrence pattern of an event is different from past event occurrence patterns. To create a story, we need to find the cause of the unusual events after automatically detecting them. However, automatically finding the cause of unusual events is very difficult. Many works employ association rules to find causal relationships.

However, because unusual events are rare by definition, learning such association rules for unusual events is not easy. Also, we may not be able to find all of the causes of detected unusual events because the causes may not be sensed as real-world phenomena even with ideal ubiquitous sensors. Thus, we employ a method in which an agent asks users for the cause of automatically detected unusual events. Users select a possible causal event from candidate events presented by the agent or directly input text that describes the cause. Inputs are used for story creation and accumulated in the system for the future use.

4   Interactive Story Creation System

Figure 1 shows an overview of our system. The "EventDetectors" module recognizes events from sensor data obtained from sensor nodes embedded in daily environments and puts the events into the "EventDataBase." The "UnusualEventDetector" module detects unusual events from event data stored in the "EventDataBase," and puts them into the "UnusualEventDataBase." The "QuestionCreator" module creates questions about the causes of detected unusual events. The "Story Creator" module creates stories from the answers and posts them to a weblog. We implemented the system in our home-like experimental environment where we installed fifty sensor nodes with acceleration and direction sensors, four microphones, and eight cameras attached to daily objects such as chairs, coffee pot, coffee cups, rice cooker, toothbrushes, and vacuum.

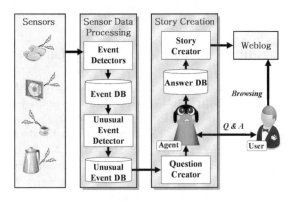

Fig. 1. Story creation system

4.1   Event Detection

Our system contains four kinds of real-time event detectors. The conversation detector detects periods of conversation from microphone signals. The physical-phenomena detector detects objects' movement and falling. The object event detector detects events specific to approximately ten kinds of objects, such as opening/closing of doors, cabinets, and drawers. The activity of daily living(ADL) detector [9] uses machine learning to detect roughly 20 kinds of ADLs such as cooking pasta or rice and listening to music.

4.2   Unusual Event Detection

We use histograms of event occurrence to detect day to day unusual events day-to-day. The detection is performed independently for each event class; e.g. Tom's slipper is moved, the door is open. The event histogram has a different bin number n (proportional to detecting window size) for each class, and is denoted by an event vector $x \in \mathbb{R}^{n \times 1}$. We collect event vectors over past m periodical samples[1] to form an event matrix $X = [x_1 \dots x_m]^T \in \mathbb{R}^{m \times n}$ and evaluate the latest event vector x_m. The evaluation is performed by using the *singular value decomposition* (SVD) analysis of X and whether it is usual or unusual against past days. As is known, the SVD of X is $X \equiv U\Sigma V^T$ where $U \in \mathbb{R}^{m \times r}$, $\Sigma \in \mathbb{R}^{r \times r}$, and $V \in \mathbb{R}^{n \times r}$. The columns of V are the orthonormal basis of the event vectors within X, and have the properties of occurrence frequency of past m samples. We define a basis reduction matrix, $V' := [v_1 \ v_2 \ \dots \ v_k \ 0 \ \dots \ 0]$ where $V' \in \mathbb{R}^{n \times r}$, $k < r$, and v_i is the columns of V corresponding to the i-th highest singular value of Σ. Here, we compute an angle, $\theta = \arccos(\frac{<x_m, VV'^T x_m>}{\|x_m\| \|VV'^T x_m\|})$ where $V'^T x_m$ means x_m projected onto V'. Because the size of θ means the difference of event occurrence frequency between present and past, when θ is larger than a heuristic threshold, we decide that x_m is unusual.

4.3   Question Answering Interaction

When an agent encounters a user, it asks her/him about the cause of the computed unusual event with voice and display. It displays the latest histogram of the unusual event and the related information such the as event's name and the time of occurrence. Also, to reduce the burden on users during the input task, the agent presents candidates of causal events selected from usual/unusual events detected by the "EventDetectors" and the "UnusualEventDetector." Candidates have high co-occurrence probabilities with the unusual event of the agent's question. Users can respond by selecting possible causes from candidates by touchscreen. Only when users can not do this, they input an answer by keyboard.

4.4   Story Creation

The "StoryCreator" module makes stories by connecting an unusual event and causal information. For example, if the cause of unusual vacuuming from 16:20 to 16:30 corresponds to the event of Tom's cup dropping between 16:10 to 16:20, the "StoryCreator" module creates the following story "From 16:00 to 16:30, vacuum_use occurred because Tom's cup_drop occurred from 16:10 to 16:20."

---

[1] The sampling period can be, for instance, one day during which unusual events occurred.

5   Preliminary Experiment

The aim of this experiment is to confirm the effectiveness of our story creation system. We used Robovie-R2 [10] as an agent. Eight subjects (five males and three females) had the task of answering the agent's questions when passing by the agent. The subjects are workers in our environment. The experimental period ran for four days during which the system was activated from 10:00 to 18:00. At the end of a day, our system posted story-based and non-story entries to a weblog. Subjects read both weblog entries and rated them for "importance," "specialness," and "usefulness" on a 5-point scale. A non-story entry does not include causal information but only unusual event information.

5.1   Results

Figure 2 shows the average ratings of story-based and non-story entries. The ratings of story-based entries were higher than non-story. For all criteria, the numbers of high rating (≥ 4) for each criterion were increased by story creation. As result of two sided t-tests between ratings of story and non-story for each criterion, the "usefulness" criterion showed significant difference ($p < 0.05$).

The highest rated story was "From 10:30 to 11:00, Cook_Rice occurred for a Hinamatsuri   from   12:00   to   13:00"(Importance:4.0,   Specialness:4.4, Usefulness:4.1). This story received a high rating because a Hinamatsuri is a Japanese annual event where people celebrate the lives of girls with specially prepared rice and users could know that cooking rice is a part of the memorable story.

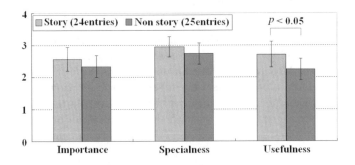

Fig. 2. Average ratings for each criterion

6   Conclusion

In this paper, we presented a method and an evaluation of semi-automatic story creation about important daily events using events detected by ubiquitous sensors and question-answering interaction between an agent and users. Our preliminary experiment clarified the effectiveness of story-based lifelogging.

References

1. Lamming, M., Flynn, M.: Forget-me-not: Intimate computing in support of human memory. In: Proc. FRIEND21: International Symposium on Next Generation Human Interface, pp. 125–128 (1994)
2. Maekawa, T., Yanagisawa, Y., Kishino, Y., Kamei, K., Sakurai, Y., Okadome, T.: Object-blog system for environment-generated content. IEEE Pervasive Computing 7(4), 20–27 (2008)
3. Tulving, E.: Elements of episodic memory. Oxford Clarendon Press (1984)
4. Wyer, R.S.: Knowledge and memory: The real world. Lawrence Erlbaum Association, Hillsdale (1995)
5. Byrne, D., Jones, G.J.F.: Towards computational auto-biographical narratives through human digital memories. In: Proc. ACM International Workshop on Story Representation, Mechanism and Context, pp. 9–12 (2008)
6. Gemmell, J., Aris, A., Lueder, R.: Telling stories with MyLifeBits. In: Proc. ICME 2005, pp. 20–27 (2005)
7. Appan, P., Sundaram, H., Birchfield, D.: Communicating everyday experiences. In: Proc. ACM Workshop on Story Representation, pp. 17–24 (2004)
8. Riessman, C.K.: Narrative analysis. Saga Publications, Thousand Oaks (1993)
9. Tapia, E.M., Intille, S.S., Laarson, K.: Activity Recognition in The Home Using Simple and Ubiquitous Sensors. In: Ferscha, A., Mattern, F. (eds.) PERVASIVE 2004. LNCS, vol. 3001, pp. 158–175. Springer, Heidelberg (2004)
10. Robovie-R2, http://www.atr-robo.com/

SAGE: A Logical Agent-Based Environment Monitoring and Control System

Krysia Broda[1,*], Keith Clark[1], Rob Miller[2], and Alessandra Russo[1]

[1] Department of Computing, Imperial College London
{k.broda,k.clark,a.russo}@imperial.ac.uk
www.doc.ic.ac.uk/{~kb/,~klc/,~ar3/}
[2] Department of Information Studies, University College London
rsm@ucl.ac.uk
www.ucl.ac.uk/infostudies/rob-miller/

Abstract. We propose SAGE, an agent-based environment monitoring and control system based on computation logic. SAGE uses forward chaining deductive inference to map low level sensor data to high level events, multi-agent abductive reasoning to provide possible explanations for these events, and teleo-reactive programming to react to these explanations, e.g. to gather extra information to check abduced hypotheses. The system is embedded in a publish/subscribe architecture.

Keywords: Environmental Control, Logic, Event Calculus, Logic Programming, Abduction, Multi-Agent Reasoning, Teleo-Reactive Programs.

1 Introduction

SAGE (Sense, Abduce, Gather, Execute) is an agent based environment monitoring and control system we are building based on computational logic. Its key components are: (1) the use of the event calculus [7] and forward chaining deduction to map low-level time-stamped sensor reading events into inferred higher-level composite events using specialist agents for each type of sensor, (2) the use of multi-agent abductive reasoning [6] to co-operatively infer unobserved events or actions as possible explanations of the composite events, (3) the use of agents executing persistent teleo-reactive [9] control procedures that automatically respond to possible explanations, to gather auxiliary information about the state of the environment or to execute goal directed and robust control responses, (4) the use of a formal logical ontology to specify application dependent event terms, facts and action descriptions, and (5) the use of publish/subscribe servers [12] as a communication infrastructure enabling easy integration of new components and agents that have only to conform to the application ontology regarding the notifications they publish and the subscriptions they lodge.

The key advantage of using computational logic is that it allows high level declarative representation of an application domain. It greatly facilitates extensibility and re-engineering for different domains.

---

* Authors are listed in alphabetical order, not in order of their relative contribution.

M. Tscheligi et al. (Eds.): AmI 2009, LNCS 5859, pp. 112–117, 2009.

Throughout this paper we will provide further commentary on the features listed above with reference to the following example scenario. Ann, Bob and Carl live in a sheltered housing complex which employs SAGE. At 9:30:00am and 9:30:09am respectively, adjacent sensors s34 and s35 detect movement down the main corridor of the complex. The building agent infers that someone is moving down the corridor and consults with the intelligent agents of its residents to either confirm or eliminate them as a possible explanation. Ann's agent confirms the likelihood that it is her, because she has an dental appointment at 10am that requires her to leave the building, so the building agent positions the lift appropriately. Later, the building agent infers a similar but faster movement down the same corridor, but this time Ann's and Bob's agents rule themselves out as possibilites, because Ann is at the dentist, and Bob's recent ankle sprain prevents him from moving that quickly. Carl's agent has learned that if he forgets to take his medication he tends to wander around the building, and so prompts the nurse to check his medication pack. The nurse confirms that Carl has forgotten his medication and so Carl's agent is therefore unable to confirm his likely whereabouts. So the building agent seeks another source of confirmation by asking the security agent to locate Carl, which it attempts by displaying a query message on the (human) security guard's computer screen. The system simultaneously considers the possibility of an intruder, and seeks extra confirmation of this by asking the perimeter camera agents to swivell round searching for signs of forced entry. Camera c92 locates a broken fence, and there is no previous log of this information. Meanwhile the security guard ascertains that Carl is elsewhere and responds to the computer query accordingly. The building agent now has sufficient evidence to support the explanation that an intruder is in the building, and reacts accordingly, locking doors, alerting the staff, etc.

Notation: using Prolog convention, variables start with uppercase and constants with lowercase. Variables are universally quantified with maximum scope.

2   Agent Communication via Publish and Subscribe

To integrate the various components of SAGE we use a publish/subscribe server called Pedro [12] which matches subscriptions with notifications using Prolog unification technology. Additionally, Pedro supports peer-to-peer address based communication, as commonly used in agent applications and assumed in the FIPA agent communications language [11]. Asynchronous messaging systems that support publish/subscribe message routing [2] have been found useful for developing open distributed applications [8], and particularly so for complex event processing [5] and open multi-agent applications such as ours.

Pedro messages are strings representing Prolog terms. For example, a subscription is a string of the form "subscribe(T,Q,R)" where T is a message template (a Prolog term, usually with variables), Q is an associated Prolog query using variables that appear in T, and R is an integer which can be used by the subscriber as a subscription identifier. Pedro automatically forwards any notification it receives to all processes that have a current subscription S that *covers* the notification, preceded by its identifier R. A subscription *covers* a notification N iff the Prolog query T=N,Q succeeds. Here, = is term unification, a generalisation of pattern matching in which both T and N can contain variables.

As an example of the use of Pedro, a motion detection sensor s34 might send the notification "motionDetected(s34,time(9:30:00))" at time 9:30. This is covered by the subscription:

```
subscribe(motionDetected(S,_), (member(S,[s34,s35]), 1)
```

which might have been lodged by the agent monitoring a corridor with two sensors s34 and s35. If so, Pedro forwards the notification to this agent, preceded by the subscription identifier 1. If the same agent now receives a similar notifications from the sensor s35 mentioned in its subscription, with time value 9:30:09 it might infer and then post the notification:

```
movement(hall1,vel(south,6),during(9:30:00,9:30:09))
```

to Pedro to be picked up by any (possibly unknown) agent interested in this information. Such an interested agent will have lodged a subscription such as:

```
subscribe(movement(Pl,Vel(Dir,Sp)),(3=<Sp,Sp=<8), ..)
```

The range restriction on Sp is because the agent is only interested in movement of a walking or running person, not, say, an electric cart.

The key advantage of using Pedro for an application which involves both event processing and control responses is that all that has to be decided is the ontology for event notifications and control messages. The system is then open. As monitoring agents are added they subscribe for the event notifications of interest to them, which they can update at any time. These agents then attempt to exert control over the monitored system by issuing action requests. No component needs to know the identities of other components, or even what other components there are.

3   Interpreting Sensor Data via Forward Chaining

The corridor monitoring agent subscribing to the sensor readings in our example might use an implication such as the following to deduce (by forward chaining) the movement notification that it posts:

```
[motionDetected(S1,T1) ∧ motionDetected(S2,T2)   ∧
coLocated(S1,S2,Loc,Dir,Dis) ∧ speed(Dis,T1,T2,Sp)]
                   → movement(Loc,Vel(Dir,Sp),during(T1,T2))
```

where the coLocated and speed conditions are part of the agent's background knowledge. This is a (much simplified) example of an event calculus "counts as" rule, defining a complex event in terms of simpler ones. The event calculus additionally allows us to infer persisting properties that are initiated and terminated by events, e.g. the event of moving the lift from floor 2 to floor 1 initiates the property that it is at floor 1 and terminates it being at floor 2.

4   Explanation Generation via Distributed Abduction

As mentioned above, SAGE uses *abduction* to generate possible explanations of (directly or indirectly) observed changes or events in its environment. In the scenario of Section 1, for example, various explanations for the detected corridor movement are abduced by different agents. Formally, abduction is the process of finding a set of sentences Δ that can be (consistently) added to a theory T so that $T \wedge \Delta \models G$, for a given "goal" G. Δ cannot contain arbitrary sentences but must be composed only of "abducible" sentences (usually literals), the set of which is domain-specific. In the present context Δ is an explanation of an event or change in circumstance G (e.g. corridor movement) deduced from sensor data. The environmental knowledge T is spread among different agents (the building agent, the residents' agents, etc.) as logic programs with integrity constraints, and so we make use of the distributed logic program abductive procedure DARE [6]. Distributed abduction involves the cooperation of different logical agents in constructing explanations Δ which draw upon their combined knowledge and respect their combined consistency requirements. DARE has the advantage, crucial to SAGE, of being an *open* proof procedure: agents can join or leave the cooperative abductive process during its execution without affecting the correctness of the outcome. This openess is facilitated by the use of Pedro (see Section 2) for inter-agent communication during the abduction.

As a (simplified) example, in our scenario the building agent may have a rule:

```
movement(Loc,vel(Dir,Sp),during(Begin,End)) ←
    3 ≤ Sp ∧ Sp ≤ 8 ∧ at(Person,Loc,walking,during(Begin,End))
```

which can be invoked by matching its head with the details of a particular detected movement `movement(hall1,...)` that needs explaining. Anne's agent is able to help satisfy the conditions of this rule by adding `at(anne,hall1,...)` to the current set Δ, since her set of abducibles contains literals of this form, and it is consistent with current beliefs and conjectures. Later when Anne is at the dentist her agent will be unable to abduce a similar explanation because of the integrity constraint ¬[at(X,L1,...) ∧ at(X,L2,...) ∧ L1≠L2].

5   Teleo-reactive and Information Gathering Procedures

For agent actions we use Nilsson's TR (Teleo-Reactive) procedures [9] for robot control embedded in a multi-threaded agent architecture [13]. TR procedures have the form:

```
p(X1,..,Xk){c1 -> a1.    c2 -> a2.    ...    cn -> an}.
```

where X1,...,Xk are parameters and the body is an ordered sequence of condition-action rules. The conditions can access the current store of observed and inferred (i.e. deduced or abduced) events and any other beliefs about the state of the environment and inhabitants. The event and belief stores are continuously and asynchronously updated as a procedure executes.

The rules' conditions are constantly re-evaluated to find the first rule with a true condition to fire. Once a rule is fired its action is persistently executed until *another* rule is fired. A special `exit` action terminates a procedure. The actions can be information gathering actions that indirectly result in new sensor events (e.g. video capture images) being added to the event store, which may result in another rule being fired. The following is a TR procedure that might be invoked to pan a surveillance camera to look for a sign of entry through a perimeter fence. `FT` is the time when the camera pan should terminate if the analysis of the camera images has not detected some sign of entry, such as a broken fence:

```
lookForSignEntry(FT){
        broken_fence or gate_open or current_time > FT -> exit.
        true   -> pan_camera. }.
```

6   Conclusions and Related Work

The key features of SAGE are that it provides a flexible, distributed, open and component-based approach to environmental monitoring and control, and that its computational processes reflect natural, multi-stage, collaborative human reasoning: when events are detected it forms and tests hypotheses about these before reacting appropriately. Its multi-agent and multi-threaded architecture allows it to form and act upon different hypotheses concurrently. Space limitations prevent us from commentating on all the features of SAGE hinted at in our example scenario, such as agent learning capability and human intervention supplementing its reasoning processes. Work on SAGE is currently at the specification stage (hence this short paper format), although some of its key components already have implementations. Our next stage will be to provide a full implementation and to test this with a simulated example environment, using the event calculus to "run" different scenarios and measure the likely success of our approach.

Space limitations prevent a detailed comparison of related work, but [1] is another ambient intelligent system that uses a publish/subscribe architecture to integrate a disparate set of components, [4] uses the event calculus for a distributed agent environment, [3,10] are examples of logic based agent architectures for ambient intelligent systems.

References

1. Anastasopoulos, M., et al.: Towards a Reference Middleware Architecture for Ambient Intelligence Systems. In: Building Software for Pervasive Computing, OOPSLA 2005 (2005)
2. Baldoni, R., Contenti, M., Virgillito, A.: The Evolution of Publish/Subscribe Communication Systems. In: Schiper, A., Shvartsman, M.M.A.A., Weatherspoon, H., Zhao, B.Y. (eds.) Future Directions in Distributed Computing. LNCS, vol. 2584, pp. 137–141. Springer, Heidelberg (2003)

3. Bikakis, A., Antoniou, G.: Distributed Defeasible Contextual Reasoning in Ambient Computing. In: Aarts, E., Crowley, J.L., de Ruyter, B., Gerhäuser, H., Pflaum, A., Schmidt, J., Wichert, R. (eds.) AmI 2008. LNCS, vol. 5355, pp. 308–325. Springer, Heidelberg (2008)

4. Bromuri, S., Stathis, K.: Distributed Agent Environment in the Ambient Event Calculus. In: DEBS 2009 (2009)

5. Luckham, D.: The Power of Events: An Introduction to Complex Event Processing in Distributed Enterprise Systems. Addison Wesley Professional, Reading (2002)

6. Ma, J., Russo, A., Broda, K., Clark, K.: DARE: a system for distributed abductive reasoning. Autonomous Agent Multi-Agent Systems 16, 271–297 (2008)

7. Miller, R., Shanahan, M.: Some Alternative Formulations of the Event Calculus. In: Kakas, A.C., Sadri, F. (eds.) Computational Logic: Logic Programming and Beyond. LNCS (LNAI), vol. 2408, pp. 452–490. Springer, Heidelberg (2002)

8. Muhl, G., Fiege, L., Pietzuch, P.: Distributed Event-Based Systems. Springer, Heidelberg (2006)

9. Nilsson, N.: Teleo-Reactive Programs for Agent Control. Journal of Artificial Intelligence Research 1, 139–158 (1994)

10. Stathis, K., Toni, F.: Ambient Intelligence Using KGP Agents. In: Markopoulos, P., Eggen, B., Aarts, E., Crowley, J.L. (eds.) EUSAI 2004. LNCS, vol. 3295, pp. 351–362. Springer, Heidelberg (2004)

11. Foundation for Intelligent Physical Agents, Fipa Communicative Act Library Specification (2002), http://www.fipa.org/specs/fipa00008/XC00008H.html

12. Robinson, P.J., Clark, K.L.: Pedro: A Publish/Subscribe Server Using Prolog Technology. Software Practice and Experience (2009) (submitted)

13. Clark, K.L.: AgentMT(TR): a Multi-threaded Agent Architecture Using Teleo-Reactive Plans (in preparation)

Using Video with Active Markers

Jussi Mikkonen, Jung-Joo Lee, and Ilpo Koskinen

University of Arts and Design, Hämeentie 135, 00560 Helsinki, Finland
{jussi.mikkonen,Jung-Joo.Lee,ilpo.koskinen}@taik.fi

Abstract. The designers have started to use technological means in increasing fashion, with tools aimed for them readily available. In order to manage the task of designing and analysing a prototype, we focus on using video as a storage of data by embedding the information with active markers. Based on a small survey of methods, characteristics of active markers are developed and a test program written. Using interactive prototyping projects as a test material, we form a direction for prototype development and video analysis.

Keywords: video, design, prototyping, infrared, active marker.

1 Introduction

Drawing from the emergence of software [1] and hardware [2] tools aimed at the designer audience, and due to industrial designers tackling with the technical issues [3][4], it could be interpreted that their field is getting more technical. In order to create concepts and prototypes of increasing complexity, e.g. such as in experience prototyping[5], the need for technical solutions and methods has been noted. In order to lighten the load of prototyping and analysing the user tests without getting side-tracked from the actual prototyping, we explore simple means for the information gathering in different phases of the design process. We aim to create an understanding of a few basic means for augmenting video, in combining the design and evaluation during the prototyping process, and to create a direction for the development of open source video analysis environment.

2 Background

The video is usable in different aspects and phases as a tool for design[6]. It might be used in the divergent phase, as in observing what people do and collecting visual data. It can be used during the analysis and in order to create an understanding, such as video card game[7] and creating video collages[8]. As a means of explaining, spreading the information and explaining the future scenarios to others, the video is very well utilised with a plethora of methods[6]. The video camera might be used again, from a different perspective, when the process has produced a prototype, which needs to be analysed.

The natural interaction of using hands with different tasks, such as image manipulation[9], has emerged in different contexts. It provides a direction for the interaction

M. Tscheligi et al. (Eds.): AmI 2009, LNCS 5859, pp. 118–122, 2009.

regarding the environment for video analysis, as it is directed towards designers and how they naturally interact with physical images.

For a more direct interaction with a large display, work has been done using an infrared laser pointer and an infrared tracking device[10]. It is also noted that a CCD camera or a video camera could be used for detecting the infrared. The infrared LEDs have been used in tracking situations[11]. Active markers have also been used in mobile devices, to create a virtual display usable with a HMD or an EGD[12]. A similar setup might be used to transmit complex information to a video system.

It is clear that infrared and active markers can be used in embedding the data to the video, but to also act as a basis for an user interface in a larger scale, in order to create the environment for analysing the video.

3   Characterising the Active Markers

A single marker could be used as an indicator of an event, or a threshold for the physical action. It can represent binary information, such as an interesting event, something being switched on, or simply to test if something is blocking the line of sight to the camera. In the event of using it for transmitting on/off -information, the marker should be placed so that users or objects do not obstruct it during the test. There is also a possibility to use a single active marker as a serial communication output, where the data is transmitted in binary format over time. The single marker can also be tracked with a camera, thus creating a simple user interface, or a possibility to track the location of the test device.

Multiple markers with a single context could be used to convey much more complex information in a single frame, such as the orientation, the state of the device under test, or numerical values from the sensors on the device under test, in addition to the properties of a single marker. The multiple markers can also be thought of as being equivalent to a parallel communication bus.

In the user test situations, the users or the observers can control the markers directly or indirectly, e.g. by observing an interesting event and marking it for the analysis phase, or by using the device, with changes in the state being visible in the video. On the other hand, the device-controlled markers might represent sensor information, which could be analysed to deduce why and how the user reacted.

If the markers are static, i.e. they are not moving, the test situation can be designed so that the markers are not obstructed, unless that is the purpose of the test. The dynamic marker position requires tracking capability from the analyser.

The visibility of the markers could be determined by the nature of the user test and the relevance of the information they represent to the users. In the case of using e.g. the infrared to transmit the information, the camera must be tested in order to verify the visibility of markers. Not all cameras are capable of sensing the infrared.

Based on this and the research, a simple program was written with processing, and used for analysing an active marker in different videos. The location of the marker can be selected in the video with a mouse, and the activation of the marker is shown with a white circle.

4   Test Videos and Origins

In order to teach the students the ways of prototyping, we developed the interactive prototyping course[13]. During the nine weeks the course is in progress, the students do a background research on a given subject, an user research, a concepting phase, a design phase, building a prototype based on a concept and design, and in the end, user testing the prototype. The tight schedule of the course leaves room for little else than doing just the necessary electronics and programming work. In spite of time constraints, the course is sometimes used as a test bed for new design research ideas.

Fig. 1. The lights of the visual-talk table as active markers, left: white dot on selected light, right: reaction on the activation of the light

During the spring 2007 the first IP course was held, and one of the prototypes was the visual-talk table[14]. The pattern on the table is reacting to the speech with visible light patterns, with the pattern area proportional to the speech characteristics, and thus can be used as visible active markers. The video from observation is analysed using our program, as shown in figure 1. This way, it could be used to mark the moments when certain people start talking during the test.

In the spring 2009 the course focused on the notion of cooking together, which could be understood e.g. from a service design point of view or as a product development process. In order to gain new insights, a few groups of students conducted video observation. While preparing their scenes for the observation, one such group was asked to place an infrared LED as an active marker, shown in figure 2, controllable by the student recording the situation. During the filming, if there was something interesting happening, the student switched the infrared LED on for a short period of time in order to mark the situation to the video. A single LED is fairly simple to use, and easily manageable by the students. Some groups used visible LEDs to get additional information from their prototypes during debugging. It is trivial to replace them with the infrared LEDs to provide means for embedding information to the video without disturbing the test situation.

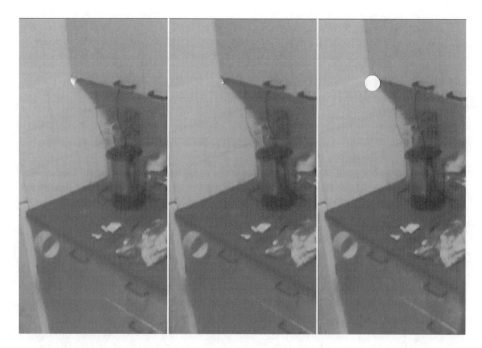

Fig. 2. Video observation of the kitchen, left: an active marker signal as captured by the video camera, middle: selecting the active marker with a dot, right: a reaction on the activated marker

5 Discussion

The active markers can be used to embed information to videos, as shown with examples of using a single infrared LED during the research phase, and by using natural information from a working prototype. Markers can be implemented without too much extra work, and the video is usable as storage. While the software we built for analysing the markers reacted with a very simple visual element, it provides solid groundwork. The intended next steps in development are enhancing the program to use the markers for extracting key video segments for use in video card game, and to build an open source analysing environment. Finally, the question of practicality and the usable limits for storing data within a video need to be addressed more thoroughly.

Acknowledgements. Authors would like to thank Salu Ylirisku for providing insight to the video analysis and RHSK team of IP09 for the extra effort.

References

1. Processing, http://processing.org/
2. Arduino, http://www.arduino.cc/
3. Hulkko, S., Mattelmäki, T., Virtanen, K., Keinonen, T.: Mobile probes. In: Proceedings of the Third Nordic Conference on Human-Computer interaction, NordiCHI 2004, Tampere, Finland, October 23 - 27, vol. 82, pp. 43–51. ACM, New York (2004)

4. van den Hoven, E., Frens, J., Aliakseyeu, D., Martens, J., Overbeeke, K., Peters, P.: Design research & tangible interaction. In: Proceedings of the 1st international Conference on Tangible and Embedded interaction, TEI 2007, Baton Rouge, Louisiana, February 15 - 17, pp. 109–115. ACM, New York (2007)
5. Buchenau, M., Suri, J.F.: Experience prototyping. In: Boyarski, D., Kellogg, W.A. (eds.) Proceedings of the 3rd Conference on Designing interactive Systems: Processes, Practices, Methods, and Techniques, DIS 2000, August 17 - 19, pp. 424–433. ACM, New York (2000)
6. Ylirisku, S., Buur, J.: Designing with Video. Focusing the user-centred design process. Springer, London (2007)
7. Buur, J., Soendergaard, A.: Video card game: an augmented environment for user centred design discussions. In: Proceedings of DARE 2000 on Designing Augmented Reality Environments, DARE 2000, Elsinore, Denmark, pp. 63–69. ACM, New York (2000)
8. Buur, J., Jensen, M.V., Djajadiningrat, T.: Hands-only scenarios and video action walls: novel methods for tangible user interaction design. In: Proceedings of the 5th Conference on Designing interactive Systems: Processes, Practices, Methods, and Techniques, DIS 2004, Cambridge, MA, USA, August 01 - 04, pp. 185–192. ACM, New York (2004)
9. Lucero, A., Aliakseyeu, D., Martens, J.-B.: Augmenting Mood Boards: Flexible and Intuitive Interaction in the Context of the Design Studio. In: TABLETOP apos 2007. Second Annual IEEE International Workshop on Horizontal Interactive Human-Computer Systems, October 10-12, pp. 147–154 (2007)
10. Cheng, K., Pulo, K.: Direct interaction with large-scale display systems using infrared laser tracking devices. In: Pattison, T., Thomas, B. (eds.) Proceedings of the Asia-Pacific Symposium on information Visualisation, vol. 24, Adelaide, Australia. ACM International Conference Proceeding Series, vol. 142, pp. 67–74. Australian Computer Society, Darlinghurst (2003)
11. Kavakli, M., Taylor, M., Trapeznikov, A.: Designing in virtual reality (DesIRe): a gesture-based interface. In: Proceedings of the 2nd international Conference on Digital interactive Media in Entertainment and Arts, DIMEA 2007, Perth, Australia, September 19 - 21, vol. 274, pp. 131–136. ACM, New York (2007)
12. Hong, Y., Lee, S., Lee, Y., Kim, S.: Mobile pointing and input system using active marker. In: Proceedings of the 2006 Fifth IEEE and ACM international Symposium on Mixed and Augmented Reality (Ismar 2006), October 22 - 25, pp. 237–238. IEEE Computer Society, Washington (2006)
13. Koskinen, I., Mikkonen, J., Ahde, P., Eckoldt, K., Helgason, T., Hänninen, R., Jiang, J., Niskanen, T., Schultz, B.: Hacking a Car: Re-Embodying the Design Classroom. In: Proceedings of the Nordic Design Research Conference, Nordes 2009, Oslo, Augest 30-September 1 (2009)
14. Lee, J.-J., Koskinen, I., Mikkonen, J.: The Visual-Talk Table: Understanding Co-Experience in a Cross-Cultural notion, Interactive poster. In: CSCW 2008, San Diego, California, USA, November 8–12 (2008)

An Event-Driven Approach to Activity Recognition in Ambient Assisted Living

Holger Storf[1], Thomas Kleinberger[1], Martin Becker[1], Mario Schmitt[1],
Frank Bomarius[1], and Stephan Prueckner[2]

[1] Fraunhofer-Institute Experimental Software Engineering
Fraunhofer-Platz 1, 67663 Kaiserslautern, Germany
Firstname.Lastname@iese.fraunhofer.de
[2] Department of Anaesthesiology and Emergency Medicine
Westpfalz-Klinikum GmbH, Hellmut-Hartert-Strasse 1, 67655 Kaiserslautern, Germany
stephan.prueckner@med.uni-muenchen.de

Abstract. One central challenge of Ambient Assisted Living systems is reliable recognition of the assisted person's current behavior, so that adequate assistance services can be offered in a specific situation. In the context of emergency support, such a situation might be an acute emergency situation or a deviation from the usual behavior. To optimize prevention of emergencies, reliable recognition of characteristic Activities of Daily Living (ADLs) is promising. In this paper, we present our approach to processing information for the detection of ADLs in the EMERGE project. The approach is based on our multi-agent activity recognition framework EARS with its special definition language EARL. An evaluation with controlled experiments has proven its suitability.

Keywords: Information Processing; Activity Recognition; Ambient Assisted Living; Multi-Agent Systems; Complex Event Processing.

1 Introduction

In most industrialized countries, demographical, structural, and social trends are driven by an increasing number of elderly people and single households. Consequently, more and more elderly people are living alone longer, leading to a large number of emergencies reported late or remaining undiscovered. This has dramatic effects on public and private health care, emergency medical services, and the individuals themselves.

An emergency incident often results in the loss of a self-determined, independent life and reduced quality of life for the elderly person. A very common example of an emergency are falls leading to immobilization. Literature surveys and our own epidemiological studies [1] show that the likelihood of falling increases with age, and peaks when a person is in his/her eighties. In the district of Kaiserslautern, Germany, about 30% of elderly persons over the age of 65 still living at home experience a fall at least once a year. 50% of the persons in this group fall several times a year, and 20% of these recurring falls occur within 6 months. In the worst case, the fallen person remains lying on the floor, unnoticed for hours or even days, with corresponding

M. Tscheligi et al. (Eds.): AmI 2009, LNCS 5859, pp. 123–132, 2009.
© Springer-Verlag Berlin Heidelberg 2009

follow-up complications such as decubitus ulcer, hypothermia, or pneumonia. The epidemiological study [1] also shows that current state-of-the-art "Personal Emergency Response Systems" such as emergency push buttons may not be appropriate for preventing such dramatic situations in all cases. As some of the main problems we found that (i) the assisted persons do not wear the respective alarm devices, as they do not expect an emergency event to happen or do not like to be stigmatized, and (ii) they are not able to activate them appropriately in case of an emergency. We conclude that there is an urgent need for a next generation of emergency recognition and prevention solutions that detect potential emergency situations automatically based on ambient and unobtrusive sensors.

In the project EMERGE [2], a system concept for early detection and prevention of emergencies at home is being conceived, developed, and validated. Our system monitors the behavior patterns of assisted persons through unobtrusive sensors embedded into the home environment. It reasons on sensor data, extracts typical behavior patterns, detects behavior deviations, and assesses the functional health status of the assisted person.

The remainder of the paper is structured as follows: In section 2, we present an overview of the EMERGE system, explaining the system mission and identifying significant requirements. In section 3, we explain the general way of the information process. Section 4 then describes the approach of the activity recognition framework of EMERGE and related approaches as well as the way sensor information is processed in order to detect specific situations where assistance should be offered. The practical experiences we made during implementation and evaluation are presented in section 5. In Section 6, we finally draw conclusions about our approach and provide an outlook on future work.

2   EMERGE System Overview

The mission of the EMERGE system is not only to provide reliable emergency assistance in case an acute emergency such as a sudden fall occurs, but also to offer proactive prevention of emergencies by analyzing daily behavior and comparing behavior trends with typical behavior over extended periods of time. Timely detection of and reaction to an acute emergency is very helpful. Nevertheless, especially the prevention of potentially arising emergencies with long-term behavior monitoring promises to sustain the quality of life for the assisted persons and to reduce follow-up costs in the health care system. The main user requirements to be addressed are a) to provide fully automatic detection of potential emergencies without active user involvement (e.g., without pressing buttons) and b) to find an unobtrusive sensor constellation that gets accepted and does not influence daily life.

By employing a range of ambient and unobtrusive sensors such as presence detectors, reed contacts, or pressure mats, our approach initially detects Activities of Daily Living (ADLs) [3]. Vital data is additionally monitored with an unobtrusive wrist-mounted device, a weight scale, and a blood pressure measurement device. At the core of the EMERGE system is a model for analyzing recurring behaviors of the assisted persons on top of ADLs to detect potentially precarious deviations from their typical daily routine. Fig.1 shows the EMERGE system in a simplified overview.

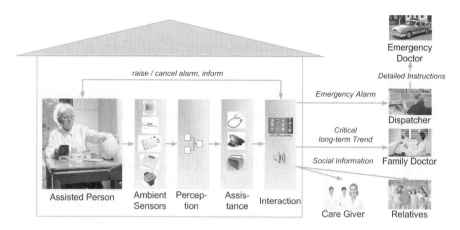

Fig. 1. EMERGE System Overview

In the context of automated emergency detection, we distinguish situations such as: (i) automatic, reliable, and immediate detection of acute emergency events that develop within a short time (sudden falls, cardiac arrest, or helplessness), and (ii) long-term deviations from typical behavior or critical trends of vital parameters. From the medical point of view the analyses of long-term trends act as indicators of changes in the mental or cognitive state, e.g., dementia or depression, or other age-related chronic diseases such as cardiac insufficiency or arthritis. Based on the recognized situation and health condition, adequate assistance services can be rendered in a proactive and preventive way. In addition to that, the rate of false alarms can be reduced if knowledge about the current situation is available.

Of special interest in behavioral monitoring and health state assessment are the so-called Activities of Daily Living (ADL), which were initially defined in the Katz index [3]. Based on ADLs, long-term trend analyses can be performed and checked against normal behavior and preexisting information about the assisted person.

In workshops with clinical experts it has been found that an accuracy of 80% for detecting ADLs as a basis for long-term trend detection is sufficient. The hypotheses for the evaluation were defined accordingly.

3   Information Processing in EMERGE

In EMERGE, the installed sensors and aggregating components provide and process several types of information for behavior monitoring. Detection of characteristic situations is performed by processing raw sensor data in a hierarchical way in the "Perception" subsystem. In order to strictly separate different concerns, it is structured into self-contained perception components that perceive context information, aggregate it, and provide the information to other components as illustrated in Fig. 2. In order to hide sensor-specific details (communication technology, protocols, etc.) from the component developers and to allow for easier integration of sensor devices into software applications, we abstract from the concrete devices by using a Sensor

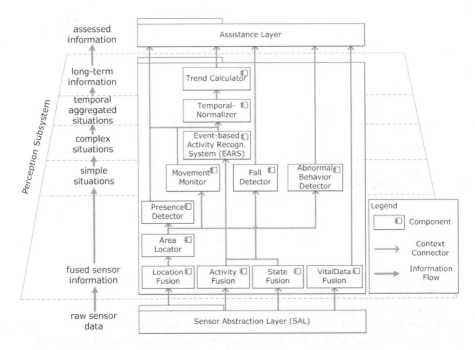

Fig. 2. Perception subsystem of EMERGE

Table 1. Perception Components

Component	Description
LocationFusion	fuses basic location information from different available sources into one location information with the currently highest quality.
ActivityFusion	fuses basic activity information, so overlapping or causal information can be merged into one resulting information with higher quality.
StateFusion	fuses basic state information, e.g., room temperature or humidity.
VitalDataFusion	fuses basic vital data, which can be emitted by several devices (e.g., wrist watch, pressure mat, blood pressure meter).
AreaLocator	identifies the entering and leaving of defined areas, e.g., based on defined areas of interest or rooms.
PresenceDetector	identifies whether no one is present, or whether one or several persons are present.
MovementMonitor	monitors the general movement and activity of the user and generates a characteristic daily score.
FallDetector	detects sudden falls, based on several spatial indicators.
AbnormalBehavior-Detection	detects irregular deviations from a person's usual activity pattern (motionlessness situation).
Event-driven Activity Recognition System (EARS)	aggregates simple activities, e.g., movement or device usage, into complex activities, e.g., ADLs by using a hybrid reasoning approach.
TemporalNormalizer	normalizes relevant context information over time, e.g., lack of information due to absence or visit periods.
TrendCalculator	calculates trends on different time ranges. These will be assessed with the help of the clinical knowledge (HCM) in the *Assistance Layer*.

Abstraction Layer (SAL) [4]. SAL provides a simple and standardized interface for discovering, managing, and accessing a wide range of different sensor types. In addition to data provided by the sensors, the interface exposes semantic information on the sensors as well as on the measured data. The pro-active reactions to the detected critical situations are planned and triggered in the "Assistance" subsystem. The assessment of the person's long-term behavior with the help of a Human Capability Model (HCM) [5] is also located there. The HCM represents the clinical knowledge, created with the help of medical experts.

The functionality of each component in Fig. 2 is briefly described in Table 1.

Information exchange between the components is supported with a context management system in a publish-subscribe manner. The context information is represented in a uniform data format and is characterized with quality attributes, e.g., accuracy. This supports the various system components with access to context information in a device- and component-independent manner. For instance, components can register for the best available location information, independent of how this information is gathered.

4 Activity Recognition in AAL

Our Event-driven Activity Recognition System (EARS) of the Perception Layer for the detection of ADLs and other activities of interest is described in this chapter.

4.1 Challenges and Related Approaches

One key challenge faced by Ambient Assisted Living systems is the choice of the reasoning approach for detecting complex human activities such as ADLs out of a continuous sequence of events measured by an array of sensing systems. Such sensors are supposed to be unobtrusive and are therefore usually integrated into the environment, i.e., not mounted on a person's body.

Quality demands have to be considered, e.g., timely recognition and reliability in terms of precision and recall. One important issue that complicates the selection of appropriate approaches is the fact that the sensor configuration is specific for every system instance, depending on the layout of the apartment, the sensor and communication devices deployed, and the type of sensor data provided to the activity recognizer, such as raw, fused, or already aggregated data. Furthermore, recognition of an ADL is complicated by inter- and intra-personal variances in the behavior of people resulting in a diversity of event or activity sequences. In some cases, the typical activity sequence may show a clearly identifiable temporal distribution. In other cases, these sensor information sequences appear to be almost randomly ordered. Examples include the ADLs "Toilet Usage" and "Preparing Meals". In general, toilet usage can be defined as a clearly structured sequential chain of subactivities. Contrary to this, the preparation of a meal has very high diversity, because the concrete occurrence may be anything from buttering a slice of bread to preparing a complex meal.

In addition to this, the sequences of several activities may overlap and also vary heavily in their occurrence depending on the habits of the operating person. Consequently, the activity recognizer component has to ensure a high level of adaptability towards the basic surrounding environment and the aspired activities.

One important requirement in the context of the Ambient Assisted Living system is that the defined activity should be detected as soon as possible after its appearance. In addition, the chosen approach should be efficient due to the limited processing power of the hardware.

Many algorithms that deal with the detection of special patterns with and without the consideration of the time aspect are known in the fields of Artificial Intelligence and Complex Event Processing (CEP). Hein and Kirste [6] have analyzed the most prominent ones in terms of their suitability in this context and have divided the approaches into Model-Free / Non-Temporal, Model-Free / Temporal, and Model-Based / Temporal approaches. They conclude that each approach has its own advantages and disadvantages, but no single approach exists that meets all of the specific demands of activity recognition in the AAL domain as described above.

In the context of our system design, a few well-known approaches are of special interest. One idea is to follow the timemap approach [7] for defining a typical temporal network of the sensor events that are included in the activity. The Complex Event Recognition Architecture (CERA) allows non-fuzzy recognition of special event occurrences with basic temporal dependencies. The rules are defined externally in a Lisp-like syntax [8]. The event pattern language RAPIDE is a strong-typing declarative computing language for CEP, which provides basic event patterns, pattern operators and temporal operators [9]. Tapia et al. have chosen naive Bayesian classifiers with an extension to sequential relationships for the automatic detection of activities in elderly people's homes [10].

4.2 EARS: A Multi-agent-Based Approach

In order to tackle the aforementioned problems, our Event-driven Activity Recognition System (EARS) follows a hybrid combination of the different approaches, which appears to us to be a promising way to solve most of the addressed problems in one component. Furthermore, we decided to approach the complex activities (ADLs) in a divide-and-conquer approach by decomposing them into atomic activities. Atomic and complex activities are detected by a specialized detection agent that has its own special logical unit. In order to enable arbitrary communication structures between the agents, they communicate by exchanging typed facts represented in a common data structure.

The detection agents conform to the idea of intelligent agents defined by Wooldridge and Jennings [11]. The functionality of an agent can be summarized as follows: It receives temporally shifted data, stores them in cache memory, analyzes the data, and reports when a defined constellation has been identified.

From a semantic point of view, we can classify incoming data as low-level sensor data, e.g., device usage or movement, or activities already classified by other kinds of reasoning components or by other detection agents. The number of possible incoming facts is not limited, in contrast to the outgoing activity fact, which has to be unique and is generally at a higher information level than the incoming ones. Practical experience has shown that feedback of events can be of interest, too. This means that an agent may process information that it has provided itself at an earlier time.

The functional characteristics of the detection agents comply with the capabilities of software agents [11], namely:

- Reactivity
- Proactiveness
- Social Ability

The detection process of EARS is event-triggered. The agents are activated as they receive new facts (standardized communication format). They cache the fact annotated with the time of its arrival. The agent's detection algorithm proceeds as soon as the characteristic activity pattern is present (Reactivity). In order to improve the overall performance, agents receive only those facts they are interested in. These facts of interest and the functionality of the reasoning algorithm are encoded in predefined rules; they are checked against the already stored facts (Proactiveness). After the decision is made as to whether a defined activity has occurred or not, the agent falls back into sleep mode. If the activity has been detected, a corresponding fact is emitted to the environment, so that other agents that may be interested in this activity will be triggered (Social Ability).

Splitting the overall reasoning approach for detecting ADLs into specialized agents that detect atomic activities makes sense for several reasons. Every fact needs to be stored in memory only once. A set of facts may be necessary for the recognition of one activity. The same fact may be of interest for several agents. As an example we take the interpretation of the fact "Bathroom door closed". This fact can contribute to the detection of the sub-activities "Person enters Bathroom" as well as "Person leaves Bathroom". In turn, both sub-activities are needed for the detection of higher-level activities in the bathroom, such as the ADL "Personal Hygiene". Sub-activities can be supported by concurrent facts like "Motion in the Bathroom". In general, a fact can be interpreted in different ways and results in other facts at a higher level.

Splitting the functionality into manageable parts assigned to agents is also an advantage in terms of execution performance. Only those parts of the overall functionality are invoked that are actually affected.

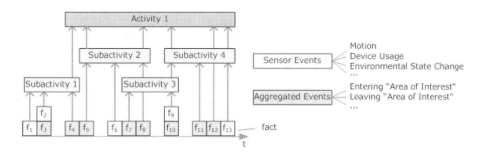

Fig. 3. Exemplary Activity Recognition with EARS

In Fig. 3, an example of a timeline with three-stage activity recognition is illustrated. At the bottom, the facts with their unique timestamps are shown as they arrive over time. These facts may originate from sensors (motion, device usages, etc.) or may be aggregated events from underlying continuous data streams, such as spatial or vital data. In the middle, agents that detect sub-activities are illustrated. The more complex activities are located towards the top. From the system point of view, there is no difference between sub-activities and activities.

4.3   Event-Driven Activity Recognition Language (EARL)

The logical units of the agents do not encode rule definitions inside their functional code. Rules are defined in an external file in order to enable quick and easy adaptation of the rule base to specific problems. The structure of activity rules is shown in Fig. 4. Table 2 lists attributes of the elements in a clearly represented way. A rule header comprises declarative information about an activity, e.g., its name – which is also the name of the fact emitted if the activity is detected –, the maximum storage time of the cached facts, the duration of a latency period during which incoming facts will be ignored after positive detection, and the threshold value for fuzzy reasoning that applies for every case with no individual threshold.

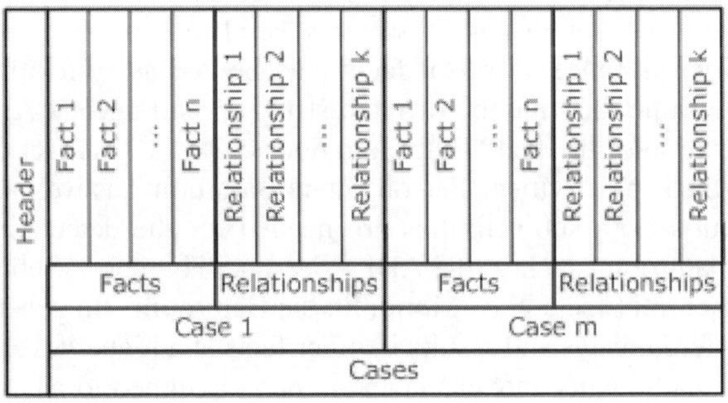

Fig. 4. Structure of EARL

By means of several cases, different occurrences of the activity can be distinguished. Optionally, each case may have a specific threshold instead of the threshold in the header. Basically, a variant consists of at least one fact, and an arbitrary number of relationships. Both types are equipped with individual characteristics. The characteristics of a fact include a well-defined ID and name. A relationship consists of the references to the starting fact and the ending fact, and the minimum time elapsed between them. Facts as well as relationships have special characteristics for controlling the further flow of the activity detection process. One of these characteristics is a weight used to support fuzzy decisions. In addition, facts or relationships can be defined as being mandatory or sufficient.

Table 2. Characteristics of EARL

Elements	Attributes
Header	activity name, monitoring duration (msec), general threshold, latency duration. (msec)
Case	case-specific threshold (optional)
Fact	fact ID, fact name, weight, mandatory, sufficient
Relationship	start fact ID, end fact ID, min. in-between time range (msec), weight, mandatory

An activity can be described by an unlimited number of weighted facts, relationships, and cases. Examples of EARL rules for a sequential and a fuzzy activity are shown in [12].

5   Practical Experiences

The rule-based multi-agent approach EARS has been implemented and integrated into the Ambient Assisted Living Environment at Fraunhofer IESE. In addition to the actual functionality, a graphical user interface (GUI) for visualizing the results using a timeline and an XML editor, which allows easy management of the agents and rules, are provided.

In a systematic evaluation, the accuracy of the detection of the ADLs "Toilet Usage", "Personal Hygiene", and "Preparing Meals" has been tested by randomly playing scenarios with test persons in the AAL apartment with manually defined rules. An overview of the setting is given in the following table. The test persons were unbiased students who had not been involved in AAL projects before. The hypothesis was that the accuracy (number of correct detected scenarios / number of all scenarios) of EARS for each ADL is higher than 80 % (chapter 2).

Table 3. Summary of evaluation results [13]

ADL	Number of all scenarios	Number of pos. scenarios	Number of neg. scenarios	Number of test persons	Accuracy
Toilet Usage	100	50	50	6	98.0 %
Personal Hygiene	54	33	21	5	83.3 %
Preparing Meals	66	45	21	4	94.0 %

The conclusion was that in general, our approach seems to be well suited for the on-the-fly detection of activities in the domain of Ambient Assisted Living.

6   Conclusion and Future Work

In this paper, we described the motivation of EMERGE and the situations we want to detect based on information from ambient sensors in order to provide assistance in a proactive way. The general information processing approach and the system architecture were described. We focused on describing our approach for the recognition of activities (EARS), based on the experiences we made in the domain of AAL. We first described the theoretical view on our approach by giving examples, and then its practical realization and the experiences we made in a scenario-based evaluation.

In summary, we conclude that our approach to information processing and activity recognition is capable of detecting activities of varying complexity, sequential or almost random, and overlapping with other activities as well. Regarding the sensor environment and the behavior of an elderly person, the recognition functionality can be adapted individually. Incompletely received information will be considered, and incomplete knowledge can also be modeled using the given rule structure.

In the future, the general suitability of EARS will be verified by configuring more activities. In addition, the general suitability of the EMERGE system will be verified in advanced evaluations in field trials in Greece and Germany. Further steps include enforcing the development of the advanced decision process, including medical knowledge based on ADL detection.

Acknowledgement. Part of this work has been funded by the European Commission under project no. FP6-IST-2005-045056 EMERGE [2].

References

1. Nehmer, J., Becker, M., Kleinberger, T., Prueckner, S.: Electronic Emergency Safeguards for the aging generation; Gerontology: Regenerative and Technological Gerontology. In: Special Section Technology and Aging: Integrating Psychological, Medical, and Engineering Perspectives. Karger Verlag (2009)
2. EMERGE: Emergency Monitoring and Prevention, Specific Targeted Research Project (STREP) of the EC, Project No. 045056, http://www.emerge-project.eu
3. Katz, S., Ford, A.B., Moskowitz, R.W., Jackson, B.A., Jaffe, M.W.: Studies of Illness in the Aged: The Index of ADL: A Standardized Measure of Biological and Psychosocial Function. Journal of the American Medical Association 185(12), 914–919 (1963)
4. Van Megen, F., Sugar, R., Latour, L., Neugebauer, M., Gefflaut, A.: Supporting Diabetes Treatment through Wearable Sensor Integration. In: Proc. WSNHC (2007)
5. Prueckner, S., Madler, C., Beyer, D., Berger, M., Kleinberger, T., Becker, M.: Emergency Monitoring and Prevention - EU Project EMERGE. In: Ambient Assisted Living Proc. 1st German AAL-Congress (2008)
6. Hein, A., Kirste, T.: Activity Recognition for Ambient Assisted Living: Potential and Challenges. In: Proc. 1st German AAL-Congress (2008)
7. Pollack, M.E.: Intelligent Technology for an Aging Population - The Use of AI to Assist Elders with Cognitive Impairment. In: American Association for Artificial Intelligence (2005)
8. Fitzgerald, W., Firby, R.J., Phillips, A., Kairys, J.: Complex Event Pattern Recognition for Long-Term System Monitoring. In: Workshop on Interaction between Humans and Autonomous Systems over Extended Operation (2004)
9. Luckham, D.: The Power of Events: An Introduction to Complex Event Processing in Distributed Enterprise Systems, pp. 145–174. Addison-Wesley, Reading (2002)
10. Tapia, E.M., Intille, S.S., Larson, K.: Activity Recognition in the Home Using Simple and Ubiquitous Sensors. In: Ferscha, A., Mattern, F. (eds.) PERVASIVE 2004. LNCS, vol. 3001, pp. 158–175. Springer, Heidelberg (2004)
11. Wooldridge, M.: An Introduction to MultiAgent Systems, p. 16. John Wiley & Sons, Chichester (2002)
12. Storf, H., Becker, M., Riedl, M.: Rule-based Activity Recognition Framework: Challenges, Technique and Learning. In: Proc. PervaSense Workshop, Pervasive Health (2009)
13. Kleinberger, T., Jedlitschka, A., Storf, H., Steinbach-Nordmann, S., Prueckner, S.: An Approach to Evaluations of Assisted Living Systems using Ambient Intelligence for Emergency Monitoring and Prevention. In: Proc. 13th International Conference on Human-Computer Interaction (2009)

EMon: Embodied Monitorization

Davide Carneiro[1], Paulo Novais[1], Ricardo Costa[2],
Pedro Gomes[1], and José Neves[1]

[1] DI-CCTC, University of Minho, Braga, Portugal
{dcarneiro,pjon,jneves}@di.uminho.pt,
pg12890@alunos.uminho.pt
[2] College of Management and Technology - Polytechnic of Porto,
Felgueiras, Portugal
rfc@estgf.ipp.pt

Abstract. The amount of seniors in need of constant care is rapidly rising: an evident consequence of population ageing. There are already some monitorization environments which aim to monitor these persons while they remain at home. This, however, although better than delocalizing the elder to some kind of institution, may not still be the ideal solution, as it forces them to stay inside the home more than they wished, as going out means lack of accompaniment and a consequent sensation of fear. In this paper we propose EMon: a monitorization device small enough to be worn by its users, although powerful enough to provide the higher level monitorization systems with vital information about the user and the environment around him. We hope to allow the representation of an intelligent environment to move with its users, instead of being static, mandatorily associated to a single physical location. The first prototype of EMon, as presented in this paper, provides environmental data as well as GPS coordinates and pictures that are useful to describe the context of its user.

Keywords: Ambient Intelligence, Monitorization, Mobility, Portable Monitorization, Wearable Computers, Pervasive Computing.

1 Introduction

Population ageing is a problem that nowadays affects almost every country in the world. According to its definition [1], population ageing is a shift in the distribution of a country's population towards greater ages. However, population ageing means much more as there are both social and economical costs associated to this problem that cannot be ignored [2]. According to a report prepared by the United Nations [3], the number of older persons has tripled over the last 50 years and will more than triple again over the next 50 years.

These seniors frequently have special needs and require a close and personalized monitoring, mainly due to health related issues [4]. The most common answers are the elder moving to a relative's house or to a senior institution. The first option generally carries major changes to the routine of the host family and not all families are willing

M. Tscheligi et al. (Eds.): AmI 2009, LNCS 5859, pp. 133–142, 2009.

to or able to carry that burden. The second one carries increasing economical costs which not every family member is able to support, neither is it a good option for the elder, since they usually show reluctance when being moved out from their normal habitat where they have their life [5], their friends and their routine. It is desired that older people can age and maintain their well being while dealing with all the diseases and limitations that arise, for as long as possible.

New approaches have therefore to be devised for dealing with this problem. The answer, in our opinion, relies on the coming together of a group of fields such as Artificial Intelligence techniques, Human-computer interaction, ubiquitous computing, sensors and network technologies. By merging insights from these fields of research, it is possible to build the so-called Intelligent Environments. These environments are able to sense their users and their surroundings, analyze the information gathered and take actions with the objective of increasing the security and well-being of the persons in the environment. In this context of aged population, the advantages of these environments can be even more deeply exploited, acting as a way of increasing the autonomy and independence of seniors, especially the ones living alone [6].

1.1 The VirtualECare Project

The VirtualECare project [7, 8] aims at a Multi-agent based architecture in support of computational systems that seek to monitor and provide personalized health care services to its users or patients. These systems will interconnect healthcare institutions, leisure centres, patients and their relatives, on a common network, i.e., the VirtualECare architecture stands for a distributed one with its different nodes corresponding to a different role, either in terms of a call centre, a group decision support system or a monitoring device, just to name a few.

The nodes of the architecture depicted in the previous picture have been object of the work of this research team. However, in the ambit of this paper, we want to focus on the *Supported User* (Figure 1). This node of the architecture represents the person in need of care and is, therefore, constantly monitored inside his environment. We want, however, to extend this Monitorization to outdoor settings, following the person on-the-move, enriching the VirtualECare with this important feature. The work done in implementing this feature is described in this paper.

1.2 Ambient Assisted Living in Healthcare

Ambient Assisted Living (AAL) is a sub field of application of Ambient Intelligence. It builds on recent developments of IT and aims to promote the advantages that these technologies can have when put to work together to proactively assist their users in the day-to-day activities. Such a technology is able to lighten common and routine tasks, or even to replace their users in their execution. If to a regular user this means more comfort or free time to be spent in other activities, to senior or impaired users an assisted environment may mean autonomy, independence and security.

Indeed, these environments have known a significant growth in their use in the domain of the healthcare provision. At the MIT research has recently begun on the possibilities of AAL environments in the monitorization of patients in rural areas, that cover most of the territory of the countries but whose inhabitants generally lack access to health care [9]. We can also mention the Living Lab for Ambient Assisted Living in the Municipality of Schwechat that is a space where people from the community join together and share ideas and visions to implement technologies that support the independent living of seniors [10]. Another example is ALZ-MAS 2.0 which is an Ambient Intelligence based multi-agent system aimed at enhancing the assistance and health care for Alzheimer patients living in geriatric residences [11].

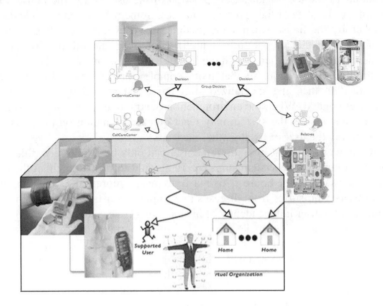

Fig. 1. The VirtualECare architecture, highlighting the components addressed in this paper

AAL-based projects can result in the direct benefit of both caregivers and patients. For caregivers, it may represent a more efficient time schedule, the automation of determinate tasks, or a more close and constant contact with their patients. For the patients, an AAL environment may be synonym for a supportive system that constantly monitors them and proactively takes actions that ensure their safety. More than that, these environments can take care of the supervision of the house, ordering goods, controlling the temperature and humidity of the air or the access of other persons. These environments constitute therefore an important improvement to the healthcare delivery sector, being only bound by the restriction of being physically associated to a place. In this paper we intend to take the first steps to create mobile assistive environments that follow their users while they move.

2 Embodied Monitorization

In the ambit of the VirtualECare project, this team has developed a monitorization platform intended to monitor seniors in their environment [12]. This platform is placed in the Home component of the architecture visible in Fig. 1. It is responsible for collecting all the information about the environment considered important for the well being of the user, study the behaviour of the user in terms of the management of the house and infer rules for that management that are then applied by the system in an attempt to adapt the house settings according to the user's preferences [13]. In a few words, this monitorization platform helps to describe the context of the user. The information collected may comprise the temperature, luminosity or humidity of the several rooms of the user's house, the position of the user inside the house, the persons visiting or the state of the several appliances. Some reactive and simple decisions can be taken by the house when some predetermined events occur (e.g. turn on air conditioning when the temperature is high). Moreover, the information about the environment may also be shared with the higher level components of the architecture, namely the Group Decision, so that more complex or important decisions can be taken. More than that, the specialized staff has constant and updated information about the user context. When the environment around the user, by some reason, is not safe or recommendable, the system may react quickly by acting on the house actuators, by notifying the user or by any other measure.

This has however a great limitation: the user can only be monitored while he is inside the environment. The system stops receiving vital information about the user the moment he steps out of the house. This may, obviously, represent a risk, mainly when we talk of users who suffer from diseases that imply a constant accompaniment. The will to monitor the user independently of his location drove us to idealize EMon.

EMon has as objective to make monitorization so portable that it may, eventually, be worn by the user the same way he wears a watch or a necklace. With such a device, the user can be accompanied while he is on the move, increasing his self-assurance, autonomy and security. Although there are already some devices in the market with the objective of monitoring their users while they move, none of them provides a complete and integrated solution. Some are simple GPS-based locators while others monitor one or some vital signs.

What we propose is an integrated device that can provide a full range of important information to describe the context of the user and make it so small that it can comfortably be carried by its users. What we expect to achieve is that intelligent environments are no longer static environments, mandatorily associated to a single physical location, but can instead move while their users move, following them wherever they go.

We do not believe that a device for such a purpose is possible to develop at the present since, although the devices necessary become smaller every day, they still too big to be integrated in a single device that can be comfortably worn. We however believe that the concept can be proved to be valid by means of a working prototype, and its usefulness demonstrated through positive changes in the routines of seniors that wore them.

2.1 Devices and Features

In order to implement the prototype of EMon we initially had to consider which functionalities to implement. One of the more important features nowadays and the first one to be considered by us given the domain of the problem is the location. If the system has information in real time about the location of the senior, help can immediately be sent in case of an emergency. Moreover, location-based services can be provided to the senior such as suggesting nearby interesting places according to the preferences or providing directions to the closest health facility if not feeling well. Another important feature would be to inform the senior about nearby friends, relatives or persons in the same situation, with the same interests with whom he eventually would like to interact. Adding to this the common functionalities of location based systems like guiding a person to a specific place or saving favourite places in a list, we obtain a very complete solution that can be advantageous for any senior and especially for seniors suffering from conditions like Alzheimer's disease.

In order to implement these features, we are using a PDA's Global Positioning System (GPS) integrated module together with software developed to implement some of the said features. The software is responsible for constantly reading the NMEA strings from the GPS receiver and provide them to the system. Among the functionalities implemented by this software, we can mention the record of the path travelled by the senior, the current position or the smallest path to walk to a predetermined location (Fig. 2. The output file from the *GetPathTo* service visualized on Google Maps. In this case the client is in University of Minho and wants to go to the nearest hospital in the database which is located at lat: 41.547407, lon: -8.423090.). All these functionalities are implemented using Google Maps and Google Earth API.

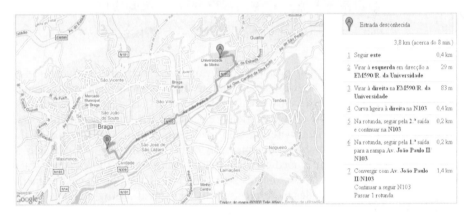

Fig. 2. The output file from the *GetPathTo* service visualized on Google Maps. In this case the client is in University of Minho and wants to go to the nearest hospital in the database which is located at lat: 41.547407, lon: -8.423090.

An important factor that conditions the health of the elder is the quality of the environment around him. This quality may be given in terms of factors like airborne pollutants, the humidity or the temperature. Our conviction that the monitorization of the environment around the elder is mandatory for ensuring his safety and well being is also shared by [14].

The importance of the air quality is even higher when we talk of seniors with diseases like asthma, bronchitis or cancer [15]. Having this in mind, we decided to incorporate into the prototype sensors which could provide the system with some information about the environment. Our purpose is that the system is able to warn the user if he is in a place where the environment is not safe or recommendable, according to his conditions. We have therefore decided to enrich the first prototype with temperature and luminosity sensors, embedded in the sleeve of the elder's jacket (Fig. 3). If, in one hand, the sensors chosen for the prototype are not of major importance as our objective in this first stage of the work is to present a proof of concept and test the architecture defined, in the other hand temperature and luminosity are two of the parameters that more influence our well being.

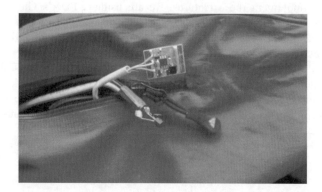

Fig. 3. The sensors embedded in the sleeve of the elder's jacket

The last device added to the prototype of EMon was a webcam. The webcam has several purposes. In one hand, we verified that the GPS system is not always accurate in an urban environment, especially when used around obstacles that can prevent the signal to be received in the best conditions (e.g. high trees, buildings). The image provided by the webcam can therefore help to determine the exact location of the elder in case of need, acting as a complement to the GPS module. An example of application could consist in a medical team that is being sent to the location of the elder in need but whose GPS coordinates are not precise. Using the image, the medical team could locate the elder more precisely by looking at nearby buildings, landmarks or monuments. This image can be requested by the elder if he feels threatened or endangered or can be remotely taken by the system, if some pre-determined event occur (e.g. a sudden rise in the heartbeat). The elder can also request a picture of something he likes and save it, like a common photo.

2.2 A Service Based Architecture

The architecture for implementing such a prototype has some specific issues. First of all, it must be a portable architecture as it will be traveling with the user. It must provide a constant connection to some network (e.g. Wi-Fi, GPRS, GSM, UMTS, HSDPA) so that the data gathered by the devices is constantly being routed to the higher level VirtualECare components. The architecture must also accept very different devices or components and provide means for their intercommunication. It should be dynamic and expansible, ready to accept new functionalities as we expect to

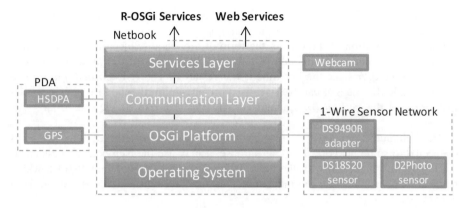

Fig. 4. The architecture of EMon

continue adding new devices. Last but not the least, the architecture must be light-weight so that it may be implemented in portable, low battery-consuming devices.

We decided to base our architecture on two open service-oriented standards: OSGi [16] and Web Services. OSGi is a standard designed to promote the interoperability of applications and services over networks. It allows for java programs to be encapsu-lated into OSGi bundles, which are modules able of providing and using services of other bundles. The result is a modular way of building applications based on the junc-tion of bundles, being the expansion of the application as easy as adding new bundles. For accessing and providing remote services, an extension to OSGi is used: R-OSGi. Web Services can be seen simplistically as a way of sharing information over a net-work. Each component that provides information declares Web Services that are then requested by the other components which need to access that information.

These two technologies are the base of our architecture. With this base, we gain in-teroperability and platform independence. This means that services can be used by any member of the VirtualECare architecture, independently of the platform or the device providing them. This also means that EMon can be used by any other higher level architecture similar to VirtualECare and use services provided by that architecture, therefore sharing advantages. It also results in a very expansible architecture as it is easy to add new components, which does not affect the components already present.

Let us now describe in more detail each component of the current EMon prototype and its place in the architecture (Fig. 4). The Netbook is the central core of our archi-tecture. It provides support to all the other modules and is responsible for running the OSGi platform and the web services as well as for connecting all the devices. The OSGi platform being used is the Knopflerfish OSGi, an open source OSGi service platform. Two of the bundles running in this platform are the GPS and the 1Wire bundles. The first one is responsible for constantly reading NMEA strings from the PDA and parse them. The second one regularly reads the values of the sensors. These two bundles provide as services the values read so that other bundles can have easy access to that information. In the case of the sensor values, they are simply sent to the VirtualECare platform. As for the values of the GPS bundle, they can be used for three main purposes: the *getPathTo* service uses it to obtain the current position of the user and, through the Google Maps API, calculates a walking path to the destination provided by the user; the *getLastValidLocation* service simply provides the value of the last valid location of the user in the form of a Location object, a java object that encodes the latitude and longitude of the user; the *getRecordedPath* service returns the path of the user since the last time it was restarted. The *getRecordedPath* service generates a KML file that can be visualized on Google Earth while the *getLastValid-Location* and the *getPathTo* generate HTML files that can be viewed in any web browser.

The communication layer is responsible for ensuring that the system is always connected to some network. For that purpose, it may use the Netbook wireless capabilities or the connection with the PDA which has access to mobile networks, which nowadays cover almost all the inhabited areas and have considerable speeds for data transfer.

Fig. 5. The prototype of EMon with its components connected: a netbook, a PDA, a webcam and two sensors

As for the services layer, its task is to provide support for the Web Services. In this first prototype of the system, only the data from the wireless webcam is provided via Web Service. To provide the services of the webcam the GlassFish application server is being used. The application developed consists of an online interface, accessible thru a web browser that, by means of the java media framework, enables to remotely control the camera (i.e. take pictures). When a picture is taken, it is visible on the web browser and automatically transferred, via Web Service, to a folder on the server. If the user intends to take a picture, he must also use the same interface and the picture is also transferred to the server so that he may later have access to it.

The prototype, as depicted here, is made of only a few devices so the functionalities are still limited (Figure 5). The architecture however, by being based on open and service-oriented technologies, allows for virtually any devices to be connected, ensuring that the prototype is highly expansible and multifaceted.

3   The Future of EMon and Similar Projects

EMon has much to evolve in order to become what the authors envisioned: a device small enough to be comfortably carried by its user, nevertheless completely monitoring him and his surroundings. In order to achieve this vision, several issues have to be solved. In one hand, the devices in question must become smaller and more portable: it is, although their small size and weight, impracticable to go around carrying a netbook embedded in our clothes.

EMon will also be empowered with more sensors to enrich its features. One of the more important will be the ability to monitor the elder's vital signs in real time as they configure the most important health information one can have about an individual. Another important enhancement will be to add sensors for sensing the quality of the air and initiate actions for adapting this quality. This will allow to monitor people who are intolerant to some specific gases or particles with the objective to avoid respiratory conditions.

Concerning the web cam, we are currently only sending via Web Service still images. It is our desire to provide EMon with the ability to send live video when needed or to record video as well as audio. The webcam will also need to be replaced by a smaller camera. Another improvement would be to develop the system or at least the backbone of it in washable electronics so that the jacket could easily be washed by its user. At last, we will develop an intuitive integrated interface showing in real time all the information generated by the system, that can be accessed locally by the user in its handheld device or remotely by authorized personal of the VirtualECare platform.

The fields of application of projects similar to EMon are however much more extensive that just the healthcare sector. There are similar applications of the same technologies in the most different fields with the common objective of monitoring persons or their surroundings while on-the-move. As an example we can mention a chest belt being used by the USA military that is able to provide automatic ECG measurements [17] and that is now being applied to sports clothing, with the support of Adidas. Another good example is Ericsson Mobile Health, which intends to provide healthcare professionals with vital and objective information about the patients, allowing the assessment of their health status while on the move and avoiding unnecessary routine checkups, letting patients live more normal lives.

4   Conclusion

In this paper we have presented the EMon prototype. We integrated some different components in a common architecture with the aim of providing monitorization to seniors while on the move. If in one hand the device is still too big to be comfortably carried around and has little functionalities, in other hand we have proved that the concept is valid and feasible. In our tests we concluded that the GPS system is not very effective when used in some urban scenarios although it is very accurate when used in open air spaces, without nearby obstacles. To try to minimize this problem, we integrated a web cam with the objective of providing additional information about the location of the person. The implementation of the architecture presented revealed itself easy, mainly due to the experience this team gained in developing previous monitorization projects. It is our conviction that this new project constitutes a major improvement to the VirtualECare platform, and that the concept presented in this paper is the path to ensure the security and accompaniment of seniors while outside their environments.

References

1. Weil, D.: Population Aging. Department of Economics, Brown University and NBER (2006)
2. Turner, D., Giorno, C., Serres, A., Vourc'h, A., Richardson, P.: The Macroeconomic Implications of Ageing in a Global Context. OECD Economics Department Working Papers, No. 193. OECD Publishing (1998)
3. United Nations: World Population Ageing: 1950-2050. UN (2002)
4. Malmberg, A.: Industrial Geography: agglomeration and local milieu. Progress in Human Geography 20, 392–403 (1996)
5. Al-Hamad, A., Flowerdew, R., Hayes, L.: Migration of elderly people to join existing households: some evidence from the 1991 Household Sample of Anonymised Records. Environment and Planning A 29(7), 1243–1255 (1997)
6. Bahadori, S., Cesta, A., Iocchi, L., Leone, G., Nardi, D., Pecora, F., Rasconi, R., Scozzafava, L.: Towards Ambient Intelligence For The Domestic Care of the Elderly. In: Ambient Intelligence, pp. 15–38. Springer, Heidelberg (2005)
7. Novais, P., Costa, R., Carneiro, D., Machado, J., Lima, L., Neves, J.: Group Support in Collaborative Networks Organizations for Ambient Assisted Living. In: Oya, M., Uda, R., Yasunobu, C. (eds.) Towards Sustainable Society on Ubiquitous Networks. IFIP International Federation for Information Processing. Springer, Heidelberg (2008)
8. Costa, R., Novais, P., Machado, J., Alberto, C., Neves, J.: Inter-organization Cooperation for Care of the Elderly. In: Wang, W., Li, Y., Duan, Z., Yan, L., Li, H., Yang, X. (eds.) Integration and Innovation Orient to E-Society. IFIP International Federation for Information Processing. Springer, Heidelberg (2007)
9. Havasi, F., Kiss, Á.: Ambient Assisted Living in Rural Areas: Vision and Pilot Application. In: Constructing Ambient Intelligence, pp. 246–252 (2008)
10. Panek, P., Zagler, W.: A Living Lab for Ambient Assisted Living in the Municipality of Schwechat. In: Miesenberger, K., Klaus, J., Zagler, W.L., Karshmer, A.I. (eds.) ICCHP 2008. LNCS, vol. 5105, pp. 1008–1015. Springer, Heidelberg (2008)
11. García, O., Tapia, D., Saavedra, A., Alonso, R., García, I.: ALZ-MAS 2.0; A Distributed Approach for Alzheimer Health Care. In: 3rd Symposium of Ubiquitous Computing and Ambient Intelligence, pp. 76–85 (2008)
12. Carneiro, D., Costa, R., Novais, P., Machado, J., Neves, J.: Simulating and Monitoring Ambient Assisted Living. In: Proceedings of the ESM 2008 - The 22nd annual European Simulation and Modelling Conference (2008)
13. Carneiro, D., Novais, P., Costa, R., Neves, J.: Case-Based Reasoning Decision Making in Ambient Assisted Living. In: Omatu, S., et al. (eds.) IWANN 2009, Part II. LNCS, vol. 5518, pp. 787–794. Springer, Heidelberg (2009)
14. D'Amato, G., Liccardi, G., D'Amato, M., Cazzola, M.: Outdoor air pollution, climatic changes and allergic bronchial asthma. European Respiratory Journal 20 (2002)
15. Oberdörster, G.: Pulmonary effects of inhaled ultrafine particles. International Archives of Occupational and Environmental Health 74, 1–8 (2000)
16. O.S.G.i: OSGi Service Platform, Release 3. IOS Press, Amsterdam (2003)
17. National Defense Magazine, Heart Monitoring for Soldiers on the Move (August 2008), http://www.nationaldefensemagazine.org/archive/2007/August/Pages/TechTalk4893.aspx

Interoperation Modeling for Intelligent Domotic Environments

Dario Bonino and Fulvio Corno

Politecnico di Torino, Dipartimento di Automatica ed Informatica
Corso Duca degli Abruzzi 24, 10129 - Torino, Italy
{dario.bonino,fulvio.corno}@polito.it

Abstract. This paper introduces an ontology-based model for domotic device inter-operation. Starting from a previously published ontology (DogOnt) a refactoring and extension is described allowing to explicitly represent device capabilities, states and commands, and supporting abstract modeling of device inter-operation.

1 Introduction

Traditional problems connected to Home Automation systems such as the lack of interoperability, intelligence, adaptivity and integration with other systems (e.g., entertainment or the web) can be gracefully overcome by applying strong model-based abstraction and inference mechanisms. Interoperability, in particular, is a well-known issue in the Home Automation domain, and no valid general solutions have currently been devised. In this paper, an ontology model for domotic device inter-operation is designed, starting from a formerly published ontology, DogOnt v1.0.2 [1]. DogOnt is currently exploited by an open-source home gateway [2] designed for transforming already existing domotic installations into Intelligent Domotic Eenvironments.

The original *functionality/state* modeling of domotic devices adopted in DogOnt is extended to support the explicit representation of *commands*, accepted by domotic devices, and *notifications*, generated by suitable control devices (a specific subclass of domotic devices). Such an abstract modeling is complemented by the definition of SPARQL query mechanisms for extracting associations between controller and controlled devices, and to further specialize the same associations in terms of interacting notifications and commands. Extracted information provides the basis for designing network-independent, general and scalable device inter-operation solutions.

The paper is organized as follows: Section 2 provides a brief review of related works on home and context modeling while Section 3 summarizes the main DogOnt v1.0.2 features. Section 4 describes new device modeling in DogOnt v1.0.3, whereas Section 5 tackles inter-operation modeling. Finally, Section 6 draws conclusions and discusses future research directions.

M. Tscheligi et al. (Eds.): AmI 2009, LNCS 5859, pp. 143–152, 2009.

2   Related Works

Different approaches have been developed, in literature, to solve the issues related to the interoperation problem, however they are mainly devoted at supporting home/building-wide integration of domotic plants, smart appliances and wireless sensor networks. Among the home/building wide approaches interoperation issues are often addressed by defining "interoperation middlewares" and only few solutions are based on a stronger model-based design.

In the domain of interoperation middlewares Moon et al. [3] worked on the Universal Middleware Bridge for allowing interoperability between domotic networks. Sumi Helal et al. [4] addressed network-level interoperation with a very distributed approach where each device is represented by an OSGi bundle. Tokunaga et al. [5] defined a device-level interoperability solution, which tackles the problem of switching from one-to-one protocol bridges to one-to-many conversions by means of so-called home computing middlewares. These solutions rely on application-specific environment models, often hard coded in the middleware framework. However the same models can seldom be exploited as a basis for building high-level interoperation policies, e.g. inter-network scenarios based on rules, or to support more sophisticated inferences. In this sense the DogOnt approach is more general since it supports automatic interoperation modeling (and execution through the DOG [2] gateway) as well as complex inferences based on logic and rules [6].

The work of Miori et al. [7] represents one of the few solutions that can be directly compared to the proposed approach. Similarly to DogOnt (and DOG) the system-level framework introduced by Miori, called DomoNet, addresses domotic interoperability by exploiting a formal environment model called DomoML and widely accepted technologies such as Web Services, XML and Internet protocols. DomoML [8,9] stems from the EHS taxonomy[1] and provides a full-blown set of ontologies for representing household environments. Three main ontologies define the available modeling primitives: DomoML-env, DomoML-fun and DomoML-core. DomoML-env provides base classes for describing all "fixed" elements inside the house such as walls, furniture and doors, and supports defining the house layout by means of neighborhood and composition relationships. DomoML-fun allows describing the abstract functionalities of each house device. It defines basic control objects such as sliders and knobs, and is able to model complex functions such as heating control and scenarios. Eventually, DomoML-core provides the glue layer between DomoML-env and DomoML-fun concepts, and defines shared classes, e.g. physical quantities. With respect to DogOnt, DomoML shows some shortcomings in the description of current domotic systems. First, it mixes too different levels of detail in modeling, sometimes adopting questionable modeling choices, e.g., gates and barriers are both modeled as subclasses of doors. Second, DomoML does not model device states, which are fundamental for operating real systems. Finally, DomoML doesn't offer facilities for either querying

---

[1] The European Home System, http://www.ehsa.com

or auto-complete models, thus requiring a cumbersome modeling effort whenever a new house must be described.

On the pervasive computing side several models can be found either related to or overlapping the DogOnt knowledge domain. Among them, the SOUPA ontology [10] provides a modular modeling structure that encompasses vocabularies for representing intelligent agents with associated beliefs, desires and intentions, time, space, events, user profiles, actions and policies for security and privacy. SOUPA is organized into a core set of vocabularies, and a set of optional extensions. Core vocabularies describe concepts associated with person, agent, belief-desire-intention, action policy, time, space and event. These concepts are expressed as 9 distinct ontologies mapped to well known vocabularies such as FOAF [11], DAML Time [12], OpenCyc [13] and RCC [14]. SOUPA cannot be directly applied to support interoperability and intelligence for domotic systems since most of the needed domain-specific concepts are lacking (e.g., no primitives are provided for modeling devices, functionalities, etc.), however it can be exploited in a modular approach to house modeling, where DogOnt acts as domain-specific ontology, defining low-level, operative knowledge, and SOUPA provides mid-level definitions easing the design of pervasive, context-aware ambient intelligence solutions.

3   DogOnt v1.0.2

DogOnt v1.0.2 is an ontology model for Intelligent Domotic Environments that has been presented in [1] and is briefly summarized in this section. It is organized along 5 main hierarchies of concepts (in bold in Figure 1) and allows explicitly representing: (a) the domotic environment structure (rooms, walls, doors, etc.), by means of *BuildingEnvironment*; (b) the type of domotic devices and of smart appliances (*BuildingThings* of type *Controllable*); (c) the working configurations that devices can assume, modeled by *States* and *StateValues*; (d) the device capabilities (*Functionalities*) in terms of accepted events, i.e., *Commands*, and generated messages, i.e., *Notifications*; (e) the technology-specific information needed for interfacing real-world devices (*NetworkComponent*) and (f) the kind of furniture placed in the home (*BuildingThing* of type *UnControllable*).

DogOnt models devices in terms of functionalities (modeling device capabilities) and in terms of states (modeling the stable configurations that a device can assume). Functionalities are represented by the concept hierarchy rooted at the *Functionality* concept. Three kinds of functionalities are considered: *ControlFunctionalities*, modeling the ability of a device to be controlled by means of some message or command; *QueryFunctionalities* modeling the ability of a device to be queried about its internal state; *NotificationFunctionalities* modeling the ability of a device to issue notifications about state changes. Each Functionality sub-class has a single instance that is associated to every device characterized by the modeled capability. In addition, each device possesses a unique *State* instance, which models the current stable configuration. States are organized in a concept hierarchy stemming from the *State* concept that encompasses *ContinuousStates*, modeling continuously changing properties of devices

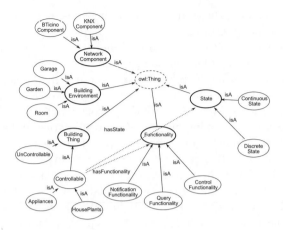

Fig. 1. A bird-eye view of the DogOnt v1.0.2 ontology

(e.g., the temperature sensed by a thermal sensor), and *DiscreteState*s, modeling properties that can only abruptly change, e.g. switching a Lamp on or off.

4   Device Modeling

Modeling inter-operation between (domotic) devices requires to formally describe device-to-device interaction patterns where a device can either control, or be controlled by, other devices, without any "a priori" assumption on the device role. Inter-operation can be seen as a mapping problem where changes in the state of one device (i.e., notifications) must be mapped to commands issued to one or more devices either connected to the same or to a different domotic network. This requires to revise and extend the DogOnt v1.0.2 ontology for describing

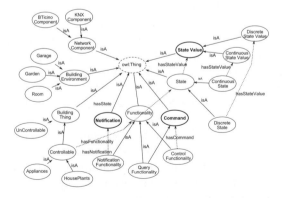

Fig. 2. An overview of DogOnt v1.0.3 (new concepts in bold)

notifications sent by controller devices, commands accepted by controlled devices and connections between them, i.e., to model which commands are generated by a given notification. These informal requirements drive the new DogOnt v1.0.3 ontology design, and are reflected in three major changes (Figure 2) involving:

(a) **Functionality modeling** (Section 4.1): the single-instance assumption is removed and the modeling detail is increased by defining 2 new ontology sub-trees stemming from the *Notification* and the *Command* concepts, respectively;

(b) **State modeling** (Section 4.2): the modeling granularity is increased by associating states with newly defined state values, i.e., concepts stemming from the new *StateValue* concept;

(c) **Inter-operation modeling** (Section 5): two new semantic relationships are defined allowing to abstract device inter-operation, on one side, and to support automatic inter-operation processes through querying and inferencing, on the other side.

4.1   Functionality Modeling

To model device-to-device interactions, functionalities must be detailed down to single commands and notifications. In order to support this increased modeling granularity, DogOnt v1.0.3 moves from the single instance assumption of the former 1.0.2 version to a more classic modeling pattern where each device instance is associated to a specific and distinct functionality instance.

The ontology tree stemming from the *Functionality* concept is integrated by 2 new ontology trees stemming from the *Command* and *Notification* concepts, respectively. In particular, *ControlFunctionalities* are connected to *Command* instances by means of a new *hasCommand* relationship (shown in bold in Figure 3a), while *NotificationFunctionalities* are associated to suitable *Notification* instances by means of a new *hasNotification* relationship (Figure 3b).

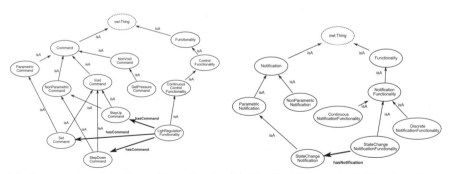

(a) Commands and ControlFunctionali- (b) Notifications and Notification Func-
ties.   tionalities.

Fig. 3. Control and Notification Functionalities in DogOnt v1.0.3

Commands are modeled according to two orthogonal domains : the number of involved parameters ,either 0-*NonParametric* or >0-*Parametric*, and the expected return values, either none-*VoidCommands* or one-*NonVoidCommands*.

Every parametric command(or notification) is further detailed by means of suitable restrictions defining the number of accepted parameters (*nParams*, usually 1), the allowed values (*paramValuesEnum*) for enumerable values, etc.

4.2   State Modeling

Reflecting the need of increasing model granularity, the *State* sub-tree, originally available in DogOnt v1.0.2, has been complemented by a newly designed *StateValue* tree, which allows to explicitly represent values of device states as concept instances. This design choice permits to reach a uniform modeling detail with respect to the granularity of functionality modeling, and provides the modeling base for defining associations between commands and current, or future, device states (not yet included in DogOnt v1.0.3). StateValues are divided (disjoint) into *Discrete* and *Continuous*. *Discrete* state values model properties that can only assume discrete values like "on" and "off", whereas *Continuous* values model continuously changing features, e.g., the temperature measured by a thermal sensor. DogOnt *States* and *StateValues* are associated by means of the *hasStateValue* relation (in bold in Figure 4).

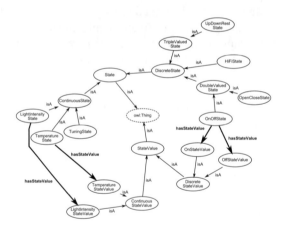

Fig. 4. State modeling in DogOnt v1.0.3

5   Inter-operation Modeling

5.1   Model

Inter-operation between domotic devices, either connected to the same or to different domotic plants (or networks), is modeled by associating notifications of "controller" devices with commands of "controlled" ones. This association is formally represented by two relationships instantiated at the device level (*controlledObject*) and at the functionality level (*generatesCommand*), respectively.

At the device level, interoperation is modeled with a very light master-slave approach: every device can control or can be controlled by another device, and may also change its role in time due to home configuration changes. As an example, an Hi-Fi amplifier usually acts as controller for the Hi-Fi components, e.g., the CDPlayer and the Tape Recorder. Nevertheless, it can also assume the role of controlled device, e.g., if it is remotely controlled by a PC. In general, while some devices (e.g., thermostats, Hi-Fi systems, etc.) can play both as controller and controlled device, other, simpler, domotic devices can only behave as "controlled" devices, e.g., Lamps. The ability to act as "controller" is therefore explicitly modeled in DogOnt v1.0.3 by defining a new *Control* ($\sqsubseteq$ *Controllable*) class[2]. All *Control*s are connected to their controlled devices by means of the *controlledObject* relation. The *controlledObject* relation defines the interaction roles played by the real objects modeled in DogOnt. However, to enable automatic inferences on device-to-device interoperation, e.g., to automatically generate interoperation rules, a higher modeling detail is needed. A finer grained relationship has therefore been defined between *Notification* and *Command* instances: *generatesCommand*. This relation allows defining specific command(s) generated by specific notification(s) associated to functionalities of a specific *Control* device. For example it permits to associate the *OnNotification* of a simple *Switch* to the *OffCommand* of a Home Entertainment System.

Example - Controlling a Dimmer Lamp. Building upon Example 1, we can now model how a dimmer lamp is controlled by a 2-way switch (*OnOffSwitch*). Two-way switches always have an *OnOffFunctionality* instance, describing their ability of being switched on or off. The *OnOffFunctionality* instance is in turn associated to 2 *Notification* instances: a *OnNotification* and a *OffNotification*, respectively. If the Dimmer Lamp shall be lit at 50% when the switch is in the on position and shall be switched off when the switch is off, then the *OnNotification* of the switch shall be connected to the *SetCommand(50%)* of the DimmerLamp. Accordingly, the *OffNotification* of the 2-way switch shall be connected to the *OffCommand* of the dimmer lamp. Figure 5 shows the involved instances.

5.2   Automatic Interoperation

Modeling primitives defined in previous sections encode the base knowledge needed to support automatic device interoperation scenarios. For the sake of simplicity, in this paper we assume that automatic interoperation is achieved through rule-based reasoning (as in [6]), and that suitable communication primitives are included in the rule language, allowing to listen for real device notifications and to send commands.

---

[2] Please notice that in DogOnt the semantics of *Controllable* is: "a device that can be interfaced by a domotic gateway".

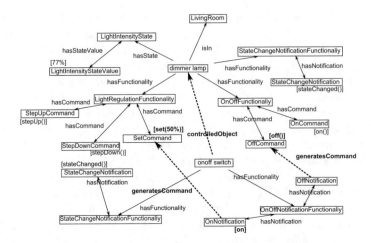

Fig. 5. Inter-communication between a 2-way switch and a dimmer lamp

Figure 6 shows a prototypical rule, where the **when** clause represents the rule antecedent and the **then** clause the rule consequent. It is important to notice that the rule structure is completely independent from the device type and technology.

```
when
  device:?x
  receivedNotification(?x, ?v)
then
  device: ?y
  sendCommand(?y, ?cn, [?cv])
```

Fig. 6. An sample interoperation rule, values in brackets are optional

To enable automatic interoperation the ?x,?v, ?y, ?cn and ?cv variables shall be automatically extracted from DogOnt device, notification and command instances. This requires to first compute the transitive closure of the DogOnt model instantiation to derive all direct and inherited information involving declared device instances, e.g. to infer that an *OnOffSwitch* instance is also an instance of *Switch, ElectricComponent, Controllable*, etc. Secondly, SPARQL querying is exploited to extract, for each controller device ?x, the list of controlled devices ?y and to further retrieve the controller device notifications ?v and the commands accepted by the controlled device ?cn (and their values ?cv, when available). Figure 7a shows the query for devices accepting *DiscreteCommands*, a similar query (Figure 7b) is defined for *ContinuousCommands*, also retrieving the command values.

```
SELECT DISTINCT ?x ?n ?v ?c ?d ?class
?cn WHERE
{
?x a dogont:Controllable .
?y a dogont:Controllable .
?x dogont:controlledObject ?y .
?x dogont:hasFunctionality ?f .
?f dogont:hasNotification ?n .
?n dogont:notificationValue ?v .
?n dogont:generateCommand ?c .
?d dogont:hasFunctionality ?f2 .
?f2 dogont:hasCommand ?c .
?c rdf:type ?class .
?class rdfs:subClassOf
dogont:DiscreteCommand .
?class rdfs:subClassOf [rdf:type
owl:Restriction; owl:onProperty
dogont:realCommandName;
owl:hasValue ?cn]
}
```

(a) discrete commands

```
SELECT DISTINCT ?x ?n ?v ?c ?d ?class
?cv WHERE
{
?x a dogont:Controllable .
?y a dogont:Controllable .
?x dogont:controlledObject ?y .
?x dogont:hasFunctionality ?f .
?f dogont:hasNotification ?n .
?n dogont:notificationValue ?v .
?n dogont:generateCommand ?c .
?d dogont:hasFunctionality ?f2 .
?f2 dogont:hasCommand ?c .
?c rdf:type ?class .
?class rdfs:subClassOf
dogont:ContinuousCommand .
?class rdfs:subClassOf [rdf:type
owl:Restriction; owl:onProperty
dogont:realCommandName;
owl:hasValue ?cn]
?class rdfs:subClassOf [rdf:type
owl:Restriction; owl:onProperty
dogont:CommandValue;
owl:hasValue ?cv]
}
```

(b) continuous commands

Fig. 7. The SPARQL query for extracting interoperation data

6   Conclusions

This paper introduced the new DogOnt v1.0.3 ontology, highlighting the differences with the formerly published DogOnt v1.0.2. DogOnt v1.0.3 is designed for explicitly supporting interoperation of domotic devices, by modeling interactions between "controller" and "controlled" devices. Thanks to simple, yet clear, modeling choices and to the adoption of standard modeling and querying patterns, DogOnt easily fulfills the requirements of automatic interoperation support, as demonstrated by exploiting a simple rule-based reasoning approach.

References

1. Bonino, D., Corno, F.: DogOnt - Ontology Modeling for Intelligent Domotic Environments. In: Sheth, A.P., Staab, S., Dean, M., Paolucci, M., Maynard, D., Finin, T., Thirunarayan, K. (eds.) ISWC 2008. LNCS, vol. 5318, pp. 790–803. Springer, Heidelberg (2008)
2. Bonino, D., Corno, F.: The DOG Gateway: Enabling Ontology-based Intelligent Domotic Environments. IEEE Transactions on Consumer Electronics 54(4) (November 2008)
3. Moon, K.-D., Lee, Y.-H., Lee, C.-E., Son, Y.-S.: Design of a Universal Middleware Bridge for Device Interoperability in Heterogeneous Home Network Middleware. IEEE Transactions on Consumer Electronics 51, 314–318 (2005)
4. Helal, S., Mann, W., El-Zabadani, H., King, J., Kaddoura, Y., Jansen, E.: The Gator Tech. Smart House: A Programmable Pervasive Space. IEEE Computer 0018-9162/05, 64–74 (2005)

5. Tokunaga, E., Ishikawa, H., Kurahashi, M., Morimoto, Y., Nakajima, T.: A Framework for Connecting Home Computing Middleware. In: International Conference on Distributed Computing Systems Workshops, ICDCSW 2002 (2002)
6. Bonino, D., Corno, F.: Technology Independent Interoperation of Domotic Devices through Rules. In: 13th IEEE International Symposium on Consumer Electronics, ISCE 2009 (2009)
7. Miori, V., Tarrini, L., Manca, M., Tolomei, G.: An Open Standard Solution for Domotic Interoperability. IEEE Transactions on Consumer Electronics 52, 97–103 (2006)
8. Sommaruga, L., Perri, A., Furfari, F.: DomoML-env: an ontology for Human Home Interaction. In: Proceedings of SWAP 2005, the 2nd Italian Semantic Web Workshop, Trento, Italy, December 14-16. CEUR Workshop Proceedings (2005)
9. Furfari, F., Sommaruga, L., Soria, C., Fresco, R.: DomoML: the definition of a standard markup for interoperability of human home interactions. In: EUSAI 2004: Proceedings of the 2nd European Union symposium on Ambient intelligence, pp. 41–44. ACM, New York (2004)
10. Finin, H.C.T., Joshi, A.: The SOUPA Ontology for Pervasive Computing. In: Ontologies for Agents: Theory and Experiences, pp. 233–258. Birkhäuser, Basel (2005)
11. Brickley, D., Miller, L.: FOAF Vocabulary Specification 0.91 (November 2007), http://xmlns.com/foaf/spec/
12. Hobbs, J., Pustejovsky, J.: Annotating and Reasoning about Time and Events. In: 2003 AAAI Spring Symposium (2003)
13. Reed, S.L., Lenat, D.B.: Mapping Ontologies into Cyc. In: AAAI 2002 symposium (2002)
14. Li, S., Ying, M.: Region Connection Calculus: its models and composition table. Artificial Intelligence 145(1-2), 121–146 (2003)

Intertwining Implicit and Explicit Awareness of Wellbeing to Support Peace of Mind and Connectedness

Pavan Dadlani[1], Panos Markopoulos[2], and Emile Aarts[1,2]

[1] Philips Research, High Tech Campus 34, 5656AE, Eindhoven, The Netherlands
[2] Department of Industrial Design, Eindhoven University of Technology,
P.O. Box 513, Den Dolech 2, Eindhoven, 5600 MB, The Netherlands
pavan.dadlani@philips.com, p.markopoulos@tue.nl,
emile.aarts@philips.com

Abstract. An awareness system was designed to provide peace of mind and a sense of connectedness to adults who care for an elderly parent living alone. Our empirical research, including a field trial of six months, confirms the potential of awareness systems to support both generations suggesting that future research should examine, firstly, how to convey long-term trends regarding the wellbeing of the elderly and, secondly, how to intertwine the communication of awareness information with expressive forms of communication. We discuss implications of our studies for the design of ambient intelligent systems supporting awareness between elderly and their adult children.

Keywords: Ambient intelligence, awareness, connectedness, assisted living.

1 Introduction

The elderly population is expected to grow rapidly in developed countries in the next 50 years. This trend inflates the 'sandwich' generation: adults with children *and* an aging parent to take care of. We explore the potential of ambient intelligence [4] to offer peace of mind to adults who are peripherally involved in the care of their parents and also address the desire of both sides for a sense of *connectedness*, understood as a positive emotional experience, characterized by a feeling of staying in touch within ongoing social relationships [6].

Several studies examine the scenario of monitoring a remote elder; most notably CareNet [1], Digital Family Portrait (DFP) [3] and Diarist [2]. Such studies provide converging evidence regarding the potential of awareness systems, understood here as systems that help connected individuals stay informed regarding the activities and status of each by providing frequent and partly automated updates. Actual deployments of awareness systems supporting the scenario of monitoring a remote elder are scarce and the evidence they report regarding their benefits is still tentative. Furthermore, driven by the aim to bridge distance, earlier works have focused on supporting awareness at a relatively fine time-scale: moment-to-moment presence, or activities of daily living. Taking a step back, this research questions what are the needs for awareness between seniors and their adult children. Compared to those earlier works, more emphasis is also put on the hardware design and its aesthetics, which are often argued

M. Tscheligi et al. (Eds.): AmI 2009, LNCS 5859, pp. 153–158, 2009.
© Springer-Verlag Berlin Heidelberg 2009

to be important in this field, see for example [3]. Section 2 summarizes the design and initial evaluation of Aurama, which led to its redesign reported in Section 3. Section 4 describes a field trial, involving five participants for a period of six months. We end with several implications and conclusions from this work.

Fig. 1. Intelligent photo frame jewelry provides explicit awareness of affections

2   Design of the Awareness System

Four focus groups (N=19) and interviews (N=8) with caregivers, and interviews with seniors (N=7) (participants were different and not related in each of these studies) questioned several elements that are adopted in related research prototypes discussed above. Rather than detailed trivia of daily activities, or synchronous updates regarding whereabouts, care giving children wish to obtain high-level overviews about their parents' wellbeing. Rather than a constant feed of information, they wish to be informed of changes to known patterns, and of gradual shifts in lifestyle that may not be easy to notice during visits or direct communication. Although they value the possibility to see historical data, they found the idea of receiving a daily status reports or a 'story' with detailed schedules and activities. Participants favored ambient displays such as interactive digital photo frames, over direct channels such as SMS and e-mail.

To verify the reported preference of long-term trend awareness we designed and implemented a system supporting awareness of presence at home, sleep patterns, and weight variations regarding the lone elder. The system includes an interactive photo frame which emits colored light 'auras' presenting at-a-glance information regarding the elder (see Figure 1). If the elder is at home, a blue aura appears on the child's frame, which disappears if the elder leaves. To provide awareness of changes of patterns a yellow or orange aura is formed, depending on the severity of the change. The touch screen displays charts showing long-term trends of the elder's data.

Presence at home is detected via a wireless tag transmitting RF signals and placed on a keychain carried by the elder. Weight is measured with load sensors placed under each leg of the bed. The same load sensors are used to monitor the number of times the elder gets up during the night and the amount of sleep the elder gets. This information is used to measure their sleep quality. Our approach is not presented here as the best way to measure sleep quality; it is chosen to provide though a realistic and accurate measure to allow participants to experience first hand what remote monitoring of sleep quality would be like for both parties, the 'watcher' and the 'watched'. Data about sleep and weight was assessed once a day to identify unusual events.

2.1   Laboratory Evaluations and Short Field Trials

Participants (N=6) in lab-based trials were invited to test the usability of the system and obtain an overall impression of the application. These were different than the participants in the original inquiries. They appreciated the concepts and were assured that the system will help them access wellbeing information easily and help them be more involved in their parents' wellbeing. We then conducted two field trials of two weeks each, to test the experience of the awareness system under realistic conditions and focus on its added value to bring elderly and their children closer.

Users appreciated the design aesthetics of the display and valued the colored auras to indicate the status information of a close relative. Users valued the emphasis on coarse grain information, confirming our choice to deviate from earlier designs, see for instance [2]. Participants expressed a major interest for the positive aspects in their parents' lives rather than the negative events that the system focused upon. Often the younger adults fear being intrusive, even though their parents claim that they do not mind sharing the information. A detailed report of these studies can be found in [7].

3   Second Generation of the Awareness System

Based on lessons learnt from the first field trials, several changes were made to the awareness system. To further examine the interest for users of long-term trend information, in addition to sleep and weight charts, we developed an overview of presence at home over time, which allows the detection of abnormal patterns and changes in habits. To allow the expression of positive messages, affective messaging was supported by means of *intelligent photo frame jewelry* (Figure 1) allowing users to express emotions playfully: placing a tagged object (*smiley*, *love* or *cry*) on the picture frame creates a colored aura on the frame at the remote site, together with a graphical representation of the emotion. To reduce or eliminate asymmetry, the revised design allows presence information and affective messages to be bidirectional. Figure 2 shows the system's architecture and examples of long-term trends.

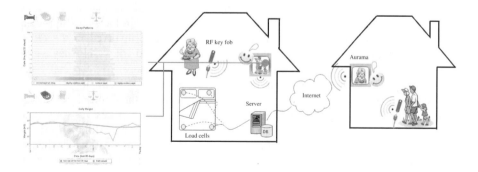

Fig. 2. System's architecture and sample charts for sleep and weight patterns

4 Long-Term Field Trial

To evaluate the revised system, a 6-month field trial was conducted with five participants: an 85-year old woman living alone and at a distance (70km) from her son, his
wife and her two granddaughters. The trial consisted of three phases: (1) the sensor
infrastructure was installed and data was collected for three months, (2) the ambient
display was installed on both locations where awareness of presence and wellbeing
was provided (10 weeks), and (3) intertwining this with explicit exchange of affective
messages (four weeks). Interviews and questionnaires were conducted before install-
ing the system and after each phase. Due to technical problems, the system could not
be used for three weeks in phase 2. Figure 3 shows the usage patterns of the family.

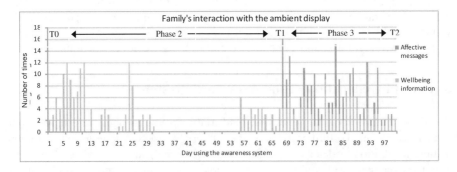

Fig. 3. Sample usage patterns for the remote family in the second and third phase of the study

During the second phase, the grandchildren and daughter in law checked every 2-3
days every wellbeing parameter presented in the frame. The son, however, would not
check that often directly, but preferred to learn about it through his family, preferring
them to act as intermediaries to get the information.

The elder did not sleep well for several nights throughout the study and as a result
yellow auras appeared on the child's frame. The family called to inquire if she had a
bad night of sleep and felt 'obliged' to react, but they considered that an act of care
and a responsibility they want to have, instead of a burden. In fact, they appreciate
receiving such 'negative' news because they can get more involved in the elder's
wellbeing. Further corroborating with our preliminary field trials [7], they valued
seeing wellbeing information that they have no access to otherwise; especially non-
detailed long-term patterns gave them rich information to assess wellbeing.

The experiences of the five participants were surveyed at three times, T0, T1, and
T2 (Figure 3). At T1 they reported feeling that the system is not necessary yet because
the elderly is still healthy, active and can call if there is a problem. Although she does
not mind sharing the information with them and finds it pleasant to get calls when she
is not sleeping well, she feels she has enough contact and that it would be more useful
for frailer elderly or be more relevant for her if she would not be living in a care facility. They do see the value, nevertheless, as a way to assess gradual decline.

At T2, participants reported that they enjoyed communicating emotions by means
of the 'jewelry' and the auras. They exchanged emotions multiple times a day. *Love*

and *smiley* were used the most. Although they considered that presence and wellbeing awareness made them think more about each other, they reported feeling more connected during the third phase. Several times, an exchange would trigger a phone call. The granddaughters, for example, confirmed that the number of contacts increased during the third phase. The exchange of affective messages was also used as a reassurance mechanism. For example, the family learnt to expect every morning affective auras from the elder. A few times when this was missed from the elder, the family would take the initiative of sending her an emotion, and she would reply back. The elder also felt the same: '*If you see the smiley aura then you know that everything is fine*'. This feature created a level of obligation and expectation. If they receive an emotion, they felt they had to reply and if they sent one, they would expect a reply.

Participants were satisfied with the three emotions and thought that more would confuse the elder. There is, however, a need for more meaningful and short messages, *e.g., good morning, hello!*, and the ability to talk through the ambient display. The physical objects were preferred over screen-based emotions because the tangibility of the interaction was considered more fun and natural.

5   Discussion and Implications for Ambient Intelligent Systems

This paper summarizes several user studies that informed the design of Aurama, and that helped evaluate it as a design concept. They support several conclusions regarding the design of awareness systems for connecting elderly and their adult children:

Pre and post calamity. Our participants considered the function of the system more appropriate for frailer elderly than the elder mother of our case. This is consistent with Morris et al. [5], who derived a model of actual (decline) vs. perceived (denial) functioning of elderly. Our data helps elaborate the awareness needs pertaining to different stages of the model. It is only after an event (*e.g.,* a fall or heart attack) that target users would perceive an awareness system to be important to have and the awareness of wellbeing is the primary goal. On the other hand, for those elderly who have not experienced such events, the primary goal of a system should be providing new ways to communicate (*e.g.,* easy text messages, video chat, or affective messages), and wellbeing information kept secondary or as an additional feature.

Awareness of what? Children want to be aware of changes they cannot grasp easily, looking at long-term trends. They do not want to receive very detailed information, but just enough such that if there is some indication of change of patterns it would trigger them to call to obtain details. The aim is to trigger them to have more contacts and not replace them. They prefer that physiological measurements (*e.g.,* blood pressure, glucose levels) be sent to a doctor.

Positive and negative news. Typically, people do not want to share negative news. In the field trial, both parties refrained from sending the *cry* emotion preferring to not explicitly provide awareness of negative feelings. However, when the system assessed bad nights of sleep and informed the family, it was perceived positively, given the reactions that they provoked. Elderly find it nice that children care for them and their family appreciate being involved in their wellbeing.

Intertwining implicit with explicit awareness of wellbeing. While implicit awareness of presence and wellbeing can provide peace of mind, its combination with the explicit exchange of affective awareness can further foster reassurance and connectedness. We have seen the value of this in the extensive field trial.

Allow for 'symmetric sharing'. During the preliminary trials, the system was mainly one-way flow of awareness information (from elderly to child). This gave a sense of a monitoring 'big brother' system. Having a two-way flow of awareness is essential for acceptance. Although awareness needs may be different between elderly and their children, there should be some symmetry on sharing awareness information.

6   Conclusions

This paper has presented the design and evaluation of an awareness system to support awareness of elderly living alone. Two trials of two weeks each and an extensive trial of six months confirm earlier findings regarding the potential of this class of applications. We have shown the need to transcend momentary awareness of commotion, or mundane activities and to focus long-term trends in their elderly parents' wellbeing. To motivate the adoption of such a system and to enhance the connectedness between elderly and their children, our study suggests coupling awareness information with a bi-directional communication; an abstract symbolic mapping of emotions to colored auras was found appropriate in this design as it helped trigger direct contacts.

References

1. Consolvo, S., Roessler, P., Shelton, B.: The CareNet Display: Lessons Learned from an In Home Evaluation of an Ambient Display. In: Davies, N., Mynatt, E.D., Siio, I. (eds.) Ubi-Comp 2004. LNCS, vol. 3205, pp. 1–17. Springer, Heidelberg (2004)
2. Metaxas, G., Metin, B., Schneider, J., Markopoulos, P., Ruyter, B.: Diarist: Aging in Place with Semantically Enriched Narratives. In: Proc. Interact (2007)
3. Rowan, J., Mynatt, E.: Digital Family Portrait Field Trial: Support for Aging in Place. In: Proc. CHI 2005, pp. 521–530. ACM Press, New York (2005)
4. Aarts, E., Harwig, H., Schuurmans, M.: Ambient Intelligence. In: Denning, J. (ed.) The invisible future, pp. 235–250. McGraw-Hill, New York (2001)
5. Morris, M., Lundell, J., Dishman, E., Needham, B.: New Perspectives on Ubiquitous Computing from Ethnographic Study of Elders with Cognitive Decline. In: Dey, A.K., Schmidt, A., McCarthy, J.F. (eds.) UbiComp 2003. LNCS, vol. 2864, pp. 227–242. Springer, Heidelberg (2003)
6. van Baren, J., IJsselsteijn, W., Markopoulos, P., Romero, N., Ruyter, B.: Measuring affective benefits and costs of awareness systems supporting intimate social networks. In: Nijholt, A., Nishida, T. (eds.) CTIT workshop proc. series (2), Proc. of SID (2004)
7. Dadlani, P., Sinitsyn, A., Fontijn, W., Markopoulos, P.: Aurama: Caregiver awareness for living independently with an augmented picture frame display. To appear in: Artificial Intelligence & Society. Springer, Heidelberg (2010)

NICA: Natural Interaction with a Caring Agent

Berardina De Carolis, Irene Mazzotta, and Nicole Novielli

Dipartimento di Informatica – University of Bari
www.di.uniba.it

Abstract. Ambient Intelligence solutions may provide a great opportunity for elderly people to live longer at home. Assistance and care are delegated to the intelligence embedded in the environment. However, besides considering service-oriented response to the user needs, the assistance has to take into account the establishment of social relations. We propose the use of a robot NICA (as the name of the project *Natural Interaction with a Caring Agent*) acting as a caring assistant that provides a social interface with the smart home services. In this paper, we introduce the general architecture of the robot's "mind" and then we focus on the need to properly react to affective and socially oriented situations.

1 Introduction

The development of Ambient Intelligence (AmI) solutions that provide assistance to elderly people in order to improve their quality of life at home is a very fervid research field [1,2]. In this vision, assistance and care are delegated to the intelligence embedded in the environment. Obviously, technology should not represent a further obstacle in achieving the user goals and therefore, besides providing efficient infrastructures for managing domestic automated services, it is necessary to put the emphasis on human-technology interaction. The environment should provide an easy and natural interface in order to make service fruition effective and adapted to the user needs. We propose the use of a robot NICA (as the name of the project *Natural Interaction with a Caring Agent*) aiming at increasing the quality of life by acting as a social interface between the user and the home services. NICA, combining the interpretation of the user moves (sentences, actions, etc.) and sensors data, provides proactively and reactively the needed assistance. The level of assistance, however, has to take into account not only service provision but also the establishment of social relations. Social and affective factors become even more relevant when the system has to be used by elderly people since they need not only service-oriented assistance but also a friendly companion [3].

In this paper we present the general architecture of NICA that, acting as a mediator between the user and the environment, provides a natural interface to Smart Home Environment (SHE) services establishing, also, a social relation with the user. We focus on the integration of a social and affective reactive layer in the robot deliberative architecture. To test our approach we decided to use LegoMindStorm for embodying NICA and at present we simulate the interaction with the user and the environment using a simulation tool and the robot is acting in a "toy" house.

M. Tscheligi et al. (Eds.): AmI 2009, LNCS 5859, pp. 159–163, 2009.

2   Learning from Human Caregivers

To define and implement feasible behaviours of NICA, we started from real data. To collect them we asked two families in a similar situation to record the experience of two human caregivers about the assistance of two elder women affected by chronic diseases during a period of one month. Both women lived alone, they had a son/daughter living in another town, which could intervene only in case of need and for solving relevant medical and logistic problems. Everyday the caregiver had to write on her paper-diary two kinds of information: i) the schedule of the daily tasks and ii) the relevant events of the day (Table 1).

Table 1. Two entries from the diary

time	event		reason	action	affective action
10.45	Maria	is	medical	I go toward Maria and	encourage
	worried		visit	ask about her state.	
11.00	-		medical	I call the daughter to	-
			visit	remind her.	

From these data we extracted knowledge needed to build the reasoning strategies of the robot, to try to make it behave as a human caregiver. In particular, this labelled corpus of about 900 entries was used for understanding which were the events and context conditions relevant to goal and action triggering and learning causal relation among data and for determining the possible action plans. Then, starting from this experience we depicted the following scenario to test our agent framework:

"Maria is an elder woman living alone in her smart house equipped with smart sensors and devices typical of an AmI system. She suffers of a serious form of diabetes and a mild form of heart disease. Her daughter lives in another town and she is quite busy. NICA has the role of taking care of Maria. One day Maria has to go to the doctor for discussing results of blood tests. NICA's plan includes the following actions: to remember Maria about the appointment, to suggest about the dressing according to the weather situation, and to call her daughter to remember to go to get Maria to the doctor. After these, NICA has to ask to the smart phone to send a remind message to the daughter. Suddenly Maria, sitting on a chair waiting for her daughter, starts whispering and moaning. NICA approaches the woman and asks about her complaints, encouraging with appropriate sentences."

Working on a simulation of this scenario let us abstracting from many technological issues that are outside the scope of this paper. Instead, in this scenario, we want to outline the importance of integrating the social aspects of taking care of a person with service-oriented assistance.

3   Overview of NICA's Architecture

NICA is based on the BDI model and the goal processing cycle is a simplification of the model presented in Castelfranchi and Paglieri [4] and is based on the following steps: PERCEPTION, INTERPRETATION, GOAL ACTIVATION, EVALUATION and CHECKING, PLANNING and EXECUTION .

NICA's mental state uses reasons on and stores different types knowledge:

- the **World Model** that represents a set of relevant beliefs about context.
- the **User Model** that contains the representation of user's beliefs. For example, long terms factors concern user stable data (i.e. sex, age, chronicle diseases, allergies, main personality traits, interests, etc.) and short term factors concerns the current user's situation, physical and affective state, health conditions, recognized goals etc.
- the **ToDoList** that represents the agenda of scheduled daily activities that should be performed by the user. This agenda is planned everyday and it is revised when new events have to be scheduled (i.e. an appointment is postponed, etc.).
- the **Agent Social Memory** stores structured information about feelings associated with an event. It holds not only information about when, what and how an event happened, but also a `valence' tag. It is used to learn relations about events and the user affective state. The importance of this feature at the aim of establishing empathy with the elder person was outlined several times by the human caregivers during the data collection phase.

As the agent reasons and updates beliefs, infers goals, plans actions and executes them, it keeps an image of this process in its mental state where we represent *actions* to be performed in the environment (i.e. Administer(NICA drug)), *communicative actions*(i.e. Remind(NICA USER Take(drug))), *properties of objects or states, predicates* (i.e. Feel(U,sad)), *Beliefs, Intentions, Persistent and Contingent Goals. Persistent goals* never change because denotes the agent's nature, its mission, and guide its reasoning (i.e. keep the wellness of the user). Their achievement is then interleaved with the achievement of contingent *goals* that are triggered by the situation. Since uncertainty is typical of this we indicate in the representation of beliefs, intentions and goals their probability to be true.

3.1 Perception and Interpretation

The PERCEPTION phase allows collecting data from sensors present in the environment and to handle the user input (speech or actions in the environment). These data are then sent messages to the INTERPRETATION Metareasoner. This module evaluates changes in the world and user state that are relevant to the robot reasoning. The received messages are then transformed into a set of beliefs that are evaluated and stored in the agent's mental state. In order to handle the goal processing steps, these beliefs are classified into the agent mental state as:

Maintenance Beliefs: these beliefs support P-GOALs and must be kept true with a high level of certainty in order to support the mission and motivations of the agent.

Triggers Beliefs: this set stores beliefs that denote changes in the world, after the belief revision that may trigger new contingent goals.

Preference Beliefs: in this set are stored beliefs that indicate a preference about a certain action over another one.

Cost Beliefs: represents costs in terms of time, resources, etc. useful for the estimation of the utility of goals or plans.

3.2 Goal Triggering and Planning

In the considered scenario we set the persistent goals shown in Table 2. These goals are the ones that human caregivers indicated as important in their daily assistance.

Table 2. Persistent goals considered in the scenario

persistent goal	Maintance beliefs supporting goals
keep the well-ness of the user	(P-GOAL N (BEL N (Feel(U,comfort))))
	(P-GOAL N (BEL N (Has(U,normal(health_state)))))
	(P-GOAL N (BEL N NOT(Is(U,Negative(affective_state)))))
schedule daily ToDoList	(P-GOAL N (Int-To-Do N Plan(N ToDoList)))
execute actions in ToDoList	FORALL z element of ToDoList:
	(P-GOAL N (Intend-To_Do N z))

The goal processing of the agent is constituted by different steps. The first one is Goal ACTIVATION. In this phase, goals are triggered on the bases of the current beliefs and these can be then pursued after the EVALUATION step.

Indeed this phase uses a reasoning model that allows to relate beliefs stored in the agent's mental state with the activation of the goals. Possible goals belong to two categories: service-oriented task execution and socio-emotional related goals.

This step is based upon a mixed model: starting from the beliefs about the current state and from the agent's persistent goals, using a set of reasoning rules the model selects the influence diagrams (ID) [5] describing the possible contingent goals in the current context. In particular it models the relation between goals, random uncertain quantities (e.g. context situation) and values (e.g. utility of the goal).

Figure 1 shows the high-level diagram used for deciding the utility of the possible affective goals triggered by the situation. **Square box** denotes the decision of selecting a goal G at time t_i; **round nodes** are chance variables denoting the situation before (t_i) deciding to achieve one of the goals and after (t_{i+1}); **rhombus nodes** represent the utility deriving from an improvement in the user affective state when G is selected and the correspondent plan will be executed.

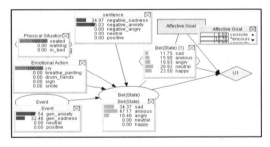

Fig. 1. An example of goal activation

Each activated goal will have then a utility defining how much it is worth to be pursued. Then, the Evaluation Phase decides whether or not active goals can in principle be pursued, according to the beliefs in the mental state of the user. For example conflicts, resources etc, are checked. After this checking, goals with the maximum utility are selected. When there are goals of the same type, it is possible to use preferences or priority rules. The example shown in Figure 1 describes how the goal triggering model works in the scenario described previously: Maria is crying and the event *"going to the doctor"* generates anxiety in Maria. Moreover, the linguistic and prosodic features of the spoken sentence denote a high level anxiety. NICA chooses to activate the "encourage" goal, because it is the one with the higher utility since it let to raise the wellness level of the affective state of the user, leading to a probable lowering of the probability of being sad and anxious and to a raising of the probability of being in a normal state. Once a goal has been selected, actions are planned selecting the plan from a library. Planning of service-oriented actions, related to the ToDoList, is made using plans that allow calling the services provided by the smart home. Planning of social and affective actions is made using plans that actually drive the communicative behaviour of NICA. Figure 2 illustrates an example of conditional instantiated plan.

```
<Plan Name="Encourage">
<SelectCond> <Cond var="affective_goal" value="encourage"\>
<Body>
<Act name="Move" to="Maria" />
<Cond var="know_reason" p-down="0" p-up="0,49">
<Act name="Ask" to="Maria" var="Why(Maria,anxious)"/>
</Cond>
<Cond var="know_reason" p-down="0,5" p-up="1">
<Act name="Inform" to="Maria" var="Understand(NICA,MARIA)"/>
</Cond>
<Act name="Express" to="Maria" var="Encourage(NICA,MARIA)"/>
<Act name="Inform" to="Maria" var="WhatToDo(MARIA)"/>
...
```

Fig. 2. A portion of instantiated plan

4   Conclusion and Future Work

Research presented in this paper has been developed in the context of the NICA project. NICA is a social robot acting as a caring assistant for elderly people living in a smart home. Besides performing service-oriented tasks, the robot has to establish a social relation with the user so as to enforce trust and confidence. In this paper we have presented an approach to planning social and affective reactions in the robot behaviour. This approach is based on the integration of logical rules, probabilistic models and conditional plans. The first results are encouraging, however we did not have yet the possibility to evaluate the system with real users. In this phase of the project we performed a quantitative evaluation of the decisions and plans executed by the agent compared to the behaviours of human caregivers collected in the initial phase of the project. Results of the evaluation indicate that the system performance is quite good since the percentage of pattern matching between robot and human actions in the dataset is 79. At the moment we are testing and refining the reasoning strategies of the robot in order to improve its performance.

References

1. McFadden, T., Indulska, J.: Context-aware Environments for Independent Living. In: Proceedings of 3rd National Conference of Emerging Researchers in Ageing, ERA 2004 (2004)
2. Consolvo, S., Roessler, P., Shelton, B.E.: The CareNet display: Lessons learned from an in home evaluation of an ambient display. In: Davies, N., Mynatt, E.D., Siio, I. (eds.) UbiComp 2004. LNCS, vol. 3205, pp. 1–17. Springer, Heidelberg (2004)
3. Reeves, B., Nass, C.: The media equation: how people treat computers, television, and new media like real people and places. Cambridge University Press, New York (1996)
4. Castelfranchi, C.C., Paglieri, F.: The role of beliefs in goal dynamics: Prolegomena to a constructive theory of intentions. Synthese 155, 237–263 (2007)
5. Jensen, F.V.: Bayesian Networks and Decision Graphs. Statistics for engineering and information

Ambient Rabbits
Likeability of Embodied Ambient Displays

Thomas Mirlacher, Roland Buchner, Florian Förster,
Astrid Weiss, and Manfred Tscheligi

ICT&S Center, University of Salzburg
Sigmund-Haffner-Gasse 18, 5020 Salzburg, Austria
{thomas.mirlacher,roland.buchner,florian.foerster2}@sbg.ac.at,
{astrid.weiss,manfred.tscheligi}@sbg.ac.at

Abstract. This paper discusses the possibility of using embodied Ambient Displays for presenting information in a public setting. For embodying an Ambient Display, a Nabaztag rabbit was used, the information displayed was a weather forecast. Throughout four weeks of alternating traditional visual Ambient Displays and Nabaztag testing, differences and commonalities in terms of perceived usability and likeability have been investigated. Special focus has been put on the likeability and comprehension differences. Results show a correlation between perceived usability and likeability for the traditional Ambient Display as well as a better comprehension over time for both Ambient Displays. However, significant differences in terms of perceived usability and likeability could only be revealed for the traditional Ambient Displays.

Keywords: Ambient Intelligence, Ambient Display, Ambient Information System, Embodied Display.

1 Introduction

Since Weiser's groundbreaking article about calm computing [1], Ambient Intelligence (AmI) is on the rise, and with it Ambient Displays. The development of Ambient Displays historically includes many different technologies and naming conventions. Ubiquitous-, Disappearing-, Tangible-, and Pervasive-computing describe just a handful of the technologies and concepts, which gave birth to AmI and Ambient Displays. Ishii et. al [2], Matthews et. al [3], Stasko et. al [4], Mankoff et. al [5] and others came up with their own definition. In this paper however, we use the term Ambient Displays interchangeable with Ambient Information System (AIS) as defined by Mankoff et. al [5]:

"Ambient Displays are abstract and aesthetic peripheral displays portraying non-critical information on the periphery of a user's attention."

Ambient Displays are a way to produce cues in the environment (see Tscheligi et. al [6]). Specifically, visual Ambient Displays are designed to visualize information, which is not to be explicitly used by users, but perceived in their periphery.

M. Tscheligi et al. (Eds.): AmI 2009, LNCS 5859, pp. 164–173, 2009.

What happens if these Ambient Displays are not simple screens or colors on the wall, but represented as physical entities to the spectator? This paper raises this question and presents a study comparing perceived usability and likeability of traditional visual Ambient Displays with a physical embodied display, showing the same kind of information.

Fig. 1. Nabaztag - a smart rabbit

For the study, we used a Nabaztag rabbit as physical embodied entity (see Figure 1). The Nabaztag is capable of producing sound, visual cues through multicolored LEDs as well as physical information by (re-)positioning of its ears. For the sake of comparability, an abstract display has been designed in a way to present information similar to its embodied counterpart (see Figure 2). The information displayed in both Ambient Displays was a two-day weather forecast in a public setting. Following hypothesis are going to be evaluated by this paper:

- H1: The likeability of the Nabaztag is higher than the one of an Ambient Display presented on a traditional display.
- H2: Likeability influences the perception of information.
- H3: The longer the experiment lasts, the easier it is for participants to interpret the display.

2   Related Work

There are many examples of visual Ambient Displays, presenting a wide variety of information. It seems that embodied Ambient Displays are not covered in depth by literature, nevertheless, general concepts for designing Ambient Displays and methods for evaluating them can be applied. This section examines some of the foundations, used for the research this paper depends on.

Selecting Data. Neely et. al [7] describe several criteria for choosing suitable data. The five characteristics for Ambient Displays, as highlighted by them are: (1) Precision (2) Criticality (3) Periodicity (4) Interpretability (5) Self Descriptiveness.

Design. The design for the PC Display has been largely restricted by the physical properties of the Nabaztag. Nevertheless, for designing the interfaces, we reused the goals stated by Jafarinaimi et. al [8]. These goals are: (1) Abstract - display the information in a rather abstract way, far away from raw sensor data and a really concrete depiction of the information. (2) Non-intrusive - avoid pollution of the room, either by noise produced by the Ambient Displays (which would also explicitly draw the attention of the user to the display), nor by any visual cues distracting the user. (3) Public - this can be a problem with Ambient Displays when the display adjusts to the people in the environment, and would potentially display private information. (4) Aesthetic - the design of the display and the presentation of the information should follow aesthetic rules. Since we did not have any control over the shape nor type of presentation of the Nabaztag, we tried to apply the same design principles used on the Nabaztag, presenting the same information in a similar manner on a tablet PC.

Evaluation. Hazlewood et. al organized a workshop about AIS [9]. The topics, amongst others, included examples of heuristics, taxonomies and design principles as well as appropriate methods for evaluating Ambient Information Systems. Neely et. al [10] noted, factors needed for evaluating Ambient Displays cannot be reproduced in a lab setting, but field studies are challenging as well. As they remarked, a single approach for evaluating every AmI scenario is unrealistic, so we combined multiple approaches, which fit our problem best.

As suggested by Holmquist[11], we also evaluated the comprehension of Ambient Displays. This allows finding out more about: (1) *That* information is visualized (2) *What* kind of information is visualized (3) *How* the information is visualized For more detailed results on comprehension, see Figure 7.

Pousman et. al [12] stated the existence of two paradigms: the functionalist and the social relativist research paradigm. We tend to focus on the more computer science orientated side - the functionalist approach. This approach includes following items in the evaluation of the Ambient Display. (1) Heightened Awareness - through the availability of information through opportunistic glances. (2) Time Saving - convenient for users, providing information without the need to go somewhere else. (3) Anxiety/Stress - no need for the user to find and monitor the information by himself, the Ambient Display takes care of that, and provides the information whenever needed. (4) Distraction of presentation - an Ambient Display saves time and decreases anxiety and stress, and should not distract a user from her daily business - it should provide information in the background or periphery. (5) Learnability of mappings representations - a system that remains hard to learn and understand cannot be a success.

3   Study Setup

For this study, two kinds of displays were used. A tablet PC as visual Ambient Display and a Nabaztag as embodied Ambient Display. The study was conducted at the ICT&S Center at the University of Salzburg. We chose the lounge as the place to install the display as it is frequented by the 45 people working at the institute. People meet there in order to have breakfast, lunch, they sometimes choose it as alternative workplace or gather for meetings.

3.1   Design of the Ambient Information

We began the study with a brainstorming phase on what information should be presented via the two Ambient Displays. Literature research and evaluation of different displays helped to gathered ideas. Finally, we decided to go with an ambient weather forecast service as we judged this information most relevant for the different people attending the lounge. In order to be able to compare the perception of a traditional Ambient Display with an embodied display, the same information was presented on both (see Figure 2).

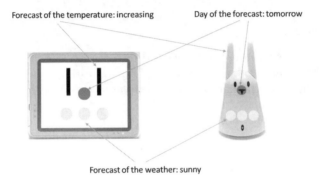

Fig. 2. Tablet PC displaying the weather forecast for tomorrow. The same forecast is shown at the right picture with the Nabaztag.

As foundation for the information design, Nabaztag's weather forecast service was used. It provides a forecast for the next few hours using Nabaztag's light language. We modified (simplified) the light language, added information and evaluated our design during a pretest (details from the pre-test phase can be found in 3.2). The final information for the display consisted of three elements: (1) A light at the nose of the Nabaztag respectively in the middle of the display indicated the day the forecast was for: a red light indicated that the weather forecast was for tomorrow, while a purple light indicated the day after tomorrow. (2) Below, three lights in a row indicated the predicted weather condition (sunny, fair, cloudy, overcast, rain). The lights were blinking: three seconds visible and one second invisible. The blinking should provide a feedback to the audience that the Ambient Displays are "alive" or have a "heartbeat" - a fundamental requirement in natural communication.(3) The ears of the Nabaztag, respectively two bars on the traditional display indicated how the temperature would change in comparison to the current temperature. If the present day had 15 degrees and the temperature for tomorrow was 17 degrees, the cars or the two bars of the display were adjusted vertically.

The forecast continuously altered every 30 seconds between tomorrow and the day after tomorrow. Enough time to process the information by the people around the display.

As source of the weather forecast a website[1] providing a three-day forecast was chosen. If the website predicted light showers, the granularity of the displays allowed only to depict a rain condition. A forecast of both displays is shown in Figure 2, which depicts the prediction for tomorrow (the red dot), which should be sunny (three yellow dots) with increasing temperature (ears up on the Nabaztag or the two bars up on the display). For reasons of simplicity the display was updated manually every morning before the first person entered the lounge. For the tablet PC, a set of weather images was created and then loaded as a full screen presentation by a local Java application. For the Nabaztag, a perl script was used to indicate control of the rabbit and the weather information.

3.2   Procedure

The study consisted of a pre-test, followed by a four-week period of alternating Ambient Display and embodied Ambient Display testing. Due to the abstractness of how the weather-information was displayed, a codebook was provided to the participants and placed next to the display. Such an approach was also used by Shen et. al [13], providing bypassers a description of the display's content. In order to get information on how embodiment influenced users, the content of both codebooks was identical (see Figure 3, Figure 4).

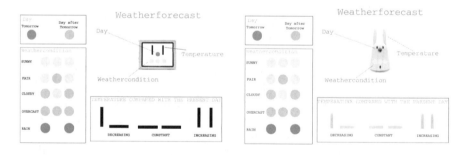

Fig. 3. Codebook for the tablet PC   **Fig. 4.** Codebook for the Nabaztag

Pretest. Before going into the field a pre-test was conducted for five workdays. The first design for the ambient information used in the pre-test included a forecast for the next three days as well an extensive number of possible weather conditions. Twelve people were asked to filled out a questionnaire (7(m) and 5(f),

---

[1] http://at.wetter.com/oesterreich/salzburg/ATAT30532.html

avg. age=30.8) after the pre-test week. It yielded information about usefulness and overall usability of the displayed information, and showed that people have enough interest in weather forecasts. The pre-test revealed that users had difficulties to understand the great variety of information. Only five out of twelve people (41.67%) could answer the comprehension question "Which weather is being displayed?" correctly. They remarked the high cognitive load of processing weather forecasts for more than two days in advance. This showed that a simplification was necessary. We therefore reduced the forecast to two days and redesigned the light language, reducing the granularity to five possible weather conditions.

Ambient Display Study. After redesigning the information displayed the actual study was started. It lasted for four weeks. In the first week (five work days, Monday to Friday) the tablet PC (see Figure 3) was placed in the lounge. In the following week the tablet PC was replaced by the Nabaztag. In the third week we put up the tablet PC, exchanging it in the fourth week once again by the Nabaztag. At the beginning of each follow up week, a questionnaire was handed out to the people regarding the display placed in the lounge the week before. This point in time was chosen so that people needed their long-term memory for the recollection part and had no possibility to look at either the display, the Nabaztag or the corresponding code-books while filling in the questionnaire. All in all 32 unique participants (14(m) and 18(f); from 24 to 36 years; mean age=28.5, SD=3.51), distributed over a period of four weeks, took part at the study.

3.3   Design of the Questionnaire

To investigate the differences in the perception of the traditional Ambient Display and the embodied Ambient Display, a questionnaire was designed addressing the factors: perceived usability, likeability, perceived usability, and comprehensibility. In order to measure the perceived usability of the system, six suitable questions from the System Usability Scale (SUS) questionnaire were extracted (see [14]). Likeability was measured by using the likeability part of [15]. The comprehension questions were: "Which information was being displayed?", "For which days was the weather predicted?", "Which weather is being predicted on this showcase picture?" Furthermore the questionnaire included questions on demographic data and usage behavior. In total the questionnaire consisted of 24 items, which had to be rated on a 5 point Likert-scale (1 = negative, 5 = positive) and eight additional open-ended questions.

4   Results and Discussion

In total 32 unique participants were interviewed with the questionnaire, which was adapted in wording to "Ambient Display" and "Nabaztag Rabbit" depending on the study week. Table 1 details the distribution of participants over the four weeks.

Table 1. Participant Distribution over the four weeks

Week	Participants	Gender	Mean Age (SD)
1	21	11(m) 10(f)	28.23 (3.39)
2	18	9(m) 9(f)	28.78 (4.08)
3	15	8(m) 7(f)	27.87 (3.68)
4	16	7(m) 9(f)	27.00 (2.94)

Twelve participants took part in only one week of the study, seven in two weeks, eight in three weeks and five participants in all four weeks. The first open-ended question asked in general which information was displayed. The data indicates that the displayed information (weather forecast) was intuitive for almost all participants (week1: 17 out of 21, week2: 15 out of 18, week3: 14 out 15, week4: 16 out of 16 identified the correct information). When asking participants how often they use the Ambient Display, a tendency could be determined (see Figure 5) that participants had the feeling that they used the embodied display (Week2 and Week4) more often than the traditional display (Week1 and Week3).

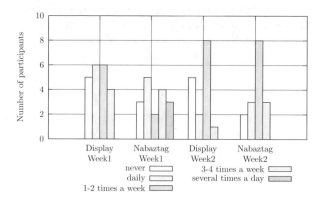

Fig. 5. Distribution of participants over time

Since the third study week none of the participants stated that they need the manual any longer to interpret the displayed information. Regarding the usage of the different displays in a public or private setting, minor differences between the traditional display and the Nabaztag could be observed. For private settings like the personal work place or at home participants rated the Nabaztag (work mean=2.94, SD=3.25; home mean=2.69, SD=3.00) better than the traditional display (work mean=1.86, SD=1.00; home mean=2.09, SD=1.00). However, the larger standard deviation for the Nabaztag indicates that participants answers were more heterogeneous than for the traditional display. Interestingly, participants perceived the traditional display as slightly more suitable for a public place, than the Nabaztag (display mean=2.14, SD=2.00; Nabaztag mean=1.93, SD=1.5). Questions regarding the type of information participants experienced as suitable for the different types of displays also revealed an interesting result. Participants would prefer personalized context aware information more for the embodied (mean=3.25, SD=2.31) than for the traditional display (mean=2.31, SD=2.50), but for personalized private information they would prefer the traditional Ambient Display (mean=2.31, SD=1.00) versus the embodied Ambient Display (mean=1.69, SD=1.00). However, both differences are not significant regarding a t-test for independent samples.

Likeability was one important factor concerning the distinction between the two kinds of displays. Our likeability questionnaire resulted in a Cronbach α of 0.884, which allows to conclude that the questionnaire has sufficient internal consistency reliability. Hereby, a t-test between likeability of the tablet PC display and the Nabaztag shows a significant difference. The difference could be confirmed through a non-parametric Wilcoxon-Test, through the ratio Z=-2.03 (p<.05), which confirms the hypothesis "The likeability of the Nabaztag is higher than the one of an Ambient Display presented on a traditional display". Figure 6 depicts the relative difference of the likeability between tablet PC and Nabaztag.

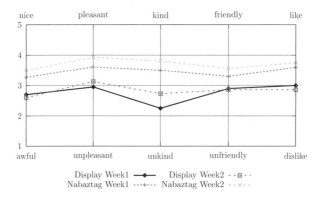

Fig. 6. Comparison of the likeability between traditional display and Nabaztag

In order to measure the perceived usability of both systems, the extracted question of the SUS were cross checked with Cronbach's α test, resulting in a value of 0.98. This discloses a very high internal consistency reliability of the remaining SUS questions. As one goal of the study was to find out if embodiment influences the perception of an Ambient Display, Spearmans ρ between the perceived usability and the likeability of both systems was calculated. Interestingly, the test reveals a strong correlation (r=0.823, significance p<.05) between the likeability of the display and its perceived usability. This allows the conclusion for the tablet PC, that a bad perceived usability leads to a low likeability of the display and good perceived usability would increase likeability ratings. Spearmans ρ resulted in -0.75 (significance p<.05), ruling out accidental or random results. Although the Nabaztag was rated poorer in terms of usability, the relative likeability is still higher than the displays. This leads to the conclusion that a lower perceived usability has no influence on the likeability of the Nabaztag. An explanation is that people see the display more as a tool, whereas the Nabaztag as a toy. The results of the study also confirmed that the longer the study lasted, the better the people could interpret the information of both displays. Figure 7 displays the comprehension distributed over the four weeks of the study.

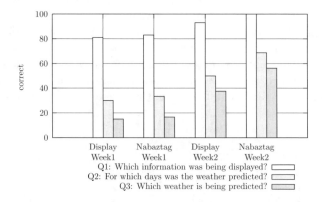

Fig. 7. Comprehension during the duration of the study

5   Conclusions and Future Work

Still a problem is the determination of the usability of an Ambient Display, since it's not directly or explicitly used - so classic usability testing cannot be applied. Due to the small sample size and an even smaller number of participants taking part for the full length of the study, side effects cannot be ruled out. The study should be with more participants, for a longer period of time (as proposed by Hazlewood et. al [16]) and in different settings. More participants and a longer runtime could result in a higher significance rating.

Ambient Displays in general have been accepted for presenting information in a public setting, while embodied Ambient Displays has been rated more positive. In a future iteration of the prototype display, the presentation should be somewhat simplified, so the representation of the data is even more intuitive and the codebook could be left out all together. Results show a correlation between perceived usability and likeability of Ambient Displays. Further studies should deepen the insight into this area, and should also shed light into age and gender differences.

References

1. Weiser, M.: The computer for the 21st century. Scientific American 265(3), 94–104 (1991)
2. Ishii, H., Ullmer, B.: Tangible bits: towards seamless interfaces between people, bits and atoms. In: CHI 1997, pp. 234–241. ACM Press, New York (1997)
3. Matthews, T., Dey, A.K., Mankoff, J., Carter, S., Rattenbury, T.: A toolkit for managing user attention in peripheral displays. In: UIST 2004, pp. 247–256. ACM, New York (2004)
4. Stasko, J., Doo, M., Dorn, B., Plaue, C.: Explorations and experiences with ambient information systems. In: Workshop on Ambient Information Systems at Pervasive 2007, May 2007, pp. 36–41 (2007)
5. Mankoff, J., Dey, A.K., Hsieh, G., Kientz, J., Lederer, S., Ames, M.: Heuristic evaluation of ambient displays. In: CHI 2003, pp. 169–176. ACM, New York (2003)
6. Tscheligi, M., Reitberger, W., Obermair, C., Ploderer, B.: perCues: Trails of Persuasion for Ambient Intelligence. In: IJsselsteijn, W.A., de Kort, Y.A.W., Midden, C., Eggen, B., van den Hoven, E. (eds.) PERSUASIVE 2006. LNCS, vol. 3962, pp. 203–206. Springer, Heidelberg (2006)
7. Neely, S., Stevenson, G., Nixon, P.: Assessing the suitability of context information for ambient displays. In: Workshop Ambient Information Systems at Pervasive 2007, May 2007. CEUR Workshop, CEUR-WS.org, vol. 254 (2007)
8. Jafarinaimi, N., Forlizzi, J., Hurst, A., Zimmerman, J.: Breakaway: an ambient display designed to change human behavior. In: CHI 2005, pp. 1945–1948. ACM, New York (2005)
9. Hazlewood, W.R., Coyle, L., Pousman, Z., Kyung Lim, Y.: Ambient Information Systems 2008 - Introduction. In: 2nd Workshop on Ambient Information Systems, September 2008. CEUR Workshop, vol. 402 (2008)
10. Neely, S., Stevenson, G., Kray, C., Mulder, I., Connelly, K., Siek, K.A.: Evaluating pervasive and ubiquitous systems. IEEE Pervasive Computing 7(3), 85–88 (2008)
11. Holmquist, L.E.: Evaluating the comprehension of ambient displays. In: CHI 2004: Extended abstracts, pp. 1545–1545. ACM, New York (2004)
12. Pousman, Z., Stasko, J.: Ambient Information Systems: Evaluation in Two Paradigms. In: Workshop Ambient Information Systems at Pervasive 2007, May 2007, pp. 25–29 (2007)
13. Shen, X., Eades, P., Hong, S., Moere, A.V.: Intrusive and non-intrusive evaluation of ambient displays. In: Workshop Ambient Information Systems at Pervasive 2007, May 2007. CEUR Workshop, vol. 254 (2007)
14. Brooke, J.: SUS: A 'quick and dirty' usability scale. In: Usability Evaluation in Industry, pp. 189–194. Taylor & Francis, Abington (1996)
15. Bartneck, C., Croft, E., Kulic, D.: Measuring the anthropomorphism, animacy, likeability, perceived intelligence and perceived safety of robots. In: Metrics for HRI Workshop, Technical Report 471, University of Hertfordshire, pp. 37–44 (2008)
16. Hazlewood, W.R., Connelly, K., Makice, K., Lim, Y.k.: Exploring evaluation methods for ambient information systems. In: CHI 2008, pp. 2973–2978. ACM, New York (2008)

Contextual Interaction Design:
The Case of Pause Buddy

David V. Keyson and Hannah J. Doff-Ottens

ID-StudioLab,
Faculty of Industrial Design Engineering, Delft University of Technology
Landbergstraat 15, 2628 CE, Delft, The Netherlands
D.V.Keyson@tudelft.nl, h.j.doff@hnnh.eu
http://studiolab.io.tudelft.nl/scid/

Abstract. This paper describes a range of design techniques which have been elaborated upon by Industrial Designers to create novel interactive products in which context and social interaction play a central role in the user experience. The techniques described here can be broadly grouped under Context Mapping and Research through Design. The methods are presented as part of a design process, from "fuzzy front end" to a working field prototype. To illustrate how the methods can be applied, the design of a prototype product that was developed to reduce office stress by stimulating short breaks and social interaction pauses is described. The results of a field study are reported following by a reflection on the value of applied design methods.

Keywords: Context Mapping, Research through Design.

1 Background

In the current paper a design study called Pause Buddy, is presented which focused on how to reduce office stress by encouraging social interaction through a monitoring device. The design research was conducted as part of a project sponsored by the Dutch Ministry of Finance called Smart Surroundings (www.smart-surroundings.org). A central aim of the project work package on interaction design, was to consider how new interactive technology and sensors could be used to improve well being in the workplace.

In terms of office-related stress, working under a high mental workload for a prolonged period of time can be detrimental for an individual's well-being and may eventually lead to several (psycho)somatic complaints, e.g. shoulder-pain, excessive fatigue, etc. [1]. Furthermore, office worker absence relating to illness is a major economic issue for companies in the Netherlands. Over 12% of reported office worker absence can be attributed to mental and psychological factors. According to the Dutch Central Bureau of Statistics, some 30000 employees are declared to be unfit for work every year as a result of stress (www.cbs.nl). From this group 16% of the complaints are directly related to repetitive strain injury (RSI). In this context, the Dutch government is actively pursing research aimed at reducing stress in the work environment [2].

M. Tscheligi et al. (Eds.): AmI 2009, LNCS 5859, pp. 174–185, 2009.

Many approaches towards reducing office stress focus on the physical side of monitoring and feedback, such as work pace tools, workplace exercise programs, feedback of physiological information, including galvanic skin conductivity and skin temperature (e.g., using the Logisens mouse), and electronic coaches or a mouse that provides tactile feedback after a certain time threshold (e.g., Hoverstop Mouse). However examples of products that trigger timely social interaction pauses, as a means to reduce office related stress, are less common. Office buildings may include a relaxation area which has been shown to reduce stress [3] or at least a coffee corner where colleagues can mingle with each other. Social support has been shown to be an important factor in coping with stress [4], including regular informal contacts in the workplace [5].

In developing context rich products and services it is essential to examine in depth the user context of interaction towards creating an experience that fits in daily routines. While there is no consensus of the definition of 'experience', the notion that experiences are holistic, situated and constructed [6] has held the test of time. The user experience of a product does not exist in a vacuum, but rather involves the dynamic relationship between people, places and objects [7]. Pleasure in interaction directly impacts the use experience [8]. Methods towards understanding the user experience such as observations, field visits, interviews, focus groups, and applied ethnography have been applied in a range of fields. More recently design research methods have emerged from the design discipline itself, such as cultural probes and generative techniques [9]. Cultural probes [10], design probes [11] and generative techniques [12] make use of a designer's skill in order to create eliciting assignments. Context mapping combines these research methods to generate rich experience information, while involving a small number of representative subjects. The technique is in particular valuable in industry where time to market is of the essence and only a limited number of subjects might be available to the design team. In terms of gaining insight into what people say, do and know or feel, it maps different methods to different types of desired knowledge [9] (see Figure 1). In the case study described below context mapping was deployed. The key steps to context mapping are preparation, sensitization, sessions, analysis, sharing, and conceptualization. Preparation involves setting a well-defined goal, sensitizing takes place prior to sessions with users and typically involves sending a package of probes to record daily routines of interest. During the sessions the users 'make' things such as collages, storylines, 3D models to

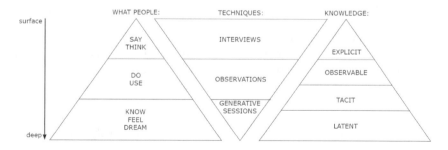

Fig. 1. Different levels of knowledge are accessed by different methods [9]

express their experiences along with information collected by themselves using the sensitizing tools. In stage 4, the design research analyzes the data, and form categories and models. Finally, in the conceptualization phase the analyzed material is used as deep user insights to generate product or service concepts [9].

2 Case Study: Pause Buddy

Based upon an extensive review of literature on office related stress, five key considerations for Pause Buddy were identified, namely:

- Encourage social interaction pauses in the workplace
- Include a sense of empathy in Pause Buddy, given relation agents as computational artifacts, result in a higher degree of trust and care given postural and facial cues [13].
- Provide a rich form of multimodal interaction while balancing for control to create an engaging product [14].
- Create a sense of awareness for the need to pause in an unobtrusive manner. Given the difficulties of measuring negative stress reliably, enable the user to set their own boundary conditions for work pauses based on predefined time intervals and to ignore pause cues. Expect users to take micro pauses of a few seconds without requiring prompting [15].

3 Procedure

In developing Pause Buddy, context mapping was applied to gain an insight into the context of the office worker faced with stress. The study consisted of the following four steps: (1) a sensitizing step, (2) creative sessions, (3) concept generation, and (4) user testing.

Eight target users were selected for the study. Participant 1 and 2 were employed at companies with more than 100 people, participants 3, 4 and 5 worked at small companies with the remaining three working in companies of about 40 employees. Each participant was asked to complete a Dutch version of the Spielberger State-Trait Anxiety Index (STAI) [16], to quantify individual degree of anxiety proneness.

3.1 Sensitizing Step

Following an initial pilot study a box was given to each participant with exercises spread over the course of a working week (Figure 2). The box contained: (a) a disposable photo camera, removed from packaging and modified with a sticker of a clock on the back of the camera. The participants were encouraged to use the camera to take pictures to help clarify their responses, including pictures of stressful and relaxing moments in their working and living environments, (b) a "stress card" (Figure 3) with words that could be encircled to show causes of stress and daily irritations at work and a "relax card" with words that could be circled to show what helps to relax at home and to relax at work , (c) a time line card in which participants were asked to indicate what activities they did during the course of a typical chosen work day and how they would have liked to have spent their time during that same day and (d) a diary booklet with several items including a list in which subjects were asked to mark the top three of nine possible product wishes or write their own wishes for an ideal stress relieving product. Within the diary the participants were asked to indicate where physical stress was felt, explain the origin, and to indicate how they deal with it (Figure 4). The last day of the diary, contained instructions for the participants to create a drawing of their ideal stress relieving product, and the resulting emotion the product should trigger, during the course of the week using the diary. They were instructed to use stickers or other visual materials and explain in text their idea.

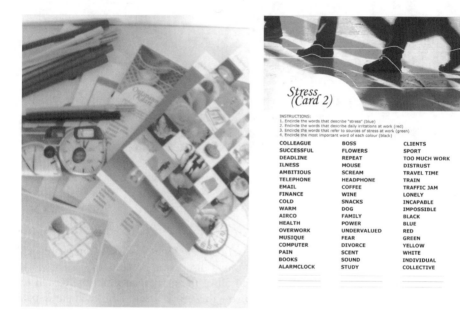

Fig. 2. Probe package, containing disposable camera, stickers, diary, and the time, relax, and stress cards as well as pens

Fig. 3. Participants were instructed to fill in a Relax and Stress card to indicate ways to rest at home and at work and types and causes of stress at work, as one of the cultural probe exercise

The most common words marked in the stress card were "deadline" and "workload" with health being the main implication. In terms of relaxation, the words "humor" and "friends" were circled most frequently. Note, for the group of eight participants, the STAI values for anxiety proneness average was 34.6 (std 4.3) which is "normal" according to the index.

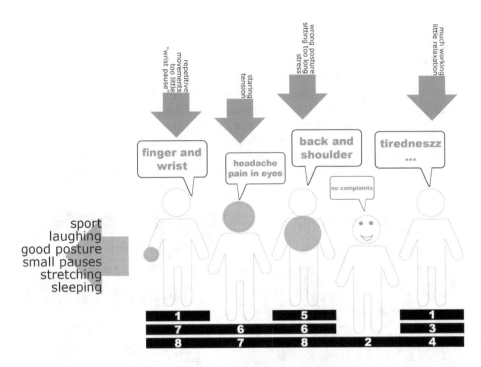

Fig. 4. The cultural probe included a card in which participants were instructed to indicate on a manikin where they felt physical stress and the related cause

3.2 Creative Sessions

Following the sensitizing exercises as described above creative sessions were held with four participants. During a 50 minute long discussion on stressors in the workplace and personal coping mechanism with all of the participants and the design researcher, comments were annotated. Following this group discussion, each participant was encouraged to sketch themselves in relation to how they experience and cope with stress. A second discussion was held lasting 53 minutes. The participants were then giving clay and materials and asked to form a stress reducer in a creative session (Figure 5). For example one of the participants formed a body like object that could monitor stress and give feedback based on changes in posture. The subsequent group discussion on the mockups ran for about 90 minutes, and all of the comments per participants were annotated for later analysis.

3.3 Analysis

The results from the diary exercise in which participants were asked to express their desired stress relieving product emotion were visually summarized as a tree of related terms, with most frequently occurring words being portrayed larger graphically.

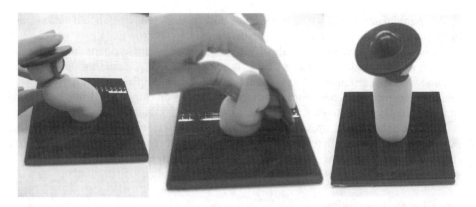

Fig. 5. One of the forms developed by a participant in the creative session to convey stress by form posture

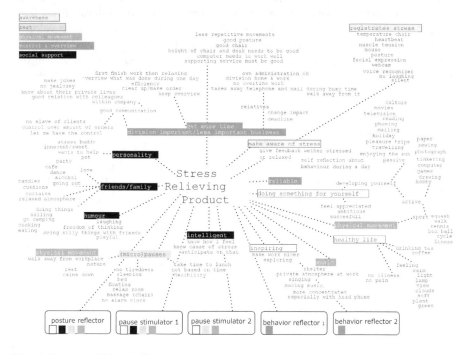

Fig. 6. A range of ideas falling under each of the five colour coded categories of stress reduction were plotted in a mind map by the design researcher

The participants stated wishes relating to how a stress relieving should act, as one of the diary exercises, were also graphically mapped.

To combine and characterize all of the qualitative insights on participant experiences in relation to dealing with office stress, four fictional personas groupings were developed, characterizing the input from each of the participants. Each persona was described in terms of their work environment, spare time individual activities and spare time collective activities, in relation to stress and coping mechanisms.

The five criteria for a stress reducing product derived from the literature review as mentioned above were ranked according to frequency of reporting, derived during the stages of context mapping. The ranking, from highest to lowest was as follows: (1) social support, (2) rest, (3) physical movement, (4) control and (5) awareness.

3.4 Concept Generation

Following the analysis phase a number of potential ideas falling under each of the categories were plotted in a mind map (Figure 6). The design researcher then started creating sketches of product ideas such as the posture reflector and pause stimulator, which would collapse when a worker sits longer than a user-defined threshold without taking a break or chatting with a colleague. Several prototype ideas were developed in the lab and tested in a local design lab with staff and students during working hours. Designs were manipulated remotely by the design researcher working in the lab. The participants were instructed to work as usual. The final resulting concept developed was given the name Pause Buddy.

4 Pause Buddy Design

The Pause Buddy was constructed as a round ball with LEDs and limited range Bluetooth technology with signal strength detection to detect if another Pause Buddy is in the vicinity of 50 cm. The basic prototype was rapidly built using an Arduino board and MAX MSP to record Pause Buddy usage events, once the Pause Buddy was placed back in the docking station. Furthermore, the Pause Buddy units each contained a small motor with an offset-weight on the shaft to create a vibration in the ball. The device shows one blinking red LED light to indicate that the user needs to take a pause of at least 3 minutes. The user can decide whether or not to pause alone or with someone else. If the user does not react to Pause Buddy after 15 minutes it begins to vibrate and displays three blinking red lights. Based on a user defined threshold the pause buddy can indicate it is time to take a social interaction break via a yellow emitting light.

5 User Testing Results

Three usage scenarios storyboards were developed to test the Pause Buddy concept as depicted in Figure 7, 9 and 10. Two alternative uses to the physical carrying of Pause

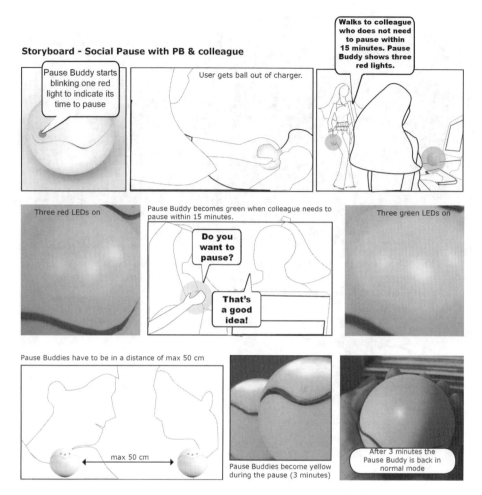

Fig. 7. Storyboard 1: Sequence of events when pausing with a colleague

Buddy were included. The RFID condition refers to use of an RFID positioned under Pause Buddy that could be taken, rather than the device itself when taking a social break with an other Pause Buddy user. The second alternative was use of a pressure sensor in the office chair to detect leaving the workspace without requiring taking Pause Buddy along. In the latter case, social interaction feedback could not be given to the user, but a signal that a longer break was taken could be given. Following pilot testing and debugging, a functional prototype of Pause Buddy was distributed in a package as depicted below with instructions to each of 6 participants, with three participants per company over a testing period of four days (Figure 8).

As depicted in the scenarios, there was only one kind of pause cue, triggered by a blinking red LED, namely the need for users to take a macro-pause, being a break

Fig. 8. The package contained an instruction book, the Pause Buddy and its charger

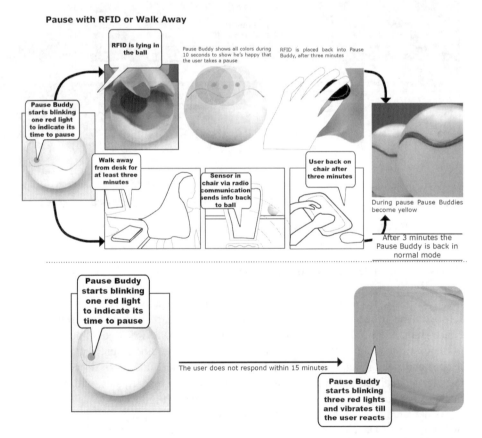

Fig. 9. Storyboard 2: Taking a break, but only taking the RFID tag from Pause Buddy rather than the entire device along

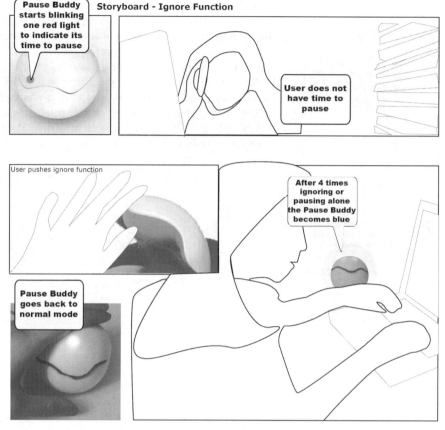

Fig. 10. Storyboard 3: Sequence of events when Pause Buddy is ignored

longer than three minutes. The user could decide whether to pause alone or with someone else. There was no rule that users had to take a social pause, only that the user had to pause seven times a day for at least three minutes and leave the desk chair. The ignore function as detailed in Figure 10 was implemented.

With permission from the participants a web camera was placed at each participant's workstation, the video was remotely recorded. Furthermore, a questionnaire containing 25 questions, on a seven point Likert scale, was included with the package. The scales were based on measures of Appeal [17], including ergonomic and hedonic factors and an overall impression dimension. The subjective appeal ranged from slightly positive with mean rankings higher than 3.0 to very positive for factors such as Attractiveness and Sympathy. The lower observed scores relating to control, value and fragility could have been due to technical problems, such as the unit overheating at one of the sites, and the occasional loss of the Bluetooth signal. The overall pausing behavior is summarized in Figure 11.

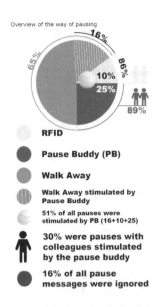

RFID

Pause Buddy (PB)

Walk Away

Walk Away stimulated by
Pause Buddy

51% of all pauses were
stimulated by PB (16+10+25)

30% were pauses with
colleagues stimulated
by the pause buddy

16% of all pause
messages were ignored

Fig. 11. Overview of types
of pauses taken during user
testing

As can be seen in Figure 11, in 25% of the pause cases, Pause Buddy was taken along when the Pause Buddy indicated to the office workers that a social pause should be taken. Ten percent of the social pauses were taken without taking Pause Buddy along. In 65% of the pause cases, the participant left or "walked away" from the desk and took a pause. It cannot be ascertained if these were social pauses, however, 16% of these pauses occurred while Pause Buddy was flashing.

6   Conclusions

The context mapping method could be considered as an effective means to gain deep insights into target users, in relation to relevant experiences for new product development. The method integrated aspects of cultural probes [10] with co-creation sessions involving the user. In industry settings, designers may not have access to large user groups or time to conduct an extended field survey. By creating a well defined target group, a relatively small number of users can be well utilized, given a wealth of qualitative methods are applied as demonstrated in the case study. Secondly, the empirical research through design method [18] whereby design variables are translated into a working field prototype and tested in the field, proved to be an effective way to gain externally valid results and reflect back on user needs. For example, by not requiring the user to take a social pause, it was possible to see the added value of Pause Buddy or use of the RFID tag in triggering social pauses. While the subjective ratings for appeal of Pause Buddy were generally positive, further research is needed over an extended period to determine the long term effects of such a device as compared to a similar control group in which no device is present.

Although the current case involved the design of a physical product, context mapping combined with research through design could also be used to develop service based applications. In short, structured methods can be applied in the "fuzzy front" end of design, which is the critical part of the design process in terms of developing creative and innovative concepts. The wealth of rapid prototyping hardware and software tools available today such as Adrino's and Max MSP provide a means to support the research through design method which can build on the early design conceptualization work.

References

1. Arnetz, B.B., Wiholm, C.: Technological stress: psychophysiological symptoms in modern offices. Journal of Psychosomatic Research 43, 35–42 (1997)
2. Schaufeli, W.B., Kompier, M.A.J.: Managing Job Stress in the Netherlands. International Journal of Stress Management 8(1), 15–34 (2001)
3. Varkevisser, M., Keyson, D.V.: The impact of VDU Tasks and Continuous Feedback on Arousal and Well-Being: Preliminary Findings. In: Dainoff, M.J. (ed.) HCII 2007 and EHAWC 2007. LNCS, vol. 4566, pp. 151–156. Springer, Heidelberg (2007)
4. Metaal, N., Jansz, J.: Psychologie de stand van zaken. Swets & Zeitlinger B.V., Lisse (1999)
5. Sepmeijer, J., Scheurs, P.n.d.: Wat is werkstress en hoe voorkom je het, World Wide Web: http://www.werkenstress.nl/downloads/Werkstressdef.htm (Accessed June 26, 2009)
6. Dewey, J.: Arts as Experience. Berkley Publishing Group, New York (1934)
7. Buchenau, M., Fulton Suri, J.: Experience Prototyping. In: DIS 2000, New York, pp. 424–433 (2000)
8. Jordan, P.W.: Designing pleasurable product. An introduction to the new human factors. Taylor & Francis, London (2000)
9. Sleeswijk Visser, F.: Bringing the everyday life of people into design. PhD dissertation, Delft University of Technology (2009)
10. Gaver, W.W., Dunne, T., Pacenti, E.: Cultural Probes. Interactions 6(1), 21–29 (1999)
11. Mattelmaki, T.: Design Probes. PhD Dissertation. University of art and design Helsinki, Finland (2006)
12. Sanders, E.B.-N., William, C.T.: Harnessing People's Creativity: Ideation and Expression through Visual Communication. In: Langford, J., McDonagh Philip, D. (eds.) Focus Groups: Supporting Effective. Product development. Taylor and Francis, Abington (2001)
13. Bickmore, T., Picard, R.W.: Subtle Expressivity by Relational Agents. In: Proceedings of the CHI 2003 Workshop on Subtle Expressivity for Characters and Robots, Fort Lauderdale, FL, April 7 (2003), World Wide Web: http://affect.media.mit.edu/publications.php (Accessed June 26, 2009)
14. Rozendaal, M.C., Keyson, D.V., de Ridder, H.: Product features and task effects on experienced richness, control and engagement in voicemail browsing. Personal and Ubiquitous Computing 13(5), 343–354 (2009)
15. Slijper, H.P., Richter, J.M., et al.: The effects of pause software on the temporal characteristics of computer use. Ergonomics 50(2), 178–191 (2007)
16. Spielberger, C.D., Gorush, R.L., Lushene, R.E.: State Trait Anxiety Inventory manual. Consulting Psychologists Press, Palo Alto (1970)
17. Hassenzahl, M., Platz, A., Burmester, M., Lehner, K.: Hedonic and Ergonomic Quality Aspects Determine a Software's Appeal. CHI Letters 2(1), 201–208 (2000)
18. Keyson, D.V., Bruns Alonso, M.: To appear in the proceedings of the International Association of Design Research (IASRD) (October 2009)

Creating a Development Support Bubble for Children

Janneke Verhaegh[1,3], Willem Fontijn[2], Emile Aarts[1,3],
Laurens Boer[3], and Doortje van de Wouw[2,4]

[1] Philips Research, High Tech Campus 34, 5656 AE Eindhoven, The Netherlands
[2] Serious Toys, Kooikersweg 2, 5223 KA 's-Hertogenbosch, The Netherlands
[3] TU Eindhoven, Den Dolech 2, 5600 MB Eindhoven, The Netherlands
[4] TU Delft, Landbergstraat 15, 2628CE Delft, The Netherlands
{janneke.verhaegh,emile.aarts}@philips.com,
willem.fontijn@serioustoys.com, l.m.boer@student.tue.nl,
doortjevdwouw@gmail.com

Abstract. In this paper we describe an opportunity Ambient Intelligence provides outside the domains typically associated with it. We present a concept for enhancing child development by introducing tangible computing in a way that fits the children and improves current education. We argue that the interfaces used should be simple and make sense to the children. The computer should be hidden and interaction should take place through familiar play objects to which the children already have a connection. Contrary to a straightforward application of personal computers, our solution addresses cognitive, social and fine motor skills in an integrated manner. We illustrate our vision with a concrete example of an application that supports the inevitable transition from free play throughout the classroom to focused play at the table. We also present the validation of the concept with children, parents and teachers, highlighting that they all recognize the benefits of tangible computing in this domain.

Keywords: Ambient Intelligence, child development, tangible interfaces, validation.

1 Introduction

The vision of Ambient Intelligence (AmI) presumes similar technological developments as visions like Ubiquitous Computing [1] and Pervasive Computing [2], i.e. computing power available everywhere and in everything. However, in contrast, AmI focuses on the needs and desires of people and not on the technology [3]. This different viewpoint causes AmI research to look into distinctive aspects of human computer interaction related to context awareness, personalization, adaptation and anticipation [4].

AmI addresses the problem of bridging the gap between what is technologically possible and what the user is able to handle. As the latter is a widespread problem, AmI is relevant for a wide variety of application domains. But there is more. AmI can not only make life easier within a domain, like the home, but it can also facilitate the integration of aspects of everyday life such that they span domains. One example is integrating healthcare and wellbeing not only at home, but also in public spaces and in

M. Tscheligi et al. (Eds.): AmI 2009, LNCS 5859, pp. 186–195, 2009.

institutions like hospitals [5]. In the end the borders between wellbeing en healthcare, between at home and away, between self medication and professional care all fade, resulting in a continuous, homogeneous and persistent 'care bubble' around the user, that supports the user wherever he goes, whatever he does, demands little from the user and yields the best personal health and wellbeing possible.

Another example is personal development. With AmI children may experience a smooth transition from playing at home to learning at school without compromising on the fun experienced or on educational effectiveness. In fact both can be enhanced at the same time. In this paper we explore this vision.

1.1 Some Characteristics of Ambient Intelligence

Of the many aspects of AmI we will focus on those most pertinent to this paper. First of all, AmI takes people as a starting point when designing (computer) interfaces to the pervasive computer power of the future. It reads computer interfaces here but the point of AmI, Pervasive Computing, Ubiquitous Computing and the like is that computers will be everywhere. So in fact it can be any interface. Actually, if we take the human centric approach seriously the interface used may not be recognizable as a computer interface to the user, not even as an interface to a computer [6].

The interface between user and computer should be *easy to use* and *easy to learn to use*, not requiring the user to adapt to the computer, as is done until now, but instead adapt the computer to the user. The threshold to start to use an application should be as low as possible, and using the application should require a minimal (or no) effort from the user. To achieve this shift of the burden, the interface needs to become more intelligent. One could say that the interface will have a better understanding of users rather than vice versa. For the user the interface should be like the interface a human would use if the computer would accept anything. This suggests the interface should be close to what evolution prepared us for to use, tangible interfaces. Fortunately, there is a lot of research in this field being conducted, e.g. [7,8].

There is another challenge related to this. As more and more non-technical domain experts are employed to understand the user and adapt the system to the user, it would be beneficial if these people could create applications themselves, without having to explain themselves to technical experts who are not domain experts. AmI applications should be *easy to create* and hence AmI can also apply to the tooling used to create applications. In such a case the domain expert becomes the end-user and the tooling should be tailored to their needs. Research in this field is emerging [9].

The second distinctive aspect we mention is personalization of the responses of the system. The system will get to know its users. It will learn things about them when they interact with it. And by knowing its users the system can tailor its responses to better fit each individual user. This goes beyond merely recording preferences and acting on them. The system should identify the strengths and weaknesses of the user and follow them over time to be able to adapt to them. Also, the acquisition of this information should be done without the user noticing. The gathering of personal information should not burden the user but be embedded, engrained, hidden within the application.

1.2 Enhancing Children's Development with Ambient Intelligence

To assess the suitability of AmI for child development support, one only has to look at the characteristics of AmI: embedded, context aware, personalized, adaptive, anticipatory and realize that these, apart from social aspects, pretty much describe a good parent or teacher. AmI applied to child development holds a promise to ensure a smooth transition from play at home to first play at school and then learning at school, but also an integration of play at home and learning at school, in the end creating a continuous, homogeneous and persistent 'development support bubble' around the child, that supports it wherever it goes, whatever it does and throughout its entire childhood. To give a sense of how this may work, we will discuss the aspects from the previous section applied to child development specifically.

The most obvious augmentation of current (pre-)school learning environments is the integration of electronics and computing, as the resulting options for interactivity and connectivity offer many opportunities to enrich the learning experience. However, care should be taken that the result fits the children and their needs. We envision classrooms where computing indeed takes a prominent role but mostly hidden from sight through the use of tangible electronic interfaces that are embedded in the learning environment. In that context, two aspects are of prime importance.

The first aspect relates to the individual child and its developing abilities. For one, the electronics should be very accessible and easy to use by young children. The interfaces used should be simple and make sense to the children and the interaction with them should come natural to the child. This implies that, rather than that the children have to adapt to the new technology, the technology is adapted to fit the children. This also holds for the applications. As the child's skills develop, the application should adapt actively to the changing abilities. Children's individual needs related to learning styles and personal interests can be taken into account as well. Tangible interfaces seem to fit these requirements to a unique degree [10].

The second aspect relates to educational yield. Electronics and computation should only be used in classrooms when they can actually improve the current educational process. This may sound obvious, but too often technology takes center stage and the benefits for education are simply assumed. Areas of improvement could be promoting the active participation of each individual pupil, enhance the possibility to share and collaborate with peers and teachers, motivate children for tasks that are currently less attractive and support the different needs of each individual, including early signaling and remedying shortfalls in development. Direct feedback and assistance through the system can be part of this.

Taking both aspects into account will result in applications that are at the same time intrinsically motivating (fun) and educationally effective. In the remainder of this paper we will report on our investigations to validate that the electronic tangible learning console we have been working on, TagTiles, fits that bill and constitutes a first step towards AmI for children's development. We took a user-centric approach to investigate the feasibility and desirability of our concept. This involved children, parents and teachers. We first developed a number of applications that were implemented and tested with children, which we will discuss in section 2. In section 3 we will discuss the studies we conducted to test the concept with teachers and parents. In Section 4 we draw some conclusions.

2   The Needs of the Children

Children are the main users and as such their needs and desires are paramount. We developed a number of games that were intended to address specific skills. Each game was built on the same device, called the TagTiles console [11]. The console includes a tabletop sensing board with an array of LED lights underneath and audio output. The games were specifically created to develop and improve distinct skills in the areas of cognitive [11], motor [12] and social development [13].

Each of these games went through a full design cycle and was evaluated with children. They demonstrate that the challenges the game offers can be tailored to fit children of different ages and with different needs. The children are intrinsically motivated to undergo the embedded training because these are presented in the form of attractive games. In addition we have observed that different skills can be trained in an integral manner with one game. Dependent on the (developmental) needs of the player(s), the challenge offered can be tuned to create the right type of training, addressing the proper combination of skills and offered at the right level. We illustrate this idea with a game that was built to train social skills, but that can be easily tuned to include training of cognitive skills such as spatial insight.

2.1   Addressing Social Skills: Playground Architect

The investigation into the potential of the TagTiles console in the domain of social skills started with identifying the main problems children face in this domain by interviewing teachers. One of the issues the teachers described was the lack of assertiveness and confidence that hinder many children in certain situations. Therefore we decided to create a game that promotes assertive behavior. Several game concepts were created and eventually 'Playground Architect' was selected for further development.

In Playground Architect (see Figure 1), 3 to 5 children can participate. One of them takes the role of Architect. The other players are Builders. The Architect's role is specifically intended for a shy child. He or she receives the Architect's pawn, and the Builders have all the playground objects, which they have to place onto the board according to the Architect's instructions.

The Architect is the only one who can access a set of narrative instructions (by using the pawn) that describe the client's wishes. These instructions are played back via the Architect's headphones. The instructions involve choices that are to be made by the Architect or by all players together, depending on the Architect's preference. If the Architect makes the decision alone, this can be seen as a sign of assertiveness or self confidence. The main task of the Architect is to communicate the client's wishes to the Builders, as the Architect himself is not allowed to build.

Forty children (mean age 9.5 years) participated in an evaluation of the game that took place at their school. Before the evaluation, they were all tested for Dominance/Shyness via a teacher questionnaire, based on which the shyest children were placed in the Architect's role.

The analysis of speech during the recorded play sessions showed that the shy children (the Architects) talked at least as much as the less shy children (the Builders).

Fig. 1. A play session in progress. The board lights up to show that all objects have been placed correctly so far.

Peer acceptance was also measured and in many cases it increased already after only a single round of play. Reviewing the play sessions with the children's teachers gave overall very positive reactions (see [13] for complete results).

2.2   Integral Skill Development with the TagTiles Console

Our applications demonstrate that you can use one skill set in optimizing the development of another. For example, the original TagTiles game [11] aimed at cognitive skills, employs fine motor skills and a social component (competition) to increase motivation. The games aimed at fine motor skills [12], use a cognitive challenge to tune the overall challenge of the game. The Playground Architect game, aimed at social skills, also uses a tunable cognitive challenge.

We therefore argue that the TagTiles console is useful for an integral approach towards skill development. Based on our evaluations, we can readily see that fine motor skills will be improved by the TagTiles game aimed at cognitive skills. We can also readily see that the spatial skills of children improve with the games aimed at fine motor skills. Furthermore, collaborative games like Playground Architect can easily be augmented to add linguistic or math challenges. As an example, the TagTiles console illustrates that electronic tangible interfaces can deliver both fun and the educational yield required. And that its applications fit the AmI characteristics.

2.3   Sample Application

For many children in the age group 3-5, it is a challenge to make the transition from free play that takes place on the floor or outdoors, to sitting at a table and completing a task as instructed by a teacher. Typically, pre-school learning environments allow both. The latter requires children to adhere to instructions, and sustained attention for a task that usually has a more serious nature than freely playing with toys. The TagTiles console can make this transition much easier, as it can make the transition more gradual by using tasks that feel like play, but also introduce the children to sitting at a table and completing a task.

We will illustrate our vision with an example of a game with which letter recognition can be trained for children aged 3-4 years. In this application, children are literally taken from play throughout the classroom to playing at a table. We chose to focus on the training of letter-sound associations. This skill typically develops during the age of 3-5 years. It is also prerequisite for learning to read and write, which is usually part of the school curricula starting when children are about 6 years old. As such, the application also serves as a test, because children that are not yet able to recognize letters can be identified at an early stage and if desired provided with extra training. Similarly, children that are ahead of the curriculum can be identified and offered more challenging tasks to keep them engaged.

Fig. 2. Sketches of children in classroom environment including ground- and table- play options (left) and of children testing the letters of the name of the cuddly animal on the interactive tabletop (right)

The game is played as follows. As a preparation the teacher has hidden tagged cuddly toy animals and letter cards throughout the classroom. The children are gathered in small teams (2-3 children). With their team they first need to find one of the animals. Once they found a toy animal, they go to the TagTiles console and place the animal on top of it. The console senses the animal and pronounces its name.

Then, the children need to search the classroom again to find the letter cards that form the name of the animal. This can be a structured process when the children can already recognize letters and know what they are looking for, but it can also be done in a trial and error fashion, by just trying a letter on the console and then listen to the response of the console which will pronounce its sound (see Figure 2). When the task is too difficult for the children, the system will notice that and help them by pronouncing and/or displaying the letters that are missing. This will train the children in making the connection between a letter symbol and its sound.

To add a game element, the teams may play in competition to be the fastest to gather the letters of the animal and place them in the right order onto the tabletop.

Once they have done this successfully, there can be a next phase in which the children need to find additional objects. Now they can place objects together on the tabletop, with which the system may provide simple sentences (via audio output) about the objects, e.g. 'the cow is next to the duck'. The children may even bring or create their own objects to develop a more elaborate or just different story.

3 Validating with Parents and Teachers

As AmI is people centric it is important that the primary carriers of the current development process of children buy into the proposition. To test our ideas and concepts with teachers and parents we conducted a series of group sessions and interviews, of which we will describe the results below.

3.1 Validation with Parents

Parents are responsible for the development of their children and they typically   decide to which play- and learning materials their child is exposed to at home. Hence, the importance of validating the concept with them. The study with parents was set up as a broad assessment of what is important to parents when it comes to child development, whether they feel a need to support the development of their children in addition to existing means and to assess which solutions they think are most suitable.

The study included parents of children aged 4-8 years old in the Netherlands, in the United Kingdom and in China. In the Netherlands and the UK 21 parents in groups of 7 participated in focus groups and 8 were interviewed individually. In China 16 parents were interviewed individually and 30 parents participated in focus group sessions in groups of 6.

Table 1. Predefined insight tested in the user study with parents

Situation	Dilemma	Solution
Parents want to have learning tools which aid the child's development (cognitive, social, physical) during leisure time, i.e. while the child is playing and having fun.	Children go for fun. They do not want to feel that games have educational purposes. So fun and learning are difficult to combine from a child's perspective.	Toys that are convincing for children and parents; the child should see it as a real toy and the parents should be able to see the educational value.

In more detail, the research objectives were to explore parents' attitudes, motives and needs with respect to the upbringing of their child(ren) and developmental aspects in cognitive, social and physical domains. Also the possible effects of cultural backgrounds were taken into account. In addition, the parents' behavior with respect to issues related to their child's behavior and how to deal with these was explored. The possible role of serious games or learning aids was discussed in relation to developmental issues. The parents were confronted with a set of predefined statements (based on our vision), to learn about their attitude towards these statements. Subsequently, the parents in the Dutch and British groups were presented with a video prototype of TagTiles, to gauge their reactions to these concepts.

For lack of space, we only present a selection of the statements discussed and we describe the parents' reactions to the presented video prototype of TagTiles. The most important statements that were tested with these parents are the following:

1. The ideal toy is a combination of fun and development, without putting pressure on the child.
2. Toys that do not include a screen are to be preferred over past times that do.

Parents in all three countries responded very positive to the first insight. In the Netherlands and the UK many toys on the market are labeled as such already. In China this was not the case. In the Chinese market most toys were either categorized as fun or as educational.

The second statement also strongly resonated with most parents in the study. The physicality of the TagTiles console was seen as a great benefit, because most parents would be happy to give toys to their children that will keep them from (continuously) playing screen-based games. Toys that have no screen trigger more active play. The parents welcomed toys without a screen especially when they are as attractive for children as computer games can be. A remark added was that this toy could become addictive (as well).

The video prototype of TagTiles was well-received. The parents were shown a video where TagTiles was played by two children, and they were only shown the original version of a pattern-copying game. TagTiles was seen as a game on an attractive high tech board and a credible device for educational purposes. The fun part was sometimes questioned. This was not very surprising to us as previous experiences of demonstrating the game had taught us that TagTiles is a game that has to be played to recognize the fun of it.

3.1 Validation with Teachers

Ten teachers from a range of different types of schools (different religions and different types of education) in the northern part of the Netherlands participated in a workshop. The workshop consisted of two parts. In the first part the teachers were asked about their general ideas on learning materials for the cognitive development of children. What do they find important aspects of learning materials? What are their wishes with respect to new learning applications? The following aspects were described by the teachers as important:

*   Autonomous use. Children should be able to use educational materials independently. Also self-assessment of the performances was mentioned.
*   Attractiveness. The materials should look inviting to use, challenging, attractive and they should be interactive.
*   Versatility of use. Multiple functionalities, options for extension of applications and addressing multiple skills at different levels were seen as beneficial.
*   Didactics. The materials should be very accessible for pupils and teachers. Language use should be clear and the tasks should be well-structured.
*   Supporting collaboration. Children should be able to play together with the materials as well as individually.
*   Registration of the user. Identification of the user and registration of performance was desired, allowing integration in existing performance-monitoring programs.
*   Practical aspects. The materials should not be too small, they should be easy to handle and robust, easy to clean and easy to store.

In the second part of the workshop a concept was introduced to the teachers by means of a video prototype. The video showed a concept similar to the TagTiles console, demonstrating how it could be used to train color recognition and spatial skills while guiding the child in a puzzle task with audio instructions through headphones.

The teachers were asked to respond to this video and identify the strong points, but also to share concerns and questions this video might have raised. In the teachers' responses, the wishes described above were all recognized in this concept. Most often mentioned as benefits were the autonomous use, versatility of tasks and didactics/easy accessibility. In addition registration of the pupils' work was seen as a strong benefit.

In the video, a rather monotonous voice guided the children through the tasks. This sounded too boring to the teachers. Also the physical aspects concerned some of them, as they thought headphones are often too vulnerable for classroom use. How the console could be self-assessing was one of the questions of the teachers. And one of them also asked if the system would be able to identify task solutions that were almost correct. In addition they wondered if the system could support remedial teaching and help to indicate when children would need this.

4   Discussion and Conclusions

The class room of the future based on tangible computing presented in this paper puts the child in the center and still emphasizes educational yield. It can address cognitive, social and fine motor skills in an integrated manner. Furthermore, it enhances the normal educational process, but also signals and treats shortfalls in development. The environment is flexible and allows for intrinsically motivating educational applications with which the child can work both independently and collaboratively. At the same time the objects used are familiar to the children and connects to their natural way of play, thus creating a natural transition from playing at home through playing in a school environment to focused learning at school.

Therefore we conclude that, in the hands of the appropriate domain experts, electronic tangible interaction consoles, like the TagTiles console, are very powerful tools indeed for the integral and personalized development of children in the areas of cognitive, fine motor and social skills for assessment, education and therapy. Furthermore, as the exercises can be presented in the form of attractive games, the children are intrinsically motivated to use them. Finally, as professionals in the field like teachers and occupational therapists pointed out, such tools can be used by the children unsupervised and hence as easily at home as in a more formal setting.

We assert that the ability to deliver this combined set of benefits in an integral manner is unique to tangible electronics.

As an example, the TagTiles console illustrates that electronic tangible interfaces fit the AmI characteristics. It is easy to use, easy to learn to use and offers great opportunities for personalization and contextualization of the developmental process. Next to showing that these benefits are real we have shown that these benefits in particular are of importance to both parents and teachers and that both also recognize that electronic learning aids based on physical computing, like the TagTiles console, deliver on these benefits.

As with such a console the requirements of teachers, parents and children are aligned, the parts of the development process taking place at home and at school can be aligned also, even integrated. This allows for the introduction of concepts like a personalized development support bubble for children that spans both contexts and can optimize the development process from pre-school throughout the school life of a child. As such, this constitutes a prime example of the application of the principles of Ambient Intelligence.

References

1. Weiser, M.: The Computer for the Twenty-First Century. Scientific American 165(3), 94–104 (1991)
2. Satyanarayanan, M.: Pervasive Computing: Vision and Challenges. IEEE Personal Communications 8(4), 10–17 (2001)
3. Aarts, E.H.L., Marzano, S. (eds.): The New Everyday: Visions of Ambient Intelligence. 010 Publishing, Rotterdam (2003)
4. Aarts, E.H.L., de Ruyter, B.: New research perspectives on Ambient Intelligence. Journal of Ambient Intelligence and Smart Environments 1, 5–14 (2009)
5. Gaver, W., Sengers, P., Kerridge, T., Kaye, J., Bowers, J.: Enhancing Ubiquitous Computing with User Interpretation: Field Testing the Home Health Horoscope. In: Proceedings of CHI 2007, San Jose, CA, USA, April 28-May 3, pp. 537–546. ACM, New York (2007)
6. Streitz, N., Kameas, A., Mavrommati, I.: The Disappearing Computer: Interaction Design, System Infrastructures and Applications for Smart Environments. LNCS, vol. 4500. Springer, Heidelberg (2007)
7. Ullmer, B., Ishii, H.: Emerging frameworks for tangible user interfaces. In: Carroll, J.M. (ed.) Human Computer Interaction in the New Millennium, pp. 579–601. Addison Wesley, Reading (2001)
8. Hornecker, E., Buur, J.: Getting a grip on tangible interaction: A frame work on physical space and social interaction. In: Proceedings of the International Conference on Computer Human Interaction, Montreal, Canada, pp. 437–446. ACM Press, New York (2006)
9. Van Herk, R., Verhaegh, J., Fontijn, W.F.J.: ESPranto SDK: an adaptive programming environment for tangible applications. In: Proceedings of CHI 2009, Boston, MA, USA, April 04 - 09, pp. 849–858. ACM, New York (2009)
10. Verhaegh, J., Fontijn, W., Jacobs, A.: On the benefits of tangible interfaces for educational games. In: Proc. of Digitel 2008, Banff, Canada, November 17-19 (2008)
11. Verhaegh, J., Fontijn, W., Hoonhout, J.: TagTiles: optimal challenge in educational electronics. In: Proc. of the 1st international Conference on Tangible and Embedded interaction. TEI 2007, pp. 187–190. ACM, New York (2007)
12. Li, Y., Fontijn, W.F.J., Markopoulos, P.: A tangible tabletop game supporting therapy of children with Cerebral Palsy. In: Markopoulos, P., de Ruyter, B., IJsselsteijn, W.A., Rowland, D. (eds.) Fun and Games 2008. LNCS, vol. 5294, pp. 182–193. Springer, Heidelberg (2008)
13. Hendrix, K., van Herk, R., Verhaegh, J., Markopoulos, P.: Increasing children's social competence through games, an exploratory study. In: Proceedings IDC 2009, Como, Italy, June 03 - 05, pp. 182–185. ACM, New York (2009)

I Bet You Look Good on the Wall: Making the Invisible Computer Visible

Jo Vermeulen, Jonathan Slenders, Kris Luyten, and Karin Coninx

Hasselt University - tUL - IBBT,
Expertise Centre for Digital Media,
Wetenschapspark 2, B-3590 Diepenbeek, Belgium
{jo.vermeulen,kris.luyten,karin.coninx}@uhasselt.be
jonathan.slenders@student.uhasselt.be

Abstract. The design ideal of the *invisible* computer, prevalent in the vision of ambient intelligence (AmI), has led to a number of interaction challenges. The complex nature of AmI environments together with limited feedback and insufficient means to override the system can result in users who feel frustrated and out of control. In this paper, we explore the potential of visualising the system state to improve user understanding. We use projectors to overlay the environment with a graphical representation that connects sensors and devices with the actions they trigger and the effects those actions produce. We also provided users with a simple voice-controlled command to cancel the last action. A small first-use study suggested that our technique might indeed improve understanding and support users in forming a reliable mental model.

1   Introduction

The visions of ambient intelligence (AmI) and ubiquitous computing (Ubicomp) share the goal of moving computers into the background, thereby making them effectively *invisible* to end-users. This design ambition is clearly present in Mark Weiser's vision of Ubicomp [14] as well as in AmI-oriented efforts such as the EU-funded Disappearing Computer Initiative [12].

If computers are to be so natural that they become invisible in use, they will often need to function on the periphery of human awareness and react on implicit input. This kind of system is called context-aware [11]: it is able to interpret and adapt to the user's current situation or *context*. These systems often react on a context change by taking a (presumably desired) automatic action on behalf of the user. In an ideal world, where the sensed context would be 100% accurate, users would then indeed not "notice" the computers embedded in their environment, but would only experience the right actions being "magically" performed at the right time.

The previous assumption is unrealistic, however. There are many aspects of context (e.g. human aspects such as our mood) that cannot reliably be sensed or inferred by machines [4]. Moreover, our behaviour is unpredictable and impossible to model accurately by computers [13]. From these arguments, it can be

M. Tscheligi et al. (Eds.): AmI 2009, LNCS 5859, pp. 196–205, 2009.
© Springer-Verlag Berlin Heidelberg 2009

concluded that it is infeasible to allow context-aware computer systems in Ubicomp or AmI environments to act *without user intervention*. However, before users are able to intervene, they should first understand how the system works and what it is trying to do. When something goes wrong, the system needs to present itself and the way it works to end-users – or essentially become *visible*.

Making clear how an AmI environment functions is not always easy to achieve because of the heterogeneous nature of these environments (they often contain several displays, speakers, sensors and computers of different sizes) and their complex behaviour. Adding to this problem is the fact that due to the focus on the invisible computer, Ubicomp and AmI systems often have little support for traditional user interface concerns such as feedback, control, and indeed "visibility" [3]. We are not the first to make these observations: a number of researchers have pointed out problems along these lines such as Bellotti et al. [4,3], Rehman et al. [9] and Barkhuus and Dey [2]. The heart of the problem lies in the fact that the lack of visibility inhibits users from forming a correct mental model of the system and exacerbates the Gulf of Execution and the Gulf of Evaluation [7]. As a consequence, users have difficulties predicting the behaviour or even the available features of the system [9]. Moreover, there is often no way for the user to override the actions taken by the system, which results in users who feel out of control [2]. Bellotti et al. [4] propose two key principles that are necessary to improve the usability of context-aware applications: *intelligibility* (or the system's capability of being understood) and *control*.

In this paper, we present a technique to make the invisible computer *visible* for end-users. We use projectors to overlay the environment with a graphical representation that shows the location and state of the different sensors and input/output devices such as displays or speakers. When the system acts on behalf of the user, an animation is shown that connects a system action with its cause and effect. Of course, constant visualisations might be distracting and contrary to Weiser's idea of calm computing [14]. We therefore believe our technique is useful mainly as a "debug mode" for end-users. The visualisations might be hidden when users have gained more experience with the system, and be called upon again whenever users have difficulties understanding the system's behaviour or when they want to know more about the reasoning behind a certain system action. Our technique allows users to consult the system state whenever necessary, thereby improving the system's intelligibility. Users receive real-time feedback about actions that happen, when they happen. In addition, a primitive control mechanism is provided that allows users to cancel an action in progress. We explored the usefulness of our technique in an informal first-use study. Results suggested that it might indeed improve understanding and support users in forming a reliable mental model.

2   A Graphical Representation of Behaviour

A simple graphical language was developed to visualize the relationships between sensors or devices and the actions executed by the system. This allows users to gct an overview of the system state at a glance. When an action is executed by the system, an animation is shown to reveal the links between this action and the different devices or sensors in the environment.

2.1 Visualising the Environment and Its Behaviour

Each sensor or input/output device (e.g. a camera, speaker or display) is visualised at its physical location in the environment with an icon and a label . These icons allow users to get a view of the devices that are present in their environment. Below the icon of each *input* device or sensor, a separate label is drawn that displays the possibilities of the device and its current state using smaller icons. *Output* devices feature only an icon and no separate label. The icon of an output device embeds its current state. For example, Fig. 1(a) shows an icon and label for a webcam (an input device) on the left and an icon for a light (an output device) on the right. In this (fictional) example, the webcam can detect the events "waving" and "moving", as indicated by the small icons in the label. In Fig. 1(a), the motion detection state is active and therefore highlighted. The light's state corresponds to its current intensity and is displayed as a horizontal bar.

We define a *trajectory* as a visualisation between two or more objects in the environment. A trajectory consists of four parts: a source device; the event that happened at this device; an action to be executed; and one or more target devices that are impacted by the action. Between each of these, lines are drawn. Dotted lines are used between events and actions, while connections between devices and other objects use solid lines.

(a) Motion in front of the webcam (input) triggers the light (output). The event "waving" of the webcam is now inactive, but could trigger another action.

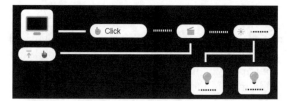

(b) A chain of events: touching the screen results in a movie being played (on the same screen). This, in turn, results in the lights being dimmed.

Fig. 1. Mockups of example trajectory visualisations

An example trajectory is shown in Fig. 1(a). Here the webcam detects motion, which triggers an action that turns on the lights. This action, in turn, impacts the light on the right side of the figure. Note that the small state icons are repeated together with a textual description. The "Waving" state is shown semi-transparently to indicate that it is not active. A bit further to the right, a graphical representation of the action is shown, connected to the light it turns on. The lines in a trajectory will be animated from source to effect, thereby possibly spanning multiple surfaces. Device icons and labels will always be shown, even if they are not active (in which case they are displayed semi-transparently). Other labels (e.g. action labels) only become visible when the connecting line crosses them. Animations will slowly fade out after they have been completed.

Trajectories can also visualize multiple actions which are triggered in sequence. Fig. 1(b) shows a trajectory with two sequential actions. In this situation, touching the screen causes a movie to be played on this screen. The action of playing a movie will itself cause another action to be executed: one that dims the lights for a better viewing experience. Likewise, it is possible to visualize more complex rules that combine multiple sensors using boolean operators (e.g. AND, OR).

2.2 Overriding System Actions: The Cancel Feature

Fig. 2 shows a mockup of the cancel command in action. Since the cancel feature is voice-controlled, it is displayed as a microphone sensor icon. The only possible state is an invocation of the cancel feature when it recognizes the word "cancel", as indicated in the corresponding label. When an action is cancelled the microphone will turn and shoot at the icon corresponding to the effect of the action, resulting in a hole in this icon. The shooting animation might again span different surfaces to reach its target. This kind of visual feedback shows users in a playful way that the effect that the action had on the environment has been undone.

Fig. 2. When the action "light off" is cancelled, the microphone shoots a hole in the light icon

2.3 Expressiveness and Limitations

The graphical notation was deliberately kept simple. It mainly targets systems that encode their behaviour as a list of if-then rules, which is a common approach to realizing context-awareness [5]. Our behaviour representation suffers from two main shortcomings. First, we are currently unable to visualize the reasoning behind machine learning algorithms, another frequently used approach to realize context-aware systems. Secondly, as with any visual language, scalability is an issue. When the notation would be used to visualize a very complex network of connected sensors and devices, the result could become too complex to comprehend for users. Despite these limitations, we believe that our notation is useful for exploring the potential of visualising the behaviour of AmI environments.

3   Implementation

We use several static and steerable projectors to overlay the physical environment with our graphical representation. The advantage of using projectors is that annotations can be displayed on any surface in the environment without requiring users to wear head-mounted displays or carry specialized devices. For more details on how to set up this kind of system, we refer to the existing literature (e.g. [8]). An overview of our implementation is given in Fig. 3.

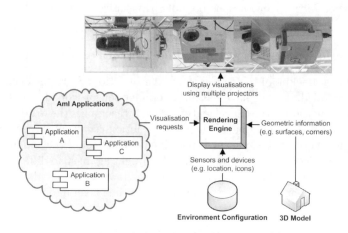

Fig. 3. Software applications in the AmI environment can send requests to the rendering engine to make their behaviour visible to end-users

Because we were mainly interested in exploring the potential of our technique, our current implementation was deliberately kept simple. The most important software component in our system is the *rendering engine*. It is implemented as a central service that allows applications to make their behaviour visible to end-users. The rendering engine is responsible for overlaying the environment with a visualisation of all devices and sensors, and for showing animations (or *trajectories*) between these elements when a software application executes an action. For this, it relies on a 3D model of the environment and an environment configuration file describing the sensors and devices in the environment. The 3D model of the environment is used to determine which of several steerable and static projectors need to be used and what image corrections need to be applied to display the annotations. The configuration file encodes the position of each device and sensor in the environment, together with their icons, possible states and a number of predefined trajectories. When software applications need to visualize a change of state in a device or the execution of a certain action, they send a request to the rendering engine containing an XML description of the required state change or trajectory.

4   Evaluation

4.1   Participants and Method

We ran an informal first-use study to investigate the suitability of our technique for understanding the behaviour of an AmI environment. Note that the aim of the study was to identify major usability problems and to drive design iteration, rather than to formally validate specific claims. The experiment was carried out in a realistic Ubicomp environment: an interactive room which features different kinds of sensors, and various means to provide users with information. We deployed a number of applications on the room's server which used sensors to steer other devices in the environment (e.g. motion detection with a webcam for controlling the lights). Applications were developed with Processing[1] and communicated with each other and the ambient projection system over the network.

Fig. 4. A user looks at an ongoing animation

The study group comprised 5 voluntary participants from our lab whose ages ranged from 24 to 31 (mean = 27.8); three were male, two female. All subjects had general experience with computers. Four out of five had experience in programming, while the fifth participant was a historian. Each individual study session lasted about 40 minutes. First, subjects were asked to read a document explaining our technique. Afterwards, subjects were presented with three situations in which they had to understand the environment's behaviour using our technique. After completing the test, participants had to fill out a post-test survey. The three tasks subjects had to perform during the study were:

---

[1] http://www.processing.org/

- **Task 1**: Subjects were asked to press a play button on a touch screen, after which a movie would start to play in the environment. This, in turn, triggered an action that turned off the lights for better viewing experience.
- **Task 2**: Subjects were given the same instructions as in the first task, but were also told to find a way to turn the lights back on afterwards. They were expected to use the *cancel* functionality to achieve this effect, which was explained in the introductory document.
- **Task 3**: In the last task, subjects were asked to walk up to a display case and were told that they would notice something changing in the environment. The display case was equipped with a webcam for motion detection, which would turn the lights on or off depending on the user's presence.

Subjects were allowed to explore the system and perform each task several times until they felt that they had a good understanding of what was happening. After completing a task, participants received a blank page on which they had to explain how they thought that the different sensors and devices were connected. This allowed us to get an idea of each participant's mental model. Subjects were free to use drawings or prose (or a combination of both).

Two of the sensors used during the test were implemented using the Wizard of Oz technique: the voice-controlled cancel feature and the webcam motion detection sensor. The other applications and devices were fully functional.

Q1	I understand how to use the visualisation of the environment.
Q2	I found the visualisation of the environment easy to use.
Q3	The visualisation of the environment was easy to understand.
Q4	The visualisation of the environment was what I wanted to know.
Q5	I understand how to use the cancel feature.
Q6	I found the cancel feature easy to use.
Q7	I find these techniques useful to allow users to understand what happens in a smart environment, and to allow them to exert control over this behaviour.
Q8	I was not confused by the visualisation of the environment.

(a) Questions used in the survey.

	Q1	Q2	Q3	Q4	Q5	Q6	Q7	Q8
P1	5	5	4	5	5	5	5	5
P2	4	4	3	3	4	5	4	3
P3	5	4	5	3	5	5	4	5
P4	5	3	4	4	5	3	4	5
P5	4	3	4	5	1	1	4	3
Mean	4.6	3.8	4	4	4	3.8	4.2	4.2
Median	5	4	4	4	5	5	4	5
σ (Std. dev)	0.548	0.837	0.707	1.000	1.732	1.789	0.447	1.095

(b) Post-test questionnaire results. Participants are numbered from P1 to P5, questions from Q1 to Q8.

Fig. 5. Post-test questionnaire

4.2 Study Results

In our post-test survey, participants ranked our technique highly for being useful to understand and control what happens in an AmI environment (Q7, mean = 4.2, median = 4 on a 5-point Likert scale, $\sigma = 0.447$); and for *not* being confusing (Q8, mean = 4.2, median = 5, $\sigma = 1.095$). In general, participants indicated that they understood how to use our visualisation technique (Q1, mean = 4.6, median = 5, $\sigma = 0.548$); that they found the visualisation easy to understand (Q3, mean = 4, median = 4, $\sigma = 0.707$); and that it provided them with the information they wanted to know (Q4, mean = 4, median = 4, $\sigma = 1.0$). However, responses were less conclusive about the cancel feature (Q5 and Q6, $\sigma > 1.7$ in each case), where one participant (P5) gave the lowest score twice. Detailed results are presented in Fig. 5. Note that the small sample size ($n = 5$) causes the standard deviation (σ) to be relatively high overall. Four out of five participants described the system's behaviour correctly for each of the three tasks. The fifth participant (P5) described the first and third task correctly, but experienced difficulties with the second task.

4.3 Discussion

Subjects were generally happy with our visualisations. One of the test participants mentioned that he found it "convenient to follow the lines to see what is happening", while another said: "it was clear to see which action had which effect". As mentioned before in Sect. 4.2, four out of five subjects were able to correctly describe the system's behaviour. We feel that this is a promising result, especially since the participant without a technical background (P2) was among these four. It might indicate that visualising the behaviour of an AmI environment can help users to form a correct mental model, which is in line with the findings of Rehman et al. [10]. However, further investigation is necessary to validate this claim.

The study also revealed a few shortcomings in our current prototype. Three subjects reported problems with recognizing the features of devices or sensors using its icons. Both the touch screen and cancel icons were found to be unclear.

During the study, we noticed that several participants experienced difficulties with keeping track of visualisations across multiple surfaces. Sometimes the visualisation would start outside subjects' field of view, which caused them to miss parts of the visualisation. A possible solution might be to use spatial audio to guide users' attention to the area of interest.

One participant (P2) commented that she sometimes received too much information, which confused her (as indicated by the neutral score on questions Q3, Q4 and Q8). She referred to the first task, in which a "click" on the touch screen was visualised as causing the movie to start playing. It might be useful to disable visualisations for actions which occur often and are obvious to users, or to implement a generic filtering mechanism.

Finally, several subjects had difficulty in invoking the cancel feature. This issue might be ascribed to two causes: an unclear icon (as mentioned before) and the unfamiliarity of participants with speech interaction. One user (P4) mentioned that he felt "uneasy using a voice-controlled command", because "he was used to clicking". Both the relatively low score by participant P4 on question Q6; and the low scores on questions Q5 and Q6 by participant P5 and his incorrect explanation of the system's behaviour, might be attributed to the difficulty of invoking the cancel command. However, further studies will be necessary to identify the exact problems that subjects face when using the cancel feature.

5   Related Work

In recent years, increasing awareness of the difficulties users encounter in AmI or Ubicomp environments gave rise to a number of techniques that try to address these issues. In what follows, we discuss interaction techniques related to the ones presented in this paper. Rehman et al. [10] describe how a location-aware Ubicomp application was enhanced with augmented reality visualisations to provide users with real-time feedback. An initial user study compared the augmented version of the application with the original one. Results suggested that the visual feedback makes for a more pleasant user experience, and allows users to form a better mental model, which is in line with our findings. The main difference with our work is that the visualisations of Rehman et al. are application-specific, while ours could be used for any application. There have been a number of other studies that deal with issues of intelligibility, control and trust. For example, Antifakos et al. [1] found that displaying the system's confidence increases the user's trust, while Lim et al. [6] suggested that answering why (not) questions posed by users could improve the intelligibility of context-aware systems. We feel that these techniques could be combined with our approach. Further investigation will be necessary to determine the ideal level of user involvement and the most suitable feedback mechanisms in different situations.

We are not the first to visualise the behaviour of context-aware systems. iCAP [5], a design tool that allows end-users to prototype context-aware applications, also represents context-aware behaviour rules visually. With our system, however, users see a visualisation of the system's behaviour in real-time and in-situ, when and where the events take place.

6   Conclusions and Future Work

The implicit nature of interaction and the invisibility of the system in AmI and Ubicomp environments have led to a number of interaction challenges. In this paper, we presented a technique that overlays the environment with a graphical representation of its behaviour. This allows users to view the system state at a glance and receive real-time feedback about events and actions that occur in the environment. Additionally, we provided users with a basic control feature that allowed them to cancel the last action. A small first-use study suggested that our visualisation might indeed improve understanding and support users in forming a reliable mental model. The study also revealed a few shortcomings of our system which we plan to address in a future design iteration. Finally, we are aware of the limitations of this study and plan to conduct further experiments to validate our findings.

References

1. Antifakos, S., Kern, N., Schiele, B., Schwaninger, A.: Towards improving trust in context-aware systems by displaying system confidence. In: Proc. MobileHCI 2005, pp. 9–14. ACM, New York (2005)
2. Barkhuus, L., Dey, A.K.: Is context-aware computing taking control away from the user? three levels of interactivity examined. In: Dey, A.K., Schmidt, A., McCarthy, J.F. (eds.) UbiComp 2003. LNCS, vol. 2864, pp. 149–156. Springer, Heidelberg (2003)
3. Bellotti, V., Back, M., Keith Edwards, W., Grinter, R.E., Henderson, A., Lopes, C.: Making sense of sensing systems: five questions for designers and researchers. In: Proc. CHI 2002, pp. 415–422. ACM, New York (2002)
4. Bellotti, V., Keith Edwards, W.: Intelligibility and accountability: human considerations in context-aware systems. Hum.-Comput. Interact. 16(2), 193–212 (2001)
5. Dey, A.K., Sohn, T., Streng, S., Kodama, J.: iCAP: Interactive Prototyping of Context-Aware Applications. In: Fishkin, K.P., Schiele, B., Nixon, P., Quigley, A. (eds.) PERVASIVE 2006. LNCS, vol. 3968, pp. 254–271. Springer, Heidelberg (2006)
6. Lim, B.Y., Dey, A.K., Avrahami, D.: Why and why not explanations improve the intelligibility of context-aware intelligent systems. In: Proc. CHI 2009. ACM, New York (2009)
7. Norman, D.A.: The Design of Everyday Things. Basic Books, New York (2002)
8. Pinhanez, C.S.: The everywhere displays projector: A device to create ubiquitous graphical interfaces. In: Abowd, G.D., Brumitt, B., Shafer, S. (eds.) UbiComp 2001. LNCS, vol. 2201, pp. 315–331. Springer, Heidelberg (2001)
9. Rehman, K., Stajano, F., Coulouris, G.: Interfacing with the invisible computer. In: Proc. NordiCHI 2002, pp. 213–216. ACM, New York (2002)
10. Rehman, K., Stajano, F., Coulouris, G.: Visually interactive location-aware computing. In: Beigl, M., Intille, S.S., Rekimoto, J., Tokuda, H. (eds.) UbiComp 2005. LNCS, vol. 3660, pp. 177–194. Springer, Heidelberg (2005)
11. Schilit, B., Adams, N., Want, R.: Context-aware computing applications. In: Proc. WMCSA 1994, pp. 85–90. IEEE Computer Society, Los Alamitos (1994)
12. Streitz, N., Kameas, A., Mavrommati, I.: The Disappearing Computer: Interaction Design, System Infrastructures and Applications for Smart Environments. Springer, Heidelberg (2007)
13. Suchman, L.A.: Plans and situated actions: the problem of human-machine communication. Cambridge University Press, Cambridge (1987)
14. Weiser, M.: The computer for the 21st century. Scientific American 265(3), 66–75 (1991)

AmIQuin - An Ambient Mannequin for the Shopping Environment

Alexander Meschtscherjakov, Wolfgang Reitberger, Thomas Mirlacher,
Hermann Huber, and Manfred Tscheligi

ICT&S Center, University of Salzburg
Sigmund-Haffner-Gasse 18, 5020 Salzburg, Austria
{alexander.meschtscherjakov,wolfgang.reitberger,}@sbg.ac.at
{thomas.mirlacher,hermann.huber,manfred.tscheligi}@sbg.ac.at

Abstract. We present AmIQuin, a virtual mannequin, which leverages an Ambient Intelligence (AmI) system within a shopping environment. AmIQuin is designed to replace a traditional shop window mannequin in order to enhance a customer's shopping experience by reacting to the customer's presence and presenting personalized information. The AmIQuin is implemented as 3D graphic representation of a mannequin displayed on a large screen situated in a shop window. In this paper, we describe the first cycle of an iterative User-Centered Design (UCD) process including the technical implementation of an AmIQuin prototype, along with an initial three days field study. The first prototypical version of the virtual mannequin presented in this paper moves its head or full body towards the beholder in response to recognizing a human face looking at it. We describe technical challenges of deploying an AmI application in the field. Our findings indicate the usefulness of an AmI application within the shopping context and give insights on customers' attitudes towards shop windows in general and the AmIQuin in particular. Furthermore, the study results reveal customers' wishes for future versions of the AmIQuin.

Keywords: Ambient Intelligence, Field Study, Shop Window, Embodied Agents, Implicit Interaction, Mannequin.

1 Introduction

The shopping context is challenging, but also particularly fruitful for Ambient Intelligence (AmI) applications [1]. Our vision is to enhance the customers' shopping experience by providing AmIQuin, a virtual interactive mannequin visualized in form of a 3D avatar on a large screen situated within a shop window. Similar to classical "real world" mannequins the AmIQuin should be seamlessly integrated into the shopping environment and display the latest fashion offered within the shop. This has the potential for new kinds of advertising based on AmI technologies (comp. [2]), that could be more compelling than traditional advertising techniques. Moreover, it should attract customers by reacting to the customer's presence based on implicit input. According to Schmidt et. al [3] implicit interaction means that the AmI environment reacts to input, which is not explicitly entered by the user. Once the AmIQuin has gained the

M. Tscheligi et al. (Eds.): AmI 2009, LNCS 5859, pp. 206–214, 2009.

customer's attention, it should enhance his shopping experience by providing general as well as customer specific information.

We position the AmIQuin project within an iterative User-Centered Design (UCD) process. This constitutes an iterative process of system design, deployment and evaluation. In this paper we present the first cycle including the design, a prototypical implementation and the evaluation of the AmIQuin. We describe an initial field study together with design implications for further iterations. The AmIQuin project includes research on the persuasive aspects of AmI technologies, which are not covered within this paper but can be found in [4].

The visual presentation of the AmIQuin prototype is based on the appearance of a conventional mannequin, situated in the shop window, which was later used to conduct the field study. Clothes worn by the AmIQuin showed the latest collection offered within the shop and were designed to represent the same clothes worn by the conventional mannequin. These design decisions were motivated by our desire to integrate the AmIQuin seamlessly into the shopping context and make it easy for the customer to compare the AmIQuin with her "real world" equivalent. Contrary to the classical headless mannequin, we decided to equip the AmIQuin with a head. The head was important for the realization of the reaction to customer's implicit interaction.

The AmIQuin reacts to a customer looking into the shop window by turning its body and head towards the customer and therefore facing him, creating the impression of being looked at. This reaction to the customer's presence aims at attracting the customer's attention. A customer perceiving the AmIQuin only peripherally when facing the shop window (e.g. while looking at other items), is expected to be attracted by the moving AmIQuin, and the customer's interest should be stimulated. Once the AmIQuin has gained the customer's attention, we envision a transaction from what Vogel et. al [5] calls the "implicit interaction phase" to the "explicit" or "personal interaction phase". This can be reached by e.g. giving the customer the possibility to change various attributes of the displayed clothes (e.g. color, style). As proof of concept we developed a functional hi-fi AmIQuin prototype, which we evaluated during a three days field study within a real shopping context. The first prototypical version of the AmIQuin presented in this paper moves its head in response to recognizing a human face looking at it, whereas the additional features described above were not yet implemented.

2   Related Work

Several researchers within the AmI community [6,7,5] have conducted research on public ambient displays. Recently these displays and other AmI applications have been exploited within the shopping context. Schmidt et. al [8] discuss how to improve the User Experience (UX) by tailoring advertisements and to improve the understanding of the advertising space. Furthermore, workshops on pervasive advertising [2] and shopping [9] have recently been conducted.

Van Doorn et. al [10] introduce the Intelligent Shop Window (ISW), which uses a transparent display for augmenting a traditional shop window. According to the presence or absence of customers in front of the ISW different information is displayed. Reitberger et. al [11] and Meschtscherjakov et. al [1] present two iterative versions of a dynamic map in retail stores to visualize customer shopping behavior. Pinhanez and Podlaseck [12] propose frame-less advertisement projections to attract customers within a retail store. Bohnenberger et al. [13] developed a decision-theoretic location-aware shopping guide. They tested their prototype in a real shopping mall and noted a behavior change in shoppers towards a more goal oriented behavior. Sukaviriya et. al [14] present text and imagery projection into physical environments for user interaction in a retail store. Spassova et. al [15] introduce the concept of Product Associated Display (PADs) which provide visual feedback to users interacting with physical objects in a shopping scenario.

Cheng et. al [16] presented the "ChroMirror" system, a digital mirror imaging system that allows users to change the color of their clothes without the need to physically change clothing. Zhang et. al [17] demonstrate an Intelligent Fitting Room (IFR) providing implicit user interaction for a responsive mirror. Our approach uses a public ambient display to enhance the customer's shopping experience and persuade customers to interact with a virtual shop window mannequin. A more general work on shopping experience is presented by Underhill [18], who points out the advantages of physical shops over online shops based on extensive field studies in retail environments.

3   The AmIQuin Prototype

The AmIQuin prototype is a virtual 3D avatar presented on a large LCD. The prototype reacts to a customer looking into the shop window by turning its full body or head towards the beholder and therefore facing him, creating eye-contact. If noone is looking directly at AmIQuin, she is performing an idle animation (i.e. continuous subtle body movements) to further an illusion of a realistic character. The design of the avatar, especially the clothes it is wearing, is so that it closely resembles the classical "real world" shop window mannequin which it replaces.

3.1   Framework

The technological framework as shown in Figure 1 has been designed to be flexible and easy to setup. Its foundation is comprised by several components connected via XML messages. An IP camera constantly takes images, which are delivered to a face-detector component, based on the Fraunhofer real-time face detector library [19,20]. This component detects faces within images and generates an XML stream containing the bounding box of all detected faces, which is passed on to the head-tracker application. The head-tracker in turn maps the detected faces into 3D space, by using a transformation depending on the camera position and alignment as well as the size of the detected faces (assuming faces bigger on the images, are faces closer to the camera). The results of the head-tracker are forwarded via XML to the CryEngine 2 [21] plug-in, allowing the AmIQuin model to look at the 3D position commanded by in-game node flowgraphs.

3.2   Implementation Issues

The technical problems we encountered reveal how environmental context factors are particularly challenging for a real world implementation. Unlike the lab setup, the test

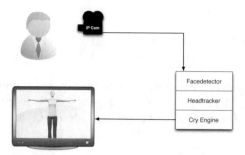

Fig. 1. AmIQuin Framework: IP cam captures image - Face-detector identifies faces - Head-tracker calculates 3D position of nearest face - Cry Engine visualizes AmIQuin facing nearest person

in a real world environment posed various challenges (see Figure 2). These challenges stem from the public place, where several people at once are looking at the display. A particular problem was induced by the placement of the camera, which was placed within the shopping window, pointing outside toward the shoppers. This introduced a reflection of the ubiquitous display in the shopping window itself, as well as lens glare and blurring effects due to highly lit shopping windows from stores at the other side of the aisle.

Fig. 2. Image as captured by the AmIQuin camera during the field study. A Reflection of AmIQuin's legs can be seen in the window (black legs covering a good part of the image). The background is very noisy.

Our system dealt with these challenges by using an error resilient algorithm, selecting only the closest person by using the calculated area covered by the detected head as a measure for the distance. This was complemented by a mean filtering of the nearest vector over a sample time of five seconds to prevent jittering between two people. The reflection, glare and blur effects were improved and finally resolved by using a camera with more advanced optics (Axis 213 PTZ instead of Axis 107MW).

4   In-Situ Study in the Shopping Context

To assess the AmIQuin prototype and get insights for the next cycle of our UCD process, we deployed the prototype in an in-situ field study. The aims of the study are:

- to evaluate the AmIQuin concept and technical implementation of the prototype
- to learn about the attitudes of different customer groups towards the AmIQuin
- to gain insights of customers' wishes for future design cycles

4.1   Study Setup

For the in-situ study, which lasted for three days, we replaced a conventional mannequin within the shop window of a sports clothes store situated in a large shopping mall (see Figure 3) and interviewed a sample of customers. In the following we define customers as people within the whole shopping mall and not necessarily within the targeted sports clothes shop. Customers who were attracted by the shop window and remained there looking into it for some time were observed. Some of them were randomly chosen and asked to take part in a structured interview lasting approximately five minutes each. The interview took part in front of the shop window. Customers had the possibility to explore the AmIQuin while answering the questions.

Fig. 3. A customer standing in front of the shop window looking at the AmIQuin and a traditional mannequin

Besides demographic issues, the structured interview included general questions about customer's attitudes towards shop windows and mannequins and specific questions related to the AmIQuin. Since the AmIQuin prototype represents the first cycle within a UCD process, one part of the interview aimed at identifying customer requests for further iterations. The customers were presented open questions as well as statements, which had to be rated on a 5-point Likert scale. During the study 102 randomly chosen customers (43f, 59m) were interviewed aged between 13 and 69 years (mean=28.15, standard deviation (SD)=15.79).

4.2   Results and Discussion

Table 1 gives an overview of the percentage of negative, neutral, and positive answers to selected items of our questionnaire. For the purpose of discussing the tendencies in customer attitudes we group the answer categories "strongly agree" and "agree" to positive answers, and "strongly disagree" and "disagree" to negative answers, "neither nor" answers fall in the "neutral" category. The first two items "Shop windows are helpful to inform while shopping." and "I enjoy looking at shop windows." refer to different types of customers regarding their attitude towards shop windows in general. The last two items "The AmIQuin pleases me." and "I prefer the AmIQuin to a conventional mannequin." refer to the attitude towards the AmIQuin specifically.

Table 1. Customers' attitude towards shop windows and the AmIQuin

statement	negative	neutral	positive
Shop windows are helpful to inform while shopping.	24.0%	15.0%	61.0%
I enjoy looking at shop windows.	20.8%	18.8%	60.4%
The AmIQuin pleases me.	30.3%	24.2%	45.5%
I prefer the AmIQuin to a conventional mannequin.	40.2%	9.3%	50.5%

Overall a majority of the people interviewed stated that shop windows are helpful (61.0%) (see Table 1) and that they enjoy looking at shop windows (60.4%). Regarding the AmIQuin 45.5% of the customers were pleased with the AmIQuin, and 30.3% did not like it. 50.5% preferred the AmIQuin versus 40.2% who preferred the conventional mannequin, and 9.3% had nor preferences. This indicates that the novel concept of a virtual shop window mannequin is a promising approach for a wide range of customers.

Within a shopping mall different types of customers can be found. While it is not possible to discuss each specific customer group in detail, we present the highlights of some selected customer types. We used a χ^2-Test to show if the deviation of our results from the equal distribution is significant.

The customers, who did *not* enjoy looking at shop windows in general stated significantly more often, that they liked the AmIQuin (65.0%; $\chi^2(2)=9.70$, p<.01) and that they preferred the AmIQuin over a traditional mannequin (65.0%; $\chi^2(2)=9.10$, p<.05). A similar trend can be found when looking at customers, who generally *deny* the helpfulness of shop windows. The majority of these customers were pleased by the AmIQuin (50.0%; $\chi^2(2)=3.25$, p<.01) and significantly rated the AmIQuin above the traditional mannequin (58.3%; $\chi^2(2)=7.75$, p<.05). These findings show that the AmIQuin especially reaches customers who previously had no affinity towards shop windows in general, without alienating customers who already had a positive perception of shop windows.

Regarding the gender of customers, women enjoyed significantly more looking at shop windows than men ($\chi^2(2)=23.98$, p<.001) and stated more often than men that they are helpful ($\chi^2(2)=10.58$, p<.01). Interestingly, the AmIQuin itself was significantly more often preferred over a traditional mannequin by men ($\chi^2(2)=9.42$, p<.01). Yet again, the AmIQuin got a particularly positive response from a customer group (men) who is rather skeptical towards shop windows in general without negatively affecting women. This is shown by the fact that regarding the likability of the prototype no significant gender differences were observed. The relative majority of both genders equally liked the AmIQuin.

We clustered the age of the customers into three approximately equal sized groups (under 18, 19-35, above 36). Regarding the attitude towards shop windows in general and the likability of the AmIQuin no significant differences between age groups were found. The AmIQuin was equally liked by the relative majority of all ages. We would like to point out that despite younger customers (under 18) stated that shop windows are *not* helpful ($\chi^2(4)$=10.18, p<.05), the majority of this group (57.14%) preferred the AmIQuin to the traditional mannequin. This indicates that the AmIQuin has the potential to appeal to this important target group, who refuse to be impressed by traditional shop windows.

Summarily we can state that the AmIQuin was well accepted throughout all customer groups. The relatively high acceptance by the above described groups "customers, who generally do not like to look into shop windows", men, and younger customers may be due to the fact that the AmIQuin represents a novel approach of interaction with a shop window. In particular men and younger customer often share an affinity towards new technologies, which might be an additional explanation for these findings. Customers who are used to virtual worlds, video games, and online shopping might be more compelled by the interactive AmIQuin than a traditional, old-fashioned mannequin. We aim at confirming this interpretation in an upcoming long-term field study.

Concerning a future version of the AmIQuin customers would have liked to have the possibility to change the color (82.4%) and the type (80.4%) of the displayed clothes. 78.2% wanted the possibility to display additional information. Women liked to have this additional feature significantly more than men ($\chi^2(2)$=8.27, p<.05). 72.4% wished a personal recommendation for suitable clothes. 68% desired that the AmIQuin would automatically adapt to one's own gender. Customers who liked to look into shop windows requested this attribute highly significantly more than others ($\chi^2(4)$=15.52, p<.01). Thus we can conclude that customer groups, with a more positive attitude towards shop windows are also more interested in additional features. More advanced features like a reaction to the customer's emotion (50.0% negative answers) and the possibility to play a game with the AmIQuin (61.8% negative answers) were rejected. This indicates that people are concerned about application features in a public space, which interfere with their private sphere.

5   Conclusion and Future Work

Regarding the sudy aims presented in Section 4 we have

- evaluated the AmIQuin concept and technical implementation of the prototype in a real shopping scenario
- learned about the attitudes of various customer groups towards the AmIQuin
- gained insights of customers' requests for future design cycles.

Above all, we have shown that the AmIQuin could attract the customer's attention. This has been achieved through the idea of the customer's implicit interaction with the

AmIQuin. Now that the AmIQuin has gained this attention, the challenge is to shift from implicit to a more explicit form of interaction in order to engage the customer. To accomplish this, the next version of the AmIQuin will include the most requested additional features. This could comprise the possibility to change the type and color of clothes using gesture input. Additional information such as price (in particular special offers), fabric, available sizes and colors could be displayed gradually based on the length of stay. Personalized recommendations could be visualized based on information stored on customers' loyalty cards (e.g. new suitable shoes based on the customer's shopping history), which could be implemented for instance through near-field communication technologies (NFC). The results form this initial study will serve as feedback for the next phase in our iterative design process.

To get a deeper understanding of the effect of the AmIQuin on the customer's shopping experience a long-term deployment and study is planned. For the current version we designed the AmIQuin as close to a traditional mannequin as possible. Future versions will include a comparison of different types of avatars (e.g. more human like, more abstract) and their influence on the customer's attitude. Currently only a few customers had privacy concerns (17.8%). Still, with the introduction of more intrusive features like personalization and privacy issues have to be taken into account and be examined in detail.

The technological framework will be extended to allow an even more flexible way of interacting with the customer. Logging facilities will be implemented to detect the number of customers dwelling in front of the shopping window with and without the AmIQuin as well as the time they are spending to look at the items on display. Regarding the representation of the first AmIQuin prototype we have chosen a LCD screen for visualization. In a next version we aim at moving the AmIQuin out of the "frame" given by the LCD screen and embedded it more seamlessly in the shop window space. This could be achieved by utilizing back projection on a semitransparent foil attached to the window glass . We hope that our work will also lead to interesting discussions and inspire further research in the area of ambient shopping and advertising.

Acknowledgements

We would like to thank our colleagues Michael Lankes and Thomas Scherndl for their support.

References

1. Meschtscherjakov, A., Reitberger, W., Lankes, M., Tscheligi, M.: Enhanced shopping: a dynamic map in a retail store. In: Proc. of UbiComp 2008, pp. 336–339. ACM, New York (2008)
2. Müller, J., Schmidt, A., Quigley, A., Begole, B.: Pervasive computing will change the future of advertising. In: Workshop at Pervasive 2009 (2009),
   http://www.pervasiveadvertising.org/
3. Schmidt, A.: Interactive context-aware systems interacting with ambient intelligence. In: Ambient Intelligence. IOS Press, Amsterdam (2005)

4. Reitberger, W., Meschtscherjakov, A., Mirlacher, T., Scherndl, T., Huber, H., Tscheligi, M., Mirnig, N., Pöhr, F.: A persuasive interactive mannequin for shop windows. In: Proc. of Persuasive 2009. Springer, Heidelberg (2009)

5. Vogel, D., Balakrishnan, R.: Interactive public ambient displays: transitioning from implicit to explicit, public to personal, interaction with multiple users. In: Proc. of UIST 2004, pp. 137–146. ACM, New York (2004)

6. Brignall, H., Rogers, Y.: Enticing people to interact with large public displays in public spaces. In: Proc. of INTERACT 2003, pp. 17–24 (2003)

7. McCarthy, J.F., Costa, T.J., Liongosari, E.S.: Unicast, outcast & groupcast: Three steps toward ubiquitous, peripheral displays. In: Abowd, G.D., Brumitt, B., Shafer, S. (eds.) UbiComp 2001. LNCS, vol. 2201, pp. 332–345. Springer, Heidelberg (2001)

8. Schmidt, A., Alt, F., Holleis, P., Müller, J., Krüger, A.: Creating log files and click streams for advertisements in physical space. In: Adjunct Proc. of UbiComp 2008, pp. 26–27 (2008)

9. Abbas, Y., Hwang, J.E., Konomi, S., Roussos, G.: Pervasive shopping pervasive shopping: Shop / i don't need help, i'm just browsing. In: Workshop at Pervasive 2009 (2009)

10. van Doorn, M., van Loenen, E., de Vries, A.P.: Deconstructing ambient intelligence into ambient narratives: the intelligent shop window. In: Proc. of Ambi-Sys 2008, Brussels, Belgium, ICST, pp. 1–8 (2008)

11. Reitberger, W., Obermair, C., Ploderer, B., Meschtscherjakov, A., Tscheligi, M.: Enhancing the Shopping Experience with Ambient Displays: A Field Study in a Retail Store. In: Schiele, B., Dey, A.K., Gellersen, H., de Ruyter, B., Tscheligi, M., Wichert, R., Aarts, E., Buchmann, A. (eds.) AmI 2007. LNCS, vol. 4794, pp. 314–331. Springer, Heidelberg (2007)

12. Pinhanez, C., Podlaseck, M.: To frame or not to frame: The role and design of frameless displays in ubiquitous applications. In: Beigl, M., Intille, S.S., Rekimoto, J., Tokuda, H. (eds.) UbiComp 2005. LNCS, vol. 3660, pp. 340–357. Springer, Heidelberg (2005)

13. Bohnenberger, T., Jacobs, O., Jameson, A., Aslan, I.: Decision-theoretic planning meets user requirements: Enhancements and studies of an intelligent shopping guide. In: Gellersen, H.-W., Want, R., Schmidt, A. (eds.) PERVASIVE 2005. LNCS, vol. 3468, pp. 279–296. Springer, Heidelberg (2005)

14. Sukaviriya, N., Podlaseck, M., Kjeldsen, R., Levas, A., Pingali, G., Pinhanez, C.: Augmenting a retail environment using steerable interactive displays. In: Proc. of CHI 1992, pp. 978–979. ACM, New York (1992)

15. Spassova, L., Wasinger, R., Baus, J., Kruger, A.: Product associated displays in a shopping scenario. In: ISMAR 2005: International Symposium on Mixed and Augmented Reality, Washington, DC, USA, pp. 210–211. IEEE Computer Society, Los Alamitos (2005)

16. Cheng, C.M., Chung, M.F., Yu, M.Y., Ouhyoung, M., Chu, H.H., Chuang, Y.Y.: Chromirror: a real-time interactive mirror for chromatic and color-harmonic dressing. In: Proc. of CHI 2008, pp. 2787–2792. ACM, New York (2008)

17. Zhang, W., Matsumoto, T., Liu, J., Chu, M., Begole, B.: An intelligent fitting room using multi-camera perception. In: Proc. of IUI 2008, pp. 60–69. ACM, New York (2008)

18. Underhill, P.: Why We Buy: The Science of Shopping, June 2000. Simon & Schuster, New York (2000)

19. Fraunhofer IIS: Real time face detector (2008),
http://www.iis.fraunhofer.de/EN/bf/bv/kognitiv/biom/dd.jsp

20. Kueblbeck, C., Ernst, A.: Face detection and tracking in video sequences using the modified census transformation. Journal on Image and Vision Computing 24(6), 564–572 (2006)

21. Crytec: Cryengine 2 (2008), http://www.cryengine2.com/

Designing an Awareness Display
for Senior Home Care Professionals

Martijn H. Vastenburg and Robbert J. Vroegindeweij

ID-StudioLab, Faculty of Industrial Design Engineering, Delft University of Technology,
Landbergstraat 15, 2628 CE, Delft, The Netherlands
M.H.Vastenburg@tudelft.nl,
R.J.Vroegindeweij@student.tudelft.nl

Abstract. Home care professionals play a central role in supporting elderly people when they need help to continue living in their own homes. Using awareness systems, caregivers might better be able to consider the actual and changing needs of individual clients, and better be prepared for the home visits. In the present situation, the functional requirements on a awareness systems for professional caregivers are unknown, and caregivers tend to be unaware of the potential use of these sensor-based systems. This paper presents a case study in which the user needs are studied using a working prototype; the prototype is used to make target users experience an awareness system in their everyday work practice, and thereby enable them to better reflect upon the user needs and the potential use of these systemsWhereas caregivers were skeptical at first, they did value the prototype in the evaluation phase. In the exit interviews, the caregivers came up with an interesting list of requirements and design directions for a future awareness display.

Keywords: awareness display, design of interactive products, contextual studies, aging in place.

1 Introduction

Elderly people generally indicate that they would prefer to continue living in their own homes as long as possible [1]. By living independently, elderly people can stay active and involved, and thereby maintain well-being [2], and at the same time they do not burden the nursing homes. In many cases, however, support is needed to continue their everyday living routines. In western countries, home care professionals play a central role in in-home support of elderly people. Without help from these professional caregivers, many elderly people would have to give up their independent situation at an earlier stage.

Clients of home care are generally visited several times a week, up to several times a day. Each caregiver visits a series of clients each day. Since the need for care per client changes in time, and due to incidental needs for extra care, caregivers need to adjust their schedules regularly.

Systems that provide awareness of the actual situation of the clients could potentially support caregivers in providing the care needed at the best time. In the present situation,

M. Tscheligi et al. (Eds.): AmI 2009, LNCS 5859, pp. 215–224, 2009.
© Springer-Verlag Berlin Heidelberg 2009

however, awareness systems are rarely used in a home care setting, and caregivers are unaware of the potential use of sensor-based systems. The requirements and design directions for awareness systems for professional caregivers are not known. To better understand these requirements, and to explore the design directions of these systems, a case study was conducted. The present paper describes the design steps that resulted in the development of a prototype awareness display for home care professionals, and the findings from a user study in the field. The case study serves as an example of how awareness systems could be used within the home care domain to support professional caregivers, and provides design directions for future awareness systems.

2 Related Work

In recent years, products including video communication systems and incident re-sponse systems have been developed to improve awareness for caregivers. These products tend to be focused at emergency detection, rather than at supporting caregiv-ers in their day-to-day work.

Several research projects have studied to potential use of awareness displays for caregivers, as a means to enable computer-supported coordinated care (CSCC). The CareNet Display [3, 4] is one of the early examples, in which an interactive digital picture frame was developed to be used in the home setting. The display is based on the Digital Family Portraits project [5]. Local members of the elder's care network, responsible for providing the elder's day-to-day care, use the display to monitor the status of the elder. The CareNet Display includes a shared calendar for sharing ap-pointments and transportation needs. The display depicts seven information clusters: falls, meals, medications, mood, calendar, activities and outings. The caregivers re-ported that they felt less stressed when using the display, and they were pleased that they did not have to ask the elders for information needed to provide proper care time and time again. For family carers, providing care tends to be a secondary activity, next to their own job and/or household. For professional caregivers, on the other hand, providing care is the primary task. Towards creating an awareness display for professional caregivers, the information need and design directions in the professional home care domain need to be explored.

Whereas CareNet display focused on functional aspects of the situation of the elder, several other projects focused on the social side. For example, Morris et al. [6] developed the *solar display* to visualize social connectivity, in order to raise aware-ness of social connectedness, and consequently contribute to overall well-being. Us-ing the solar display, caregivers could modulate their caregiving activities.

Another interesting example of sensor-based systems is the unattended autono-mous surveillance (UAS) [7] system developed by TNO, which aims to provide a sense of safety and security for elderly people living at home. The system consists of a wide range of sensors that enable automatic fall detection, wandering detection, detection of smoke and fire, video observation and communication, and an emergency response system. In case of an alarm, the system automatically contacts a call center and/or individual caregivers. Even though the system could potentially well support professional home caregivers, it is not clear whether or not the alarming and alerting approach matches the needs of the caregivers. Whereas technology seems to be in place to support professional home caregivers, the actual information need of caregivers has not been studied before. The present study aims to better understand this information need, and to find out how this information could best be communicated to home caregivers.

3 Domain Analysis

To better understand the present work situation of the caregivers, interviews were conducted with four caregivers of a local home care provider in Delft. The individual, semi-structured 1-hour interviews focused on (1) understanding the present situation, and (2) describing the potential use of awareness systems in a future situation.

3.1 Present Situation

Client population. Home care services are being provided to people of all ages, mostly aging 60 and up. Elder clients tend to suffer from an increasing number of health problems. Older clients tend to be in need of care until they move to a nursing home or until the end of their lives.

Care activities. Most of the care activities are related to personal care, such as washing and bathing clients and helping people get dressed and undressed. When needed, caregivers do make time for social activities. In some cases, caregivers train their clients to deal with their issues independently, e.g., by showing how to administer insulin injections.

Average working day. At 7:30 in the morning, the caregivers discuss the status of their clients during a staff meeting in a local care office. Information from the staff meetings is used to schedule and prepare for the home visits. Next, the caregivers conduct a series of home visits. The afternoon starts with another staff meeting, and continues with a second series of home visits and/or administrative tasks.

Responsibilities. Each caregiver acts as the central contact person for up to twelve clients and their family members; the caregiver is responsible for all care activities for these clients. In some cases, clients are visited by a dozen different caregivers a week, due to working shifts and specializations. The status of clients needs to be continuously communicated between caregivers.

Communication devices. The caregivers use smart phones for phone calls, time registration, and as an address book. All caregivers have access to a desktop computer at the local care office, which can be used for email, Internet access and administrative tasks. The participants were generally skeptical towards using new technology, since technology could create a new barrier between them and their clients.

Information exchange. A week planner is used in the local care office to share information between caregivers. Messages include "Blood pressure of client A needs to be measured each morning!", and "Client B is hospitalized with a broken hip." Diaries are used in the homes of clients to share information between caregivers and family members.

3.2 Future Situation

The interviewees were asked to reflect upon the question: "If you could have a look in the homes of your clients from a distance, what would you like to be able to see?" They were encouraged to describe in detail what information they would be interested in, at what time, and how the information would affect their work process. The caregivers mentioned 9 items they would like to see from a distance:

1. **Monitoring medicine intake** was found to be the top-priority request by each of the four caregivers. They would like to know (a) *if* medicine has been taken, (b) if the *right* medicine has been taken, and (c) if the medicine has been taken at *the right time*.
2. **Monitoring food and fluid intake** was mentioned by each of the four caregivers. They would like to know (a) if clients eat and drink sufficiently, and (b) if clients eat and drink at a regular basis.
3. **Monitoring the status of the care tasks.** Based on the actual needs and the status of scheduled tasks, caregivers can better estimate the amount of time needed for a visit.
4. **Monitoring potential emergencies.** Caregivers would like to know about *potential* emergencies, for example, when a client did not get out of bed at the normal time. In these cases, the home care organization by default sends two caregivers at the same time.
5. **Monitoring presence**. Awareness of the presence could help reduce the number of visits when clients are not at home, and caregivers could provide assistance when elderly with dementia are wandering.
6. **Monitoring the availability of supplies.** When the availability of supplies (e.g., medicine) could be checked from a distance, caregivers could pick up extra supplies before visiting the client, and/or visits could be rescheduled in order to provide extra supplies in time.
7. **Monitoring devices.** If the status of devices could be monitored from a distance, problems could be identified at an earlier stage, and time needed to manually check the status of devices could be saved.
8. **Monitoring activity patterns in time.** Caregivers would like to see changes in living routines of clients in time, in order to be able to better assess the care needs of a client, and to assess the ability of clients to continue living in their homes.
9. **Monitoring personal hygiene.** For those clients with reduced awareness of the need for personal hygiene, caregivers would like to know (a) if clients have used the bathroom and/or toilets, (b) if the clients actually washed themselves, and (c) if the clients wash themselves at a regular basis. This way, clients can stay in control as long as possible, whereas caregivers can take over when needed.

When asked for the best time to communicate the information, the participants indicated that they are primarily interested in an up-to-date status overview of their clients before starting the home visits, in order to be able to adjust the schedule of their home visits and to take with them extra materials in case of special needs.

4   Concept Development

The domain analysis showed that caregivers would like to be aware of the actual situation and care needs of their clients. Based on the findings from the interviews, it was decided to build a system which would (1) provide easy access to the status of all clients of a caregiver, thereby enabling caregivers to set their priorities based on actual needs and to visit their clients well-prepared, (2) create an easy-to-use and easy-to-learn solution, (3) provide access to presence and activity-data, a history-in-time, and a shared calendar, (4) enable notifications, and (5) allow client-specific settings. In view of time limitations, it was however decided to focus on the development of the design concept for a desktop-based tool, instead of a tool which could be accessed using both a desktop computer and a mobile device. The main views of the design concept are shown in Figure 1.

The awareness display provides access to all requested information as described in section 3.2. Rather than continuously showing the status of all information categories, it was decided to use a notification-based view of the status. Each notification represents a situation which needs attention of the caregiver. Notifications can be set up to monitor medicine intake (1), food and fluid intake (2), emergencies (4), availability of supplies (6), status of devices (7), and the status of personal hygiene (9). The active notifications are visually presented in the central *overview*.

Care tasks (3) can be viewed using the *calendar view*; tasks which have not been completed in time will result in a notification in the *overview*. Presence (5) can be viewed using the *activities view*; this presence information could also be linked to the *overview*. Activity patterns in time (8) can be viewed using both the *logbook view* and the *activities view*.

5   Evaluation

To find out how the prototype was experienced in a realistic setting with real users, and to better understand the user requirements on the system, a small-scale explorative field-study was conducted with three participants. Supposedly, participants would come up with new and more focused requirements and suggestions for a future awareness product, after they were given the possibility to use and experience an awareness product in their work setting.

Participants. Three professional home caregivers from a local care provider were recruited for the user study.

Prototype. Sensors were installed in the homes of three clients, who were living at different locations within the district of the local care office. Infrared sensors were placed in the living room and the bathroom, a pressure sensor was placed in the bed, and a reed sensor was attached to the front door (Fig. 2). Even though only few sensors were used, it was expected based on the interviews that the information provided by the system would be useful for the caregivers. Using the prototype, caregivers could see when the clients were in bed, in the bathroom, in the living room, and when they might be away.

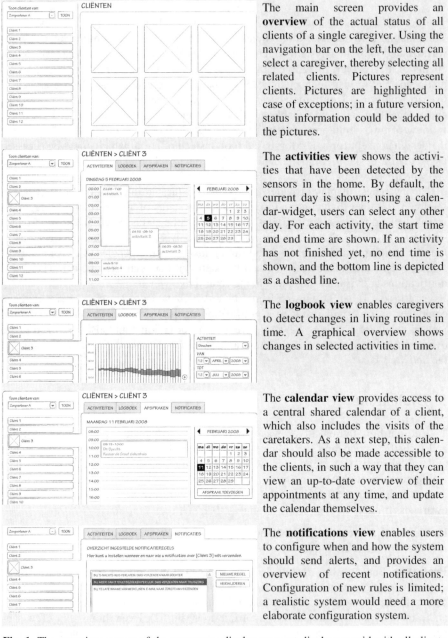

The main screen provides an **overview** of the actual status of all clients of a single caregiver. Using the navigation bar on the left, the user can select a caregiver, thereby selecting all related clients. Pictures represent clients. Pictures are highlighted in case of exceptions; in a future version, status information could be added to the pictures.

The **activities view** shows the activities that have been detected by the sensors in the home. By default, the current day is shown; using a calendar-widget, users can select any other day. For each activity, the start time and end time are shown. If an activity has not finished yet, no end time is shown, and the bottom line is depicted as a dashed line.

The **logbook view** enables caregivers to detect changes in living routines in time. A graphical overview shows changes in selected activities in time.

The **calendar view** provides access to a central shared calendar of a client, which also includes the visits of the caretakers. As a next step, this calendar should also be made accessible to the clients, in such a way that they can view an up-to-date overview of their appointments at any time, and update the calendar themselves.

The **notifications view** enables users to configure when and how the system should send alerts, and provides an overview of recent notifications. Configuration of new rules is limited; a realistic system would need a more elaborate configuration system.

Fig. 1. The overview screen of the awareness display concept displays a grid with all clients. Separate views can be selected for activities, a logbook, a calendar and notification settings.

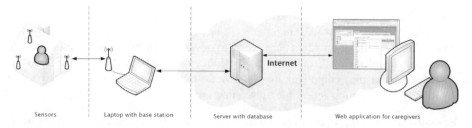

Sensors   Laptop with base station   Server with database   Web application for caregivers

Fig. 2. Data from the homes of three clients was stored in a central database, and could be accessed by the participating caregivers through a web interface at the local care office

Due to time constraints, only part of the functionality has been implemented and tested in the field study. The prototype included the overview screen and the activities view (Fig. 1). The logbook view, calendar view and notifications view have not been implemented.

Informed consent. The purpose and setup of the study was explained to the participating elderly. The clients agreed with the sensor setup and with the information that would be sent to the caregivers. Both the clients and the caregivers were explicitly told that the prototype is a system under development; the participants should never base their decisions solely on the information from the prototype tool.

Method. The prototype was deployed in the field for seven days. An introduction to the application was given to the three participants. The participants were asked to use the application whenever they liked, but at least twice a day: in the morning just before the morning round, and at noon before the afternoon round. Exit interviews were conducted immediately after the field study. Participants were asked to describe their experiences with the prototype awareness tool (ease of use, understandability of the information presented, usefulness of the prototype in relation to work practice, overall impression), and to describe the ideal awareness tool (dream functions, what should the future system definitely *not* do, dream form factor).

5.1 Findings: Experiences with the Present Prototype

Usefulness and added value. The participants were very positive on using the prototype system. Using the system, all participants felt better prepared when visiting the clients. Two participants indicated that they now better understood the living routines of their clients, and they might want to use this information to discuss issues with their clients.

Changing schedules. According to the participants, using the awareness display would have resulted in changes in their schedules, if only the system would have been validated and the data could be trusted. The participants were aware of the limitations of the prototype system; they did not make decisions based on the information presented by the system.

The participants indicated that in case information would require a change in the schedule, this change would require substantial effort; schedules are set by the minute, and weighty arguments are needed to deviate from these schedules. Caregivers do not change their schedules themselves; they need to contact a superior to do so. An awareness display could simplify the process of changing the schedules, by making relevant information accessible to the superiors.

Ease of use. Both the visual overview and the possibility to view past activities were appreciated by all participants. Two participants indicated that the activity view needs to be improved; the view was cluttered by partial activities, which could not be merged by the simple recognition module used in the prototype.

5.2   Findings: Towards the Future Awareness Tool

In the exit interview, the participants were asked to describe the dream-functions for a future awareness tool. Table 1 shows the dream-functions that were mentioned by the participants, as well as an overview of what the future system should *not* do. Based on these suggestions, it would be good to focus on creating a networked system that links to other stakeholders in the care-network. Furthermore, mobile connectivity needs to be explored in order to send updates when the caregivers are in the field.

Table 1. Dream-functions for a future awareness tool

Do's	- Show the location and status of the clients at any time of the day. - Show the room-level location of clients when entering the home. - Make the tool adapt to the needs of individual clients. - Send alerts and notifications to mobile devices. - Link to informal caregivers and family caregivers. - Link to existing emergency response systems; the awareness tool could help reduce the number of false alarms. - Show the location of other caregivers in the district, and make it easier to contact these caregivers.
Don't's	- Don't introduce technology at the expense of social contacts. - Don't show incorrect data or too many details. - Don't use cameras (supposedly not acceptable by clients).

6   Discussion and Future Work

This paper has presented the findings from an exploratory study in which the use of awareness systems in supporting professional home caregivers has been studied. A working prototype was developed and deployed in the field at a very early stage of the product design process. Caregivers were able to experience a prototype awareness display at work, and they were able to reflect upon the limitations and potentials of awareness systems in their work. The case study deliberately did *not* take the perspective of the elderly clients into account. Even though product adoption by the elderly is crucial towards creating a system which is accepted in the field, we think a different type of user study is needed in order to capture the client needs and values in relation to awareness systems. It was decided to focus on the information need of the caretakers first, before studying the perspective of the elderly in a future study.

The participants were found to be very positive towards the prototype awareness display. Not only did the study result in an understanding of how caregivers might use an awareness display in their work, the exit interviews also resulted in interesting suggestions for requirements for a future awareness display for home caregivers. These findings can be used as design directions for product developers in the home care domain.

A future awareness system could be a desktop application that provides detailed information on the actual status and the history of clients, combined with a mobile application for displaying notifications and alerts. An awareness display could be made accessible for informal caregivers and/or family caregivers, thereby making it easier to distribute care tasks to people within in the care network. In order to make optimal and efficient use of awareness tools, support from the organizational structure of the care providers involved is needed.

The use of awareness technology does raise ethical questions. For example, people tend to be willing to give up privacy, when in return safety and security are increased [8]. Even though people might be willing to give up their privacy themselves, would it be ethically correct to allow caregivers to continuously monitor the lives of their clients? And what if the use of technology leads to fewer moments of social contact between caregivers and clients? Even though these questions are considered as highly relevant by the authors, they are considered out of scope in this explorative study.

Acknowledgements. The work presented in this paper was part of the Independent at Home project, funded by SenterNovem IOP-MMI. Thanks to Peter Hermans and his colleagues from Careyn Home Care in Delft, professor David Keyson, and the participants in the user study for their valuable input throughout the design process.

References

1. Vermeulen, J.: Langer zelfstandig wonen en hoe ICT daarbij kan helpen. PhD Thesis, University of Tilburg, The Netherlands (2006)
2. Holmén, K., Furakawa, H.: Loneliness, health and social network among elderly people - a follow up study. Archives of Gerontology and Geriatrics 35(2), 261–274 (2002)
3. Consolvo, S., Roessler, P., Shelton, B.E.: The CareNet Display, Lessons Learned from an in Home Evaluation of an Ambient Display. In: Davies, N., Mynatt, E.D., Siio, I. (eds.) UbiComp 2004. LNCS, vol. 3205, pp. 1–17. Springer, Heidelberg (2004)
4. Consolvo, S., Roessler, P., Shelton, B.E., LaMarca, A., Schilit, B.: Technology for Care Networks of Elderly. Pervasive Computing, April-June 2004, 22–29 (2004)
5. Mynatt, E.D., Rowan, J., Jacobs, A., Craighill, S.: Digital Family Portraits: Supporting Peace of Mind for Extended Family Members. In: Proceedings of the SIGCHI Conference on Human Factors in Computing Systems, Seattle, Washington, pp. 333–340 (2001)

6. Morris, M.E.: Social Networks as Health Feedback Displays. IEEE Internet Computing 9(5), 29–37 (2005)
7. Unattended Autonomous Surveillance system, TNO Defense and Safety,
   `http://www.tno.nl/downloads/zelfstandig_wonen.pdf`
8. Hoof, J., van Kort, H.S.M.: Unattended autonomous surveillance in community-dwelling older adults: a field study. In: Proceedings of ISG 2008, Pisa, Italy (2008)

A Framework to Develop Persuasive Smart Environments

Pedro Lobo[1,2], Teresa Romão[1,2], A. Eduardo Dias[1,3], and José Carlos Danado[4]

[1] Research Center for Informatics and Information Technologies (CITI-DI/FCT/UNL)
[2] DI-Faculty of Sciences and Technology/New University of Lisbon,
Quinta da Torre, 2829-516 Caparica, Portugal
[3] DI-University of Évora, R. Romão Ramalho, 59, 7000-671 Évora, Portugal
[4] YDreams, Edifício YDreams, Madan Parque Sul, 2829-149 Caparica, Portugal
pjglobo@gmail.com, tir@di.fct.unl.pt,
aed@di.uevora.pt, jose.danado@ydreams.com

Abstract. This paper presents a framework for the creation of context-sensitive persuasive applications. The framework allows the authoring of new persuasive smart environments producing the appropriate feedback to the users based on different sensors spread throughout the environment to capture contextual information. Using this framework, we created an application, Smart Bins, aimed at promoting users' behavioural changes regarding the recycling of waste materials. Furthermore, to evaluate the usability of our authoring tool, we performed user tests to analyze if developers could successfully create the Smart Bins application using the framework. A description of the Smart Bins application, as well as the results of the user tests, are also presented in this paper.

Keywords: Persuasive technology, contextual awareness, ubiquitous applications authoring.

1 Introduction

Ubiquitous computing can extend the persuasive power of a physical location or appliance. The use of sensors allows the capture of contextual information that can later be used to determine the most appropriate feedback from an application in order to persuade its users to adopt certain behaviours. Different sensors can be used to analyze the user's current actions, as well as to examine environmental variables, which will then be applied to set the most suitable reaction from a computer device or application.

We developed a framework to facilitate the creation of interactive smart environments that act as persuasive tools and social actors [1]. Our project idea was developed thinking on both the person who needs to develop persuasive applications and the people who will be using them. The main objective of this generic framework is to provide users without programming skills with the adequate tools for the rapid authoring of persuasive smart environments using multimedia resources and sensors.

This paper addresses the functionalities of the framework and introduces an application – Smart Bins – produced using it. Smart Bins aims at persuading people to recycle in order to contribute to preserve the environment.

M. Tscheligi et al. (Eds.): AmI 2009, LNCS 5859, pp. 225–234, 2009.

The paper is structured as follows. The next section summarizes research work related with this project. Section 3 presents our design concept, describing the developed framework. To study the use of this framework to build new persuasive applications, we created a prototype application - Smart Bins – which is presented in section 4. We also performed user tests to analyze if application developers could successfully create the Smart Bins application using this framework. Section 5 describes those tests and their results. Finally, we present the conclusions and orientations for future work.

2 Related Work

This work relates to the study of computers as persuasive technology – Captology - which focuses on the design, research, and analysis of interactive computing products created to change people's attitudes and behaviours [1]. We have been also inspired by Mark Weiser's vision of ubiquitous systems [2]. Mark Weiser brought a new vision to Human-Computer Interaction: computers should weave into human's lives, being as invisible as possible, instead of being the main focus of attention.

By merging the concepts of *captology* and *ubiquitous computing,* we can build systems that subtly guide the users through planned appropriate actions, which may change their attitudes or behaviours. These systems can act as computer tools that provide ways to simplify user's tasks and interaction, according to people's needs and system's goals. Moreover, these systems can play the role of social actors, rewarding people with positive feedback and even showing users how their actions can contribute to the achievement of a certain goal.

Oinas-Kukkonen and Harjumaa [3] present a conceptual framework for the design and evaluation of persuasive systems. Based on the works of Fogg [1], they define persuasive design strategies and guidelines.

According to Picard [4], if we want computers to be "intelligent" and to interact naturally with us, we must give computers the ability to recognize, understand, and even to express emotions. Emotions can play an important role in decision making and consequently in behaviour changes. A system's visual and audio messages can be more effective if they also express emotions according to the contextual situation.

Studies show that just-in-time motivation messages are one of the keys to persuade people to change. Stephen S. Intille [5] stated that an effective strategy to motivate behaviour change is to present a simple message that is easy to understand, at just the right time, the right place, and in a non-annoying way. The use of sensors embedded in physical objects throughout the environment, allows for the selection of the most appropriate moment to present relevant information, given the context.

Situational awareness can be used to reduce the amount of explicit input a person has to give to a computer system. The value of context-aware computing comes from interpreting the sensors' output, in order to determine the users and environment characteristics and activities, therefore simplifying the user scenario and reducing the teaching needed to accomplish tasks [6].

CleanSink [7] explores the use of augmented physical interfaces to persuade users to keep their hands clean. This system was designed for places that required employees with absolutely clean hands, like hospitals. It uses RFID sensors to identify users and a camera to detect if they have washed their hands.

Several other projects considered the use of sensors in the development of persuasive systems, combining context-sensitive system behaviour with persuasive content [8, 9, 10].

The framework we conceived was also influenced by the works of Streitz et al. [11] and Vogel and Balakrishnan [12]. The former considered situated interaction and the use of smart artefacts to facilitate awareness and communication in ubiquitous work environments. The latter developed an interaction framework for interactive public ambient displays that support the transition from implicit to explicit interaction with both public and personal information. They both considered the distinction between several interaction zones depending on user's location, orientation and actions. Moreover, end-user programming is also a focus of the framework being created with inspiration from tools such as Yahoo Pipes [13]. The authoring tool should support the developer and be as natural as possible for him.

3 The Framework

We created this framework to support the development of ubiquitous persuasive applications with a minimal programming effort. We aimed at providing application developers with a tool that helps them to assemble different sensor devices, blend them in the environment and create a context-sensitive application using a form-based authoring tool. In section 4, we describe one such application developed with this framework.

However, this framework can be used to build different ubiquitous persuasive applications, such as interactive advertising installations or augmented physical objects. Therefore, the proposed framework seeks to contribute to the study of how computer systems can be used as persuasive technologies to change people's attitudes and behaviours.

The architecture is supported by sensors that detect users and surrounding context. The set of characteristics collected by sensors, within the system vicinity, is used to trigger a state transition. An authoring tool was developed to allow developers to establish the application's interaction model. Consequently, for distinct patterns detected by sensors, different multimedia resources can be provided to the users of the developed application.

The following sections describe the framework architecture and current implementation, showing how contextual awareness is achieved.

3.1 Framework Architecture

The proposed architecture relies in four main modules: Multimedia Display, Context Processor, Database and Sensor Processor. The diagram shown in Fig. 1 represents the different modules and shows how they exchange information between them.

This architecture allows the system to evolve through time, because the modules are independent, relying on common interfaces to exchange information between

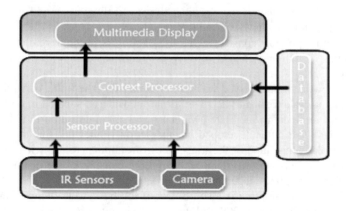

Fig. 1. Persuasive Framework architecture

them. Therefore, new features can be easily integrated within each module to fit the needs of different applications and additional sensors can be incorporated in the system. The framework works as follows.

First, the Sensor Processor receives data from the sensors, filters it, and sends it to the Context Processor. Then, the Context Processor analyzes the data provided by the Sensor Processor module and accesses the Database to gather additional information and present it through the Multimedia Display. Finally, the Multimedia Display is the module that provides the user with the result of each interaction with the system.

Visual and audio stimuli are the primary output of the system, but additional stimuli can be added, namely olfactory or tactile. Output stimuli, shown to the users within the Multimedia Display, result from the analysis of contextual information (gathered by the sensors) performed within the Sensor Processor.

The framework is supported by an authoring tool, which eases the development of new applications. The authoring tool allows users to define the interaction model for the application under development. During the usage of the authoring tool, modules are configured and further information is added to the platform in order to be used within the application. Moreover, existing interaction models can be further modified and adjusted for specific purposes. Thus, while the framework can evolve over time, new applications can also evolve to integrate new features added to the framework.

The authoring tool explores three major concepts: frames, resources and links. Frames correspond to the major interaction points in an application, since they reflect an application state within the interaction model. A frame aggregates the remaining two concepts: resources and links.

Resources correspond to the media used to compose the frames and are able to provide the stimuli to the user within the application. Resources can be in the form of images, videos, text, audio or flash animations. Links correspond to application state transitions. A link establishes a move from one frame to another (from one application state to another) and defines the conditions (set of context variables) that activate that transition. When a specific sensor pattern, matching the condition to trigger a link in the current application frame, is achieved the corresponding link is activated and the application automatically jumps to the defined interaction frame.

While defining a frame, its media content and the possible links to other frames must be specified. The resources which compose the frames, have to be gathered and prepared in advanced. Moreover, when creating a new environment the users have to know which stimuli will be presented in each frame, in order to create the application.

3.2 Framework Current Implementation

While developing a new application or editing an already developed one, the authoring tool creates a set of files that will be used to provide the different settings to operate each module of the architecture. Mainly, those are XML files that will be operated by the architecture when the application is executed. These files are created through a simple set of forms edited by the application developer, from which the authoring tool collects the necessary information to allow the framework to establish the application interaction flow. The authoring tool provides an easy way to create the frames that will be shown to the users in every application state and to add resources and links to each frame. Although a frame may resemble a visual interface, applications can be built based on other stimuli, namely auditory stimuli. Thus, frame is a concept aggregating the stimuli supplied in an interaction point.

While running an application, when a specific context is sensed, a link is activated and a new frame is conveyed to the user with the appropriate content in order to inform or persuade her or him to adopt a certain procedure. Indeed, based on the descriptions built with the support of the authoring tool, the framework is able to detect a particular context, activate a particular frame and provide the correct stimuli.

The context is gathered based on defined patterns from sensors. In the current implementation, we considered the following types of sensors:

- Infrared (IR) sensors – To measure distance. A certain distance threshold from a user or object to these sensors may be used to activate a link.
- Digital camera – The camera is prepared to detect Data Matrix patterns that can be used to identify items from the real world. A link can be activated when the camera detects a certain item.
- Time based – It is possible to define a period of time, after which a certain link is activated. In such cases, a new specific frame is shown. This allows for defining default links to be activated when no action from the user is detected for a certain period of time.
- Number of visits to a specific frame – This option allows the user to define to which frame the system will go after being in a specific frame a certain number of times.

To support the authoring of new applications, making it easier to keep track of the application structure, we have added a graphical support window that shows developers a graph representing the frames already created and the links between them. This way, developers do not need to remember the whole application structure. Furthermore, application developers can easily modify an application by editing the forms provided by the authoring tool to describe the frames. The framework will then automatically update the corresponding XML files.

After creating an application, developers are immediately able to preview it. Context Processor loads data from the interaction model, including information regarding frames, resources and links and starts the application. A first frame is then shown to the developer, usually a first interaction point inviting users to start using the application. Afterwards, the application will evolve according to the defined structure, the user's actions and the context parameters. Fig. 2 describes how different framework elements evolve during the execution of an application.

Each column shows the correspondence between the elements at different levels and how they evolve in order to persuade a user into a new behaviour.

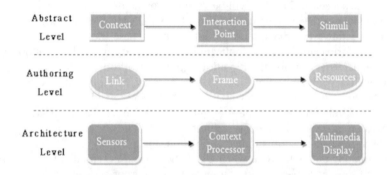

Fig. 2. Elements evolution in an application

4   The Smart Bins Application

In order to test the presented framework, an application was created using the authoring tool. Smart Bins aims at increasing young children's conscience towards recycling. It was designed as an augmented recycling bin, composed by three physical recycling containers (blue, yellow and green), able to detect if users are placing the objects to be recycled in the right container. Smart Bins is also able to communicate simple persuasive messages and inform users about the effects of their behaviours.

A set of sensors, composed by four IR sensors measuring distances was used for the development of Smart Bins. The application also uses a camera to recognize Data Matrix images that are used to identify the type of objects to be recycled.

4.1   Application Description

Smart Bins was designed as an educational game intended to change users' behaviour towards environmental issues. Target users are 7-10 year old children. With Smart Bins we created a smart environment that approaches a serious problem, the need for recycling, as a funny activity, teaching children how to recycle correctly and why they should do it. The proposed application addresses recycling in an affective way, also enabling children to earn conscience on the subject.

The application gives "life" and "intelligence" to the recycling containers, making them communicate with the children through visual and audio messages. Humanized animated characters, representing the recycling containers, provide users with useful stimuli, guiding them and establishing an affective relationship with children. Fig. 3 shows the Smart Bins environment.

Smart Bins works as follows. When no one is close to the system, the display shows a video about recycling. As soon as someone approaches the augmented recycling bin (detected by the IR sensors) one of the recycling bins characters tells the children how to play the game and start recycling.

To play Smart Bins, children have to place a set of objects inside the recycling containers, aiming at selecting the correct container for each object. A Data Matrix image is attached to each object to identify its type (paper, plastic or glass). Thus, to identify an object the user has to place the object in front of the camera and then place the object in a recycling container.

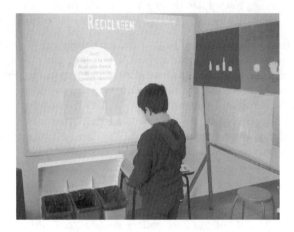

Fig. 3. Smart Bins environment

Each container has an IR sensor, thus whenever an object is dropped inside, it is detected and stimuli is provided to children telling them whether the object was placed in the correct container. An effusive compliment is heard if so, and a disappointed, but encouraging message if not. In order to reinforce the success of the user's action or to motivate the user to keep trying, the recycling containers characters provide both visual and audio feedback.

Smart Bins can be set to end after a period of time or after the recycling of a predefined number of objects. When children identify all the objects, or time is over, results are displayed and the system conveys messages about the user's actions.

Using the framework support, we were able to build Smart Bins application in about 20 minutes. The content (videos, images, sounds) was produced in advance and we have formerly planned the application workflow.

5 User Studies

User tests were performed in order to test the proposed architecture and the authoring tool. We asked participants to use this framework to create the Smart Bins application, giving them the application's description in the form of a storyboard. The storyboard explained the multimedia resources and the sensors they should use for each interaction frame, and described the application work flow. We intended to find out if the developers understood the framework functionalities and if they could successfully develop Smart Bins. The tests were divided in four parts:

- Introductory questionnaire to collect developers' personal data, such as age, gender, background or computer experience.
- Briefing of the framework, the objectives of the test, and an explanation on how Smart Bins should work.
- Application development by filling the system's forms according to a storyboard of the application.
- A final questionnaire to evaluate the potential of the framework and to understand developers' opinions concerning its usage and usability in creating the application.

After the introductory questionnaire and the briefing, developers started to create Smart Bins according to the storyboard they received. To do that, participants had to perform 74 actions. These actions included all elementary steps users had to perform in order to achieve their goals, e.g. choosing the background image for one frame or defining a link that establishes the transition from one frame to another. During this part of the test, an observer watched the developers and registered their performance in each of the actions. The tests were carried out individually and the developers' performance in each task was scaled from 0 (not completed task) to 3, (easily completed task).

5.1 Participants

The tests were performed on a population of 6 voluntary participants, 4 of them male, and 2 of them female. All of them were college students, from different study areas as Physics, Biomedical and Computer Science, with ages between 23 and 30, yielding an average age of 25.3. All the participants had their first contact with the framework during the test.

5.2 Questionnaire

Besides gender and age, the questionnaire covered general data on developers' aptitude to work with a computer and with forms. To conclude the tests, the participants had to complete a nine-question questionnaire. In the first two questions, participants had to rate how easy it was to build Smart Bins using the framework and their overall impression about it. To answer, developers had to circle a response on a 5-point Likert-type scale. On this scale a response of 1 means very poor and a response of 5 very good. The remaining questions were open-ended and covered participants' opinions on the potential use of this framework to create different persuasive applications, as well as their likes and dislikes about the framework and their ideas on how to improve it.

5.3 Results

Regarding the introductory questionnaire we noticed that 2 of the 6 developers knew the concept of ubiquity, 4 had a general idea of the meaning of persuasive technology, they were all regular computer users and also had previous contact with form menus. Table 1 shows the results of the tasks performed by the participants to configure the Smart Bins application (and the automatically generated XML files). For each participant, considering the scale presented above in this section, we counted how many actions were accomplished within each level of performance.

The results were very satisfactory. Developers understood quite well how to create the application using the framework menus, as most of the tasks were easily completed (MEAN = 2.92, SD = 0.24).

Concerning what they liked best about the framework, the answers were diverse, and included the simplicity of the framework, its versatility, and the fact that during the edition of the Smart Bins application, they could observe the evolution of the application structure (as a graph) as they create new interaction frames and establish the links between them. The weakest point of the framework identified by the developers was the limited help functionalities available to assist novice users.

Table 1. Participants tasks performance results

	0	1	2	3
Participant 1	0	1	2	71
Participant 2	0	10	0	64
Participant 3	1	0	3	70
Participant 4	0	0	2	72
Participant 5	0	0	1	73
Participant 6	0	0	4	70
Evaluation Count	1	11	12	420

All participants agreed that the interface graphical design should be improved. One participant wanted to have a way to respond to sound inputs.

In general, the participants understood the functionalities of the framework and considered it useful and easy to use. The tests' duration ranged from 30 minutes to 1 hour depending on the developers' understanding of how Smart Bins should work. Developers considered the establishment of the transitions between interaction frames as the hardest part to accomplish. That may have been caused, at least partially, by the fact that they were trying to build an application they did not design.

6   Conclusions and Future Work

Context-sensitive systems and smart physical objects or environments are increasingly being used for persuasive purposes. We developed a framework that allows the authoring of new persuasive smart environments producing the appropriate feedback to the users based on different sensors spread throughout the environment to capture contextual information. Using this framework we have created an application prototype, Smart Bins, aimed at promoting the recycling of waste materials. We have performed user tests to assess the easiness of building a context-aware persuasive application using our framework, which includes an authoring tool. The results were very satisfactory.

As users suggested, we are planning to improve the graphical design of the interface and develop a context-sensitive help. We also intend to develop a new mechanism to facilitate the incorporation of new types of sensors without the need for programming. This mechanism will make it easier to create a configuration file for each new sensor type.

Acknowledgements

We would like to thank YDreams, and particularly David Palma, for all the support in developing the sensors platform.

References

1. Fogg, B.J.: Persuasive Technology – Using Computers to Change What We Think and Do. Morgan Kaufman, San Francisco (2003)
2. Weiser, M.: The computer for the 21st century. Scientific American 265(3), 94–104 (1991)
3. Oinas-Kukkonen, H., Harjumaa, M.: A Systematic Framework for Designing and Evaluating Persuasive Systems. In: Oinas-Kukkonen, H., Hasle, P., Harjumaa, M., Segerståhl, K., Øhrstrøm, P. (eds.) PERSUASIVE 2008. LNCS, vol. 5033, pp. 164–176. Springer, Heidelberg (2008)
4. Picard, R.: Affective Computing. MIT Press, United States (1998)
5. Intille, S.S.: Ubiquitous Computing Technology for Just-in-time Motivation of Behavior Change. Proceedings of Medinfo. 11(Pt) 2, 1434–1437 (2004)
6. Selker, T., Burleson, W.: Context-Aware Design and Interaction in Computer Systems. IBM Systems Journal 39(4), 880–891 (2000)
7. Arroyo, E., Bonnani, L., Selker, T.: Waterbot: Exploring Feedback and Persuasive Techniques at the Sink. In: Proc. ACM CHI, Portland, OR, April 2-7, pp. 631–639 (2005)
8. Chi, P., Chen, J., Chu, H., Lo, J.: Enabling Calorie-Aware Cooking in a Smart Kitchen. In: Oinas-Kukkonen, H., Hasle, P., Harjumaa, M., Segerståhl, K., Øhrstrøm, P. (eds.) PERSUASIVE 2008. LNCS, vol. 5033, pp. 116–127. Springer, Heidelberg (2008)
9. Obermair, C., Reitberger, W., Meschtscherjakov, A., Lankes, M., Tscheligi, M.: perFrames: Persuasive Picture Frames for Proper Posture. In: Oinas-Kukkonen, H., Hasle, P., Harjumaa, M., Segerståhl, K., Øhrstrøm, P. (eds.) PERSUASIVE 2008. LNCS, vol. 5033, pp. 128–139. Springer, Heidelberg (2008)
10. Romão, T., Hipólito, J., Correia, N., Câmara, A., Danado, J.: Interactive Public Ambient Displays for Environmental Persuasion. In: de Kort, Y.A.W., IJsselsteijn, W.A., Midden, C., Eggen, B., Fogg, B.J. (eds.) PERSUASIVE 2007. LNCS, vol. 4744, pp. 1–11. Springer, Heidelberg (2007)
11. Streitz, N.A., Röcker, C., Prante, T., Stenzel, R., Van Alphen, D.: Situated Interaction with Ambient Information: Facilitating Awareness and Communication in Ubiquitous Work Environments. In: Tenth International Conference on Human-Computer Interaction (HCI International 2003), Crete, Greece, June 22-27, pp. 133–137 (2003)
12. Vogel, D., Balakrishnan, R.: Interactive Public Ambient Displays: Transitioning from Implicit to Explicit, Public to Personal, Interaction with Multiple Users. In: Proceedings of the 17th annual ACM symposium on User Interface Software and Technology, Santa Fe, NM, US, October 24-27, pp. 137–146 (2004)
13. Yahoo: Yahoo Pipes, http://pipes.yahoo.com

Measuring the Response Bias Induced by an Experience and Application Research Center

Boris de Ruyter[1], Rick van Geel[2], and Panos Markopoulos[3]

[1] Philips Research Europe, HTC34, AE5656 Eindhoven, The Netherlands
[2] University of Tilburg, The Netherlands
[3] Eindhoven University, Den Dollech 4, 5656 Eindhoven, The Netherlands

Abstract. In recent years we have observed the rise of Experience and Application Research centers (EARC). These EARCs simulate realistic environments and are used for the empirical evaluation of interactive systems in a controlled setting. Such laboratory environments are intended to facilitate data collection without influencing the data itself. Accumulated experience in the use of EARCs has raised concerns that test participants could be impressed by the environments and have raised expectations for advanced systems they expect to encounter; this brings about the danger of systematic bias in subjective report data collected with EARCs. To evaluate the impact of an EARC as an instrument, a controlled experiment with 40 test participants was conducted. This experiment involved the replication of a traditional usability test in both the EARC and a traditional laboratory environment. The results of this study provide evidence regarding the validity and reliability of EARCs as instruments for evaluating interactive systems.

In recent years we have seen the rise of Experience and Application Research Centers (EARC). An EARC is best described as an advanced research infrastructure that supports multi disciplinary teams of researchers and designers to study human technology interaction and test new applications of technology. A differentiating aspect of these infrastructures is their high level of realism to simulate real life settings and the sophistication of technological embedding. In contrast to traditional research laboratories, these environments aim at providing a naturalistic context for end users to engage in interactions with applications of advanced technologies. In traditional research laboratories the emphasis is on the standardization of the research context and the removal of any potential additional influencing factors that could stem from the testing environment.

While these EARC have been successfully deployed in evaluating the user system interaction with applications of advanced technologies ([18]), the response bias elicited by these infrastructures as assessment tools on the collected data, has not been studied. Yet, in other research areas interested in assessing the user experience, it is known that the contextual settings can be of influence on the collected data ([13] [16] [2]).

One concern that is raised with a testing environment such as the ExperienceLabs is thus its potential influence in the collected data. This concern is

M. Tscheligi et al. (Eds.): AmI 2009, LNCS 5859, pp. 235–244, 2009.
© Springer-Verlag Berlin Heidelberg 2009

strengthened with observation where end users inside such environments have high expectations of finding advanced technological applications. To evaluate this potential threat for empirical research, a controlled study was conducted in which an empirical study was replicated in both a standard and low tech environment and the HomeLab. It is important to note that the testing environment (or any other system installed in this environment other than the system to be evaluated) did not play an active role during the experiment.

Response bias can be describes as any systematic tendency of a respondent to manifest particular response behavior for an extraneous reason which is not part of the experimental manipulation. In the past, various researchers ([5] [12] [9]) demonstrated the influence of specific facets of the environment on consumer behavior. To measure potential response bias, a controlled experiment was conducted in an EARC environment. This experiment involved the replication of a traditional usability test (of an experimental system for video editing through the use of an interactive television set) in both the EARC and a traditional laboratory environment. While the application to be tested was exactly the same in both environments, the EARC environment presented a better integration of the system into the environment and provided an overall more natural situation. The experiment and its findings are discussed below.

1   Experiment

1.1   Method

A total of 40 participants, who were unfamiliar with the EARC used in this study, were recruited. The experiment was designed as a within subject design consisting of two experimental sessions separated by a time interval of one week. It was suggested to participants that there would be an improvement of the system's usability between the sessions (see Table 1) based on their input during session 1. In reality however, only minor changes (e.g. user interface colors) were made to the system in order to be able to compare the findings from both sessions. In both sessions we conducted a typical usability test of the same interactive system.

Table 1. Experimental design

	Session 1	Session 2
Group 1	EARC	EARC
Group 2	EARC	Laboratory
Group 3	Laboratory	EARC
Group 4	Laboratory	Laboratory

1.2   Procedure

Setup as a typical usability test, the ease of use of a video editing system through an interactive television set was assessed in both the EARC and in a traditional laboratory environment. The laboratory environment is less attractive and realistic compared to the EARC environment. The most importance difference between both environments is the embedding and presentation of the experimental system as part of a home like environment. Other properties of the system (e.g. the interaction and display devices) and the environmental settings (e.g. lighting conditions) would be the same for both environments. A set of questionnaires was preceded by a short introductory text that differed depending on the experimental setting the participant was about to enter. In the introduction participants were told they were taking part in a research on the usability of a recently developed video editing system. Consequently, participants were given some information on the system to make it possible that certain expectations could be evoked. Next, the participants were told the usability test had been divided in two sessions with one week in between in which the video editing system would be adjusted on the basis of first sessions results. During the second session the participants were asked to evaluate the system again.

1.3   Materials

The experimental system deployed in the usability test is a TV-based video editing system that is able to automatically convert a home video into an edited version, which is essentially a summary of the raw footage. By means of a remote control, the user can edit and modify this automatically created summary by, during the viewing of the summary, pausing the desired shot and subsequently selecting one of the editing functions (e.g. adding music, adding effects). During the usability test, participants were requested to complete a given set of tasks with this system. Several usability and contextual measures were collected during the experiment. The instruments used for this data collection are discussed briefly.

– *Brief Mood Introspection Scale (BMIS)*
  In order to measure participants mood, the Brief Mood Introspection Scale (BMIS) by [11] was applied. The BMIS consists of 16 adjectives which are based on eight mood states: (1) happy, (2) loving, (3) calm, (4) energetic, (5) fearful/anxious, (6) angry, (7) tired and (8) sad.
– *Software Usability Measurement Inventory (SUMI)*
  The softwares usability was measured with the Software Usability Measurement Inventory ([8]). The SUMI consists of 50 statements and three item Likert scales on which the participants have to indicate whether they agree, are undecided or disagree with the statement. The SUMI contains statements like I enjoy my sessions with this prototype, It is obvious that user needs have been fully taken into consideration and The prototype has a very attractive presentation.

- *Pleasure, Dominance and Arousal scale (PDA)*
  In order to measure the degree to which participants are satisfied with the two different environments, the semantic differential Pleasure, Dominance and Arousal scale was used. [12] designed this widely used instrument to investigate how consumer behaviors are influenced by atmospheres ([6]). This instrument is based on three dimensions to describe an individuals emotional responses to an environment: pleasure, arousal and dominance. These dimensions have been subdivided into six opposing states of mind each. Each opposing pair is rated along a seven point Likert scale.
- *NASA Task Load Index (TLX)*
  The task load evoked by the performance of the assignments is measured by means of the NASA Task Load Index ([7]. In order to measure mental workload, the TLX uses six bipolar scales to assess task load on six dimensions: mental demand, physical demand, temporal demand, performance, effort and frustration ([17]). The mean task load value represents how demanding the participants experienced the execution of the tasks.
- *(Dis)confirmation of expectations*
  In order to measure the (dis)confirmation of expectations a commonly applied seven-point semantic differential scale is used ([1] [10] [15] [19] [20]). The scale ranges from The experimental system was worse than expected to better than expected. In order to measure participants expectation level ([4]) seven-point semantic differential scale was used. The range of this scale goes from My expectations about the experimental system were too high: it was poorer than I thought to My expectations about the experimental system were too low: it was better than I thought.

1.4 Results

The data analysis of the results obtained with the different questionnaires is now presented.

Brief Mood Introspection Scale (BMIS). Table 2 shows the mean scores on mood state for each group preliminary to the first session.

Table 2. Mean group scores on mood state corresponding to session 1 (score is at least 1 and at most 7; N group = 10)

	Group 1	Group 2	Group 3	Group 4
Session 1	3.62 (0.38)	3.64 (0.38)	3.80 (0.36)	3.68 (0.47)

The results of a One-Way ANOVA show that there was no significant difference between the four groups on the mean mood state scores concerning session 1 ($F(3,36) = 1.60$, $p = .21$). In table 3 the mean scores on mood state for each group preliminary to the second session are presented.

Table 3. Mean group scores on mood state corresponding to session 2 (score is at least 1 and at most 7; N group = 10)

	Group 1	Group 2	Group 3	Group 4
Session 2	3.67 (0.25)	3.79 (0.45)	3.84 (0.32)	3.76 (0.63)

Again, a One-Way ANOVA was conducted. The results show that, concerning the second session, the four groups did not differ significantly from each other on the mean mood state scores ($F(3,36) <1$, $p = .91$). Subsequently, in order to check whether there was a significant difference between the scores of session 1 and session 2, for each group an Independent Samples t-test was conducted. There was no significant difference found for group 1 ($t(18) = 1.96$, $p = .07$) just as for group 2 ($t(18) = 1.34$, $p = .20$), group 3 ($t(18) <1$, $p = .95$) and group 4 ($t(18) <1$, $p = .89$).

Software Usability Measurement Inventory (SUMI). The group mean scores for satisfaction as measured by the SUMI in session 1 are presented in table 4.

Table 4. Mean scores on satisfaction (based on SUMI) corresponding to session 1 (score is at least 1 and at most 3; N group = 10)

	Group 1	Group 2	Group 3	Group 4
Session 1	2.45 (0.26)	2.41 (0.23)	2.40 (0.15)	2.55 (0.17)

The results of a One-Way ANOVA show that, regarding session 1, the groups did not differ significantly from each other concerning mean satisfaction scores ($F(3,36) <1$, $p = .57$). Table 5 shows the groups mean scores on satisfaction for session 2.

Table 5. Mean scores on satisfaction (based on SUMI) corresponding to session 2 (score is at least 1 and at most 3; N group = 10)

	Group 1	Group 2	Group 3	Group 4
Session 2	2.47 (0.20)	2.40 (0.14)	2.40 (0.25)	2.50 (0.27)

Also here a One-Way ANOVA was conducted to check for significant differences in mean satisfaction scores between the groups. The results show, once more, that there was no significant difference between the groups ($F(3,36) <1$, $p = .57$). Finally, an Independent samples t-test was conducted to check for significant differences in mean satisfaction scores within each group between session 1 and session 2. The results show that neither for group 1 (t(18) <1, p = .36) nor group 2 (t(18) <1, p = .92), group 3 (t(18) = 1.06, p = .31) and group 4 (t(18) <1, p = .93) were there significant differences between both mean scores.

Pleasure, Dominance and Arousal scale (PDA). In Table 6, for each group the mean scores on the PDA-scale corresponding to session 1 are presented.

Table 6. Mean scores on feeling evoked by environment corresponding to session 1 (value is at least 1 and at most 7; N group = 10)

	Group 1	Group 2	Group 3	Group 4
Session 1	4.44 (0.59)	4.55 (0.45)	4.34 (0.73)	3.99 (0.52)

The result of an One-Way ANOVA indicated that the four groups did not differ significantly from each other concerning session 1 (F(3,36) = <1, p = .42). Table 7 shows for each group the mean scores on the PDA-scale corresponding to session 2.

Table 7. Mean scores on feeling evoked by environment corresponding to session 2 (value is at least 1 and at most 7; N group = 10)

	Group 1	Group 2	Group 3	Group 4
Session 2	4.42 (0.57)	4.28 (0.65)	4.55 (0.70)	3.59 (0.49)

A One-Way ANOVA was conducted to check whether the mean scores differed within session 2. Just like in session 1, there was no significant difference between the mean scores concerning session 2 (F(3,36) = <1, p = .44). Finally, an Independent samples t-test was carried out in order to find out whether there was a matter of significant difference within the mean group scores between session 1 and session 2. However, the results show that within group 1 (t(17) <1, p = .89), group 2 (t(17) <1 p = .41), group 3 (t(18) <1, p = .63) and group 4 (t(17) <1, p = .35) there were no significant differences between the sessions.

NASA Task Load Index (TLX). In Table 8, for each group the mean values on task load corresponding to session 1 are presented.

A One-Way ANOVA showed that the first sessions results of the groups did not differ significantly from each other (F(3,36) = 1.37, p = .27). Secondly, within the first session the mean scores of group 1 and group 4 and group 2 and group 3 were also compared. However, neither between group 1 and 4 (F(1,18) = 1.49, p = .24) nor group 2 and 3 (F(1,18) <1, p = .42) any significant differences

Table 8. Mean task load values corresponding to session 1 (value is at least 5 and at most 100; N group = 10)

	Group 1	Group 2	Group 3	Group 4
Session 1	26.67 (13.56)	31.08 (9.92)	33.58 (11.08)	26.67 (12.90)

Table 9. Mean task load values corresponding to session 2 (value is at least 5 and at most 100; N group = 10)

	Group 1	Group 2	Group 3	Group 4
Session 2	18.47 (5.64)	31.50 (9.52)	27.33 (9.33)	26.17 (11.62)

were found. Table 9 shows for each group the total mean value on task load corresponding to session 2.

A One-Way ANOVA was conducted to check whether the second sessions results differed significantly between the groups. The results show that there was again no significant difference between mean values ($F(3,36) < 1$, p = .55). The results of a One-Way ANOVA show that group 1 and 4 ($F(1,18) = 1.73$, p = .24) and group 2 and 3 ($F(1,18) < 1$, p = .49) did not differ significantly from each other with regard to session 2. Furthermore, to find out whether there was a matter of significant difference between the groups mean scores between session 1 and session 2, an Independent samples t-test was carried out. The results show that there was only a significant difference between the mean scores for group 1 ($t(18) = 2.35$, p < .05, explained variance = 18.4 percent) and not for group 2 ($t(18) < 1$, p = .63), group 3 ($t(18) < 1$, p = .64) and group 4 ($t(18) < 1$, p = .88).

(Dis)confirmation of expectations. In table 10, the mean scores per group on (dis)confirmation of expectations towards the experimental system measured in session 1 are presented.

Table 10. Mean scores on disconfirmation of expectations measured in session 1 (value is at least 1 and at most 7; N group = 10)

	Group 1	Group 2	Group 3	Group 4
Session 1	4.40 (1.17)	4.80 (1.09	4.45 (1.09)	5.05 (0.93)

The results of a One-Way ANOVA show that the mean scores of the groups did not differ significantly from each other ($F(3,36) = < 1$, p = .49). The mean scores of each group corresponding to the second session are presented in Table 11.

Table 11. Mean scores on disconfirmation of expectations measured in session 2 (value is at least 1 and at most 7; N group = 10)

	Group 1	Group 2	Group 3	Group 4
Session 2	3.90 (0.91)	5.15 (1.31)	4.20 (0.95)	4.35 (1.11)

Once more, the results of a One-Way ANOVA show that there was no significant difference in mean scores between the four groups (F(3,36) = 2.44, p = .08). An Independent samples t-test was conducted to check if there were significant differences in mean scores between session 1 and session 2. However, there was no significant difference found for group 1 (t(18) = 1.07, p = .30) just as for group 2 (t(18) <1, p = .52), group 3 (t(18) <1, p = .59) and group 4 (t(18) = 1.53, p = .14).

2   Conclusions

While there is a growing interest in the use of Experience and Application Research Centers for studying user system interaction with applications of advanced technologies, there have been no studies reported in literature on the potential response bias induced by such testing environments. This is remarkable since the field of user system interaction research has been building on methodologies borrowed from the psychological research domain ([3]) while the notion of response bias and empirical research paradigms to avoid this effect, are a key element in the psychology research domain.

The present study investigates the presence of a potential response bias induced by an EARC during evaluations with users of advanced technology applications. The main finding of this study is that there is no statistical significant difference between the usability measures obtained in the EARC and those obtained in a traditional usability laboratory. The study presented follows on, from an earlier unpublished experiment [14], which similarly did not provide evidence of any response bias. It appears conducting user evaluations in the context of an EARC does not bias subjective report as compared to evaluating the same system in a traditional laboratory environment.

During the debriefing at the end of the second session, several participants explained that because of performing the video editing tasks and filling in questionnaires they had paid hardly any attention to the environment. These remarks suggest that when testingsystems that are more integrated in the environment participants could be paying more attention to the environment. Consider for example the evaluation of voice controlled environments in which there is no single point of interaction but in which the user will interact with or through the environment as a whole. To extend the generalizability of the findings reported future research should replicate this experiment with such applications that are more tightly embedded in the physical environment of the testing laboratory.

Neverhteless, the absence so far for any evidence of response bias that is caused by the environment constitutes an important argument towards the validity and reliability of empirical research in environments such as the EARC.

Acknowledgements

The authors acknowledge Gerard Hollemans for the original inpsiration for this study and Karin Nieuwenhuizen for her initial experimental study on response bias of EARCs and her advice at the early stages of this work.

References

1. Aiello, A.: Scaling the heights of consumer satisfaction: An evaluation of alternate measures. In: Day, R.L. (ed.) Consumer Satisfaction, Dissatisfaction and Complaining Behavior. School of Business, Indiana University, Bloomington (1977)
2. Bell, R., Meiselman, H.L., Pierson, B.J., Reeve, W.G.: Effects of adding an Italian theme to a restaurant on perceived ethnicity, acceptability, and selection of foods. Appetite 22, 11–24 (1994)
3. Carroll, J.: Human – Computer Interaction: Psychology as a science of design. Annual Review of Psychology, 48–61 (1997)
4. Churchill Jr., G.A., Surprenant, C.: An investigation into the determinants of customer satisfaction. Journal of Marketing Research 19, 491–504 (1982)
5. Donovan, R.J., Rossiter, J.R.: Store atmosphere: An experimental psychology approach. Journal of Retailing 58, 34–57 (1982)
6. Foxall, G.R.: The emotional texture of consumer environments: A systematic approach to atmospherics. Journal of Economic Psychology 18, 505–523 (1997)
7. Hart, S.G., Staveland, L.E.: Development of NASA-TLX (Task Load Index): Results of empirical and theoretical research. In: Hancock, P.A., Meshkati, N. (eds.) Human Mental Workload, pp. 239–250. North-Holland Press, Amsterdam (1988)
8. Kirakowski, J., Corbett, M.: SUMI: The Software Usability Measurement Inventory. British Journal of Educational Technology 24(3), 210 (1993)
9. Kotler, P.: Atmospherics as a marketing tool. Journal of Retailing 49, 48–64 (1974)
10. Linda, G., Oliver, R.L.: Multiple brand analysis of expectation and disconfirmation effects on satisfaction. Paper presented at the 87th Annual Convention of the American Psychological Association (1979)
11. Mayer, J.D., Gaschke, Y.N.: The experience and meta-experience of Mood. Journal of Personality and Social Psychology 55(1), 102–111 (1988)
12. Mehrabian, A., Russell, J.A.: An approach to environmental psychology. MIT Press, Cambridge (1974)
13. Meiselman, H.L.: The contextual basis for food acceptance, food choice and food intake: The food, the situation and the individual. In: Meiselman, H.L., MacFie, H.J.H. (eds.) Food choice acceptance and consumption, pp. 139–263. Blackie Academic and Professional, Glasgow (1996)
14. Nieuwenhuizen, K.: First Investigation of the Potential Halo Effect of High-End Usability Laboratories on User Evaluation Questionnaires, Stan Ackermans Institute, USI programme, graduation thesis, Eindhoven University of Technology, The Netherlands (2006)

15. Oliver, R.L.: Effect of expectation and disconfirmation on postexposure product evaluations: An alternative interpretation. Journal of Applied Psychology 62, 480–486 (1977)
16. Petit, C., Sieffermann, J.M.: Testing consumer preferences for iced-coffee: Does the drinking environment have any influence? Food Quality and Preference 18, 161–172 (2007)
17. Rubio, S., Díaz, E., Martín, J., Puente, J.M.: Evaluation of subjective mental workload: A comparison of SWAT, NASA-TLX, and workload profile methods. Applied Psychology: An international review 53(1), 61–86 (2004)
18. Russel, S., Cousins, S.B.: IBM Almaden's User Sciences & Experience Research Lab. In: Proceedings of the ACM Conference on Human Factors of Computer Systems, Vienna, Austria, April 24-29, pp. 1079–1080 (2004)
19. Swan, J.E., Trawick, I.F.: Consumer satisfaction with a retail store related to the fulfillment of expectations on an initial shopping trip. In: Day, R.L. (ed.) Consumer Satisfaction, Dissatisfaction and Complaining Behavior. School of Business, Indiana University, Bloomington (1980)
20. Westbrook, R.A.: Intrapersonal affective influences upon consumer satisfaction. Journal of Consumer Research 7, 49–54 (1980)

The Assisted User-Centred Generation and Evaluation of Pervasive Interfaces

Karin Leichtenstern and Elisabeth André

Institute of Computer Science
Multimedia Concepts and Applications
Universittsstr. 6a
D-86159 Augsburg
{Leichtenstern,Andre}@informatik.uni-augsburg.de
https://mm-werkstatt.informatik.uni-augsburg.de

Abstract. The usability of a pervasive interface is crucial because it is a quality criterion which can determine about the success or the failure of a product. The application of the user-centred design is a possibility to reach a good design. However, this process requires combined knowledge of software and usability engineering. A lack of these skills can cause long development times and additional costs as well as badly usable interfaces. We address these problems and support interface developers with a tool-based assistance which reduces the required programming and interface design skills of the developers in order to more efficiently conduct the user-centred design. In this paper we describe this tool-based assistance for the user-centred generation and evaluation of pervasive interfaces for mobile phones as well as its evaluation.

1 Introduction

Ubiquitous Computing and its synonyms *Pervasive Computing* and *Ambient Intelligence* become more and more important in our everyday life ([21],[8]). Their common idea is to make the computer invisible in our everyday life for interactions with everything, everywhere at any time [7]. The first real pervasive interaction devices are mobile phones. Almost everybody owns a mobile phone and takes it around constantly. Recent phones support novel hardware and network facilities which enable different mobile interactions to pervasive environments. Ballagas and colleagues [2] give a comprehensive overview about the different mobile interaction techniques available with todays smart phones. For example, the mobile phone's camera can be used to recognize visual markers or built-in RFID reader can be used to receive information stored on RFID tags. Consequently, interactions with the user's ambient world, e.g. RFID-tagged posters become possible. Compared to the development for desktop settings, developing pervasive interfaces for mobile phones adds new layers of complexity. For instance, the developer has to cope with the limited input and output capabilities of the mobile devices [8]. Ensuring usability in this context is challenge. A user-centered design process ([17], [10]) is one possibility to obtain a good design

M. Tscheligi et al. (Eds.): AmI 2009, LNCS 5859, pp. 245–255, 2009.

for pervasive applications. A characteristic feature of this process is an iterative design which includes several iterations of implementing prototypes along with continuous user evaluations of these prototypes. The iterations are required to build the interface as usable as possible for different contextual conditions in a pervasive environment. This user-centred design requires advanced usability and software engineering skills in order to efficiently and correctly develop a pervasive interface for mobile phones. One option to solve this problem is the usage of software tools which adapt these skills and assist in the user-centred design of pervasive interfaces. Our approach of the tool-based user-centred design supports interface developers in the iterative design with an assisted generation and evaluation of dynamic pervasive interfaces for mobile phones which are compliant with approved mobile phone guidelines. Before our tool-based approach is described more detailed, we first reflect existing tools on the requirements of the assisted user-centred design. At the end of the paper we introduce a preliminary study which shows benefits and problems of the assisted user-centred design with our tool.

2   Related Work

Until now, several tools or frameworks have been implemented which support developers in order to generate pervasive interfaces. Hull [1] classified four different categories of tools: ubiquitous middleware, ubiquitous modules, prototyping tools and content&behaviour tools. Middleware and modules ([18], [19]) provide developers with valuable software components and architectures whereas prototyping tools assist in building up a sketch of a concept [14] or a specification of particular rules, e.g. for context-aware applications [6]. Content&behaviour tools ([1], [4], [16]) provide assistance for the generation of interfaces as well as for the specification of their services and content. The specification of services and content is crucial in order to generate interfaces which content is dynamically loaded and displayed at the runtime. All of these four introduced types of tools only support in the interface's generation but not in their evaluation. To support assistance for the user-centred design process in all stages, approaches are required which also support in the conduction and analysis of user evaluations. Thus, we added two further types of tools to Hull's categories: evaluation tools and user-centred design tools. Evaluation tools ([9], [3]) assist in conducting user evaluations whereas user-centred design (UCD) tools ([13], [5]) support in the generation and evaluation of interface's prototypes. We evaluated these six categories of tools if they assist the user-centred design process in all stages (Generation and Evaluation) in order to quickly and easily develop pervasive interfaces for mobile phones which are compliant with some approved mobile phone guidelines (Guidelines). Additionally, we investigated whether these tools enable the dynamic content presentation on the mobile device (Dynamic Content) as well as the support of different mobile interaction techniques (Pervasiveness). The results of this evaluation are illustrated in table 1[1].

---

[1] The rating scale ranges from a very weak (- -) to a very strong support (++).

Table 1. Tool Categories and the Assisted User-Centred Design's Requirements

	Generation	Evaluation	Dynamic	Pervasiveness	Guidelines
Middleware	+	- -	++	++	- -
Modules	+	- -	++	++	- -
Prototyping Tools	+	- -	-	- -	- -
Content & Behaviour Tools	++	- -	++	+	- -
Evaluation Tools	- -	++	- -	- -	- -
Todays UCD-Tools	++	++	-	- -	- -
UCD-Tools: MoPeDT	++	++	++	++	++

Only UCD-tools assist in the generation and evaluation of interfaces. For this category we consider a lack of tools as our review only revealed two UCD-tools: SUEDE [13] and d.tools [5]. Both tools neither support in the compliance of approved guidelines nor assist in the development of pervasive interfaces for mobile phones. SUEDE assists in the development of speech interfaces whereas d.tools addresses the development of physical computing applications. In summary, our literature review revealed no known tool which assists interface developers in the user-centred generation and evaluation of pervasive interfaces for mobile phones which follow approved mobile phone guidelines and support the presentation of even dynamic content.

3 Assisted User-Centred Design

Our literature review proved the lack of an appropriate tool-based assistance for pervasive interface developers. We provide such a tool called MoPeDT (Pervasive Interface Development Toolkit for Mobile Phones). Different mobile interaction techniques can be used in order to generate pervasive interfaces for mobile phones which dynamically load and display content of a database. These generated interfaces are compliant with approved guidelines, e.g. a consistent layout. In contrast to other tools, our approach also assists in the conduction and analysis of user studies. For example, the assistance automatically annotates captured videos on different contexts which emerge in the pervasive environment. Thus, our tool meets all requirements of the assisted user-centred design of pervasive interfaces (see Table 1). In this section we describe the three components of MoPeDT more detailed: the architecture, the mobile phone framework and the IDE (Integrated Development Environment).

3.1 MoPeDT - The Architecture

The architecture is the basic component of MoPeDT. It enables the integration of different components which emerge in a pervasive environment. Figure 1 shows this architecture which consists of a main server and a database as well

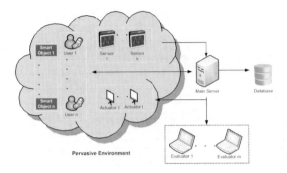

Fig. 1. The Architecture of MoPeDT

as several smart objects, users with mobile phones, sensors, actuators and evaluators. Smart objects, such as pictures or domestic home appliances are tagged objects in a pervasive environment. Users can address these objects by using the pervasive interface of the mobile phone in order to load or store persistent multimedia content about the objects via the main server. Other components of the architecture are the sensors and actuators. They can be used to collect and display additional information about the pervasive environment. Sensors, such as a temperature or a humidity sensor can collect, interpret and broadcast context to the main server. The main server can forward this context to interested users or actuators. Actuators, e.g. a public display can receive and display context or other information, such as video content. The last component of the architecture is called evaluators which are a special kind of actuators. They are required to perform user studies and log user interactions. For all these components software modules exist in Java.

3.2   MoPeDT - The Mobile Phone Framework

A special software module of MoPeDT's architecture is the mobile phone framework. The framework adopts software and usability engineering aspects, such as the implementation of the network communication, the support of different mobile interaction techniques and the support of screen templates which are grounded on approved mobile phone guidelines. Instead of considering and implementing these aspects, developers only need to specify the pervasive interface's interactions and behaviour via XML files.

The current version of the mobile phone framework supports four different mobile interaction techniques: Keyboard-based, NFC-based, Speech-based and Location-based. Thus, the framework not only enables the development of location-based applications but also of pervasive applications which require the other interaction techniques. Using the XML file for the interaction specification, developers can specify these mobile interaction techniques and map their emergence to contexts. For instance, in this file the GPS position of a location can be defined and mapped to trigger an action depending on a certain context,

e.g. the context HOME. Now, whenever a user has entered a specified location or performed a defined interaction technique, the framework automatically
triggers and processes contexts. These triggered contexts can induce transitions
and change the pervasive interface's behaviour on the local device or on other
components in the architecture. The contexts can also be used whenever user
studies are conducted. They are automatically logged and later on used in order
to annotate the captured audio-visual content.

The behaviour of the pervasive interface is specified via state-chart diagrams
which is common practice for integrated development environments (e.g. [13],
[5]). We use *State Chart XML* [20] to represent the diagram in XML. These
XML files can be interpreted by the mobile phone framework to generate the
corresponding screen or to handle the corresponding events because each state
of the diagram represents a screen of the interface and each transition of a state
represents triggerable context. For example, figure 2 shows a very simplified
state-chart diagram which consists of two states: the Main Menu screen and
the Hello World screen as well as one transition: HOME. In this example, the
Hello World screen is only loaded once the context HOME has been triggered
by a location-based interaction. Hence, in order to load the Hello World screen,
the user has to enter the specified location of the context HOME. Using our
approach, transitions can also be specified for contexts triggered by Keyboard-
based, NFC-based and Speech-based interactions. In contrast to the developers

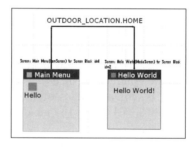

Fig. 2. Behaviour Specification of a Pervasive Interface via a State-Chart Diagram

of d.tools and SUEDE, we apprehend sources of errors when giving developers
free options to specify the interface's states and transitions in the state-chart diagram due to several inducible usability problems, e.g. the non-compliance of the
consistency. Thus, when specifying states in the state-chart diagram, we support
developers with an expandable set of screen templates which follow approved
usability guidelines from Nokia [15]. For instance, these templates consider a
consistent layout, softkey usage and navigation style. Each screen has a heading, content and a softkey part. In the softkey part the left softkey is used for
options whereas the middle key is applied for confirmations and navigations and
the right softkey is utilized for negative actions (back, cancel or exit). Additionally, each screen contains a contextual help and an option to return to the main

menu. From each screen the user can return to the previous state automatically. Thus, each screen provides a back, cancel or exit option.

The current version of the framework supports templates for various kinds of menu screens, media input and output screens as well as feedback screens, e.g. a waiting or error screen. Developers can use these screen templates and define their static or dynamic content, e.g. the heading, the items and the options of a menu screen. In contrast to static screens, dynamic screens add new layers of complexity to the specification task due to several reasons. Static screens display unchangeable content whereas dynamic screens are generated and adapted to the content at the runtime. For instance, the number of items in a dynamic menu screen or the media type of a dynamic media output screen are not known at the development time. Thus, screen templates are expected to dynamically adapt their layout, e.g. on the loaded media type (text, image, audio and video). Certainly, these dynamic screens are crucial for pervasive interfaces of mobile phones because several content are context-adaptive loaded. For instance, once a user has selected a smart object, a dynamic screen automatically loads and displays all services and their content for the just selected smart object. Our screen templates enable the dynamic screen definition by means of a simplified scripting language and thereby enable the dynamic presentation of content defined in the database.

3.3 MoPeDT - The Integrated Development Environment (IDE)

Although MoPeDT's architecture and mobile phone framework support the generation of dynamic pervasive interfaces and provide a platform to conduct user evaluations, MoPeDT also supplies an integrated development environment (IDE). This IDE simplifies the interaction and behaviour specification of pervasive interfaces as well as the conduction of user studies due to its provided graphical user interfaces (GUIs) for all stages of the user-centred design process. Figure 3 and 4 illustrate the GUIs for the generation and evaluation of a pervasive interface.

In the generation phase of an interface, the user of our IDE is assisted with a GUI in order to define the database content and the interface's interaction and behaviour files for the mobile phone framework. At the end of the specification, a high-fidelity prototype is automatically generated which runs on emulators or real mobile phones. So far, we have tested generated prototypes on the Nokia N95 and the Nokia 6131 NFC.

After the generation, a user study can be conducted, e.g. to investigate the usability or the user's behaviour. For instance, a user study can reveal whether the wording of items and options is comprehensible or not and which mobile interaction technique fits best to which situation. Therefore, videos have to be captured and later on reviewed and labeled on corresponding features, such as the user's interactions. Without tool-based assistance this task called annotation is very time-consuming and error-prone. With MoPeDT we release interface developers from performing this annoying task. During the user study, audio-visual data, live annotations and task descriptions can be stored while relevant contexts are

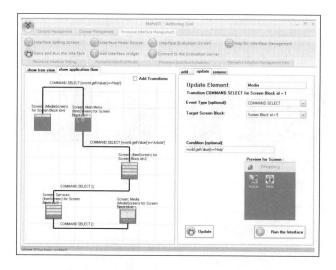

Fig. 3. Prototype Specification: The GUI for the specification of the prototype with the state chart view and options to specifiy the screen templates

logged automatically. After having conducted an evaluation, the captured data can be analyzed by means of an extended version of ANVIL [12] which automatically annotates the captured auto-visual data on the logged contexts. ANVIL is a tool which has been widely used for the annotation of audio-visual material containing human-human dialogue or human-computer interactions. It supports annotation at various freely definable tracks which makes it highly application-independent. The extended version of ANVIL displays the captured videos, a time-line with the logged contexts as well as the screen shots of the pervasive interface. This assistance helps developers to review the already pre-annotated data. For instance, interface developers can scroll through the video or jump to intended contexts of the time-line in order to investigate the user's behaviour in different contextual situations, e.g. to find usability problems or user preferences. Additionally, the extended version of ANVIL supports the export of the annotated data in different formats of statistic tools, such as SPSS in order to investigate the probability of occurrence for an intended context or behaviour.

4   Evaluation of MoPeDT

To investigate if our approach of the tool-based development of pervasive interfaces improves the conduction of the user-centred design process, we accomplished a user study with seven subjects having intermediate software engineering skills (between one and five years) and minor usability engineering skills (less than one year). We were interested whether using MoPeDT reduces the generation and evaluation time of a pervasive interface as well as the number of usability problems compared to traditional approaches. We were also interested

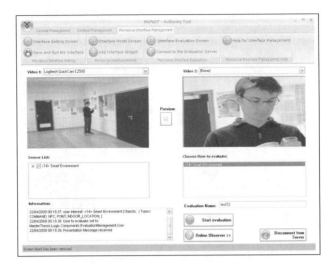

Fig. 4. Prototype Evaluation: The GUI shows the cameras and the supported options, e.g. an option to store live annotations

in the comments and wishes our participants had for our tool-based approach. Thus, after the test we interviewed the participants and asked them for their mind about our tool-based assistance. In order to evaluate the potential benefits of MoPeDT, the subjects had to create and evaluate a particular pervasive interface in two different settings. In the first setting the subjects used classical development and evaluation platforms, such as Eclipse or Netbeans to generate and evaluate a pervasive interface whereas in the second setting the subjects had to use MoPeDT for the same task. In both settings a shopping assistant had to be implemented and evaluated which helps users receive information about articles in a shopping store, e.g. about the ingredients of articles. In the evaluation videos,users had to be captured and later on analyzed in order to find usability problems, e.g. wording problems. For the generation and the evaluation of the interfaces we determined the required generation and evaluation time and counted the number of violation against the Nokia guidelines [15]. All subjects were previously skilled in these guidelines and reminded to deploy them.

The results of our tests proved our assumptions. On average, the required generation and evaluation time in minutes without MoPeDT (M = 900.71, SE = 245.16), was significantly higher than when using MoPeDT (M = 184.28, SE = 37.71),$t(6) = 3.41$, p <0.05, r = 0.94. When not using MoPeDT, the network and GUI programming required much more time in the prototype generation phase. In the evaluation phase, the annotation and analysis of the captured videos decelerated the user-centred design process when not using MoPeDT because the developers had to manually synchronize the logged events with the captured videos which is done automatically when using MoPeDT. Beside the reduced generation and evaluation time, the number of usability problems and violation against the Nokia guidelines could also be reduced. The interfaces developed without MoPeDT had significantly more usability problems (M = 4.43, SE = 0.20) than when using MoPeDT (M = 0.71, SE = 0.29), $t(6) = 10.33$, p <0.001, r = -0.06. Figure 5 shows screen shots of interfaces generated without and with MoPeDT which illustrate two usability problems. When not using MoPeDT, a common problem is the non-observance to display items with both icons and text. A further usability problem is using scrollbars instead of side-to-side scrolling which causes a user's higher cognitive load. The interviews conducted with the participants of our study showed benefits and problems of MoPeDT. The most acute problem is the limitation in the scope of supported operations, e.g. the number of the supported mobile interaction techniques and screen templates. Highlighted benefits of MoPeDT are the less required programming and interface design skills as well as the saved time and improved quality of the interfaces.

Fig. 5. Screens shots of the interfaces developed without (left screens) and with MoPeDT (right screens)

5 Conclusion and Discussion

In this paper we introduced requirements concerning user-centred design tools and illustrated MoPeDT as an example software which meets these requirements. MoPeDT is the first known UCD-tool which maps the user-centred design process in order to assist interface developer in the generation and evaluation of pervasive interfaces for mobile phones. Our study approved MoPeDT as a promising tool-based assistance for pervasive interface developers because it saves time and improves the interface's quality. Consequently, this saved time can be applied in order to concentrate on the concept development and content management of the application as well as the investigation of the user's behaviour in user studies, e.g. to investigate different multi-user settings of pervasive games [11].

References

1. Hull, R., Clayton, B., Melamed, T.: Rapid authoring of mediascapes. In: Davies, N., Mynatt, E.D., Siio, I. (eds.) UbiComp 2004. LNCS, vol. 3205, pp. 125–142. Springer, Heidelberg (2004)
2. Ballagas, R., Borchers, J., Rohs, M., Sheridan, J.G.: The smart phone: a ubiquitous input device. Pervasive Computing, IEEE 5(1), 70–77 (2006)

3. Carter, S., Mankoff, J., Heer, J.: Momento: support for situated ubicomp experimentation. In: CHI 2007: Proceedings of the SIGCHI conference on Human factors in computing systems, pp. 125–134. ACM, New York (2007)
4. Correia, N., Alves, L., Correia, H., Romero, L., Morgado, C., Soares, L., Cunha, J.C., Romao, T., Dias, A.E., Jorge, J.A.: Instory: a system for mobile information access, storytelling and gaming activities in physical spaces. In: ACE 2005: Proceedings of the 2005 ACM SIGCHI International Conference on Advances in computer entertainment technology, pp. 102–109. ACM, New York (2005)
5. Design, T.I., Hartmann, B., Klemmer, S.R.: Reflective physical prototyping. In: Proceedings of UIST 2006 Symposium on User Interface Software and Technology, pp. 299–308. ACM, New York (2006)
6. Dey, A.K., Hamid, R., Beckmann, C., Li, I., Hsu, D.: a cappella: Programming by demonstration of context-aware applications. In: Proceedings of CHI 2004, pp. 33–40. ACM, New York (2004)
7. Gopal, G., Kindberg, T., Barton, J., Morgan, J., Becker, G., Caswell, D., Frid, M., Krishnan, V., Morris, H., Schettino, J., Serra, B., Spasojevic, M.: People, places, things: web presence for the real world. In: Proceedings WMCSA 2000, pp. 365–376 (2000), http://www.cooltown.hp.com/papers/webpres/webpresence.htm
8. Gorlenko, L., Merrick, R.: No wires attached: Usability challenges in the connected mobile world. IBM Syst. J. 42(4), 639–651 (2003)
9. Howarth, J., Smith-Jackson, T., Hartson, R.: Supporting novice usability practitioners with usability engineering tools. Int. J. Hum.-Comput. Stud. 67(6), 533–549 (2009)
10. Kangas, E., Kinnunen, T.: Applying user-centered design to mobile application development. Commun. ACM 48(7), 55–59 (2005)
11. Leichtenstern, K., André, E.: Studying Multi-User Settings for Pervasive Games. In: 11th International Conference on Human-Computer Interaction with Mobile Devices and Services, Mobile HCI, pp. 190–199 (2009)
12. Kipp, M.: Anvil - a generic annotation tool for multimodal dialogue. In: Proceedings of the 7th European Conference on Speech Communication and Technology (Eurospeech), Aalborg, September 2001, pp. 1367–1370 (2001)
13. Klemmer, S.R., Sinha, A.K., Chen, J., Landay, J.A., Aboobaker, N., Wang, A.: Suede: a wizard of oz prototyping tool for speech user interfaces. In: UIST 2000: Proceedings of the 13th annual ACM symposium on User interface software and technology, pp. 1–10. ACM Press, New York (2000)
14. Li, Y., Hong, J.I., Landay, J.A.: Topiary: a tool for prototyping location-enhanced applications. In: UIST 2004: Proceedings of the 17th annual ACM symposium on User interface software and technology, pp. 217–226. ACM Press, New York (2004)
15. Nokia. Design and user experience library (2009), http://library.forum.nokia.com/
16. Pan, P., Kastner, C., Crow, D., Davenport, G.: M-studio: an authoring application for context-aware multimedia. In: MULTIMEDIA 2002: Proceedings of the tenth ACM international conference on Multimedia, pp. 351–354. ACM, New York (2002)
17. Rosenbaum, S., Rohn, J.A., Humburg, J.: A toolkit for strategic usability: results from workshops, panels, and surveys. In: CHI 2000: Proceedings of the SIGCHI conference on Human factors in computing systems, pp. 337–344. ACM, New York (2000)
18. Salber, D., Dey, A.K., Abowd, G.D.: The context toolkit: aiding the development of context-enabled applications. In: CHI 1999: Proceedings of the SIGCHI conference on Human factors in computing systems, pp. 434–441. ACM, New York (1999)

19. Serrano, M., Nigay, L., Demumieux, R., Descos, J., Losquin, P.: Multimodal interaction on mobile phones: development and evaluation using acicare. In: MobileHCI
2006: Proceedings of the 8th conference on Human-computer interaction with mobile devices and services, pp. 129–136. ACM, New York (2006)
20. W3C. State chart xml (2009), http://www.w3.org/TR/2009/WD-scxml-20090507/
21. Weiser, M.: The computer for the 21st century. Scientific American (February 1991)

Increased Robustness in Context Detection and Reasoning Using Uncertainty Measures: Concept and Application

Martin Berchtold and Michael Beigl

Distributed and Ubiquitous Systems, TU Braunschweig
Muehlenpfordtstr. 23, 38106 Braunschweig, Germany

Abstract. This paper reports on a novel recurrent fuzzy classification method for robust detection of context activities in an environment using either single or distributed sensors. It also introduces a classification of system architectures for uncertainty calculation in general. Our proposed novel method utilizes uncertainty measures for improvement of detection, fusion and aggregation of context knowledge. Uncertainty measurement calculations are based on our novel recurrent fuzzy system. We applied the method in a real application to recognize various applause (and non applause) situations, e.g. during a conference. Measurements were taken from mobile phone sensors (microphone, accel. if available) and acceleration sensory attached to a board marker. We show that we are able to improve robustness of detection using our novel recurrent fuzzy classifier in combination with uncertainty measures by ~30% on average. We also show that the use of multiple phones and distributed recognition in most cases allows to achieve a recognition rate between 90% and 100%.

1 Introduction

The detection of surrounding situations or contexts has been an interesting area of research for almost a decade. Robust context recognition could have many applications in office or industrial environments. In this paper we focus on a more playful application area, that is nevertheless very challenging: the detection of clapping events. The recognition system we present does not assume any a-priori knowledge regarding the sensors being used or their placement. As sensors we use mobile phones with microphones and optional acceleration sensors. The phones may be carried in a pocket or rest on the table. Our system is able to handle unsteady detection quality, aggregate classifications from different sources and still classifies situations correctly to a high percentage. In context recognition, measures to express the confidence of a detected context can be very helpful to improve the overall robustness. Some authors, e.g. Bucholz et al. [1] refer to this confidence level as "Quality of Context (QoC)". [2] shows the design of quality extensions for context ontologies and how fuzzy set theory can be used for context ontology matching under uncertainty. None of these publications describes a method how such a quality could be derived. We show

M. Tscheligi et al. (Eds.): AmI 2009, LNCS 5859, pp. 256–266, 2009.

how systems can be designed that deliver a QoC measure, although we use the term "Uncertainty" instead of "Quality" in reference to the wording in classical AI literature. Support for reasoning about uncertain contexts with probabilistic logic, fuzzy logic and Bayesian networks is described in [3]. How to model uncertainty in context-aware computing is described in [4], but the method for uncertainty measure calculation is not described and there is also no evidence given how uncertainty measures can improve robustness in reasoning. We will present uncertainty measures, their computation and also evaluate their benefits in this paper. In our proposed approach uncertainty measures are derived using a recurrent fuzzy inference system (sec. 3). We also evaluate how uncertainty can be used throughout the further inference processes - e.g. fusion and aggregation of contexts - to increase reliability of classification (sec. 4+5). Furthermore, the paper contains a first system architecture typification for systems and classifiers that are able to produce uncertainty measures (sec. 2).

2   Various Methods of Calculating Uncertainty Measures

There are three general methods of computing an uncertainty value in a context classification system. These three methods correspond to possible system architecture styles or types for uncertainty measurement derivation, as shown in figure 1. Which of these styles are suitable depends on the classification method, but also on the specific setting in an application context. The most general architecture style is Parallel Uncertainty Calculation (fig. 1(a)). In this system architecture style a context classifier works in parallel to an uncertainty detector (here called classification fuzziness). The uncertainty classifier thus behaves like an independent observer that constantly evaluates the output of the context classifier. Such systems are useful if methods for classification and evaluation of the classification differ. [5] shows that this approach is very beneficial for filtering contexts. A more compact classification is the Implicit Uncertainty System Architecture (fig. 1(b)). An examplary implementation of this architecture style are Fuzzy Inference Systems (FIS)[6]. Here, fuzziness from within the mapping FIS can be used to derive the uncertainty level. E.g. in a TSK-FIS the outcome requires interpretation of the mapping outcome using a membership function.

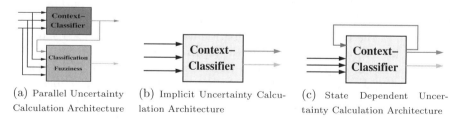

(a) Parallel Uncertainty   (b) Implicit Uncertainty Calcu-   (c) State Dependent Uncer-
Calculation Architecture   lation Architecture   tainty Calculation Architecture

Fig. 1. Different system architecture styles to compute uncertainty of a context classification

The disadvantage of this method is, that only the fuzziness of the mapping model can be detected, with only small variations among different classes. The uncertainty of the system configuration itself will thus not be taken into account when calculating the uncertainty level. The third architecture style is State Depended Uncertainty calculation 1(c). An implementation example of this architecture are recurrent fuzzy classification systems. Here it might be possible to solve problems arising in Implicit Uncertainty Calculation Architectures. Although this paper focuses on the use of uncertainty measures for filtering, we will also show in our system implementation how the measure is computed. Our system implements filter-like behavior and provides a fuzzy uncertainty on which a fusion or aggregation step is significantly improved when using uncertainty measures.

3   Offline Identification and Online System

3.1   Offline Identification Algorithm for RFIS-Classifier

A Recurrent Fuzzy Inference System (RFIS) is used to map sensor data features onto a classifiable linear set. The general idea behind Recurrent Fuzzy Systems (RFS) can be found in [7]. This soft system needs to be identified upon an annotated training feature set via a combination of a clustering algorithm and linear regression. Usually the identification of a Fuzzy Inference System (FIS) needs only one step of clustering, but since we use a recurrent one, each new mapping result leads to a new set of input data, upon which another iteration of clustering needs to be performed. The algorithm for identifying the RFIS consists of the following steps:

1. Data Separation: The training data is separated according to the class the data pairs belong to. Clustering on each subset delivers rules that can be assigned to each class. **2. Subtractive Clustering:** Subtractive clustering [8] per subset identifies the number of rules and the membership functions of each rule's antecedent without having to declare how many clusters there are. **3. Least Squares:** A linear regression identifies the linear functional consequence of the rules. The least squares method minimizes the quadratic error, which is the quadratic distance between the desired output and the actual output of the TSK-FIS classifier for the training data set. Minimizing the quadratic error leads to an overdetermined linear equation to be solved. **4. Recurrent Data Set:** The recurrent TSK-FIS is obtained over a data set that has the output of the previously identified FIS shifted by one, so the first data pair of the training set has a zero in the recurrent dimension. All data pairs for time $t > 1$ have the output of the FIS mapping of $t - 1$ in the recurrent dimension. For this data set the steps 1 to 3 are repeated. **5. Stop Criterion:** We could not find a general stop criterion, since two demands need to be met. The resulting classifier needs to have high accuracy and the outcome needs to have an uncertainty level that is of profit for reasoning. Therefore the developer has to decide, according to a separate check data set, what good results for the classifier and its uncertainty levels are. The steps 1 to 4 are repeated and graphically observed until the developer recognizes a good outcome.

The RFIS identified through this algorithm is the key component of the sensor data classifier. This RFIS also provides the desired fuzzy uncertainty described previously.

3.2   Online Recurrent Fuzzy Classifier

The online recurrent fuzzy classifier consists of several steps of processing from a real world value to a tuple of class and fuzzy uncertainty. The first step is the sensory, that converts the real world signal into a digital measurement. Secondly, the desired features are extracted from the measurement. In the third step the Recurrent Fuzzy Inference System (RFIS) maps the features onto a classifiable linear set. The outcome of the mapping at time t gets fed back as part of the input at $t+1$. The linear set gets fuzzily classified according to designated fuzzy numbers in the last step. All steps are diagrammed in figure 2.

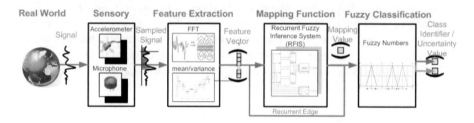

Fig. 2. Online system architecture for classification and fuzzy uncertainty

1. Feature Extraction: The features used for activity recognition with acceleration measurements are mostly variance and mean values, since they are easily calculated and give good classification results. These features were used to preprocess the accelerometer data from the "OpenMoko" phones and the "Freescale ZSTAR". For audio data the standard extraction method is a "Fast Fourier Transformation (FFT)", which is also used to extract the frequency features for the audio classification. The audio sources are the microphones of the "OpenMoko". **2. Recurrent FIS Mapping:** Takagi, Sugeno and Kang [9] (TSK) fuzzy inference systems are fuzzy rule-based structures, which are especially suited for automated construction. Within a TSK-FIS, the consequence of the implication is not a functional membership to a fuzzy set, but a constant or linear function. A TSK-FIS is used to map the extracted features onto a linear set, whose values can be assigned to a class identifier in a separate classification process. The outcome of the mapping at time t is fed back as additional input dimension for the TSK-FIS mapping at $t+1$. The recurrency not only delivers the desired uncertainty level, but also stabilizes and improves the mapping accuracy. **3. Fuzzy Classification:** The outcome of the TSK-FIS mapping needs to be assigned to one of the classes the projection should result in. This assignment is done fuzzy, so the result is not only a class identifier, but also a membership identifying the fuzzy uncertainty of the classification process. Each class identifier is interpreted as a triangular shaped fuzzy number. The mean of the fuzzy number is the identifier itself, with the highest membership of one. The crisp decision, which identifier is the mapping outcome, is carried out based on the highest degree of membership to one of the class identifiers. The overall output of the RFIS mapping and the classification is a tuple (C_A, μ_A) of a class identifier and the membership to it.

4   Reasoning with Uncertainty

The reasoning about uncertain contexts is residing on the second level of information processing, where context information has been already inferred from sensor data. On this level logics or ontologies are usually used to infer new contextual knowledge. After our classification process we end up with tuples of class identifiers and fuzzy uncertainty measures, e.g. (C_A, μ_A). The usual fuzzy modus ponens used to derive new knowledge has various definitions throughout the literature, e.g. [10]. These inference methods are complex and need a brief introduction, if they are used. Since we focus on fuzzy uncertainty and how it can improve accuracy, the consequences information content and the further inference, we used a different, simpler method to prove our point. The inference of the contexts is done crisp with simple propositional logic and the derivation of the uncertainty is done accordingly through a fuzzy t-norm/t-conorm.

4.1   Fusing Equal Contexts with Uncertainty

The idea behind the fusion of contexts is to use equal contexts from different sources in order to achieve mutual confirmation. In the crisp case contexts get fused based solely on their occurrence in the same time period. Although the overall probability is improved with each mutual confirmative crisp context included in the fusion, the reliability of each fusion member and outcome can vary strongly. This variation in reliability of each context is lost in the merging of crisp contexts and all fusions with the same number of members have the same probability of correctness. Fusion based on a fuzzy uncertainty level has a lot more to offer. If the fusion is done fuzzy according to the uncertainty level of each context, the confidence is not lost in the fusion process. Even if many mutual confirmative contexts each have a low confidence level, the fused context gains reliability. For the fusion of uncertainty we used the fuzzy equivalence to a crisp disjunction, the t-conorm. Many different t-conorms appear throughout the literature, we decided to use the probabilistic sum $(S_P(x, y) = x + y - x \cdot y)$. The result of the probabilistic sum is higher than each input of the t-conorm, which suits our understanding of the fusion process. An example for the fusion of context C_C out of the two contexts C_A and C_B and the fusion of the fuzzy uncertainty accordingly, is the following:

$$
\left.
\begin{array}{c}
C_A \vee C_B \quad \rightarrow \quad C_C \\[4pt]
S_P(\mu_A, \mu_B) = \mu_A + \mu_B - \mu_A \cdot \mu_B \\
= \mu_C
\end{array}
\right\} (C_A, \mu_A) \vee (C_B, \mu_B) \rightarrow (C_C, \mu_C) \tag{1}
$$

4.2 Aggregate New Contextual Knowledge with Uncertainty

Through aggregation contextual knowledge of many sources is combined to new contextual facts. The crisp decision is a typical application for propositional and predicate logic. The antecedent part in combination with the rule determines the conclusion, which is the typical modus ponens inference. In this kind of inference the reliability of each input source is not taken into account. Also the general uncertainty of each context classification is not considered. These uncertainties have a huge impact on the outcome of the inference process. We will show how a fuzzy aggregation can improve the outcome in the evaluation section. For the aggregation of new contexts we used simple propositional logic and for the inference of the uncertainty we used a t-norm. Since the result of the fuzzy inference needs to be less reliable than any of the inputs, the best t-norm is in our understanding the product norm $(T_P(x, y) = x \cdot y)$. An example for the aggregation of context C_C out of the contexts C_A and C_B and inference of the fuzzy uncertainty according to the context aggregation, is the following:

$$\left.\begin{array}{rl} C_A \wedge C_B & \rightarrow \quad C_C \\ T_P(\mu_A, \mu_B) = & \mu_A \cdot \mu_B \\ = & \mu_C \end{array}\right\} (C_A, \mu_A) \wedge (C_B, \mu_B) \rightarrow (C_C, \mu_C) \tag{2}$$

5 Evaluation - "Detecting Acclamation"

To evaluate the classification, fusion and aggregation we used parts of the office scenario. The aim was to show that, compared to the simple fusion of context classes, the reliability for fusion of identical context classes from different sources improves, if a uncertainty value is used as weight. The second argument for using an uncertainty value in the inference process is the aggregation of new contextual knowledge. The weighted aggregation should show improvement in reliability towards crisp inference. We used two "OpenMoko Freerunner" devices and one "Freescale ZSTAR" demo as sensor data sources. For the "Freerunner's" two recurrent FIS (RFIS) classifiers were used, with the following classes each:

1. 10-point FFT, 1000-sample window, audio at 4kHz $\Rightarrow$ 10-dim. input vector

"silence"	(class no. 1) $\Rightarrow$	no audio except noise
"talking to audience"	(class no. 2) $\Rightarrow$	speech data
"knocking appreciation"	(class no. 3) $\Rightarrow$	knocking on table
"clapping applause"	(class no. 4) $\Rightarrow$	clapping hands

2. variance and mean, 8-sample window, two 3-axis accel. $\Rightarrow$ 12-dim. input vector

"lying still"	(class no. 1) $\Rightarrow$	no movement of device
"knocking appreciation"	(class no. 2) $\Rightarrow$	knocking on table with device next to it
"sitting"	(class no. 3) $\Rightarrow$	device in users pocket whilst sitting
"standing"	(class no. 4) $\Rightarrow$	device in users pocket whilst standing
"walking"	(class no. 5) $\Rightarrow$	device in users pocket whilst walking

The "ZSTAR" was attached to a board marker and was running also a RFIS classifier, classifing on the following classes:

3. variance and mean, 8-sample window, two 3-axis accel. $\Rightarrow$ 6-dim. input vector

"lying still"	(class no. 1) $\Rightarrow$	no movement of device
"knocking appreciation"	(class no. 2) $\Rightarrow$	knocking on table with marker next to it
"sitting"	(class no. 3) $\Rightarrow$	marker in users pocket whilst sitting
"standing"	(class no. 4) $\Rightarrow$	marker in users pocket whilst standing
"writing"	(class no. 5) $\Rightarrow$	writing on whiteboard

Data was recorded on several controlled test runs with five subjects. A sequence of the classes was simulated to reflect a conference event.

5.1   Fuzzy Classifiers vs. Recurrent Fuzzy Classifiers

One feature of the recurrent fuzzy classifier is the desired classifications fuzzy uncertainty, the other one is the improvement of the classification process towards normal non-recurrent classifiers. To show the improvements in accuracy, we compared a normal FIS based classifier with our RFIS classification process. FIS uses the same algorithm as RFIS, except there is only one iteration of clustering and linear regression. The feedback of the RFIS stabilizes the classification process significantly. The most incorrect classifications are made when there is a change from one class to another one. To evaluate this disadvantage we used a check data set that reflects this insufficiency. The check data set consists of subsets (30 data pairs each) of class specific patterns (many subsets per class), which where randomly ordered: **1. "OpenMoko" audio** - 1530 training data pairs (TDP) (382,5 sec) $\rightarrow$ $\sim$51 successive class changes (SCC); 1500 check data pairs (CDP) (375 sec) $\rightarrow$ $\sim$50 SCC. **2. "OpenMoko" acc.** - 1410 TDP (352,5 sec) $\rightarrow$ $\sim$47 SCC; 1770 CDP (442,5 sec) $\rightarrow$ $\sim$59 SCC. **3. "ZStar" acc.** - 660 TDP (165 sec) $\rightarrow$ $\sim$22 SCC; 450 CDP (112,5 sec) $\rightarrow$ $\sim$15 SCC.

The feedback before the first classification is always 0, which means not identifying any class. Despite these challenges RFIS performed significantly better for all three classifiers than FIS. The confusion matrices for both phone classifiers, FIS and RFIS classifiers are shown in table 1 and 2. Table 1 shows the results of the accelerometer data classifier, where the overall correct classifications of FIS are $\sim$62% and for RFIS $\sim$94%. This shows an improvement of about 32%. The results of the RFIS audio classifier show even more improvement. As displayed in table 2, the RFIS classifier shows an enhancement from $\sim$24% to $\sim$92%. The classification accuracy of the FIS classifier indicates that the patterns are not separable with this method. The improvement for the "ZSTAR" attached to a

Table 1. Conf. mat. of FIS $\sim$62% (left) and RFIS $\sim$94% (right) accel. class. phone

		classes classified onto				
		1	2	3	4	5
designat. classes	1	0	100.00	0	0	0
	2	0.74	99.26	0	0	0
	3	0	8.33	90.00	1.67	0
	4	0	0	0.3344	99.67	0
	5	2.33	0.33	0.33	10.33	86.67

		classes classified onto				
		1	2	3	4	5
designat. classes	1	90.50	3.00	2.33	4.17	0
	2	0.74	96.67	2.5926	0	0
	3	0	0.33	94.67	3.67	1.33
	4	0	0	0	99.67	0.33
	5	0	0.33	0.67	8.00	91.00

Table 2. Confusion mat. of FIS ∼24% (left) and RFIS ∼92% (right) for audio class

		classes class. onto						classes classified onto			
		1	**2**	**3**	**4**			**1**	**2**	**3**	**4**
desig. classes	**1**	0.0	98.50	1.50	0.0	desig. classes	**1**	88.83	5.50	3.17	2.50
	2	0.0	35.74	63.65	0.60		**2**	0.20	99.80	0.0	0.0
	3	0.0	22.71	65.22	12.07		**3**	0.0	7.25	82.61	10.14
	4	0.0	14.16	63.01	22.83		**4**	0.0	0.0	7.31	92.69

board marker is not as significant as with the phone classifiers, but still amounts about 2% (from ∼88% to ∼90%). This results shows the advantage of recurrent classifiers in the field of sensor data processing.

5.2   How Fusion with Uncertainty Improves the Accuracy

The aim in this evaluation is to indicate the improvement of fuzzy context fusion towards normal crisp fusion in overall accuracy. To show this, the fusion of context classes which vary in classification correctness and according to that in accuracy needs to be made. The differentiation between the classes "lying still" and "knocking appreciation" of the marker classifier provides the desired uncertainty and shaky classification. The fusion with a more precise classification of the context "knocking appreciation" should improve the overall classification. Improvement is achieved through filtering upon the fused uncertainty level. The aim is to sort out the false classifications according to a lower uncertainty level. How a threshold for filtering can be found was shown in [5] and is generally known as "receiver operator characteristics". Another classification qualifies for fusion, the classification of the audio data on "knocking appreciation" when the phone is carried in the pocket. This classification should also improve if being fused with the same classification of a phone lying freely on a table. The following combinations of contexts, devices and device states are fused:

1. Phone A is lying on the table and phone B is in users pocket. Both should recognize context class "knocking appreciation" through the audio classifier.

2. Phone A is lying on the table recognizing "knocking appreciation" through audio and the board marker is also lying on the table recognizing the same class through the accelerometer classifier.

In the following plots the different fuzzy uncertainty levels of the fused contexts are plotted along with the samples from the test data set. The bounded areas which are signed out with "correct classified" show time periods the contexts actually happened. Mean values of the fuzzy uncertainty for correct and incorrect classifications are plotted in the figures as dashed lines. The greater the distance between these dashed mean lines is, the better correct classifications can be separated from incorrect ones. The results of fusion (1) can be seen in figure 3(a). The filtering on the uncertainty level at threshold $\tau = 0.9$ improves the accuracy by about 6% from ∼90% to ∼96%. In this example samples are not as clearly separable as in the following one, but still an improvement can be achieved. The

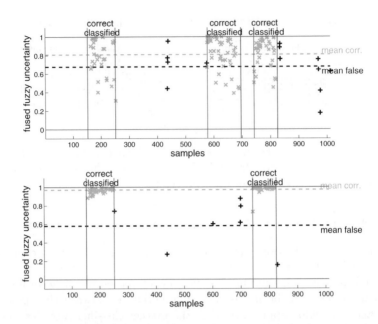

Fig. 3. Fusion (1-top) of fuzzy uncertainty for phone A and phone B classifying on "knocking app.", with correct class. marked 'x' (gray) and incorrect '+' (black). Fusion (2-bottom) of uncertainty for phone B and marker class. on "knocking app.".

results of fusion (2) are shown in figure 3(b), where the filtering on threshold $\tau = 0.9$ improves the accuracy by about 3% from ~97% to 100%. The problem with filtering is, that along with incorrect classifications also some correct ones are filtered out. Also the amount of classifications is reduced. The trade-off can be influenced through the developer via the threshold level. In our experience it is better to exclude some correct classifications from the following reasoning process or the application using the contexts, than have incorrect classifications result in faulty system states. The reduction of samples is of less significance, since much more samples are processed than needed in most applications.

5.3   Aggregated Contextual Knowledge Improved with Uncertainty

In the last section we have shown that filtering upon the fuzzy uncertainty after a fusion improves accuracy. An aggregation of new context classes is improved through the filtering on the uncertainty level. Since aggregation combines different contextual knowledge to new information, the reliability depends on every part of the input. The following combination of contexts, devices and device states are aggregated to new contexts:

1. Phone A is lying on table recognizing "clapping applause" with audio classifier and the board marker is in a users pocket classifying on "standing" which is resulting in the implication "standing ovations".

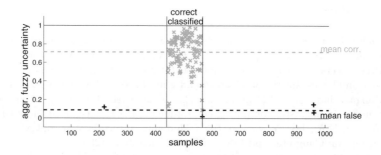

Fig. 4. Uncertainty for aggregation of "standing ovations", correct 'x' & incorrect '+'

The results of the aggregation can be seen in figure 4. For filtering, a threshold $\tau = 0.2$ was chosen, since the fuzzy uncertainty for the test set is spread over the whole interval $[0, 1]$. This circumstance is the result of the product t-norm which was chosen for the aggregation. The accuracy after filtering improves by about 2% from $\sim$98% up to 100%. The improvement up to 100%, as in the last two examples, is rather unusual. But the examples show that the presented approach is in principle and in practice capable to squeeze out the last 4% (in average) of detection accuraccy to reach absolute correct classification.

6   Conclusion and Future Work

This paper shows how uncertainty measures are created and used in context reasoning applications. Our contribution to the computation of uncertainty measures was a recurrent fuzzy classifier (RFIS) system. The evaluation shows that even in application settings with deliberately unfriendly conditions - especially fast changing contexts - more than 92% recognition rate can be reached. We also infer uncertainty measures and used them for filtering outliers after data fusion and aggregation. This approach boosts our classification result about 4% to almost 100% recognition rate. The shown application (acclamation detection) requires only a one-step fusion process. It is to be expected that the effect of using uncertainty measurement in applications with complex fusion and aggregation processes will be even more prominent. Future work will also research the inclusion of probabilities combined with the investigated fuzziness in the inference process and the utilization of recurrence in classification.

Acknowledgements. This work is partially funded by the State of Niedersachsen in the "IT-Ecosystems" project and the European Commission founded project "Cooperative Hybrid Objects Sensor Networks (CHOSeN)". We also wish to thank Matthias Budde for his corrections on grammar and general understanding of this paper and Henning Guenther for his technical support.

References

1. Buchholz, T., Kuepper, A., Schiffers, M.: Quality of context: What it is and why we need it. In: Workshop of the HP OpenView University Association (2003)
2. Preuveneers, D., Berbers, Y.: Quality extensions and uncertainty handling for context ontologies. In: W. on Context and Ont. Theory, Practice and Appl. (2006)
3. Ranganathan, A., Al-Muhtadi, J., Campbell, R.H.: Reasoning about uncertain contexts in pervasive computing environments. IEEE Pervasive Computing (2004)
4. Truong, B.A., Lee, Y.K., Lee, S.Y.: Modeling uncertainty in context-aware computing. In: Computer and Information Science, ICIS (2005)
5. Berchtold, M., Decker, C., Riedel, T., Zimmer, T., Beigl, M.: Using a context quality measure for improving smart appliances. In: IWSAWC (2007)
6. Berchtold, M., Riedel, T., Beigl, M., Decker, C.: Awarepen - classfication probability and fuzziness in a context aware application. Ubiq. Intell. and Comp. (2008)
7. Gomni, V., Bersini, H.: Recurrent fuzzy systems. IEEE Fuzzy Systems (1994)
8. Chiu, S.: Method and software for extracting fuzzy classification rules by subtractive clustering. IEEE Control Systems Magazine, 461–465 (1996)
9. Tagaki, T., Sugeno, M.: Fuzzy identification of systems and its application to modelling and control. Syst., Man and Cybernetics (1985)
10. Weisbrod, J.: Unscharfes schliessen. Diss. zur Kuenstlichen Intelligenz (1996)

Synthetic Training Data Generation for Activity Monitoring and Behavior Analysis

Dorothy Monekosso[1] and Paolo Remagnino[2]

[1] CSRI, University of Ulster, Jordanstown, UK
dn.monekosso@ulster.ac.uk
[2] CISM, Kingston University, London, UK
p.remagnino@kingston.ac.uk

Abstract. This paper describes a data generator that produces synthetic data to simulate observations from an array of environment monitoring sensors. The overall goal of our work is to monitor the well-being of one occupant in a home. Sensors are embedded in a smart home to unobtrusively record environmental parameters. Based on the sensor observations, behavior analysis and modeling are performed. However behavior analysis and modeling require large data sets to be collected over long periods of time to achieve the level of accuracy expected. A data generator - was developed based on initial data i.e. data collected over periods lasting weeks to facilitate concurrent data collection and development of algorithms. The data generator is based on statistical inference techniques. Variation is introduced into the data using perturbation models.

Keywords: Synthetic data generation, perturbation model, statistical analysis.

1 Introduction

This paper describes an Activity of daily Living (ADL) data generator to assist with the development of methodologies in the context of assisted living. The simulator produces observations consistent with activities of daily living in a smart home. The goal of our work is to monitor the well-being of a single occupant in a home; this is achieved by observing activity and analyzing behavior. We aim to detect gradual changes and atypical (sudden changes in) behavior. Our smart home is equipped with sensors that monitor directly environmental conditions and indirectly the occupant. Activity is inferred from observations and models of behavior are built. In general, data analysis and modeling require large data sets collected over long periods of time to achieve the level of accuracy needed. To allow the development of algorithms to proceed concurrently with data collection, synthetic data is generated based on perturbation methods. Generative models of the smart home systems are built and perturbed. The distribution parameters of a short data collection exercise are used as the initial values in generating data from the simulation models.

In the Section 2, related work is discussed. In Section 3, we describe the methodology. In Section 4, we present results followed by discussions and conclusions in Section 5 and 6 respectively.

M. Tscheligi et al. (Eds.): AmI 2009, LNCS 5859, pp. 267–275, 2009.
© Springer-Verlag Berlin Heidelberg 2009

2 Related Work

Intelligent Environments (IE) employ embedded sensors to record activity. Dependent on the application goal, various machine learning and statistical techniques are used to analyze and infer from the data generated by the sensors. A number of research projects addressing issues of intelligent environments have been published; including Microsoft's EasyLiving project [1], the Intelligent Dormitory iDorm [2], the Interactive Room iRoom [3], the HyperMedia Studio [4], and The MavHome project [5]. Examples of IE can be found in health applications [14] to [15]. The sensors range from arrays of relatively simple devices that record on/off status, temperature and lighting level [12], [6] to more complex sensors to record sound and images [8], [9]. Supervised ([6], [7], and [8]) and unsupervised learning ([10] to [13]) algorithms have been applied to learning a model of activity.

In the above mentioned papers, the problem is one of pattern classification solved with machine learning techniques. These techniques generally require a large dataset for training; the lack of data hinders progress in algorithm development in many applications such as sign language, speech and handwriting recognition, and human face classification. Improvement of pattern classification with sample size was investigated in ([16] and [21]). Methods for generating synthetic data include Ber resampling of face images [17], genetic algorithms to produce new face images [18], mean shift algorithms for sign language [19] and perturbation models for handwriting recognition [21]. The method presented in this paper is akin to the latter.

3 Methodology

The requirements of the data generator are easily understood by describing the system that it simulates. The typical home comprises a number of rooms (locations); each location contains embedded sensors and a sensor processing board to monitor environmental conditions. The sensors are of two basic types: continuous output sensors such as temperature, and discrete output sensors such as the on/off status of appliances. Communication between sensor boards and the base station is wireless. The data is noisy; comprising intermittent failure of IE equipment to measure and/or record activity, RF interference or appliance failure. Added to these noise sources are fluctuations in the occupant's daily routines. The synthetic data generator accounts for equipment noise and human variability seen in observations using statistical models.

The procedure for generating synthetic data is first to generate a base-model from the experimental data i.e. sensor observations. The sensors are classified as continuous- or discrete-output. Continuous output sensors such as temperature are digitized, binned and modeled as discrete output sensors. The discrete sensor outputs are modeled as a probability distribution for events in a given period; the parameters (location, scale and shape) of the distribution are estimated using a probability plot and the probability plot correlation coefficient.

3.1 Real Data Characteristics

In analyzing behavior, we are concerned with the daily profiles and long term trends. This analysis requires collecting sensor observations to generate a series of event-distributions that represent a typical day. In other words, observations for each day are collected over an extended period of time and merged. In analyzing long term trends, we are interested in one or a group of sensors; observations are collected to generate an event-distribution for a single period of the day. All noise sources are treated as one. The diagram in Fig. 1 shows an example of event count over time and the diagram in Fig. 2 shows an example of daily profile for a kitchen event; represented by three distributions. The event could be detected motion.

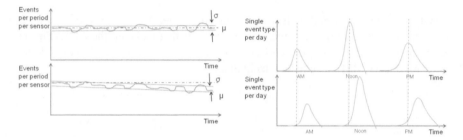

Fig. 1. Event modeling   **Fig. 2.** ADL profile modeling

3.2   Synthetic Data Generation for Events and Event Trends

Before discussing data generation, a few terms are defined. Events are classified as either primitive or compound. When a sensor is sampled; this is referred to as a *primitive event*. *Compound events* are defined by the start and end of an activity. Furthermore days are divided into *periods*; during each period the events of interested are counted. The event count for a given sensor and period is modeled as a probability distribution. The parameters for the distribution i.e. the shape, location and scale, are estimated using a probability plot and the probability plot correlation coefficient (PPCC). To generate synthetic data, the model parameters are perturbed. Modeling observations with a Weibull distribution is described below in a case study. Consider a distribution, $D_0(\mu_0, \sigma_0)$, for an event count with location, μ_0, and scale, σ_0. $D_0(\mu_0, \sigma_0)$ accounts for the expected fluctuations in ADL. Variation (noise) is added by perturbing $D_0(\mu_0, \sigma_0)$ to produce the distribution, $D_n(\mu_n, \sigma_n)$, such that $\mu_n=\mu_0\pm\Delta\mu$ and/or $\sigma_n=\sigma_0\pm\Delta\sigma$ where $\Delta\mu$ and $\Delta\sigma$ are selected according to the noise distribution. The parameters are constrained within bounds [μ_{min} , μ_{max}] and [σ_{min} , σ_{max}] determined experimentally. In practice, the base model D_0 was obtained from 'real' sensor observations.

To simulate a trend, the desired trend function, $f(t)$, modulates the chosen parameter such that at each step in time t_{i+1}, the distribution becomes $D_{i+1}(\mu_{i+1}, \sigma_{i+1}) = D_i(\mu_i, \sigma_i)+ D_i(\mu_i, \sigma_i)\times\varepsilon$, where ε is a small change applied to μ and σ. The parameters for D_i are given by $f(t)$ as shown in Fig. 3.

3.2   Synthetic ADL Profiles Data Generation

The data-generator must be capable of generating realistic daily, monthly or even yearly profiles with any granularity. Variations in a profile might be a result of

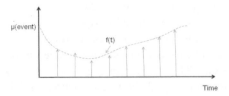

Fig. 3. Event distribution with time

seasonal variations or a trend with some diagnostic value. A behavior profile (Fig. 2) is a detectable pattern in the sequence of observations that make up the ADL (Fig. 1). A profile is modeled as a sequence of event models as shown in Fig. 4 using Hidden Markov Models (HMM), a statistical technique.

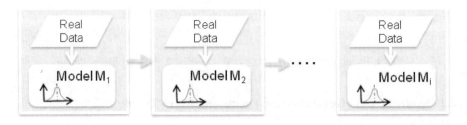

Fig. 4. Profile synthesis

The reader is referred to the work of Rabiner [22] for a tutorial on HMM. Referring to Fig. 2, the observable states are the event count. In order to generate data for a given period, we generate observable states from the appropriate distribution. Thus each of the three distributions in Fig. 2 would be represented by N symbols (one for every class of observable state). Each observation o_i belonging to the set of observations O is classified into one of the N symbol classes according to a function $f(\mu, \sigma)$, where μ is the location (mean) and σ is the scale (standard deviation) respectively for the distribution.

$$\forall o_i \in O \begin{cases} o_i > a \cdot f(\mu,\sigma) \rightarrow o_i = S_0 \\ \mu \cdot f(\mu,\sigma) > o_i \geq b \cdot f(\mu,\sigma) \rightarrow o_i = S_1 \\ \vdots \\ o_i < c \cdot f(\mu,\sigma) \rightarrow o_i = S_N \end{cases} \qquad \text{Eq. 1}$$

The parameters a, b, and c are constant such that $0 < a, b, c \leq 1.0$. The symbols thus generated, $S_1 \ldots S_N$, are employed to build the HMM model for a profile. Given an HMM model data is generated that is representative of the target profile.

4 Experimental Results

Time stamped observations (experimental data) were recorded over several weeks. This dataset form the base data for the simulation model building.

4.1 Synthetic Observations

The first step in generating synthetic data is to produce the base-model from the experimental data. Continuous output sensors such as temperature are digitized, binned and modeled as discrete output sensors. The resulting value is dealt in the same manner as for discrete output sensors observations. The observation model is a probability distribution of events in a given period; the parameters (location, scale and shape) of the distribution are estimated using a probability plot and the probability plot correlation coefficient. The goodness-of-fit is determined qualitatively (graphically) with a probability plot and quantitatively employing the Anderson-Darling test. The test allows us to confirm which distribution type the observations arise from. We elect to represent the dataset (distribution a in Fig. 5) with the Weibull distribution as a suitable distributional family. The values for parameters indicated a reasonable fit since the probability plot is near linear for the Weibull distribution and the Anderson-Darling test for the Weibull distribution supports the hypothesis at the 5% level (critical value = 0.757 and AD test value = 0.286).

The parameters are listed in Table 1. Perturbing the original dataset produces the distributions (b) and (c) in Fig. 5.

Table 1. Estimated parameters for a Weibull distribution to model observations of kitchen sensors; corresponding to (a), (b), and (c) above

Parameter	D1 (a)	D2 (b)	D3 (c)
PPCC	0.9848	0.9936	0.9961
Location	26.1057	7.6167	26.9300
Scale	15.8846	34.6466	19.5253
Shape	3	4	4

The diagrams in Fig. 5 show the base distribution and the resulting distributions for the kitchen light events (a) under normal conditions, (b) simulating later kitchen activity, and (c) greater variability in kitchen activities by varying location and scale respectively.

4.2 Modeling Behavior Profile and Effect of Dataset Size

Hidden Markov Models (HMM) are employed to generate profiles. The observed states are the event counts in a given *period*. The duration of a period is variable and can be coarse lasting 4 hours or as fine as the sensor sampling time. We build the HMM model with the distribution location parameter as the observable variable and assess the model by cross-validation; estimating the (log) probability of the model generating the profile as shown in the diagrams of Fig. 7 and Fig. 8 with an increasing

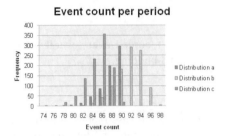
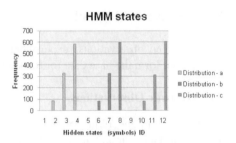

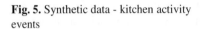

Fig. 5. Synthetic data - kitchen activity events

Fig. 6. Symbol distribution

number of hidden states. In the experiment, a day-profile is generated using three daily periods corresponding to three distributions for kitchen activity (Fig. 2). To generate a suitable sequence for modeling, the number of states is set equal to four per distribution (N=4). With three distributions, we have 64 possible combinations of symbols (encoded patterns) and a sequence of 1000 triplets (3000 sample observations).

Fig. 7 below shows the results of modeling a profile. With the exception of pattern 64 (uppermost curve), modeling with more than 6 hidden states does not improve the model as seen by the validation results and in some cases actually degrades the model as indicated by an increasingly negative log(probability). Of the 64 possible profile patterns, the five displayed in the diagram correspond to the best performance (log(probability)) i.e. the most representative. And not unexpectedly, the best performing models are those generated with the large number of samples (pattern 64 makes up 22% of the synthetic dataset). The occurrence of a pattern that appears infrequently can signify a change in equipment or human behavior and recognized through a very low likelihood.

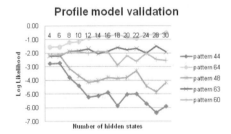
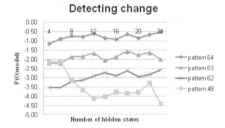

Fig. 7. Log P(O|model) vs hidden states

Fig. 8. Log P(O|model) - change in profiles

4.3 Simulating Deviations from Norm

In generating synthetic data, deviation from norm can be reproduced by altering the parameters of a single distribution. In a similar manner, the behavior profile can be changed. The diagrams in Fig. 8 compare profiles – the "normal" profile (pattern 64) against profile with relatively small changes (pattern 62, 63, and 48). Starting with pattern 64, as the norm, the other patterns were selected as these represent (after encoding) the smallest detectable state change in a profile.

Detecting differences in patterns is measured in terms of log likelihood - the probability of observing a specific sequence given the model. The curves in the diagram in Fig. 8 give an indication of the capability of the model to detect small changes.

5 Discussion

The validity of the data generator (simulator) will be fully assessed against a larger set of real sensor observations. However by combining real sensor data with the physical characteristics, individual models for sensors can be assessed. We are less concerned with the accuracy of the individual datum (sensor observation) and more with the type of the distribution. From initial results, the synthetic data is sufficiently representative to allow development of learning algorithms.

The profiles are more complex in nature. Of the 64 possible symbol combinations, only one is representative of the norm and occurs frequently. The remainder can be considered atypical; of which a high proportion are extremely unlikely to occur in real life except perhaps in extreme cases of equipment failure. This is an important issue as there is a risk of generating a distribution that cannot / should not occur in practice. However the authors believe that by 'bootstrapping' with real data and regenerating the models as more real data becomes available; this is less of a risk.

The work described here deals with a single occupant. It is proposed to extend to two or more occupants sharing one or more common areas such as a TV room or a dining area. The complexity associated with multiple-occupancy lies primarily in the fact that activities overlap. Without the use of more intrusive sensors such as visual or wearable sensors, it is difficult to distinguish between occupants.

6 Conclusions

The paper describes a simulator – a training data generator – that produces sensor observations in the form of statistical distributions. The aim is to support a project to develop a system to support independent living. The system monitors and analyses behavior detecting trends and deviations from what might be considered normal behavior of the inhabitant. Behaviour analysis is performed by gathering information such as lights snd other home appliances status, as well as motion detection; creating a model of daily activity. The nature of problem requires a solution based on statistcal techniques. These techniques for leaning models require a large amount of training data which would take years to obtained. In order to speed up the development process, a training data generator (simulator) was built. Data representative of months and years can thus be generated and variations injected to simulate change in behavior of any type.

References

1. Brumitt, B., Meyers, B., Krumm, J., Hale, M., Harris, S., Shafer, S.: EasyLiving: Technologies for Intelligent Environments. In: Thomas, P., Gellersen, H.-W. (eds.) HUC 2000. LNCS, vol. 1927, pp. 12–29. Springer, Heidelberg (2000)
2. The iDorm project home page, Essex University, UK, http://iieg.essex.ac.uk/idorm.htm
3. The iRoom project home page, Stanford, http://iwork.stanford.edu/
4. The HyperMedia studio project home page, UCLA, http://hypermedia.ucla.edu/
5. The MavHome project home page, University of Texas, Arlington (2005), http://cygnus.uta.edu/mavhome/
6. Tapia, E., Munguia, S., Intille, S., Larson, K.: Activity recognition in the home setting using simple and ubiquitous sensors. In: Ferscha, A., Mattern, F. (eds.) PERVASIVE 2004. LNCS, vol. 3001, pp. 158–175. Springer, Heidelberg (2004)
7. Mühlenbrock, M., Brdiczka, O., Snowdon, D., Meunier, J.-L.: Learning to detect user activity and availability from a variety of sensor data. In: Proceedings of the Second IEEE Conference on Pervasive Computing and Communications, Orlando, FL (2007)
8. Brdiczka, O., Vaufreydaz, D., Maisonnasse, J., Reignier, P.: Unsupervised Segmentation of Meeting Configurations and Activities using Speech Activity Detection. In: 3rd IFIP Conference on Artificial Intelligence Applications and Innovations (AIAI), Athens, Greece, June 7-9, pp. 195–203 (2006)
9. Brdiczka, O., et al.: Detecting Individual Activities from Video in a Smart Home. In: Apolloni, B., Howlett, R.J., Jain, L. (eds.) KES 2007, Part I. LNCS (LNAI), vol. 4692, pp. 363–370. Springer, Heidelberg (2007)
10. Rivera-Illingworth, F., Callaghan, V., Hagras, H.A.: Neural Network Agent Based Approach to Activity Detection, in AmI Environments. In: IEE International Workshop, Intelligent Environments (IE 2005), Colchester, UK, June 28-29 (2005)
11. Doctor, F., Hagras, H.A., Callaghan, V.: An Intelligent Fuzzy Agent Approach for Realising Ambient Intelligence in Intelligent Inhabited Environments. IEEE Transactions on Systems, Man and Cybernetics, Part A: Systems and Humans 35(1), 55–65
12. Mozer, M.C.: Lessons from an adaptive house. In: Cook, D., Das, R. (eds.) Smart environments: Technologies, protocols, and applications, pp. 273–294. J. Wiley & Sons, Hoboken
13. Rao, S., Cook, D.J.: Predicting Inhabitant Actions Using Action and Task Models with Application to Smart Homes. International Journal of Artificial Intelligence Tools 13(1), 81–100 (2004)
14. Hori, T., Nishida, Y., And Murakami, S.: A Pervasive Sensor System for Nursing Care Support. In: Ambient Intelligence Techniques and Applications, Computer Science. Springer, Heidelberg (2008)
15. Cesta, A., et al.: Robotic, Sensory and Problem-Solving Ingredients for the Future Home. In: Ambient Intelligence Techniques and Applications, Computer Science. Springer, Heidelberg (2008)
16. Baird, H.: State of the art of document image degradation modeling. In: Proc. 4th IAPR Workshop on Document Analysis Systems, pp. 1–16 (2000)
17. Lu, X., Jain, A.K.: Ber. resampling for face recognition chem. In: 4th Internat. Conf. on Audio and Video based Biometric Person Authentication, pp. 869–877 (2003)

18. Chen, J., Chen, X.L., Gao, W.: Resampling for face detection by self-adaptive genetic algorithm. In: Proc. Internat. Conf. on Pattern Recognition, pp. 822–825 (2004)
19. Jiang, F., Gao, W., Yao, H., Zhao, D., Chen, X.: Synthetic data generation technique in Signer-independent sign language recognition. Pattern Recogn. Lett. 30(5) (2009)
20. Varga, T., Bunke, H.: Effects of Training Set Expansion in Handwriting Recognition Using Synthetic Data, pp. 200–203 (2003)
21. Varga, T., Bunke, H.: Perturbation models for generating synthetic training data in handwriting recognition. In: Marinai, S., Fujisawa, H. (eds.) Machine Learning in Document Analysis and Recognition, pp. 333–360. Springer, Heidelberg (2008)
22. Rabiner, L.R.: A Tutorial on Hidden Markov Models and Selected Applications in Speech Recognition. Proceedings of the IEEE 77(2), 257–286 (1989)

Adaptive User Profiles in Pervasive Advertising Environments

Florian Alt[1], Moritz Balz[2], Stefanie Kristes[3], Alireza Sahami Shirazi[1],
Julian Mennenöh[3], Albrecht Schmidt[1], Hendrik Schröder[3], and Michael Goedicke[2]

[1] Pervasive Computing and User Interface Engineering Group
[2] Specification of Software Systems
[3] Marketing & Retailing
University of Duisburg-Essen
Schuetzenbahn 70, 45117 Essen
{florian.alt,alireza.sahami,moritz.balz}@uni-due.de,
{stefanie.kristes,julian.mennenoeh,albrecht.schmidt}@uni-due.de,
{hendrik.schroeder,michael.goedicke}@uni-due.de

Abstract. Nowadays modern advertising environments try to provide more
efficient ads by targeting costumers based on their interests. Various approaches
exist today as to how information about the users' interests can be gathered.
Users can deliberately and explicitly provide this information or user's shopping behaviors can be analyzed implicitly. We implemented an advertising
platform to simulate an advertising environment and present *adaptive profiles*,
which let users setup profiles based on a self-assessment, and enhance those
profiles with information about their real shopping behavior as well as
about their activity intensity. Additionally, we explain how pervasive technologies such as Bluetooth can be used to create a profile anonymously and
unobtrusively.

1 Introduction

In 2006, only 41% of the expenditure on advertising actually produced sale [5]. Modern advertising environments such as online stores or networks of public displays, try
to increase this ratio by not distributing or presenting advertisements to users randomly but by targeting contents towards users based on their interest. Therefore, mar-
keters need to know their customers in order to decide which products to present
where and when [6]. A common approach is that advertisers define target groups for
their ads, similar to companies defining target groups for their products in general.
When it comes to assigning users to specific target groups, two approaches prevail
today as to how information about the users' interests and shopping behavior can be
gathered and later be used to enhance the exposure of advertisements. On one hand,
users can deliberately provide these data; on the other hand, data can be gathered by
analyzing the users' shopping behavior. Based on the profiles target groups are created, which might then be selected for a specific campaign. Though target groups are
an easy and effective way of tailoring ads towards the interests of a user group, we

M. Tscheligi et al. (Eds.): AmI 2009, LNCS 5859, pp. 276–286, 2009.
© Springer-Verlag Berlin Heidelberg 2009

think that when abstracting from a user to a target group, important information gets lost that might allow for a more precise and successful targeting.

In this paper we present a platform we implemented to simulate an advertising environment in our lab. Our current setup allows for adapting advertisements towards users' interests and also lets users interact with public displays we use to show the advertisements. As a contribution we present three techniques which aims at tackling shortcomings of current approaches.

First, we present the approach of *adaptive user profiles*. It allows users to setup a profile based on a self-assessment. This profile is then automatically enhanced with data about the "real" shopping behavior. In this way, on one hand the users' subjective interests are taken into account. This is especially interesting for advertisers since it reflects the users intention and provides a strong indication whether or not a user is interested in a specific (type of) product. On the other hand, an implicit observation of the user might reveal behavior or intentions a user is not aware of or simply cannot remember or articulate. Hence, a more detailed image of the user can be drawn and advertisements be targeted more precisely as if simply assigning users to target groups.

Second, we explain how based on this sophisticated method of generating user profiles we can compare a user's activity against other users by calculating a *user activity intensity*. We use this measure when calculating the adaptive user profile and discuss its value for an advertiser.

Third, we show how pervasive technologies such as Bluetooth can be used to *create profiles in an anonymous and unobtrusive way*. Linking profile information to the MAC address of a Bluetooth enabled device, such as a mobile phone, allows for identifying a user without the need to store any personal data such as name, gender, or address. Further, a user may easily discard from using the system by switching off the Bluetooth functionality of his phone.

The paper is structured as follows: first we present the approach of adaptive user profiles, show how such profiles can be generated and critically reflect on privacy. Second, we come up with a technical concept and show how we implemented our system. Finally, we present related research and discuss future work.

2 Adaptive User Profiles

In this chapter we first provide an introduction to profiling and target groups. Second, we present an approach for creating *adaptive user profiles*. It allows for generating profiles based on user-generated information and data derived from the users' interaction with an advertisement system. Then we explain how those profiles can be used to match ads towards users. Finally, we consider the aspect of privacy and show how anonymous profiles can be used to avoid users' concerns regarding the abuse of personal data.

2.1 Introduction to Profiling and Target Groups

In order more precisely target content, information about the customer is required. Such information are gathered and stored based on profiles. In general, profiles may be created in two different ways. First, users can explicitly share this information with the advertiser. Many online stores explicitly ask users about their areas of interest when setting up their personal profile or when signing up for shopper loyalty programs. Second, data can be derived from the user's shopping behavior. While in online shops this can be done implicitly without any requirement for user interaction, e.g., by analyzing a user's click-stream, the user's cooperation is required in stores, e.g. by presenting their shopping loyalty card upon checkout.

Based on the profiles it is possible to form target groups by applying cluster analyses on the overall data set. Advertisers might then select one or more pre-defined target-groups for their campaigns.

2.2 Creating Profiles

Our approach generates profiles, which consist of ratings on a scale from 1 to 10 in several categories. Those categories depend on the advertising environment and may be adjusted to the needs of the provider, based on an analysis of the consumers or a market analysis. In our lab setup, we specified the categories for a local-scale advertising environment including local stores, events, etc. In total, ratings for 45 categories reflecting the users interest may be calculated. They include for example music, events, and places and are used to define different types of profiles: the *consumer profile, campaign profiles,* and the *target group profile* for a specific campaign.

Consumer Profiles

The consumer profile reflects the user's areas of interest and consists of two components. The first component is a self-assessment, allowing users for specifying their interest in the given categories ranging from "not interested" (1) to "very interested" (10). By providing this explicit profile to the system, a user can benefit in such a way that ads he receives are more appealing to him than random ones since they match his interests.

The second component tries to take into account the actual shopping behavior. Due to the fact that every user interaction with the system is captured, it is now possible to enrich the user's self-assessment using his behavior. The system currently tracks the following types of interaction for each category per user: *Point of Sale Visits* (A), *Event/Ad Watching on a Display* (B), *Rating of an Event* (C), and *Redemption of Coupons* (D). This set of interactions is not conclusive and further types of interaction may be considered.

Assuming that a user's visit of a sport store (A) signalizes his interest for the category "sport", this store visit should positively affect the user's profile in the assigned categories. Similarly, this is true for event/ad watching (B) and the selection of coupons (D) offered by the system as a motivation to participate. We have not yet integrated the event rating (C) into the system, because we are unsure if or how the rating can be translated into effects on users' interests. However, the impact of a certain type of interaction depends on measures such as the resulting revenue. Since we have not yet deployed and evaluate the system in the real world and hence do not have any data, we cannot provide evidence that our model correctly reflects the influence of the different types of interactions on the consumer profile. For example, can we really derive a higher interest from more frequent store visits or can we conclude that somebody's interest is lower because he missed to use his coupon on various occasions?

The consumer profile used for targeting the advertisements is calculated in three steps:

Calculating Individual Activity: For each user data is available showing, which action took place in which category. Our system aggregates the different kinds of actions to get *one* value per user per category indicating how active a user behaves with regard to a certain category. An aggregation can be displayed as a linear combination:

$$\text{Individual\_Activity} = w_1 A + w_2 B + w_3 C + w_4 D$$

with w = weights and A,B,C,D = number of actions

The weight parameter is required since a scaling is necessary depending on the impact of the action. For example, the overall amount of the redemption of coupons will be on average much lower than the amount of point-of-sale visits. However, this does not indicate that coupons are less important. Hence, the weight parameter can be used to "equalize" the different distributions in relation to their means.

Once data are available, such as a positive consumer reaction to an ad or the revenue generated by the user in this category, the weights could be estimated by using a multiple stepwise linear regression analysis. Subsequently, the weights would indicate the "importance" in relation to the influence of the action type on business relevant target measure such as the revenue. In the current state, we still have to integrate a measure to track the real impact of the advertisement, e.g., the actual sales possibly triggered by the ad.

Calculating Individual Activity Intensity: To estimate the overall user activity per category we suggest the measure *individual activity intensity*. It reflects how much the individual activity differs from the overall mean activity of all users.

For example: a value of 1.2 (0.8) would indicate that the activity lies 20% above (below) average within a certain time period. Users having a high individual activity intensity might be of special value to the advertisers since it can be assumed that their probability to generate revenue is highest among those users.

Adjusting the Profile: Since for each user the self-assessment of interests is available, the consumer profile can now be enriched using the activity intensity. An obvious approach would be to linearly increase or decrease the user's self-assessment based on whether his activity intensity is above or below average. However, this might lead to ratings beyond the scale. We use an adjusted normal distribution to assure that the value always stays within the boundaries of the scale. The profile can be calculated as follows:

Consumer_Profile =
  Profile$_{\text{self\_assessment}}$
  + f(Profile$_{\text{self\_assessment}}$ · activity_intensity)
  · ((Profile$_{\text{self\_assessment}}$ · activity_intensity) - Profile$_{\text{self\_assessment}}$)

with f(x) = adjusted normal distribution

The formula uses the self-assessment profile as an input and adjusts the value based on the user's activity intensity. The normalization function f controls how quickly or slowly the profile value changes. We plan to use the values from the campaign profile to give advertisers an influence as to how strongly their campaigns alter the users' profiles.

Campaign Profiles
Campaign profiles consist, similar to consumer profiles, of one value in each category, which can be determined by the advertiser upon creating the campaign. Its use is to characterize advertisements, coupons, and points of sale belonging to the campaign. This characterization is required to determine which category values of a user are to be adapted through a certain interaction. For example, the campaign of a sport retailer will have high values in the sport category. A consumer's visit of a point of sale, which belongs to the campaign or the retailer, will subsequently have an effect on the rating of his category sport. Since the campaign has a value zero in cultural events, a point of sale visit will not alter this category.

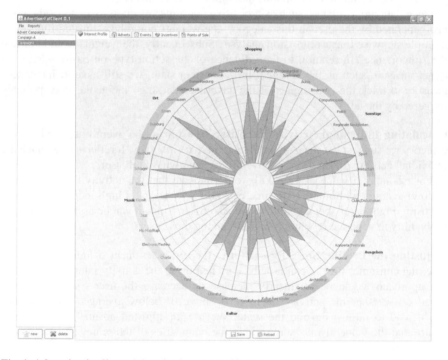

Fig. 1. Advertiser's client: Advertiser's can specify their campaign's profile (green line) defining the influence of the campaign on a user's profile, as well as the target group profile (red area) defining which user group the campaign is targeted to

Target Group Profiles
While the consumer profiles are calculated as a blend of self-assessment and actual user interaction with the system, advertisers can determine target group profiles using minimum and maximum values for each category. In addition, advertisers need to define a campaign profile for each of their campaigns, which like consumer profiles,

only hold one value for each category. This target group profile is then used to match the campaigns with the user's interests. Since advertisers can select from a range of values, they may define precisely which users they want to target the ads to and which not. For example, if a sports retailer wants to target only consumers with a high interest in sport, they might define a campaign with a target group profile ranging from values 8 to 10. **Figure 1** depicts our advertiser's client, which allows for specifying the campaigns. The red area shows the group of consumers the campaign should be targeted to (e.g., users with a value in the sports category between 8 and 10). The green line indicates how a user's profile is affected upon interacting with content related to this campaign.

An interesting idea from the marketing point of view is to identify users that stated a high interest in a certain category during the self-assessment of their interests, but do not show any activity with the system in this category. By addressing those users with an advertisement in that category, chances might be higher to trigger activity since general interest can be assumed. This case shows that having both a self-assessed user profile and an adapted user profile is very valuable for advertisers.

2.3 Targeting Content towards the Users

Based on the target group, ads to be displayed are chosen. We distinguish two cases when it comes to matching ads and users. If only a limited number of users are in the display's vicinity, ads are selected by showing the best fitting ads for only one single user taking turns in order of arrival. The main reason is that finding a best match for a small group of users might be difficult if interests among them differ fundamentally. Hence, a more promising strategy is to perform a "safe" match on the single users. With an increasing number of users at the display, we use matching algorithms to get an overall sufficient fit. Both cases require a measure indicating how well an ad fits a (group of) users. The distance measure should meet the following requirements:

- If the user's category value lies within the defined borders of the target group profile, the distance should be 0. Thus, the distance is measured between the individual value and the boundary, if the value lies beyond. Else, the distance is 0.
- It should be considered that a larger distance might indicate an aversion towards a certain category. So, it is suitable to choose a measure using squared values.

Based on those requirements, we suggest using the squared City-Block-Distance, which sums up the squared distances for each dimension. This metric takes into account that larger distances might be disproportionally worse than smaller distances. Hence, users' objections towards specific categories are well considered and the probability of targeting advertisements towards users he does not like is being minimized.

2.4 Privacy

When it comes to storing and assessing information about a user's shopping behavior, this often raises privacy concerns. Consumers are afraid of data being passed on to other companies or advertisers hence resulting in an ever-growing amount of advertisements users are confronted with. However, the success of shopper loyalty programs shows, that most of the users are nevertheless willing to give away their information in return for incentives [2][8], even though it is not entirely obvious who has access to the data.

With our approach we show that it is possible to target consumers without the need to store personal data such as name, age, gender, or address by linking a profile to a Bluetooth MAC address only. Thus, the user stays anonymous, and may at the same time deliberately decide whether or not he wants to participate in the advertising environment. This model, however, makes it essential for the success of the system to convince the user of its advantages, such as advertisements, which are personally interesting for him, and make him aware of the fact that he is virtually in control of the system at any time.

3 Technical Concept

In order to apply the profiling approach described above, we need a system that is capable of recognizing users and relating their interests to advertisements. We will first outline the requirements and general functionality of such a system; our concrete implementation will be described afterwards.

3.1 Requirements and Approach

The most important feature of this system is the management of users and their profiles. To be as pervasive as possible, users should not be represented explicitly with personal information. Instead, they should be identified implicitly whenever they connect to the system; for this purpose the identification mechanism must define a relation to the connection technologies. When a user is identified, the system can relate any data regarding profiles, interests, and advertisements to this abstract profile.

Since the system will act pervasively, the connection mechanisms play an important role, since they allow to identify and track users; an example is the MAC address of a Bluetooth device a user can utilize to connect to the system. However, we also want the system to be as flexible as possible. This means that a wide range of connection mechanisms should be supported. For each deployment of the system, a set of appropriate technologies can be selected that matches the users' target group. To illustrate this, the following exemplary scenarios using widely distributed and accepted technologies for user identification may be considered:

- The system is deployed at a traffic junction. Waiting persons can connect to it with Bluetooth-enabled mobile phones. The user range is thus limited to persons carrying such phones and being able to operate Bluetooth software, but advertisers can assume to interact with people having a technological background and can afford advanced hardware. Since no other assumptions of the user base can be made, Bluetooth devices are the lowest common denominator. Users are identified by the unique Bluetooth MAC address and can thus be recognized each time they pass by.
- The system is deployed at a university. Students at this university are used to pay in cafeterias with a student ID card that is equipped with an RFID chip

and a barcode denoting the matriculation number. The system will read either of them; the RFID chip can even be used to detect users in the vicinity of a terminal. The user base is thus limited to students of this university; however, the students can connect to the system by just using the ID cards.

The requirements are thus conflicting: Connection mechanisms must be considered to identify users, but can be very different and should not affect the architecture or limit the functionality of the system. This means that two software components are required to handle connections: First, an abstraction layer is required that decouples connections from the actual system by providing user identification at the same time; second, we must allow users to change their preferences and match different login credentials if more than one connection mechanism is offered.

The objective of the system is to employ this basic user management to offer matching advertisements. This is done by the profiling approach defined above. The system must thus handle the related data: For all users and ads, a set of *categories* must exist. Whenever a user takes an action that is of interest to the profiling algorithm, the profile values related to the categories are adjusted. While this is sufficient for basic functionality, we also want input from users. Hence, users should be able to manage their own profile and give a self-assessment, which is used as an input to the profiling algorithm.

When the system fulfills these requirements, it provides all information to advertisers for target-group-specific ads. An appropriate *ad management* allows for supplying the information about marketing campaigns. These campaigns are defined by relating them to the categories to define user interests they will match. Each campaign consists of a set of media that can be displayed to the user by display clients that connect to the system.

3.2 Interaction Types

As defined in the requirements, the user interaction must be considered carefully. So we defined the four types of user interaction with our system. We analyze these actions and use them to enhance the users' profiles.

- *Point of Sales visits*: Bluetooth scanners attached to the system are capable of sensing mobile devices in their vicinity. Thus, it is possible to gather information about shops a user visited trying to find out his preferred brands.
- *Event / Ad Watching on a Display*: Users may want to read information on an upcoming event, such as a rock concert. This can be done explicitly at displays by using a mobile phone application.
- *Event Signup and Rating*: Once a user reads information about a potentially interesting event he may sign up for this event. Though it is not (yet) possible to buy tickets for events, feedback from the users in the form of ratings or comments may be gathered asking them later to rate the event later.
- *Incentive Choice (Display Chase)*: As a motivation for users to install client software on the mobile phone, a so-called display chase is offered. Users need to walk along multiple displays and answer region-related questions. Upon successfully answering the questions, the system offers them three coupons users can choose from. Coupons can be redeemed in nearby stores.

4 Implementation

In the following chapter we describe the different components of the overall system architecture is depicted in **Figure 2**. A *central server component* is used to persistently store advertisements, events, visitor profiles, and the users' interactions with the system. Based on this information the system can calculate a user's profile as described above. This profile is matched against advertising campaigns defined by the advertisers via a web-based client. The content can be outputted to any client, e.g., a public display. The *advertiser's client* allows advertisers to specify campaigns and select user groups to target ads to. This is done using the UI depicted in **Figure 1**.

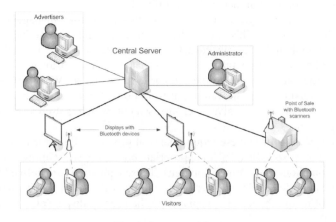

Fig. 2. System architecture

The campaigns generated by the advertisers are presented to the consumers via public displays. Each public display is equipped with a Bluetooth scanner hence the system can "identify" users in front of the display and select content according to the profile related to the scanned Bluetooth MAC address. We implemented a mobile phone client in Java ME, which can be run on most Symbian phones. The mobile client can be downloaded via Bluetooth at the public displays. We use this application for two purposes: first, users can create their self-assessed personal profile. Second, the user can remotely control the display, e.g. browsing for information on a specific event, by using his mobile phone. We use Bluetooth scanners also in so-called points of sale in order to detect, which (areas of a) store a user visited. This reveals important information on the users' interests.

Finally, an *administration client* provides means to outputting the gathered data in order to create reports. These can be used by advertisers to evaluate the success of campaigns as well as by the providers of the system for accounting purposes.

5 Related Work

Advertising is not a new research domain in pervasive computing and has already been widely explored in recent years. Rangathan et al. showed how pervasive computing technologies could be used to deliver relevant ads in suitable ways to selected consumers [6]. Sharifi et al. [7] showed how public electronic displays could improve the efficiency of advertising systems if the display is aware of the identity and the interests of the audience. [4] focuses on how contents for public displays can be selected based on the audience's preferences and areas of interest. The ad selection within their system BluScreen tries to maximize the exposure of as many ads as possible to as wide an audience as possible without any prior knowledge of the audience and need of any user action.

Further research in this domain has focused on how available technologies can be used to provide more suitable and relevant information based on profiles. Bilchev introduced the concept of a distributed user profile constructed based on different profiles that can be used for personalized online advertising [1]. Stablere et al [8] presented a platform using information extracted from a Facebook profile to target personalised ads.

Last, user interaction with pervasive environments is an important aspect, which can be considered to generate profiles; however it heavily depends on the media. Whereas in the WWW interactions can be easily assessed through analyzing a user's click-stream, tracking interactions with public displays requires additional sensing techniques. [7] explains how Bluetooth can be used to identify users in the vicinity of a public display.

6 Conclusion and Future Work

We introduced a pervasive advertising environment, which tries to tackle several issues of current deployments. First, we looked at how both the users' personal interests as well as their shopping behavior when interacting with the system can be taken into account in order to precisely target advertisements to them. Therefore, we introduced the concept of adaptive user profiles. We showed how such a profile could be generated based on a user's self-assessment, the user's individual activity, and the activity intensity compared to other users of the system. Third, we proposed a system setup allowing for anonymous and unobtrusive profiling based on Bluetooth scanners. Finally we explained a technical concept based on which we implemented our pervasive advertising system.

Our advertising environment has so far been deployed in a lab setting only and hence not been evaluated with real-world data. As a future work we plan to setup the system on the campus of the University of Duisburg-Essen and run a large-scale user study in order to evaluate the different aspects of the systems. Those aspects mainly include (1) accuracy and robustness of the profiling algorithm, (2) performance and accuracy of the matching algorithm, (3) acceptance among user as well as potential user concerns, and (4) a usability evaluation of the different types of interactions supported by the system.

References

1. Bilchev, G., Marston, D.: Personalised Advertising – Exploiting the Distributed User Profile. BT Technology Journal 21(1), 84–90 (2003)
2. Bosworth, M.H.: Loyalty Cards: Reward or Threat? ConsumerAffairs.com (April 3, 2005) (2009),
   http://www.consumeraffairs.com/news04/2005/loyalty_cards.html

3. Kern, D., Harding, M., Storz, O., Davis, N., Schmidt, A.: Shaping how advertisers see me: user views on implicit and explicit profile capture. In: CHI 2008 Extended Abstracts on Human Factors in Computing Systems, pp. 3363–3368. ACM, New York (2008)

4. Karam, M., Payne, T., David, E.: Evaluating BluScreen: Usability for Intelligent Pervasive Displays. In: Proceedings of ICPCA (2007)

5. Marsland, L.: How much advertisement actually works? SAMRA Convention, bizcommunity.com, April 15 (2006),
   http://www.bizcommunity.com/Article/196/119/9593.html

6. Ranganathan, A., Campbell, R.H.: Advertising in a pervasive computing environment. In: Proceedings of WMC 2002, New York, USA, pp. 10–14 (2002)

7. Sharifi, M., Payne, T., David, E.: Public Display Advertising Based on Bluetooth Device Presence. In: Mobile Interaction with the Real World, MIRW 2006 (September 2006)

8. Spethmann, B.: Shoppers Like Grocery Loyalty Cards Despite Privacy Worries. Promo Magazine (2005), http://promomagazine.com/incentives/
   shoppers_loyalty_cards_020205/

9. Stabeler, M., Shannon, R., Quigley, A.: Profiling and targeting opportunities in pervasive advertising. In: Pervasive 2009 workshop on Pervasive Advertising, Nara, Japan (2009)

Author Index

Printing: Mercedes-Druck, Berlin
Binding: Stein+Lehmann, Berlin